AFRICAN MUSIC, POWER, AND BEING IN COLONIAL ZIMBABWE

AFRICAN EXPRESSIVE CULTURES

Ethnomusicology Multimedia (EM) is a collaborative publishing program, developed with funding from the Andrew W. Mellon Foundation, to identify and publish first books in ethnomusicology, accompanied by supplemental audiovisual materials online at www.ethnomultimedia.org.

A collaboration of the presses at Indiana and Temple universities, EM is an innovative, entrepreneurial, and cooperative effort to expand publishing opportunities for emerging scholars in ethnomusicology and to increase audience reach by using common resources available to the presses through support from the Andrew W. Mellon Foundation. Each press acquires and develops EM books according to its own profile and editorial criteria.

EM's most innovative features are its web-based components, which include a password-protected Annotation Management System (AMS) where authors can upload peer-reviewed audio, video, and static image content for editing and annotation and key the selections to corresponding references in their texts; a public site for viewing the web content, www.ethnomultimedia.org, with links to publishers' websites for information about the accompanying books; and the Avalon Media System, which hosts video and audio content for the website. The AMS and website were designed and built by the Institute for Digital Arts and Humanities at Indiana University. Avalon was designed and built by the libraries at Indiana University and Northwestern University with support from the Institute of Museum and Library Services. The Indiana University Libraries hosts the website and the Indiana University Archives of Traditional Music (ATM) provides archiving and preservation services for the EM online content.

AFRICAN MUSIC, POWER, AND BEING IN COLONIAL ZIMBABWE

Mhoze Chikowero

Indiana University Press

Bloomington and Indianapolis

This book is a publication of

Indiana University Press
Office of Scholarly Publishing
Herman B Wells Library 350
1320 East 10th Street

Bloomington, Indiana 47405 USA

iupress.indiana.edu

The paper used in this publication meets the minimum requirements of the American National Standard for Information Sciences—Permanence of Paper for Printed Library Materials, ANSI Z39.48–1992.

Manufactured in the United States of America

Library of Congress Cataloging-in-Publication Data

Chikowero, Mhoze, [date] author.
African music, power, and being in colonial Zimbabwe / Mhoze Chikowero.
pages cm. — (African expressive cultures) (Ethnomusicology multimedia)
Includes bibliographical references and index.
ISBN 978-0-253-01768-0 (cloth : alk. paper) — ISBN 978-0-253-01803-8 (pbk. : alk. paper) — ISBN 978-0-253-01809-0 (ebook) 1. Popular music—Social aspects—Zimbabwe—History—20th century. 2. Popular music—Political aspects—Zimbabwe—History—20th century. 3. Missions—Zimbabwe. 4. Zimbabwe—Social conditions—20th century. 5. Zimbabwe—Colonial influence. I. Title. II. Series: African expressive cultures. III. Series: Ethnomusicology multimedia.
ML3917.Z55C55 2015
780.96891—dc23
2015017453

1 2 3 4 5 20 19 18 17 16 15

Amai Florence Chikowero, greatest educator, singer of hymns most beautiful and mysterious. You taught us the power of school, and the power of song. Mudhara Mugoni Chikowero, you of the Chiwashira Brothers Choir. Dova renyu iro! And to all your descendants.

Contents

Kupa Kutenda / Acknowledgments

THIS BOOK EMERGES out of a life, an upbringing, conversations, and study in the school of the Madzimbabwe everyday and the school that came. It is there that it will be celebrated or ridiculed—at the various matare where I grew up singing, listening to songs and stories, and marveling at the magical footwork of "Chapter," the village dancing professor paChikunguru paya, at Growth Points like Murambinda, in the urban dis/locations of Mbare, Makokoba, Esigodini, and Yeoville down in Joburg. The book drew energy from the contemporary iterations of the performative madariro, from the self-crafted fringes of urban joy—kwaMereki—to the nodes of indigenous knowledge regeneration such as the Mbira Centre, Dzimbanhete, Pakare Paye, Nharira, and the urbane, polite Jazz 105 (what tragedy ever shut down that splendid joint?). In these spaces I listened, thought, learned, and spoke with those driven by the spirit of song; ate gochigochi washed down with the ritual Lion lager to feel at home; or just watched the city that refuses to sleep. The stories and sensibilities of Madzimbabwe song and recreational cultures are cultivated at such places as the not-so-polite Pamuzinda, where makoronyera—those dislocated urban hunters—can crudely push you around, accusing you of robbing them as a ruse to rob you; at Sports Diner, where the more artistic of these klevas dance sideways to liberate wallets and cell phones from the naive and the distracted who dutifully "raise the flag" with both hands to superstar Karikoga Zhakata chanting, "Uri gamba wani iwe simudza mureza!" They are unpatriotic like that, those makoronyera.

The central figures in these pages are the artists, many of whom have become friends over the years. Thanks for being there always, Comrade Chinx and Mai Lenny, Bill Saidi, Mhofu Zexie, Green and Stella Manatsa, Friday Mbirimi, the late "Professor" Kenneth and Lina Mattaka, Kembo Ncube, and the numerous names catalogued in these pages. This book would have turned out very differently without Mudhara Abel Sithole's indefatigable energy, leading hand, and knowledge of where things were trying to go all those years. Gogo Jane Lungile Ngwenya, the greatest historian, teacher, and grandmother. Dhara guru, Mukanya Thomas Tafirenyika Mapfumo and Mukoma Lance, William, and Itai, thanks for the hospitality in Eugene, for sharing the stories of your lives and those majestic photos! The same goes to Austin Sibanda, the Blacks Unlimited Band Manager. Dee Mortensen at Indiana University Press believed in this book beyond ephemeral impediments. Thanks also for covering those production costs. My gratitude to the entire editorial team, especially to Shoshanna Green for the eagle eye! A version of chapter 6 was previously published in *Music, Performance, and*

African Identities; my thanks to Rochester University Press and the editors, Toyin Falola and Tyler Fleming.

A *hangry* mind was cultivated at the University of Zimbabwe, and the bounty farmers include the Economic History faculty, V. E. M. Machingaidze, J. P. Mtisi, and Pius Nyambara, and my colleagues in that record-setting honors class of 2001. Professor Ezra Chitando's hand encouraged research from the early seasons, and Josephine Nhongo-Simbanegavi not only taught me but, like the mother that she is, also ululated at the rituals of honor both in Harare and in Halifax! Jerry Mazarire, let's play more Pengaudzoke for the next book, but for now, sando dzako for opening the door for me to study history after weeks of wandering between entirely useless courses when I entered the UZ in 1999.

In 2003, I carried my archives across the Atlantic to work with Gary Kynoch, together with Phil Zachernuk and Jane Parpart at Dalhousie University. To Guy Thompson, thanks for the deep interest. Generous Killam Scholarships and History Department and Faculty of Graduate Studies fellowships underwrote the years of single-minded studying in Halifax before I skipped south to take up a postdoctoral fellowship at the Rutgers Center for Historical Analysis in New Jersey in 2008. Julie Livingstone made that fellowship profitable with the weekly "Vernacular Epistemologies" seminars and ample space to think and write.

Unlike building a house, writing a book means rewriting. And thankfully, this book did not go the way of Tizira's proverbial basket that gets weaved at one end while it unweaves at the other; support for those crucial and self-indulgent processes of writing and rewriting came in generous leave time and pockets of funding from my employers at the University of California, Santa Barbara, who granted me an IHC time-release fellowship and two UCSB Junior Faculty Research Awards, in addition to liberal sums in start-up research money, from 2009. A very generous Hellman Family Faculty Research Fellowship enabled me to sustain long-term research in Zimbabwe and Joni.

Colleagues at UCSB, including Stephan Miescher, Peter Bloom, and Sylvester Ogbechie, read versions of either the whole book or individual chapters, as did a small circle of fellow junior faculty book-writing clubbers—Ann-Elise Lewallen, Xiaorong Li, Christina McMahon, and Tess Shewry. Carol Lansing and Ed English offered their cottage on the mount in Santa Barbara; John Majewski, Lisa Jacobson, Harold Marcuse, Cecilia Mendez, John Lee, Xiaowei Zheng, and others also eased homemaking in Santa Barbara. Tayo Jolaosho, Terri Barnes, Tendai Muparutsa, Munyaradzi Munochiveyi, Mhofu Joseph Chikowero, Prof. Terence Mashingaidze, Maiguru Joyie Chadya, Wendy Urban-Mead, George Karekwaivanane, Patrick Tom, Dhagi Mpondi, Maurice Vambe, Tafadzwa Ntini, Ushehwedu Kufakurinani, Ross Larkin, Evelyn Mukwedeya and her mother, and Brian Rutledge also read either the whole manuscript or segments and furnished useful feedback at different times. Bvumavaranda Jay

Murandu, Nyamuzihwa Masimba Musodza, Mhofu Bam'nini Welly, Bam'nini Jabu, Dziva Ntini, and Mhofu Mudzingwa Munhu, thanks for convening those robust digital matare on social media. I refined aspects of this book in conversation with many who shared ideas, reading materials, and contacts on those reconfigured, virtual communal spaces. Thanks to old boy Tyler Fleming for the close reading and also, together with Nate Plageman, for presenting aspects of the work at conferences on my behalf, either because I had got stuck in Canada after misplacing a passport or because South African Airways had prevented me from traveling from Washington, D.C., to Senegal without a visa while I was not an American! Comrade-in-scholarship Mwendamberi Chakanetsa Mavhunga, the Skype dare remains ever enriching for cowriting and sharing ideas, archives, and stories. Prof. Francis Musoni, we shall dance again at Londoners (if my memory is correct that it hasn't been converted into a horse-racing lotto house like Jazz 105), at the Rainbow Towers, and elsewhere, as we did in 2012 to those thudding ngomarungundu that incensed the holy missionaries a century ago. To Allison Shutt, a dinky-two-step that offended Rhodesia will not suffice for your unstinting moral and intellectual investment into my work: those close readings, unmasking of "anonymous" historical figures, and generous sharing of archival materials, references, etc. And to my former roomie, Dr. Bisby Matinhure, for those shared long nights of bookworming in "Baghdad" at the UZ and the quaffing Pamuzinda, where you probably saved at least three lives with that threat to do quick surgery with a bottomed-out beer bottle on those cantankerous makoronyera!

Many other people too numerous to mention commented on ideas in this book at various conferences, talks, and workshops: at several African Studies Association meetings, the 2008 meeting of the Canadian African Studies Association, many NEWSA workshops in Burlington, Vermont, the vibrant and irreverent University of Zimbabwe Economic History Seminars, and at the Midlands State University in Gweru, the University of Ghana at East Legon, the University of Illinois Urbana-Champaign, CODESRIA in Dakar, the University of Cambridge, Rutgers University, UC San Diego, the University of Rochester, the University of North Carolina at Wilmington, Friends of Africa Santa Barbara, and UC Santa Barbara. Thanks to Joe Trotter and Wendy Goldman for organizing the Sawyer Seminar on the Ghetto at Carnegie Mellon University in Pittsburgh, and to Brian Larkin and Jinny Prais for inviting me to participate in the Infrastructures in Africa Workshop at Columbia University. All those matare helped me refine this book. My students, including Sarah Watkins, Hamza Mannan, Shreyas Natesan, Ryan Minor, Ross Melczer, and others, also read aspects of the work and provided useful feedback.

Hector Mugani and your team at the Book Café, time didn't allow us to extend those riveting discussions, but now I suspect we are on the right side of time. To the Zimbabwe College of Music Library, especially Dexter Mawisire, thanks for the support, and for sharing the image of August Machona Musarurwa. Thanks for weaving beautiful stories, VaChihera Sekai Nzenza and the late Mbuya Miriam Mlambo. Ndotenda Cde Earnest Mudzengi for the access to computing services at Harare's Media Centre. Sekuru Cain Chikosha, Stanley Ruziwa at Gramma Records, and homeboy Nyakudirwa O'Brien Rwafa, thanks for unlocking your record libraries; Stephen Chifunyise, Joyce Jenje-Makwenda, Gibson Mandishona, Cont Mhlanga, and Fred Zindi, you have always been available to share ideas and insights on a subject that's close to your hearts. Ngara Mwalimu Saki Mafundikwa, Humba Nyamutatanga Makombe, Dziva Boniface "Green Arrow" Mavengeni, Farai Mupfunya, Sinyoro Chiko Chazunguza and Samaita Tendai Gahamadze in those hills of Sekuru Chamatehwe, Soro Renzou Nyamasvisva Wilfred Mafika, and Samaita Albert Chimedza at the Mbira Center, thanks for advancing those shared ideas. Nyati mhenyu Takura Makoni, thanks for the support, the space, and the wholesome meals that feed the soul and loosen tongues KwaMurongo. Gono Amego Nhaka Mukucha, the task remains yours to deal with my professorially clumsy fingers on the dear ancestors' mbira. Sekuru Nhire Mutimbanepasi at ZiFM, ndinotenda for the opportunities to talk about this and other works on matare epamhepo.

Glen Ncube, teach me to be a linguist, too! Ivo Mhike, Tsheni Ntungakwa, and Mhofu Mugo waChiwashira, your foot-soldiering was critical to the completion of this book. I am deeply indebted to the dedicated staff at the National Archives of Zimbabwe and at the Harare City Council's Remembrance House (especially Mai Pondayi), to Maiguru Laina Gumboreshumba and Diane Thram at the International Library of African Music in Grahamstown, and to the war vet Enocent Msindo for helping me navigate that city that was taken. In the age of the digital and traveling archive, the UCSB Library's Document Delivery and Circulation Staff eased the burdens of this work with deliveries of the copious, scattered missionary archive. And it's always useful to strategically "deploy" one's wife at the source; Angela's trusted handbag always bulged with the dusty, precious, rotting books!

Chiwashira family, you are the ones who intercede with the ancestors and celebrate blessings. My parents Mugoni and Florence Chikowero, you are Mhondoro's greatest teachers. Madhara angu: Tsuro, Musutu, Hofisi, thanks for crooning the Chiwashira Brothers Choir tunes once more at a sacred family moment. Mukoma Josh and Maiguru Sekai, your stewardship needs no qualifying. Mhofu Tafa and Mainini Kumbi, your house in Chitungwiza chaChaminuka and your ever-ready family spirit provided an anchor throughout. Vazukuru VaChiwashira in Bulawayo, Davy "Nyangson" Nyanga and wife, Jowie, and Mai naBa'Rumbi, you are the kings. The heaviest debt is owed to Angie, the wife and mother constantly deprived by the unending wanderings, librarian, and catcher of all manner of first and repeat errors, and to our beautiful children: Kundai Z., the pianist, violinist, gwenyambira, and trumpeter; Takura Anesu, the gwenyagitari and drummer; and Takunda Maita Dombo raChiwashira, the saxophonist and gwenyambira. In addition to Piri and her ways, we now have one more thing to read, and hopefully one less alibi for not doing so! Madzimbabwe say kuwanda huuya, kwakarambwa chete nemuroyi—collective work is a virtue hated only by a witch.

AFRICAN MUSIC, POWER, AND BEING IN COLONIAL ZIMBABWE

Introduction

Cross-Cultural Encounters: Song, Power, and Being

WRITING ABOUT HER childhood in 1960s Buhera, in rural colonial Zimbabwe, Sekai Nzenza (*Herald,* December 11, 2012) reminisced about how, one Christmas Eve, her mother instructed her and her siblings to look out for a local Anglican priest, Baba Mutemarari. Once they spotted him coming, she instructed them to hide "everything that was unChristian around the village compound. We covered two big pots of the highly potent mhanga beer under sacks and blankets then closed the kitchen hut. My brother Charles dragged our famous drum [*ngoma*] called 'Zino irema' and hid that in the granary. My father reluctantly switched off his Mahlatini and the Mahotela Queens music and hid the gramophone in the bedroom."[1]

These were the dying days of the rebel British colonial state, Rhodesia, some seven decades after British settlers had invaded the country in 1890 and missionaries and the state had crusaded against African cultures unimpeded, seeking to supplant them with their Europeanized Christian doctrines. This late in the colonial era, African families that held onto their *chivanhu*—indigenous knowledges, cosmologies, and ways of being still endured continuing epistemicidal missionary crusades, campaigns to exterminate or subvert such knowledges and ways of being (Grosfoguel 2013, 74). Some deployed the time-tested, disingenuous smile to fool the bothersome village evangelist, the adoptive apostle of the foreign mission. Sekai's family was wary of Baba Mutemarari's condemnation of "beer, singing and dancing the way we did [as] unChristian and against civilised European behavior."

In Madzimbabwe and related cultures, the musical context encapsulates the people's shared cognitive forms and societal values, and their associated behaviors and underlying moral codes and concepts (Ngugi 1997, 11). Music is a vector of communication not only amongst the living, but also between the living and the world of the ancestors, *nyikadzimu.* This cosmological essence constitutes the music's sacrality and power. It is therefore not surprising that music became deeply involved in the battle of cultures that characterized the colonial encounter, with the colonists seeking to conquer indigenous knowledge in order to disarm a people who had deployed their cultures not only to resist evangelization, but also to fight the imposed alien political order. While European colonialism was intrinsically driven by economics, it was also culturally propagated, legitimated, and popularly contested. To pitch conquest as a "civilizing mission," the colonists had to systematically destroy, deliberately distort, or censor the positive aspects of Africans' cultural life while underscoring the negative. This alienation was important because, in Micere Mugo's (1992, xiii) words, "cultural zombies can neither create nor defend their birthright."

British settlers not only violently suppressed the Africans' Chimurenga (or Chindunduma) in 1896–97—one of the most tenacious anticolonial African guerrilla uprisings—they also executed its political and spiritual leaders, including the spirit mediums of Mbuya Nehanda and Sekuru Kaguvi. The Africans only dislodged the settlers in 1980 in a reignited, bloody Second Chimurenga that gathered pace in the early 1960s. Throughout the long interwar era of colonial overlordship, song was key to how Africans conceptualized their changing world, recrafted their despoiled identities, and resisted and mobilized for self-liberation. Through embodied song and oral history, they touched each other's hearts and summoned the spirits of their martyred ancestor-leaders to guide the unvanquished agenda of self-liberation. Yet the cultural elaboration of being was not unique to Africans. European imperialism itself was lodged deeply within the interstices of European cultures, variously articulated in writing, theater, public exhibitions, and songs (Said 1993). This is because, as Esther Lezra argues in *The Colonial Art of Demonizing Others* (2014), Europeans crafted works of expressive culture that created the very evil they claimed to find in others as part of the process of transfiguring themselves as defenders of civilization rather than predatory conquers and exploiters.

African Music, Power, and Being in Colonial Zimbabwe explores, on the one hand, ways in which colonists rationalized their harnessing of cultural expression, particularly music, as a weapon to undermine African sovereignty and, on the other, how Africans similarly deployed their musical cultures to tell their own stories, reclaim their freedom, and reconstitute their being. Rhodesians consistently and anxiously strived to invent a domineering settler cultural identity based on a reassertion of an alleged white epistemic superiority and African inferiority. For instance, seven decades after the settler invasion, C. T. C. Taylor (1968, 13) wrote the history of Rhodesian entertainment essentially as a story of white cultural superiority over "primitive" Africans. The land that the Rhodesians colonized, he declared, had contained "not more than a million Bantu, many of whose forebears had arrived there only 50 years before." Their life was "primitive, both in its working methods and in the nature of its infrequent amusements." By contrast, "the pioneers . . . came for the most part from environments which had all the sophistications of the nineteenth century, environments which, for their relaxation, required entertainment of the standard civilized type—theatre, music, variety." This foundational, colonizing epistemic racial discourse depended on a familiar representation of Madzimbabwe as *terra incognita*—an uncultured, unexplored, uninhabited no-man's-land. These images were culled from but also rationalized the barrage of travelogues, adventure fables, missionary publications, landscape paintings, and other cartographies of "discovery" that colonized African knowledge while caricaturing or unmapping the people, removing them from view. This "pioneer" settler self-writing formed the bedrock of colonial historiography.

The scripting of the African as the self-reflexive European's "Other" required the persistent debasement, proscription, and appropriation of selected aspects of African lifestyles, practices, signs, and symbols. Thus, while the settler state sought to install "European" cultural institutions—theaters, training schools and colleges, entertainment halls, hotels, drama clubs, and ubiquitous public-funded symphony orchestras—in efforts to foster neo-European Rhodesian identities, it conceived "native" entertainment policy to manage and reinforce notions of African primitive difference through its "native social welfare" programs.

Since ancient times, Madzimbabwe have performed their musical cultures in a wide range of secular and ritual contexts. Through *mbira* and *ngoma,* they communed with their ancestors and the creator High God Mwari (Mu-ari, "the one who is"). In this way, *mbira,* a masterpiece of historical Madzimbabwe sound and metallurgical engineering, not only mapped the people's cosmologies, it also signified the intricate connections among and ecological equilibrium of spirituality, land, technological invention, and transgenerational being. It was the music's spiritual significance that attracted missionary wrath, subverting *mbira* and *ngoma* into key indices of their negative representations and crusades to re-create a subjugated, alienated African being.

The first part of this book explores how missionaries maligned this power of African song, designating it an affront to their religious and political agenda. It dissects the psychologies that implicated indigenous musical cultures in spiritual and epistemic struggles. It reads missionary evangelization as a mission to culturally alienate and disarm this spiritual African being. Throughout these pages, I demonstrate that the recent history of Zimbabwean music reveals much more than its celebrated aesthetic ingenuity by reorienting discussion beyond the cultural rubric of mere comparison and explanation (of styles, structures, and forms) and firmly locating the power of song and its historical significance in its ability to reaffirm African being through engagement with the racialized violence of colonial dehumanization and extraction.

Cultural Alienation and Disarmament: Levers of Colonialism

Molded in nineteenth-century traditions of western epistemic ethnocentrism, most missionaries cast African musical cultures as paganism, to be destroyed if the African was to be saved. Epistemicide, the destruction of a people's spiritual and cultural foundations and sense of self-worth, would be the surest way to disarm and dominate them. Accordingly, throughout the long colonial century, all the missionary bodies, including both Catholics and Protestants, waged a determined war to destroy African music and the epistemes that informed it.

Africans did not simply submit to the colonial designs, however. They variously mediated, accommodated, appropriated, resisted, and subverted those designs. The evaluation of colonial designs therefore simultaneously highlights the dialectical relationship between colonial violence and African ingenuity and innovativeness, and acknowledges the significance of context in shaping the aporic and discursive cross-cultural encounters. This framing allows an understanding of how some Africans quickly realized that the hegemonic missionary discourse of civilization could be redeployed for counterhegemonic self-fashioning, generating new forms and third spaces that resignified elements of both the maligned indigenous cultures and incoming ideas in profound and confounding ways. In Ramón Grosfoguel's (2008) words, this was a form of resistance that resignified and transformed dominant forms of knowledge from the point of view of non-Eurocentric rationality, creating new critical spaces to engage power and devise new utopias. Africans exhibited their innovativeness in the face of epistemicidal violence through *makwaya* (choir formations), *michato* (wedding celebrations), "tea parties" and *makonzati* (concerts) of various shades, and other musical forms. Their dances soon spawned missionary outcries that, for instance, instigated a colony-wide state investigation and concerted efforts to eliminate the "evil night dances" in 1930. Africans also demonstrated their ingenuity by cloaking dances in a Christian disguise and renaming them (for instance, they "baptized" the sensuous *mbende jerusarema*) in order to evade white missionary proscription.

The epistemic violence of colonial cultural attitudes manifested in sociopolitical engineering programs in the citadels of settler power, the cities. Here, the state, capitalists, missionaries, and ethnomusicologists harnessed African music and dances not only to enact imperial spectacle, but also as tools to construct Africans into rural migrant "tribes" in order to disavow their rights in the city, performatively elaborating and ritualizing racial difference to buttress policymaking. The settler regimes harnessed African cultures to perform power not only by inscribing subjective, exploitable identities onto colonized African bodies, but also by confining them to specific, racialized physical and psychological spaces—*marukesheni*, "native locations" (sing. *rukesheni*). This appropriation and subversion of African cultures into infrastructures of colonial politics informs my critique of the orthodox, depoliticizing celebration of the vitality of such often-entrapped performances. At the intersection of policy and performance, I read a(nta)gonistic enactments of power that complicated colonial designs.

Africans variously deployed their music to contest the colonial war on their being, to regenerate their selfhoods, and to strive for self-liberation from the confinement of both the administrative kraals of urban "native" re-creation and national subjugation. Their music was informed by, and it constituted, indigenous epistemic orders that colonialism ultimately failed to subvert or destroy. They elaborated their cultures of resistance, which blossomed in the Chimurenga songs that drove the second armed war of liberation. In the closing chapters of this book, I locate these cultures of resistance in deep genealogies dating back to the advent of colonialism. The Chimurenga genealogies signify deep-seated consciousness, historical memory, and traditions of self-crafting, self-liberation, and nationalism. When Africans sang their songs on the *dariro* (the open village assembly ground) during *jenaguru* moonlight dances, on the mission school parade grounds, in the confines of *rukesheni* recreation halls, and out on the dusty urban fringes, they were performing something beyond what has been characteristically read through an exteriorizing western lens as either cosmopolitanism or exoticism. Through this musical register, many Africans did not simply imagine independence but—to speak to two influential conceptualizations (Askew 2002; Moorman 2008)—actually performed it, recentering and reasserting their marginalized humanity and epistemes.

Scholars' orthodox framing of African nationalism prior to the "mass nationalist" era (the late 1950s) as merely "reformist" highlights at least three historiographical problems. First, the framing ignores the significance of Chimurenga as historical and transgenerational sensibility and cross-class discourse that continued to shape Africans' consciousness after their military subjugation in the 1890s. Second, it reifies the myth of the colonial nation-state as the universal, originary model. And, third and more fundamentally, it betrays the scholarship's entrapment by the "western ratio" (Mudimbe 1988, x; Diawara 1990, 80), which privileges the "Europeanized," transitional, and therefore (in western eyes) most legible expressions of African being. Such extroversive legibility manifests in the overwhelming narratives of African musical practices "by outsiders who happen upon them—explorers, tourists, or anthropologists," as spectacles (MacAloon 1984, 243). While spectacle can enrich significations of power (Foucault 2007, 90), there is equal need to unravel depths that might seem mundane or inaccessible. I take the songs that villagers, urban dwellers, and students sang not just as spectacle, but as an archive of cross-class African consciousness, and utilize them to understand the political culture of African self-crafting. I read in this musical archive values, expectations, and implicit rules that expressed and shaped collective African intentions and actions, and in so doing interrogate the persistent implication that African nationalism was a belated and elite, and perhaps even alien, phenomenon. The reinsertion of these largely excluded indigenous and underclass perspectives—beyond the archival ghosts of Europe (Lezra 2014, 5)—enriches the story of African self-crafting.

The voices and agency of African underclasses have long been marginalized, impoverished, and suppressed into victimhood by elitist narratives that privilege the colonial state as organizer or originator, missionaries as tutors, ethnomusicologists as conservators, and white liberals and their African nationalist leader-pupils as the hero-agents of African history. Through reading the musical archive, the book revalues disenfranchised African underclasses as cultural agents, indigenous intellectuals, and makers of their own histories and locates power in their repressed but defiant indigenous anticolonial epistemes and anthologies of knowledge. Methodologically, it builds on Said's excellent analytical location of imperialism deep in the annals of European cultural writing and his bringing to the fore the voices of the dominated, the so-called subalterns. In doing so, it helps resolve the problem of subalterns who do not speak in scholars' works and who thus become doubly victimized—both physically and theoretically—as scholars also deny them agency to fashion change and different identities beyond colonial subalternity and ideological pupilage.

Catherine Cole (2001, 7) avers that the so-called colonial subalterns did in fact speak, thrusting the challenge back on scholars to listen to and understand what and how they spoke and what they did to reshape their own histories. Beyond Said's seminal illustration of how European cultures were vectors of imperialism, I chart a new path by examining how the colonizer also sought to appropriate, subvert, and redeploy the cultures of the colonized as an armory for domination. I venture new approaches by rereading the colonial archive and the indigenous library as loci of power in the cultures of colonialism and anticolonialism. This, then, is necessarily a project in both epistemological deconstruction and historical reconstruction, a critical aspect of which grapples with the dominant, problematic paradigms that comfortably frame much of the subject in the annals of the colonial library. A historiographical contextualization illustrates the significance of this mutually inclusive double task.

African Music Is No Mere Dancing Matter: Interrogating the Colonial Library

More than a decade ago, Kofi Agawu (2003, xiii) wrote that the "spirit of African music is . . . not always manifest in the scholarship about it." He argued that this is because, *inter alia,* the subject is dominated by foreigners whose ultimate allegiances are to the metropolis, not to Africa, and also because much of the little scholarship originating from Africa is extraverted, addressing overseas rather than local audiences. Agawu is not necessarily advocating a fundamentalist position, what Ezra Chitando (2001, 84) defined as a "culture-and-knowledge-in-the-blood" stance. He acknowledges that neither an "African" nor a "Western" approach to African music is "intrinsically good or bad as much depends on one's purposes, terms of reference, and assumptions." Agawu notes that discourse about African music, that is, not only "specific utterances but also . . . an implicit framework for the production, dissemination, and consumption of knowledge" about the music, is often very problematic and requires robust critique.

Addressing the same subject of scholarly positionality and knowledge production in his book on Zimbabwean music, American ethnomusicologist Thomas Turino (2000, 101) suggested that it is "dangerous" to privilege "cultural insiders" above specialists, because "being 'African' or a black Zimbabwean does not guarantee knowledge of indigenous African arts." Certainly, knowledge can be a matter of research, but also of reflexive practice and lived experience. As a Black Zimbabwean, I am interested in these questions of epistemology, particularly as Africans still contend with the ignominies of the historically colonizing effects of having their self-representation denied and being spoken for and defined by others who claim to be more "objective," "rational," and "disinterested" (Steyn 2001, xxxiii). Recentering *chivanhu,* African knowledge, ways of knowing (Ngara 2007), and my lived experience, I seek to deconstruct the foundational Cartesian structures and myths of westernized knowledge production in, and of, Zimbabwe. I engage a self-privileging western episteme that masks its own conditions of possibility, conditions that belie its claims to objectivity. It is through the force of this episteme that some western researchers still fancy themselves as "scholar-martyrs" or "heroes" out to "save" African music (White 2008).

In his review of Turino's book, Chitando (2001, 84) observes that urgent work is still required on this important and underresearched subject from the perspective of the (formerly) dominated. This is notwithstanding effusive praises for the book as offering "a fresh, provocative, and ultimately most convincing reading of the development of popular music in Zimbabwe" (Allen 2001, 378). Engaging this troubled politics of knowledge production is crucial, for African music is not merely about "culture," or song and dance, but also about a history of subject making, the coloniality of power and self-liberation. The apparent freshness of Turino's book is underpinned by its rejection of the orthodox position—explicitly or implicitly championed by Zimbabwean scholars A. J. C. Pongweni (1982), Alice Dadirai Kwaramba (1997), and Fred Zindi (1985)—that the Rhodesian state suppressed indigenous music before it was revived by African cultural nationalists in the 1960s. In the view of these scholars, the history of Zimbabwean music is a story of suppression and revival, or cultural imperialism and revolutionary resurgence. By contrast, Turino posits a benevolent colonial state that promoted indigenous cultures, enabling such cultures to flourish throughout the long colonial century. *African Music, Power, and Being in Colonial Zimbabwe* intervenes in this debate, arguing that both positions are problematic for different reasons.

Beyond their lived knowledge of the dominance of "western" music in the country in the first half of the twentieth century and the inherent structural and epistemicidal violence of Rhodesia the settler colony, Pongweni, Kwaramba, and Zindi do not marshal substantive evidence to reinforce the powerful thesis of suppression and revival. Few would doubt the commonsensical assumption that Rhodesia, a state that blatantly violated and exploited Africans in every way possible, would have any qualms about similarly repressing the music of the despised "natives." The problem, however, is that this narrative anticipates the sudden (re) emergence of revolutionary music in the 1960s–70s, precluding inquiry into the musical revolution and its possible genealogies. George Kahari's (1981) survey of the history of Zimbabwean "protest" song gestures a corrective long view by showing that this musical sensibility predated the colonial advent and was radically reshaped in tune with the vicissitudes of colonialism. However, Kahari's exploratory thesis remains underdeveloped: the psychosocial impact of colonial violence has yet to be fully examined, and nobody has elaborated the thesis in deeper research. I utilize a diverse written and oral archive to reinforce his thesis.

Turino's city-centric, revisionist theory draws attention to the urban entertainment programs and the recording and broadcasting of African songs on colonial radio to argue that the colonial state and capital actually promoted, rather than suppressing, indigenous music. In his view, colonial state radio promoted—if only inadvertently—African national cultural unity, "breaking down regional and so-called tribal barriers to get Zimbabweans to think of themselves as one group (Turino 2000, 99–102)." Banning Eyre (Turino 2007) criticizes Turino's radio argument for its obvious chronological telescoping. Such broadcasting began only in the mid-1940s and, more importantly, it emerged as a politicizing technology through the clandestine efforts of African organic intellectuals otherwise hired to popularize colonial propaganda radio among Africans. It was neither a design, nor an unintended outcome of the actions of, white colonial broadcasters—who, in fact, had failed to make an impact on Africans during World War II (Mhoze Chikowero 2014). By furnishing the crucial, missing historical background on Zimbabwean music in the first decades of colonial rule (1890s–1920s), *African Music, Power, and Being in Colonial Zimbabwe* enables a better appreciation of the significance of post-1920s Zimbabwean music.

Zimbabwean Music in Historical Perspective: The Missionary Factor, Ethnotheory

The period up to the 1930s was by design principally the age of missionaries, the leading Eurocentric ideologues with whom Africans interacted through church and school. What then was the impact of this missionary factor on African musical and cultural imagination? The orthodox wisdom states that missionaries suppressed African cultures (O'Callaghan 1977). Turino (2000) not only disagrees, but actually bemoans the fact that of all the arms of colonialism, missionaries have received a lion's share of the blame for direct oppression of indigenous "Shona" music and dance. But instead of elaborating or refuting this thesis with evidence to the contrary, he skirts the question by claiming that the literature regarding the missionary impact on indigenous practices is so copious that "one hardly knows where to begin" (113). However, in his extensive interview with Eyre, Turino (2007) recanted his overstatement, only to dismiss both the question and its premise out of hand: "Throughout the colonial period, indigenous dance drumming, panpipe playing, *mbira* playing, and choral music continued on within indigenous communities and in working class townships with great vitality." Without furnishing any references or substantiating his claim that "some missionaries . . . loved traditional music and dance," he concluded that the "common idea . . . that the colonial government, and missionaries, tried to stamp out indigenous musical practices" is false: "My research indicates that this is not so and that indigenous Shona music remained vibrant." Beyond the displacement of African experience and self-knowledge, the implication that there were some "good" missionaries obscures an understanding of the mission as an epistemicidal project. The mission was intended not to reinforce African (never mind "Shona") being and knowledge systems but to dismantle them, although its denominational approaches necessarily varied and a few individual missionaries went about it in subtler, quite humane ways. Method did not preclude objective.

Scholars have yet to sufficiently engage with the meaning of the missionary effect on African music, with the thin and largely dated literature limited to the work of the reformist Lutheran Reverend Henry Weman (1960), the polemical self-writing of the deported American Methodist Archbishop Ralph Dodge (1960), the more generalized short treatises of Geoffrey Kapenzi (1979) and W. R. Peaden (1970), and Wendy Urban-Mead's (2008) ongoing work on dance and gender comportment in the Brethren in Christ Church (BICC). And despite Weman's own latter-day self-interested experiments in deploying African music to revive an imperiled Lutheran mission church in the mid-twentieth century, these limited writings certainly do not tell a story of missionary love for African musical cultures. Urban-Mead shows how the BICC fiercely suppressed dancing among its converts. African musical cultures survived sustained missionary epistemicide thanks to their internal resilience. To deny the violence they endured or to attribute their survival to imagined missionary fostering is not only to misunderstand or mask the colonial epistemicidal project; it also constitutes what Sherry Ortner (1995, 174) called "ethnographic refusal"—denying people their agency through historical or textual misinterpretation. The refusal serves at least four related historiographical functions: firstly, it displaces African agency in dealing with, thriving despite, and overcoming colonial violence. Secondly, it trivializes the significance of Africans' wrestling with the alienating force that suffused every facet of their lives. Thirdly, in Lezra's (2014, 15) words, it disavows the "beastliness of Europe's systematic oppression of Black people" while, lastly, transfiguring the villains as the saviors. This book details the hitherto anecdotal and mystified story of perpetual missionary warfare on African being, revealing the depths of the violence against which they had to contend. For Africans, coming to terms with this history is critical for healing, self-rehumanization, and reasserting their displaced self-knowledge; dismissing it reinscribes that violence.

Significantly, Turino's revisionist thesis builds partly on the labors and archive of early ethnomusicologists like Hugh Tracey, Percival Kirby, and others who, often funded by colonial capital and working with or for the Southern African apartheid states, championed the study of "the African personality" through Africans' own music. These programs spawned crusades to collect and "preserve" "primitive" African music threatened by "civilization" in and beyond Southern Africa. The archive these crusades inevitably produced is an ethically problematic, fossilized index of a racist, Social Darwinist agenda. Malidoma Somé (1994, 4) and Andrew Mark (2013) observe that western colonizing regimes only started to think about preserving "native" populations (human, animal, and plant) by putting them into reserves after they had triumphed over them, often to the brink of extinction. Mark asks whether the same logic might help explain the ubiquitous, self-serving, and perennial myth of a "mbirapocalypse" (the imagined death of *mbira*) that continues to justify Euro-American ethnomusicological practices in Africa today. The historical lens allows for an interrogation of this doubly articulated triumphal coloniality, its rationalizing, duplicitous martyrdom, and the colonial foundations of (knowledge about) the "native."

For instance, how independent was the ethnomusicological "collection" of culturally significant ("primitive") African musics from the severing and "collection" of the heads of African "rebels" who "resisted civilization"? Both processes signified or were made possible by violent conquest, and the "collected artifacts"—now deposited in archival repositories and displayed (or latterly hidden) in the imperial museum, respectively—underwrote the colonial epistemic research on "the African." What then are the ethical and cultural implications of "preserving," on the one hand, Africans' culturally significant music as an ethnomusicological archive and, on the other, the decapitated heads of African ancestors whom their descendants call through the same music? In other words, did the state-funded ethnomusicological plundering of this sacred music of the ancestors and its depositing at Rhodes University and similar imperial institutions serve purposes different from those of Cecil Rhodes's decapitation of those anticolonial spirit mediums and leaders—what Andrew Apter (1999) designated "anthropology's heart of darkness"? The histories of colonial epistemicidal intervention in African spiritual and cultural health are unresolved and suppressed. African scholars need to interrogate the value and use of knowledge culled from their colonized and decapitated bodies and their disembodied spiritualities. The problematic, John and Jean Comaroff (1992, 34) pointed out, is that these sorts of questions cannot begin to be answered until this archive is "anchored in the processes of [its] production." Conquest, genocide, and plunder are the processes. In the absence of such anchoring, it becomes unclear whether one is reading indigenous African performances (mediated or invented), or an archive of "native administration" with its coercive, racialized context stripped, or "imperial spectacles" (Apter 2002) removed from their context of production. Like the severed heads—gifts to the Queen of England—this conquered archive is often fetishized and dehistoricized. Methodologically, this book therefore historicizes, interrogates, and demystifies the hegemonic ethnomusicological archive and method.

The interrogation extends Christopher Waterman's (1991) decrying ethnomusicology's reification of not only the African musical sound but particularly the forced disjunction of the music from the social and historical grounds of its existence. Waterman argues that the ethnomusicological preoccupation with difference allowed the discipline to "bracket itself outside the very real world of colonialism, power relations and the social production of knowledge" (179). Tyler Fleming and Toyin Falola (2011, 4) similarly critiqued how, in their quest for "pure" African music, early ethno-specialists condemned syncretic genres like jazz, *kwela,* and highlife as bastardizations. A necessary qualifier is that the scholarship seeks but ultimately fails to mask and distance itself from its own racializing disciplinary methodological and archival legacies. I reinforce Agawu's argument that the mainstream ethnomusicological agenda was a quest for difference not merely for its aesthetic value, but as a foundation for constructing European cultural superiority over Africans. In the age of racial imperialism, this "hunt for difference" was a process of creation, what Agawu (2003, 163) describes as "differencing the African" from the European. Or, in Achebe's (1978, 14) words, it was a quest to construct "African barbarity as a foil for European grace." Both the decapitated African ancestors' heads and their plundered music (and other wealth) constituted raw materials and a condition for a hegemonic colonial library and oppressive episteme.

Ethnomusicology cultivated difference not only as a basis and discursive justification for colonialism, but also as a project in cultural disarmament. Current ethnomusicology that silences these matrices of power through denial and sanitization betrays its ideological significance in the ongoing politics of knowledge production that its disciplinary tradition and foundational archive were implicated in producing. Ethnomusicology still often "exonerate[s] colonialism of the cultural, cartographic, and cognitive violence it wreaked on Africa" and thus remains entrapped by its racist past and racializing study of the Other (Mafeje 1991; Zeleza 2009, 124). A rehabilitative self-reading therefore silences the ways in which coloniality framed both the object and the sociopolitical context, and thus reproduces similarly hegemonic epistemes. I further this robust critique of the reification of the colonial library through a critical discourse analysis that contextualizes African music in its historical perspective.

Urban Native Social Welfare as Sociopolitical Engineering

The celebration of the colonial state's ostensible promotion of indigenous music fails both to name and to unpack Rhodesia's Native Social Welfare policy, the framework within which the state, industrialists, and allied settler organizations furnished recreational facilities to urban Africans. *African Music, Power, and Being in Colonial Zimbabwe* reads differently the copious ethnomusicological archive that this policy and others like it produced, not simply seeing the archive as a site for knowledge retrieval, but also reading the policies as processes of subject construction that were at the heart of the colonization of African being. The Southern African settler state, missionaries, industrialists, and white liberals collectively used entertainment and organized sport to control Africans sociopolitically (Shopo 1977; Badenhorst and Rogerson 1986). The logic, Ngugi (1997) observed, was that the colonial state—with its regime of borders, exits, and entrances, to which one can add *zvitupa* (passes)—constituted a macro-architecture for regulating, confining, and disciplining "the native" in particular. Superintending this kraaling of "natives" within the prison that was the colonial state were municipal officials, industrialists, and missionaries. These enactments of settler state power directly affected and reshaped African consciousness.

Equally significant, state designs molded so-called "tribal dances" into colonial cages through which African identities were cast as "tribal," politically justifying the denial to urban Africans—the "tribesmen in the city"—of any claims on the "modern" polity (unfettered presence, access to "white" entertainment venues, the right to housing, social security, and political rights). Badenhorst and Mather (1997) have shown how, through this "tribal" dismembering and recreation, the South African apartheid state and capital re-created tribalism as a political instrument for maintaining the exploitative migrant labor system while denying Africans their rights as equal humans and workers. This way, song and dance became tools of colonial ideology, elaborating and objectifying disenfranchised African subjecthood. Beyond the foundational military force, this colonial capture and abuse of African traditions constituted a deeper epistemic violation of African being that helped nurture the fiction of colonial rule as a "negotiated" project. It becomes intellectually problematic, then, to celebrate the "negotiation" (with the fragments) of the African subject while silencing the violence that made both the fragmentation and the "negotiation" possible. What price did Africans pay in such "negotiation?"

Growing up in Alexandra, a segregated Joburg ghetto, young Mark Mathabane had to make a conscious, painful decision to "reject the tribal traditions" of his ancestors that apartheid had appropriated to romanticize African identities as both disconnected from each other and backward-looking:

> Apartheid had long adulterated my heritage and traditions, twisted them into tools of oppression and indoctrination. I saw at a young age that apartheid was using tribalism to deny me equal rights, to separate me from my black sisters and brothers, to justify segregation and perpetuate white power and privilege, to render me subservient, docile and, therefore, exploitable. . . . I had to reject this brand of tribalism, and in that rejection I ran the risk of losing my heritage. (1986, xi)

According to Paulo Freire (1970), this is the classic dilemma for conquered peoples and "object societies": the cultivation of cultural ambivalence, confusion, self-doubt, and inferiority. The dominated often introject the cultural myths, values, and lifestyles of the dominators or the metropolitan society, resulting in the "duality of the dependent society, its ambiguity, its being and not being itself, and the ambivalence characteristic of its long experience of dependency, both attracted by and rejecting the metropolitan society" (59). This particularly colonial malady, a Duboisian "double consciousness," afflicted Mathabane and millions of other Africans against whom cultural and racial differences were weaponized into a province for grand "native" policymaking and social engineering. The parallels in Rhodesian and South African policy were not a fortuitous coincidence, but the result of deliberate replications of colonial wisdom for dealing with common "native problems" in the imagined "white men's countries." Similarly, many of the "native" policy architects, including ethnomusicologist Hugh Tracey and "native administrator" Hugh Ashton, alternately worked in both South Africa and Southern Rhodesia, as well as the wider network of the white settler world. This was the power of the European colonizing discourse as a traveling, transterritorial epistemic register.

Thanks to these colonial agents, choices about how one could pass time and enjoy leisure often came loaded with difficult ethical, ideological, and political implications even to the young minds of African children. The question then arises: can contemporary scholarship afford to mimic colonial discourse in its fascination with the "vitality" and "vibrancy" of indigenous musical dances while ignoring or minimizing the palpable questions of power that framed such practices? The risk is that ignoring, minimizing, or uncritically celebrating the "ethnological" archive not only reproduces the coloniality of knowledge but also perpetuates the colonial trivialization of African being and the displacement of indigenous self-knowledge by the "expertise" of self-proclaimed ethno-specialists. The result is objectified, silenced, and doubly subalternized Sekai Nzenzas and Mark Mathabanes of the African world, known and perpetually spoken for by others.

Together with its counterpart across the Limpopo, the Rhodesian state sought to appropriate African music, domesticate its versatility by distilling it into some "tribal," fossilized essence, and, ultimately, redeploy it as a weapon to reinforce and perform its hegemony over its producers. For this reason, "tribal dances" constituted a vernacularized text of colonial exploitation of cultural difference. Masked by the rubric of entertainment, this invented or reified "native" difference articulated a self-justifying discourse of conquest and domination in a process that sought to produce "the African" as a lesser, marginal, exploitable, and vaingloriously proud "tribal" being. Nonetheless, the performative nature of these colonial instruments created possibilities beyond their designs (Larkin 2008, 3), emphasizing the need to equally engage with African investment in the coproduction, disruption, and repurposing of these same structures. Therefore, to fully understand African urban recreation as a(nta)gonistic dancing with power, I conceptualize the "tribal dance" as an aspect of the colonial "traditions" that European colonists and Africans cocreated in reactionary complicity at the point of the colonial encounter. Colonists deployed such cultures as cultural technologies and weaponries of domination; and, through the magic of performativity, Africans deployed them as, *inter alia,* tools to contest that domination.

Many youngsters of ambition responded to the colonial ideology of tribalism like Mathabane, distancing themselves from the apparently captured "tribal recreations" and choosing "civilized" entertainment—"modern" bands, brass bands, ballroom dancing, quickstepping, foxtrotting, and waltzing under the patronage of colonial officialdom. And ethnomusicologists like Tracey scathingly denounced them for mimicking European culture and abandoning or bastardizing their own "authentic" cultures. The language of "civilization," progress, and class had already found its way into these aspiring middle classes' cultural toolbox. At the same time, while settlers denounced these "cheeky, mimicking natives," the Native Affairs Department (NAD), in its discourse of "native administration," celebrated law-abiding, "happy natives" who performed in "modern," "native" bands and groups that bore curious, vernacularized English names. Bedecked in European-style suits and top hats, these youngsters constituted themselves into "duos," "trios," and "quads" whose monikers referenced African American ethnic performativity, singing the idiom of progress and performing colonial dances as *chimanjemanje* (modernity) while denouncing African ways as *chinyakare* (outdated traditions).

But was this register a sign of something deeper than its assimilated and vilified (or feted) forms? Does it suggest a mere African internalization of missionary psychological witchcraft, *uroyi hwevauyi*? Or, as Christopher Ballantine (1991) suggests of the Black South African aspiring middle classes, were they literally "singing to the white man" to open the gates to upward mobility? By reinserting the power ratio into this narrative of "native spectacle," I interrogate an urban glare or city lights theory that has often blinded scholars into breathlessly celebrating, or contemptuously dismissing, African urban cultures as mere entertainment bereft of deeper significance. Yes, Africans did perform and enjoy music, dances, and "sketches." They patronized the Central African Film Unit's bioscope (Burns 2002) or otherwise passed time in the *rukesheni* recreation halls. But what else did these sanctioned and sanctioning spaces bear and the donated or appropriated rubric of civilized entertainment purvey? What were the productive capabilities of these spaces and discourses? Or were they truly circumscribed and sterilized? What were the effects of the colonial agenda to confine? What was the power of fun?

I read the close official superintendence not only as colonial paternalism but also as counterinsurgency against (the possibility of) subversion from within (and beyond) the gates. My rereading of ostensible state support as a colonizing and policing structure transcends the debate about whether or not the colonial state promoted or suppressed African indigenous music, interrogating, instead, the nature, intent, processes, and outcomes of the apparent sociopolitical engineering. Refocusing the inquiry thus allows for an evaluation of both the colonial designs and the responses of the subjects (and objects) of all this colonial expertise to this knowledge production. Africans maintained and produced their own powerful, competing epistemes.

The Limits of Colonial Power: Indigenous Libraries

Beyond evaluating the colonial mind, this story explores the power of African cultural self-determination. Africans were able to subvert the state's sociopolitical engineering stratagems and, for practical purposes, to reclaim urban space because the musical domain and recreational space remained unconquered terrains of struggle in spite of colonial designs to domesticate, enclose, control, and exclude. Thus, while the state sought to make colonial cities into geographies of white power and to consign leisure to segregated, racialized spaces, a close investigation into African cultural performativity illustrates Africans' ability to interrogate this power and to remap place and space. Africans assailed the cultural underbelly of the colonial state and articulated epistemologies of self-liberation even within the tight corners of the criminalized colonial everyday.

African Music, Power, and Being in Colonial Zimbabwe advances emergent thinking in African urban historiography that rejects the treatment of Africans as confused dupes who became culturally lost once they set foot in the "white man's town" (Ranger 2010; M. Vambe 2007). Africans deployed music, dance, spirituality, and other performative cultures to (re)assert themselves as active agents and indigenous intellectuals, to unmake their colonial marginalization and reshape their own destinies. Scholars who favor the Chimurenga-as-revolution reading of Madzimbabwe cultures and politics often dismiss the 1930s–50s as an age of high cultural imperialism. Writing on Ghana, Cole (2001, 3) finds this period politically productive, for it was then that the ubiquitous concert parties in that sister British colony "made a dramatic transition from serving as British propaganda honoring 'Empire Day' to promoting cultural nationalism." Similarly, many Zimbabwean "modern" bands, *makwaya,* and "traditional" dance troupes participated in the ubiquitous similar spectacles of imperial and Rhodesian commemoration. Yet many of those performances constituted what James Scott (1990) designated public transcripts that might disguise much less flattering subtexts. Many stories here draw out these critical subtexts and hidden (and not-so-hidden) transcripts.

African crowds often converged on sanctioned ghetto recreational spaces and mapped paths and agendas to occupy the city in organized and spontaneous demonstrations buoyed by song, violating the *cordons sanitaires* of colonial cartographies of racialized being. They not only appropriated the *rukesheni* halls and even renamed some of them after African liberation heroes; they also formed their nationalist parties and held their occasional political meetings there under the cover of authorized *makonzati.* Many of the same white-superintended "modern" bands and ballroom dance troupes also camouflaged and helped mobilize funds for political action, while they boldly demanded self-rule in many of their songs. Thanks to these preexistent cultures of resistance, by the 1960s guerrilla recruiters found popular recreation halls, *mashabhini* (*shebeens*), and *makonzati* ready sites for clandestine recruitment for the armed struggle. Thus, some of the key transformative processes in African politics can be located within the same recreational bracket that colonial administrators deployed to capture and eviscerate African being. African agency inverted the captive leisure bracket into a dangerous margin of self-regeneration.

Ultimately, *African Music, Power, and Being in Colonial Zimbabwe* demonstrates that while African cultural and political consciousness appropriated colonial infrastructures and dominant registers for self-articulation, Africans' actions were anchored in deeper indigenous consciousness that defied colonialism. This is the genealogy of the songs that would win the liberation war in the 1970s, a deeper Chimurenga sensibility that dates back to the epochal first confrontation with colonial occupiers. This was a register that colonialism largely failed to penetrate, command, and conquer. I decipher this consciousness in the ways in which African men, women, and children in the villages, the masses of factory workers and the unemployed crowds on the streets, "professional" musicians in the "locations" and criminalized underclass revelers on the dusty ghetto fringe, and teachers and students at kraal and mission schools all variously "sang for freedom" (Masiye 1977). They codified their voices into a powerful text of African self-liberation. Their capability to resist, inculturate, and appropriate shaped contemporary African nationalism as a story about assembling and weaponizing both the incoming and the preexistent cultural registers for self-liberation.

Structure of the Book

The book consists of ten core chapters weaved around three broad, interconnected thematic threads: the colonial missionary factor (chapters 1–3), colonial urbanity and African performativity (chapters 4–7), and music and self-liberation (chapters 8 and 9). Chapters 1 and 2 explore the missionary attack on African musical cultures. They argue that this attack represented an assault on the foundations of African being with the intent to disarm the people culturally as part of the process of colonial subject making. The assault was both physical and epistemological, as represented by the missionary whippings of village performers and the execution of spirit mediums and leaders of the First Chimurenga. Chapter 3 details the dramatization of these assaults in a 1930 missionary-instigated state investigation into what the missionaries called the "evil night dances." The chapters demonstrate that the latter action was made possible by the former, and that the investigation demonstrates the crisis of missionary witchcrafting of African being—that is, the spiritual and psychological subversion of African consciousness. The ethnocentric violence threw the mission church into crisis by the 1940s, as *vatendi* (African converts) increasingly demanded not just the cessation of the attacks but also the Africanization of the alien church. The ultimate irony, however, was that the embattled church soon determined that "baptizing" Africans' "heathen" songs for church use might be its only redemption, hence the belated attempt to reform by the 1940s. These chapters therefore contextualize the often-favorable image of a church (particularly the Catholic Church) that ostensibly accommodated aspects of African cultures. The chapters also furnish the missing historical background to the fledgling historiography on gospel and popular music genres in Zimbabwe and Southern Africa.

Chapters 4–7 intervene with a critical discourse analysis into the celebrated "popular culture" arena of African early colonial urbanization. Chapters 4 and 5 explore the Native Social Welfare policy that sought to capture African cultures for "native administration," while chapters 6 and 7 make sense of how Africans variously responded to those policies through appropriation, subversion, resistance, and avoidance, seeing these strategies as illustrative of complex African cultural and political consciousness. For instance, on the one hand, chapter 6 illustrates how some Africans appropriated western cultural capital and discourses to churn out a rich dialogue of self-crafting that tended both to problematically reaffirm and to disrupt the *raison d'être* of the discordant colonial modernity that justified African despoliation. On the other, through a reading of songs like "Aya Mahobho," "Nzve," and "Skokiaan," chapter 7 illustrates not only the underclass's subversion and defiance of colonial maps of racialized power but also, more importantly, its ability to celebrate such defiance in self-fashioning registers that transcended colonial negation, confinement, and classist alienation.

The last thematic cluster deals with African musical cultures and self-knowledge as weapons that Africans drew on to elaborate their self-liberation. Taken separately, chapter 8 reconceptualizes nationalism as self-knowledge, as historical memory of sovereign pasts that inspired possibilities for self-restoration. It proposes a new reading of the Madzimbabwe liberation struggle that recenters cultural reequipment and decenters the gun-centric analyses that scholars like Frantz Fanon have helped reify. Chapter 9 then further substantiates the argument by analyzing the huge archive of Chimurenga songs that "guerrilla artists"—villagers, youths, students, urban workers, political prisoners, and professional musicians—sang on various *madariro* (performance platforms) throughout the colonial era. This particular song archive illustrates that the Chimurenga sensibility as cultural self-awareness has a historically deeper and broader indigenous genealogy, which Southern African scholarship has yet to fully recognize. It shows that the culture of resistance that Madzimbabwe call Chimurenga was not limited to the epic of combatant war but had suffused the African everyday since the advent of colonialism. In effect, Chimurenga songs help to contextualize the liberation war from the grassroots, for, as my student Hamza Mannan (2014) aptly put it, "Wars are bloody affairs for which the will to fight is drawn from the deepest wells." The wells ran deeply and perennially, joining the First and Second Chimurenga into the same transgenerational project of self-liberation.

Chapter 10 is a transgenerational conversation with Gogo Jane Lungile Ngwenya about African being under colonial domination. By presenting the conversation verbatim, the chapter takes the reader to the *dare,* the African communal space and professoriate where history is authored and transacted transgenerationally and communally in ways that challenge the imposed, alienating "modern" hubris of "expert" claims to individual authorship of people's collective knowledges. Through its format, this chapter (more than any other) helps us rethink the prevalent tendency to reduce African historical figures to mere "native informants," rehabilitating them as active agents who participate in the production of their own historical knowledge.

I wrap up the narrative with an epilogue, raising questions on the enduring legacies and debates about the changing salience of song in post-colonial Madzimbabwe cultural politics of independence, nation building, and contemporary struggles over the past, historical memory, and knowledge production.

1 Missionary Witchcrafting African Being

Cultural Disarmament

Sometimes in an idle hour I amused myself by writing on the chest or back of the boys some inscription or design. A hard straw makes a whitish mark on their black skin, very much like the mark made by a pencil on a slate.

—J. H. Morrison, *Streams in the Desert*

How can one prevent the loss of respect of child for father when the child is actively taught by his know-all white tutors to disregard his family's teachings? How can an African avoid losing respect for his tradition when in school his whole cultural background is summed up in one word: barbarism?

—Steve Biko, *I Write What I Like*

In a paper that he read at the University College of Rhodesia and Nyasaland in 1961, W. F. Rea argued that European missionaries should be judged as individuals who obeyed Jesus' command to set out and teach the Christian gospel to all nations, not as people whose purpose was to further any political ideology, including the imperialism of the late nineteenth century. He contended that their work will certainly be judged, "but it is only in the Kingdom of heaven that the verdicts are published" (2). Rea's work represents missionary self-writing, one of whose tenets is self-praise for "helping poor heathens" (Chadya 1997, 6). Thankfully, the copious archive of the mission and the psychological imprint it etched in the African consciousness—deeper than Morrison's hard straw on the children's black skin and longer lasting than the ephemeral missionary pencil on the slate—allow scholars to evaluate their work and its impact, here on earth. European missionaries intruded into the nineteenth- and twentieth-century African world as potent omens of unprecedented political, social, cultural, and economic turmoil and transformation. Africans dealt with them in their various guises as colonial functionaries, traders, gunrunners, vested moral agents, technologists, educationists, healers, and settlers. As pathfinders and cobearers of the imperial flag, missionaries were key agents in the colonization of Africa and African consciousness (Jean Comaroff and John Comaroff 1991).

I open this book by examining missionary attitudes and actions and how these impacted African consciousness and sociocultural security, which I read primarily through the optic of "ritualized sound," that is, song in its constitutive politico-cultural context (Wilde 2007, 5). This deep context is crucial because song is principally a sign of larger value systems, rather than an isolated expressive trait. It was because of this deep context that missionaries assaulted African musical cultures as special manifestations of "savagery," seeking to displace them in the African consciousness and replace them with European (and) Christian songs and musical cultures. Beyond the overt military violence that planted the colonial flag, this principally psychological assault sought to witchcraft African being, that is, to subvert Africans' psychosocial worldview, to spiritually disarm them in order to facilitate their re-creation into subordinated beings amenable to alien colonial designs.

While many Africans were able to blunt the missionary assault by tenaciously holding on to their indigenous philosophies and by inculturating aspects of the mission, the assault nonetheless significantly undermined the cultural foundations of their being, *chivanhu*. From its advent, the colonial evangelical mission conflated Christianity with European cultures while condemning African cultures as paganism. To fully appreciate this assault and its psychosocial effects, I preface this chapter with a scrutiny of the idea of the evangelical mission as it developed primarily in Zimbabwe and Southern Africa. It is essential to remember this transterritorial purview because the mission was a traveling colonizing register that simultaneously served and transcended bounded territoriality.

Theorizing the Christian Mission: A Traveling Colonizing Register

The killing of the Putukezi (Portuguese) Jesuit priest Goncalo da Silveira by the Mutapa in 1561 halted the European missionary incursion, which did not return to the VaKaranga people, whom the Paris Evangelical Missionary Society's Francois Coillard called the "long neglected Banyai," until three centuries later. It returned as part of the northward expansion of empire from South Africa, the pedestal of white settlerism on the continent. In the judgment of John Buchanan of Lovedale Mission in South Africa, this mission was particularly "perilous but honourable." Hailing the effort of its head, Reverend Coillard, Buchanan (*Christian Express*, January 1, 1877) explained that the "perils" went beyond the great and terrible wilderness, with its beasts and deadly reptiles, its hunger, thirst, and wearing toils, its blazing sun, and its "reeking fever-beds." All these, he averred, shrank into insignificance "in the presence of the frightful magnitude of moral and spiritual evils to be encountered." He thus defined the mission as a direct, determined, multipronged attack on African cultures that he designated "Satan's seat, the very heart of African heathenism, the very central citadel of darkness, crime, and misery."

Considered retrospectively in the context of Coillard's subsequent snubbing and swift ejection from the country by Africans, Buchanan's characterization of this "field" reads rather like an eerie presentiment of the fate that awaited his colleague. But more importantly, his account signifies the mood of the returning European mission, garbed in the post-Enlightenment armor of cultural prejudice and fully backed by the military muscle of the incipient colonial state. The missionary discourse might certainly be read as propaganda for various purposes. My interest is neither to (dis)prove the discourse's truth claims nor to engage its various internal tensions. I analyze its deployment—that is, attitudes, sensibilities, and utterances—through the copious writings it produced (newsletters, travelogues, field notes, diaries, minutes of meetings, (auto)biographies, memoirs, and letters), seeing it both as a usable discourse and as praxis. The rich missionary archive and the variety of African experiences that I draw on allow me to dissect the attitudes, approaches, and actions this discourse betrayed, authorized, rationalized, and justified, and to think about how it affected African personhood, its object. Read both against and along the grain, this particularly copious and deeply confessional archive constituted what Esther Lezra has aptly described as the "colonial art of demonizing others."

The missionaries' new equipment lent force to their long-running rhetoric and self-construction as soldiers of Christ who bore arms against African "savagery." Following the missionaries' chronicles, one is struck by the vivid, recurrent twin imageries of the repugnant "heathen" dance and the metaphor of war. The missionaries were obsessed with the dance, projecting it into one key index of the "savagedom" that justified their very existence. The dance seemed to mysteriously give the missionaries energy to trudge on from village to village, effectively reducing African communities into citadels of the "darkness" upon which they trained their arsenal. A few quick examples help to sketch out a representative mental picture of the missionary figure spoiling for a fight on the "Dark Continent." The Methodist priest S. Douglas Gray wrote in 1923,

> See an African village as it nestles beneath the hill in all its glory of a full tropical moon, and one can delight in its picturesque beauty and artistic effect; but visit that same kraal under the searchlight of the blazing sun, and see those things that were glossed over by the gentle moonbeams, its untidiness, its litter of evil-smelling things, its filth and general unsatisfactoriness, and the first impression is rudely dispelled. (27)

This antinomic, romantic exoticization and condemnation constituted a long-running European imagination of the African cultural constitution. Back in 1894, Mrs. Louw, the young wife of A. A. Louw of the Dutch Reformed Church (DRC) at the Morgenster Mission Station near Great Zimbabwe, had similarly pondered the station's topography and "bush," and what they must hide, and framed her thoughts in the language of the popular missionary hymn "From Greenland's Icy Mountains":

> The scenery all round is very beautiful and uplifting—large, strangely-shaped rocks, deep ravines, tall, graceful trees with dense foliage, the beauties of nature on every side; and one feels inclined to say, in the midst of all God's marvelous handiwork, "only man is vile." And sad, indeed, it is to think that everywhere amongst these "koppies," hundreds and thousands are living who don't know their Maker and all that is wonderful about them. . . . We are looking forward with much longing to a time when these poor heathen shall be lifted up out of sin and darkness and shall know and serve the only true God and receive Him as their Saviour. . . . Yesterday, we two—Mr. Louw and myself—walked to Zimbabye which is about four miles distant from here. . . . I believe the general idea is that it was once a large heathen temple. It does really look like it. And if it is, the thought came to me, how glad we should be that God has honoured us to send us to proclaim the true God almost on the very place where once the grossest idolatry was practised. (*Christian Express*, December 1, 1894)

Mrs. Louw's "testimonial" echoed Theodore Bent's (1893) verdict on Ishe Mugabe after visiting him as part of his brief from Cecil John Rhodes to excavate at and "prove" the white origins of this grand Madzimbabwe site. Bent had already discovered this abode of vileness, declaring, "Here is distinctly a spot where only man can be vile; and the great fat chief, seated on the top of a rock, sodden with beer, formed one of the vilest specimens of humanity I ever saw" (88). Mrs. Louw wrote her tale in a private letter to Lovedale Mission, reporting her and her husband's progress among "the Banyai," helping to map an imagined "terrain of evil." The historical inhabitants of the Zimbabwe plateau since at least 900 AD, the VaKaranga (VaNyai)—later designated "Shona" by Rhodes's settlers—were some of the latest crop to be folded into the expanding mission project, which had extended beyond the Limpopo and Zambezi river valleys by the mid-1870s.

A nondenominational, institutionally advanced mission station, Lovedale was the principal nerve center that drove this expansion, providing training and technical support in the field. It boasted a robust press that churned out the self-reinforcing missionary discourse as the frontier expanded. The Lovedale press, together with the newer Catholic and Protestant mission presses in Rhodesia and the region, thus provides a good insight into missionary evangelism as a traveling register whose power inhered in its ability to transcend geography, to sprawl its rhizomes across expansive space. The missionary register represents both a projection of an imported European colonizing psychology and its resonance and dissonance as it rebounded on the ground. The mission station propagated and relayed such ideas through itinerant missionaries, localized diocesans, visitors from "home," settlers, and to a degree, through differently positioned *vatendi*

(African converts). Early mission stations like Lovedale worked as rear bases and relay platforms for the deployment of personnel, equipment, and the ideas that constituted the ecumenical discourse. They recruited and trained local "bright boys" into helpers and sent them back to their natal communities or into the expanding transterritorial field. Wrote S. Douglas Gray (1923, 53), "The first native helpers accompanying the missionary are usually drawn from other fields already evangelized. . . . Our first African helpers [in Rhodesia] were brought from the Transvaal." A prominent example was Mamiyera Mizeka Gwambe—baptized Bernard Mizeki—a Mozambican Anglican catechist recruited in Cape Town and deployed among VaNhowe people of eastern Zimbabwe. I discuss the Mizeki story later.

Among the "helpers" were interpreters, evangelist-teachers, carrier-trekkers, and porters who hauled the missionaries on palanquins and carry chairs, and their baggage in headloads and wagons. They also hauled the missionaries' liturgical literature, including the first hymnbooks: translations of translations—English to Zulu (or Xhosa) to Shona—set to quaint European melodies.[1] The mission was an extraordinary intervention in African life worlds, and its cultivation depended as much on African labor and resources as on the begging bowl at home.

The missionaries generally located their mission stations on high ground, often targeting places that Africans considered sacred. The Morgenster DRC Mission Station peered down on African homesteads from the Mugabe Mountains of ancient Madzimbabwe. What was the rationale for siting the stations thus?

Hunting and shooting down African "rebels" during the African uprisings in Malindadzimu (also called Matombo, rocks, corrupted Matopo) Hills in 1896, British trooper R. S. S. Baden-Powell reflected on the process of crafting the colony through cultural conquest and disarmament. He wrote to his mother in England, "[Even] when the present force has broken up the *impis* in the field, and cleared their strongholds out, there will remain a tale of work for local police to do in carrying out disarmament" (1970, 137). The settlers worried not only that African fighters would cache their weapons for another uprising, but also that such an uprising would again likely be spiritually driven. Malindadzimu—the abode for the ancestors' graves—was a burial place for African rulers, and was therefore sacred. In light of this, fellow trooper Frederick Selous (1896, 61) thus agreed that "striking terror into the hearts of wild savages" and forcing them to surrender their guns, knobkerries, spears, and bows and arrows was the easier of two tasks; beyond the physical destruction, they also had to destroy the people spiritually. This meant searching out and assassinating the priests of Mwari (M'limo), the African High God, and destroying their *mapanya* (shrines, sing. *banya*). Through the killings and physical destruction, the colonists intended to spiritually reengineer the African subject to guarantee a permanent colonial future. The destructive logic was informed by the realization that "hardly a hill or cave existed, in a landscape full of hills and caves, which did not have a religious or political historical significance" (Ranger 1987, 159). Projecting a future state of total African subjugation, Baden-Powell explained, "The doses being given . . . 'though bitter now, they're better then.'" The immense violence "seems the only way to get these men to understand there is a greater power than their M'limo; and once the lesson has been unmistakably brought home to them, there is some hope that a time of peace *en permanence* may dawn for them" (138). Mission stations were then built literally on the rubble of the *mapanya*—destroyed by cannon and the Maxim gun—completing the claiming of African cultural landscapes.

The Brethren in Christ Church (BICC), a semi-ascetic American missionary body, challenged the African cosmological order early on by holding its first mass in a cave in Malindadzimu in 1880, where Africans buried their rulers and consulted Mwari (Ranger 1999, 15). One of the church's leaders, Rev. Jesse Engle, approached Rhodes, founder of the colony, in Cape Town in 1898 with a request, and Rhodes accordingly telegraphed his lieutenant in the British South Africa Company (BSAC), Arthur Lawley, asking him to grant land to the church to establish a station in the region. Rhodes told him, "I think you might grant a farm of fifteen hundred morgen in the middle of natives, title to be given after proof of work, place say Bulalema or one of the outfalls say near De Beers grant or say in Mattoppos to deal with Umlugulu or Somabula" (L. Mahoso 1979, 16). This communiqué reaffirmed the political significance of a strategic location for the missions, signaling a shared conceptualization of the idea of a mission as a weapon for conquest. And Rhodes added matter-of-factly, as he often did by way of explanation whenever he parceled out African lands to the various denominations, "This class I think is better than policemen and cheaper" (Hostetter 1967, 26). The mission's job, Rhodes reiterated, was to epistemologically revolutionize and spiritually disarm Africans for empire. The BICC therefore duly planted its Matopo Mission Station in the natural fastnesses of the granite hills.

Africans had harnessed these topographical fortifications in fighting the colonial troops to a standstill in 1896, forcing Rhodes to negotiate for peace. These *matombo* were therefore also a fort of a different kind. They harbored the national temples of Mwari (at Mabweadziva and other shrines), whom Africans consulted through his messengers on questions of national security (wars, droughts, pestilences). Umlugulu and Somabula were key resistance leaders in this part of the country, and they worked with Mwari oracles like Mukwati Ncube to propagate the spirit of resistance. It is not surprising, then, that Rhodes deployed the BICC along the war trails that had been cut by highly equipped mercenaries like Frederick Burnham, an American who had "seen service against the Red Indians" (Baden-Powell 1970, 70). Burnham and his colleagues assassinated spiritual practitioners in the cavernous hills to demoralize the anticolonial fighters, and the incipient colonial state deployed the church to doubly subject Africans to the white man and his god. A letter to the editor of the July 1, 1871, *Kaffir Express*, signed "A Colonist," had rhetorically posed the fundamental question with reference to the Xhosa: "[How] are we to prepare the Kaffirs and make them fit to be governed by the laws of civilized and Christian communities?" Spiritual disarmament was the unambiguous answer: "It is evident that we must secure the services of Missionaries, and we must allow them to some extent to take the lead." Once Christendom has been planted, "the Kaffir himself will only too gladly and willingly seek to be subject" to colonialism.

The missionaries clearly shared this mercenary brief, as is apparent even in BICC Sister Frances Davidson's disclaimer of one. To her, the location of the Matopo Mission Station on African shrines and burial grounds for indigenous rulers indicated not a "mercenary motive" on the part of Rhodes, but rather a "conviction, borne out by experience and by long years of contact with the Africans, that missionary work and the Christianization of the natives was the only solution of the native problems" (1915, 49). Davidson is saying that the "native problem," that is, African resistance to colonialism, could be overcome more easily and thoroughly by a spiritually alienating religion than by the gun alone. Similarly, reporting on a new Catholic mission station among the Tonga people at Chikuni across the Zambezi River in 1910, the *Zambesi Mission Record* (*ZMR*) pointed out, "The missionaries' residence is built on the site of a *murende*—sacred grove of the spirits." The desecration was quite purposive, as the report indicated: "No native would venture to build on such a spot." Predictably, the mission's African builders reportedly "turned up five witchdoctors' bones on the site" (*ZMR*, July 1910). Both conceptually and in practice, therefore, the missionary functioned as a spiritual mercenary out to destroy African being for empire.

The Anglicans deployed Bernard Mizeki, a catechist, to evangelize among Ishe Mangwende's VaNhowe people of east-central Zimbabwe in the mid-1890s. He was killed there in June 1896, and the church declared him a martyr and the first African saint in the country. According to the official narrative, "during the Mashona rebellion against the Europeans and their African friends, Bernard was especially marked out, in part because he had offended the local witch doctor" (Granger 2012). The implication is that the catechist fell victim to the combined anticolonial and "heathen" fervor during the First Chimurenga. A counterstory narrates how Mizeki targeted the VaNhowe people's sacred hills for a mission station, desecrating the burial grounds of departed chiefs and erecting crosses at caves and groves that served as the people's indigenous spiritual sites. In spite of the conflict his actions caused, Ishe Mangwende reportedly gave him his daughter in marriage. But, apparently unsatisfied, Mizeki is alleged to have gone on to sleep with the two wives of Mushawatu, the chief's eldest son. Outraged, Mushawatu's younger brothers, Gomwe and Muchemwa, ambushed and murdered Mizeki at night and burned his corpse, which they adjudged unfit to be buried in their land. For this crime, according to Mushawatu's great-grandson Neddington Mushawatu, Mizeki's white patrons shot Mushawatu and scattered his family. The Anglican Church allegedly shrouded this scandal in a conspiracy of silence and threats, identifying Mizeki as a saint and designating the place of his killing a holy shrine (Mushawatu, interview). Each June, thousands of Anglican pilgrims throng the shrine of St. Bernard Mizeki today.

At the national level, Rhodes's burial in Matombo in 1902, in accordance with his will, symbolized the unity of church and state in colonial politics and represented the ultimate challenge to African cosmology. To settlers, the interment installed him as the "spirit" of the land, triumphing over the African guardians on the hills (Ranger 1999, 30–31). Settler desecration of Africans' graves and veneration of their own was a part of the design of spiritual disarmament. To generations of Africans, the entombment of Rhodes and his lieutenants—including Allan Wilson, first buried at the Great Zimbabwe site and then reinterred at Malindadzimu (Matombo), and Charles Coghlan, elected as the first settler Prime Minister of Rhodesia when BSAC rule ended in 1923—at Malindadzimu constituted mortuary defilement of the land. Similarly, it was no coincidence that the mission stations started to gain converts only after the wars of occupation had violently disrupted African societies and thoroughly desecrated indigenous spiritual institutions. The psychological impact of engineered disaster (war, famine, spiritual alienation,

"Silencing the Oracle": American mercenary Frederick Burnham's portrait of himself shooting African spirit mediums in Malindadzimu. All images in this chapter are courtesy of the National Archives of Zimbabwe.

Kaodza Gumboreshumba (the medium of Kaguvi), Nyakasikana Charwe (the medium of Mbuya Nehanda), and other captured leaders of the First Chimurenga.

Manhungetunge: shackled one to the other by the ankle, these guerrillas defiantly bond, holding one another by the arm in the spirit of Chimurenga.

Captives converted *en masse:* African women and children at Hope Fountain Mission.

social rejection, and death) then propelled a gospel of individual salvation in the shadow of the destruction of African collective security and physical displacement of people from their productive and sacral anchors. In the future, there could be no other way to maintain African subjection to the European order but a sustained "confrontation between Christianity and the fundamental features of African traditional cosmologies," as Bourdillon and Bucher (Bucher 1980, 12) insisted even as Africans were finally dislodging the colonial regime in the late 1970s. Colonial confrontation was multipronged, and it worked spatially and epistemologically, producing and thriving on the crisis in African consciousness.[2]

Writing about Bembesi, the first Free Presbyterian Church of Scotland mission station, on a supervisory visit from Scotland in 1909, Rev. John Mackay observed, "The Mission is planted in a particularly healthy spot, being on the ridge of elevated ground which separates two small tributaries of the great Zambezi River, and thus in almost every direction the view is open for many miles around" (Radasi 1966, 42). The archetypal mission station colonized landscapes that had strategic relationships to its object communities, favoring plateaus, sacred groves, and water sources—key sites of African sacrality and visuality. Architecturally, the mission's strategy was to overwhelm the African village. Thus, Reginald Smith (1950, 1) visualized Penhalonga Mission as "standing up amongst the gum trees, its corrugated iron roof a flash in the sun, its brick-built walls a warm, mellow red," contrasting with "the little round huts with thatched roofs and mud walls that go to make the African village." Similarly, through Morrison's (1969, 53) missionary eyes, one can visualize Livingstonia, planted on Mount Kondowe in Malawi, as "no doubt the most remarkable achievement in Central Africa." Africans buried their elders in *ninga,* caves under the hills, which became infused with their spirits and were therefore sacred. They propitiated the ancestors and prayed to Mwari there. "That's where we went to make offerings. We went to the mountain and would ask for rain and we would have rain," said Mushure about Chirozva Mountain, before missionaries claimed it for a mission station.[3]

This is how the mission station sought to displace the village and its sacred sites and make itself the center of African life, a beacon radiating Christian light into the abysses of the proverbial "valley of death." It posited its psychological function as the elevation of the surrounding "heathen" neighborhoods. And if, as Mrs. Louw suggested (*Christian Express,* December 1, 1894), the inhabitants of these eminent domains of God were a regrettable blot on nature's beauty, that was precisely the mission's professed *raison d'être,* its call to life. Therefore, dialectically positioned *pachikomo* (on the hilltop), the glamorous mission station constructed the African village as its depraved opposite and as an object for "civilizing." Such attacks on the village (especially the "kitchen hut"), as on the *banya,* sought to undermine its significance as the core religious and cultural space where every African family communed with its ancestors, where social life was ordered, and where rituals of passage (birth, death, and transition into the afterlife) were consummated.

Evangelizing meant drawing those labeled "pagans" from these condemned spaces of "heathendom" to the self-proclaimed "outposts of progress." It was here, on the proverbial hill, that the "uncivilized" from the "kraals" (in the demonizing colonial vocabulary) were brought to be "civilized," to be taught knowledge, "true" religion, culture, and manners, to be saved from their "sins," to be elevated and taught to sing amazing new truths. The mission station became the new locus of power in the epistemological reconstruction of African being. This is how Mrs. Louw imagined herself at Morgenster, busying herself self-consciously with the "blighted valleys":

> The work goes on. Sunday services held, kraals visited, and the evening school continued for our boys on the station.... A few weeks back, I started a sewing class for the girls. Mrs. Euvrard and the evangelists' wives help me.... We have up to twenty-two already. You would be surprised to see how nicely they manage. There is one tiny little girl, such a nice little thing, who does sew so nicely. ... While they sew, I teach them to sing, and considering they have never done any singing except their monotonous, inharmonious Native songs, they keep the tune very well. We teach them one of the four or five hymns translated into the language. (*Christian Express*, December 1, 1894)

It did not matter that Mrs. Louw did not speak "Kaffir," relying on African interpreters for communication. She was the white Father's wife, and that status and her novel technological advantage ordained her judge, teacher, and model for African women and children. This is how, positioned as a social laboratory, the mission experimented on African humanity, seeking to lead them into new socioeconomic, cultural, and spiritual realms approximating—but never equaling or rivaling—the white world (Heise 1967). From its vantage point, the mission station was also an observatory from which the missionary watched and listened to the African world, venturing out to persuade and chastise, assess, judge, and commandeer.

Missionaries framed African cultures as diabolical impediments to evangelization. They invariably condemned marriage practices, initiation rites, spirituality, medical knowledge and healing practices, "spirituous" beers, the very names of the people, and leisure practices, often identifying the "heathen dances" which appeared to drive all social life as "particularly pernicious and degrading to the extreme." These they determined to "root out" and replace with "innocent and healthy entertainment" (*Christian Express*, July 1, 1901). Like farmers on unbroken land, the missionaries surveyed the African terrain to chart the feasibility of cultivating a new "Christian personality" out of the "primitive pagan" (*South African Outlook*, January 2, 1935). This terrain—which the missionary discourse transmogrified into the African body—was imagined as "a purely heathen field," as Rev. Mackay characterized the Ndebele in 1909 (quoted in Radasi 1966, 43). It was a body-field blighted by "kaffir customs, amusements and licentiousness," evils the missionary-cultivator had to purge if he wished to produce a wholesome yield for Christ. It mattered little that "Christ" oftentimes appeared to mean the missionary himself.

Christian Villages

The mission station's ultimate strategy was to incrementally increase its influence and replicate itself spatially. Central stations gave rise to outstations as they gradually penetrated African society and their evangelizing circuits expanded. As the mission station's power solidified, it hoped to capture and transform the surrounding African villages into "Christian villages" cleansed of "heathenism."

A Madzimbabwe establishing a new home usually conducted a *bira* or *doro remusha* (family beer ceremony) to consecrate it to his ancestors, bringing their spirits home to bless and protect their progeny. A black bull without any blemish was consecrated with libations of beer—*kudira doro*—and transformed into a *diramhamba*, a symbol of the family's protective patriarchal spirit and fecundity. Christianity co-opted and subverted this ritual, so that some converts came to similarly consecrate their homes to Jesus Christ, the new, purportedly universal *diramhamba* whose body and blood converts ritually consumed. For example, one Gibson Ndowe, a Methodist catechist at a Nyadiri Mission outstation, conducted such a ritual, with Mrs. Josephine O'Farrell from the mission presiding. O'Farrell glowingly described Ndowe's homestead, which featured nicely built square houses (as distinguished from round "heathen huts") furnished with tables and chairs, a well-swept yard, and a flourishing garden boasting a variety of fruit trees, vegetables, and flowers—all providing a useful ecclesiastical lesson to his "heathen neighbors." If this "methodically reconstructed symbolic map" (Jean Comaroff and John Comaroff 1997, 182)—the physical structures and their furnishings—suggested godliness to visitors, the moving church service and dedication ceremony amply reaffirmed the intended epistemic transformation. Josephine O'Farrell (1930?) wrote,

> The service was held in front of the house with the people sitting on the ground. Gibson and his wife and three children, his mother and father and several old aunts and uncles sat on the little veranda. The choir from the nearby station furnished the music. How different that music was from the usual beatings of tomtoms in the villages for special occasions. When they sang "Lord I want to be a Christian," one couldn't help comparing it with the way we have heard it rendered at home, yet it was music to our ears. The service was very impressive, and I judged from the way one old uncle vigorously rubbed his nose with snuff from time to time, that it offered much food for thought.

After the service, the crowd drank *maheu*, an unfermented malt beverage, and "groups from several stations danced in turn around the house singing their school chants." It was such homesteads as Ndowe's that seeded Christian villages and confirmed missionaries' construction of difference through the imagination of racialized Africans and selves. The mission station thus came to exert a powerful influence on the lives of Africans in the reserves in conjunction, and sometimes in competition, with the secular state, which the Native Commissioner, *mudzviti,* personified locally.

Missions were a veritable self-contained colonizing and governing structure. Not only did they collect taxes, they also administered the hated statutory destocking, cattle dipping, *chibharo* (forced labor requisitioning), and agricultural edicts for the benefit of the state and themselves. Most importantly, as Joyce Chadya (1997) observed, missionaries were ruthless landlords on the vast, alienated mission farms. Africans' precarious survival depended on their subservient observation of the new sociocultural regulations. For example, when the government finally granted title deeds to Empandeni Mission—the oldest Catholic mission in the colony—in 1900, Sister Josephine Bullen (2008, 16) diarized that

> Fr. Prestage made them put in that he had the power to send off the estate any "obnoxious characters." A few weeks ago, he gave notice to four bad spirited polygamists to leave Empandeni and appealed to the Commissioner to enforce this order. There is what is called a Government reserve where any native may go if he had nowhere else to settle.

Reinforced by the Private Locations Ordinance (1908), which limited the number of "squatters" or tenants on private (white) land, these evictions were rampant. By 1917, twenty-six tenants had been evicted from Chishawasha for, *inter alia,* adultery, failure to send children to school, nonattendance at church, and drinking "kaffir" beer (Chadya 1997, 69). More often than not, such "repugnant natives" had a tough time finding a foothold in a "reserve" if they failed to placate the *mudzviti,* the supreme white chief presiding over these pockets of land expropriated and gifted for exclusive African inhabitation. Missions like Empandeni, Chishawasha, Kutama, and Murombedzi quickly colonized the African communities around them, dividing them into two sets. The first comprised clusters of "Christian villages" under their own "Christian chiefs," who extracted taxes and labor. These villages were located on the mission farms on condition of adherence to a battery of social regulations requiring church and school attendance and prohibiting all "heathen" customs. The "Christian chiefs" were selected or approved by the missionaries and were often deeply loathed by Africans. The second set consisted of ostracized "pagan villages" run by "pagan chiefs" (L. Vambe 1976, 5; *ZMR,* October 1908). The missionaries policed this social division as a governing structure, as the *ZMR* observed casually in January 1907: "Some pagan families were still to be found in the Christian villages. A little firmness has proved sufficient to make them move to separate pagan kraals." The Chishawasha Jesuits celebrated the benefits of this division for tax extraction: "The payment of the government poll-tax was this year accomplished in a remarkably short time, two weeks sufficing for what was at one time a very long process. . . . Our Christians have now separate tax lists, each paying under the Chief of the Christian kraal in which he lives or intends to live after marriage" (*ZMR*, January 1909).

"A little firmness" often meant the missionary and his cadets making armed forays into the villages to molest the "pagans." Such attacks were particularly common whenever the missionaries established that cultural ceremonies and "heathen" dances were taking place—not just in the so-called Christian villages, but also in the condemned "pagan" quarters. On numerous occasions, the Empandeni Mission raiding force broke up proceedings at ceremonies, pursuing the participants with dogs and whipping *masvikiro* (mediums), healers, and dancers with *sjamboks,* hippo-hide whips. On one such occasion, they destroyed the entire homestead of a *n'anga* (healer), burning down his houses and chasing him into the night with threats to hang him if he ever returned (Peaden 1970, 21; *ZMR*, 1909, 1913).

This entirely reversed the power relationship between spirit mediums and the missionaries. For instance, on July 15, 1883, DRC preachers Gabriel and Simon Buys had held their first church service at Ishe Zimuto's court, where they had been invited for a *bira* the previous day. As usual, they attracted only one person to the service, which was drowned out by the continuing ceremony. But the ritual combat went beyond the sonics. The senior of the ten possessed *masvikiro* confronted the missionaries, disapproving of their activities and leading Ishe Zimuto to eject them (Beach 1973, 37). But now this combined power of the African religious and political offices was shattered. Missions broke up many African homes, separating husbands and wives who had been living in harmony and, in the name of the missionaries' god, taking sons and daughters away from their mothers (Kunonga 1996, 66). Polygamy, wife-inheritance, and fornication were arbitrarily defined and condemned as cardinal sins for which whole families as well as individuals were banished or paraded on mission grounds in sackcloth, caricaturing the African custom of *kutanda botso.* Lawrence Vambe (1976, 3) once saw two villagers—a widow and a widower—dressed thus, kneeling in front of the church at Chishawasha for hours as penance for alleged fornication. The mission's regime of epistemic and physical violence specially targeted the intimate realm of social reproduction. All missionary bodies, both Catholic and Protestant, exercised this arbitrary power to assault, eject, or otherwise punish Africans for adhering to what they considered "repugnant" customs, defaulting on taxes, not attending church, or failing to send children to school.

Vambe was born into an ill-fated Mashonganyika village, and saw the mission parceling it out into new "Christian villages with outlandish names like 'Rosario,' 'Monserrat,' 'Manressa,' and 'Loyola.'" After agonizing over the erosion of their way of life and realizing they could not move elsewhere, Vambe's family patriarch and matriarch, Grandfather Mhizha and Grandmother Madzidza, decided to endure the pain of *chirungu*—the "European ways"—in Loyola. *Kunze kwadoka* (The sun has set), they lamented. There was no doubt in anyone's mind that

> the church, both temporal and spiritual, held the whip . . . in all the tribal affairs of the Vashawasha people in the Mission, it could if it so wished, toss out of its lands any man, woman, or family at any time and for no reason at all. The church owned the Chishawasha people; its influence over the people was overpowering. . . . The church was everywhere as much as in the loud peals of the bell which rang out continually each day and was heard for miles around as authority of its dogmatic but largely mystifying teaching (L. Vambe 1972, 5)

As the sounds of the bell and the hymn regimented the daily work and ritual routines of missionized Africans, Vambe observed, "There were no more rain-making or spirit dances, nor any of the rousing drum-beating song assemblies that often made [African] life so distinctive." The extirpative power of the missions had become hegemonic, driving otherwise adamant African cultures underground. *Kunze kwachena!* (There is light now!), cheered the missionaries.

The church forced Africans to discard their cultures and to prostrate themselves before it if they wished to remain on their expropriated lands. Children had to accede to separation from their families and enter the mission schools, which would bring them up on a diet of servile education heavily infused with settler myth, rote Bible reading, manual labor, and hymn singing—"beating them into whiteness" (Klein 2007, 142) in the style of the infamous residential schools for "natives" in North America, Australia, and New Zealand.[4] The missionaries would constitute the children into brigades of deacons, deploying them to reengineer their own societies. Using this strategy, they drove a significant wedge between African conceptions of independent self and the new, missionized African believer, *mutendi*. This is how the mission station, as a social laboratory, sought to re-create African being. As the spokesman for the American Mission testified to the Commission Appointed to Enquire into the Matter of Native Education in 1925 (*Report* 1925, para. 238), that objective, the "mak[ing of] a new man of the African," could not be achieved just by the gospel; it also required literary and industrial training. Through the metaphor of the mission brass band, the next section considers how this missionary social scalpel reordered the African future.

Embodied Evils, Transpossessing Virtues: Schooling Africans for Empire

In October 1908, the *ZMR* rededicated itself to the "white man's burden," that is, his self-awarded mandate to lead Africans' "upward movement from barbarism to civilization." This was a burden Father Andrew Hartmann assumed quite personally. He had not only led the invasion of Madzimbabwe with the "Pioneer Column" in September 1890, but had also fought to crush the African resistance alongside the British South Africa Police, defending the "Zambesi mission" and the colony, both of which he had worked hard to plant. Thus, he could authoritatively look back and, deploying personal anecdote as collective settler memory, mark time and pass a verdict on the trajectory of "progress":

> When I preached my first sermon in English in the year 1890, I committed a curious *lapsus linguat,* speaking constantly of "creature-fellows" instead of "fellow-creatures.". . . When, a few weeks ago, I again saw Chishawasha after an absence of more than twelve years I said to myself, "The people of Chishawasha have been transformed from creature-fellows to fellow-creatures!" (*ZMR,* January 1908)

One metaphor for this story of African transformation was the Chishawasha Mission Band, made up of schoolboys boarded from the surrounding communities. To follow the itineraries of the Chishawasha Band is to trace the contours of this missionary transformation of Africans from "creature-fellows" to "fellow-creatures."

The March 1903 issue of the *ZMR* vividly described one tour made by this group. On January 22, a group of eighty-one "quite young" African boys set off from Chishawasha Mission huddled in two wagons behind galloping mules on an eight-hundred-mile journey to Mafeking, South Africa. This was the Chishawasha Band, a wind and brass orchestra founded in 1892 and trained by a Jesuit priest, Father Edward Biehler, who, together with the mission station's Father Superior, Francis Richartz, accompanied them on this trip. The boys had been quickly "gathered from the workshop and veld" in response to an urgent telegram from the governor of Cape Colony, Lord Grey, asking the mission's "native band" to perform for the British Colonial Secretary, Lord Chamberlain. Chamberlain was visiting South Africa to "heal wounds" in the wake of the just-ended Anglo-Boer war. According to the *ZMR,* this band, which was "a most picturesque and novel object," caused "a furore of excitement" in Bulawayo and other places where it performed on its return trip:

> The natives in all these places simply went mad with delight, proud that boys of their despised race and colour could achieve such results. As to the white population, their interest, if less demonstrative, was no less keen, while much more deeply seated. They were prepared to see "niggers" clashing cymbals, playing on whistles and using the nigger "bones"; but they were not prepared to see young Mashonas reading music with perfect ease, provided with all the instruments and equipment of a full brass band and playing with all the precision of a first-class military band.

At Mafeking, these youngsters reportedly had to be rescued from mobbing crowds for their own safety. A detachment of the band performed at Bulawayo's Grand Hotel, earning some money, part of which they shared amongst themselves. But beyond Mammon, the band also took a detour at Empandeni "in order to give edification and show the Matabele, who are a somewhat independent and supercilious race, what the Mashonas could do." Father Sykes kept the boys for a whole week in Bulawayo, where they performed every afternoon in the town square.

Evaluated thus through the prism of the civilizing mission, the "despised Mashonas" demonstrated through their "beautiful singing" that they could measure up to the new standards the missionaries strained to cultivate in them. The Jesuits at Chishawasha—"the lords of hard work and industry"—took special pride in the fact that the boys in fact engaged in this "ornamental occupation" only to relax from their more productive exertions on the mission farms, in the classroom, and at the altar, where they served and said grace in impeccable Latin. This highly symbolic reading—and inscription—of the boys' band resonated beyond the mission.[5] Their performances were the more important, suggested the *Rhodesia Herald* (January 24, 1903), because "the Mashona has long been regarded as the lowest type of race south of the Zambezi." That a number of their youths should be brought to "such a pitch of intelligence and training," gushed the settler mouthpiece, testified to the good work of the Chishawasha Fathers.

The boys soon became a virtual colonial public spectacle. The following year, they headlined the Victoria Day events in Salisbury, entertaining settlers marking the occupation of their country. The *Rhodesia Herald* reported (May 26, 1904; italics mine),

> Away on one side of the enclosure was massed, probably over one hundred little fellows, curiously clothed, and all of them carrying a little flag or a musical instrument. As if by magic these dusky lads, *snatched from a heathen life*, crowded over the turf, yet all the while maintaining perfect order. Having played a selection of music set to waltz time and all the while parading the ground, they gave Tom Moore's "Minstrel Boy." The band, consisting of brass instruments, triangles, drums, reed instruments and tambourines, occupied the center position, while those in advance and those in the rear waved flags, on the majority of which was emblazoned the Cross of St. George's, while dominating the whole was a huge Union Jack. Now they danced, now they sang of the minstrel's departure for the wars, and so they presented a picturesque but, at the same time, weird spectacle. Little did Tom Moore think when he wrote this delightful melody that it would be sung in "Darkest Africa" by the dusky denizens of Rhodesia. Before the conclusion of their performance the youngsters *played softly and accurately* "Home, Sweet Home." This was, as far as those from England were concerned, the most affecting part of the proceedings, and many an eye was moistened. Then crashed forth once more "Rule Britannia."

The enforcers of "Britannia" in these parts, the British South Africa Police, were among those who cheered on the lads. Needless to say, in spite of his soothsaying, Rhodes had invested heavily on both sides of the coin, the mission and the police.

Barely a year after their visit, the magic of Chishawasha had rubbed off on Empandeni, thanks again to Father Biehler, "the Fighting Parson" (*ZMR*, October 1927). Out of "rough materials" and "raw labor," his hand had produced "very surprising results" from the "supercilious Matabele race": the Empandeni Band. For lack of brass instruments the boys had begun by performing on petrol tins and yet, within a year, "the band was soon brought up to the level of the older one at Chishawasha."

Meanwhile, the Chishawasha boys continued their excursions to the villages and around the country, self-consciously parading their virtues to the applause of their handlers and targeted audiences. About 1904, recalled the *ZMR* in an obituary of Father Biehler, "a world-famous singer, who was touring South[ern] Africa, was asked what impressed her most, and her reply was 'The Victoria Falls and the Chishawasha Band.'" In 1911, the band was invited to perform at the agricultural shows in Mutare and Penhalonga. The tumult at the band's performances in these two towns and on the road reportedly rivaled that of the Mafeking trip. Attired in their "pretty" uniforms of snow-white blouses, blue limbo *djira* shorts, and "pork-pie" student caps (sewn at the mission and the adjoining convent by the Sisters of the Dominican Order), the Chishawasha boys armed themselves with their brass instruments and roused Salisbury on their way to the train station. Their manager and chaperone, Father F. Marconnes (whom Ishe Chinamhora suggestively nicknamed Chidamajaha, "Lover of boys"), wrote,

> It was still early morning, about 8 AM, and the streets were comparatively deserted, but the booming of the big drum, the rolling of six small drums, and the lusty sounds of twelve bugles, besides the other fifty brass instruments, must have awakened all the late sleepers for hundreds and hundreds of yards around. . . . A huge crowd of natives very soon gathered round us as we passed on, running up from all directions, shouting and leaping with joy, scanning the boys and wondering how such small creatures and black like themselves, could possibly be the cause of such powerful and beautiful sounds. A good number of white people too, came out of their houses and stores, and stood looking and listening with evident admiration as marches and bugle calls followed one another in uninterrupted succession. (*ZMR*, January 1911)

While they waited for the train, the boys obligingly wielded their instruments once more to stage another demonstration of their enlightenment for the Superintendent of General Education, G. Duthie, who happened to be at the station. The story of Mutare and Penhalonga was a similar chronicle of unbridled spectacle, wonderment, and applause, with the agricultural show virtually turning into a show of "native intelligence, smartness and fruitful missionary enterprise" in the cultivation of a new human crop out of the "humus of savagery." They were hosted and feted by farmers, miners, and industrialists, the consumers of the cheap, disciplined African labor that the missions produced. Some of their hosts, like the family of the BSAC administrator and Rhodes's lieutenant, Leander Starr Jameson, were key benefactors of Chishawasha.

The missionaries' re/presentation and celebration of the Chishawasha boys signified their steadfast investment of time and effort in creating a new African subject being disciplined by a transplanted regime of European customs, which she or he happily mimicked. The band constituted a sort of traveling exhibition of the mission, whose good works its benefactors applauded. The boys' bodies, demeanors, and voices were an open book that testified to the power of the mission to discharge its duty in socially transforming "the African." Thus, Chidamajaha wrote that in Mutare, C. Webberley, the General Manager of the Beira and Mashonaland Railways, kindly invited them into his home—"I suppose, in order to entertain his distinguished guests, the envoys of the Mozambique Company, Capt. Monteiro Lopes and Mr. King; but also, I am sure, to give us another proof of his sympathetic interest and old attachment to Chishawasha Mission." After the boys closed their performance with "Rule, Britannia" and "Home, Sweet Home," the industrialist "congratulated them on having such a fine and good home as Chishawasha Mission, and exhorted them to ever remain faithful to the good teaching and training they received there" (*ZMR*, January 1911). Exiled nonconformist Rhodesian writer Doris Lessing (L. Vambe 1972, xv) remembered her rare visit to the mission, observing the transformative effect produced by the kraaling of the children there: "A white person visiting that Mission was like someone visiting a game reserve. . . . I remember troops of well-drilled obedient boys and girls, who stood to attention, sat down, stood up, curtsied, filed off, at the orders of the Fathers."

While the mission equally prominently paraded its students as they cut roads and erected bridges, dug water furrows, and wheeled, sawed, and hammered in the carpentry workshop, and as they weeded and harvested crops to the call and response of the hymn and the swing of the hoe, their "intelligence" and deftness seemed particularly animated on the musical stage when they struck the brass, read the score, and marched to the bugle. It was the musical show that best showcased the mission's "firm and kind discipline," showing all onlookers that the mission "has them completely in hand, both as regards music, which they play admirably, and also the complicated evolutions through which [it] puts the boys of the Band and their companions" (*ZMR*, October 1907). The musical stage articulated missionary success through the combination of faculties, often showing the boys demonstrating their "sharpness in answering orally some arithmetic problems and repeating simultaneously the multiplication tables" to tunes like "So Early in the Morning." To the missionaries, the students' bodies were a text of deeper lessons. As Hartmann asserted in the *ZMR* (January 1908), now "their bodies were well developed, and well proportioned; whilst ten or eleven years before the boys had no physique and were emaciated due to want of regular food, exercise, and the consequence of disorderly living." In Jesuit thought, music, arithmetic, and geometry were the "principle [*sic*] fields of knowledge charged with deciphering the meaning of an order that was, above all, a political and civic order" (Wilde 2007, 9). The musical parade was therefore an elaboration of the missionary reordering, rescripting, and reharmonizing of African being. This significant point requires further analysis.

In 1893, Father Hartmann had castigated the "Shona" for jeopardizing the Zambesi Mission with their "savage" and "disorderly" nature. The Jesuit had blamed the missionary failures on Africans' "dogmatic belief in witchcraft and in the spirits of their ancestors." This spiritual obstinacy, reasoned Hartmann, was causally connected with the people's physiological condition. Thus, he read "the Mashona's depraved moral code" from their physique, which was "nothing but bones and skin." Inexorably uncharitable, he branded them ugly, gluttonous, "possessed by a spirit of laziness"—an atrociously cruel, unclean, and "ingeniously superstitious" people. Riled by two and half years of evangelical barrenness, Hartmann railed, "The Mashonas are hypocritical and selfish, liars and thieves." He was repulsed by their "intense self-interestedness," asserting, "In dealing with them one soon finds out that they are full of trickery. It is their chief talent" (*Rhodesia Herald*, August 25, 1893).

Commenting on this grim opinion piece (which it reproduced), the *Rhodesia Herald* wondered rather pessimistically, "Are then the Mashonas a good material for the missionary to work upon?" Governor Grey reported on the perspective of Hartmann's colleague Biehler: "Father Biehler is so convinced of the hopelessness of regenerating the Mashonas," he wrote from Chishawasha in 1897, "whom he regards as the most hopeless of mankind that he states the only chance of the future of the race is to exterminate the whole people both male and female, over the age of 14!" (Ranger 1967, 3). This missionary genocidal wish was not new. E. H. Berman (1975, 16) observed that Basel missionaries among the Asante, and the Church Missionary Society in northern Nigeria, among others, preached this gospel of "conversion by the sword," which Iberian Catholics had perpetrated on the Incas in South America as colonial governments opened the door to missionization and vice versa. Thus, the missionary-soldiers sometimes preached physical genocide as a weapon for imposing the colonial order, and well into the twentieth century, they championed cultural epistemicide as the surest way of disarming African bodies and souls for empire, which they imposed as both Christianity and modernity. The school quickly became the key platform for waging this epistemicide. Missionary representation of African children as victims of their own families thus justified the colonial assault on the African family system and the alienation ("rescuing") of the children.

The lesson had been quickly learned that the evangelization of Africans could not depend entirely on the thinly stretched alien missionary; it had to rely "on the native catechist, the man who spoke and understood the local language and was one of the people himself" (Berman 1975, 7). Such a man had to be captured and groomed from his youth. Thus, the missions soon adopted the targeting of children, which is to say, the future of African society, as a general *modus operandi*. Richartz explained in 1905 that "it is [in] the young that the chief hopes of the Mission are placed. From grown-up pagans in these parts very little can be expected, polygamy and their fear of being contemned by others, barring their way to embracing Christianity" (*ZMR*, July 1905). Methodist Rev. S. Douglas Gray echoed the view in 1923: "If the peoples of Africa are to be brought to a knowledge of the love of God, it must be through the instrumentality of her own children" (53). The catechist would be created from the bewitched African child—the "native" fraction that Biehler would spare his panga. Thus, in the full-scale epistemicidal wars against independent African being, these cultural engineers utilized mission schooling as, in the words of J. F. Ade Ajayi (1965, 134), the "nursery for the infant church." As one missionary confessed (*Report* 1925, para. 252), "Our great object is evangelising the native. When I first came [to Southern Rhodesia] I walked from kraal to kraal and found it useless until we started schools. . . . Start with the children."

What does this say about the missionary educational agenda? Missionaries were the principal providers of schools to Africans. In 1907, settlers, missionaries, and other interested parties debated the "native education question" in Bulawayo. The question was triple-barreled: "Ought the Native to be educated? If so, to what extent? And on what lines?" Three broad positions emerged, reported the *ZMR*. The first was that "the black man, being intended by Providence to be a hewer of wood and drawer of water, should be given no education at all. Let him remain in his ignorance; then he will not be impudent and refuse to work." Second was the opposite: "Others—*fortunately they are few*—go to the opposite extreme, and say that 'the Native, being a human being, is the equal of the white man, and should be treated and educated as such.'" The editor noted that a third set of views fell between these two poles, with the majority suggesting, "Don't give the Native any book learning. Teach him to behave himself, and to be honest, and industrious—that will be quite sufficient." "No doubt," the *ZMR* agreed in a January 1911 editorial, qualifying the Jesuits' particular stance:

> But you cannot teach this without teaching a good deal more. Good conduct is founded on Christianity. If the Native is not taught his duty to God, he will not recognize his obligations to his fellow men. Unless he is taught to correct his vices and faults, and restrain his passions—and this can only be done by means of Christianity—he will not be self-respecting, honest and industrious.

As the *ZMR* pointed out, the church's logic did not diverge from "the desires of most colonists," but was only concerned with the safe limits within which schooling could shape Africans into useful colonial servants. The Catholics were even more candid in their agreement with the mainstream settler view of the dangers of unbridled "native" schooling, as their newsletter editor expounded rather impatiently:

> We have already . . . stated our views on this question, and there is no need to repeat them here. Suffice it to say that the unanimous testimony of the white population in this country affirms that "the over-educated Native is an insufferable being. He won't work; he makes others discontented; he is impudent, arrogant, and . . . he has as many vices as two savages put together" (*ZMR*, January 1911).

In light of this stance, the Native Education Commission reassuringly wrote in 1925, the mission was not out to create an African equal to the whites, but a barely literate and efficient servant through what Aimé Césaire (1972, 6) characterized as a parody of education meant to hastily manufacture a few thousand subordinate functionaries for the smooth operation of the colonial project. The missionaries and settlers confessed this mission: the disarmament and "thingification" of African personhood.

Mimicking the "native" residential schools in the United States and other neo-Europes, the missionaries therefore boarded the African children they "snatched" from their homes to "protect them from the contamination of the heathen environment" and to teach them a new life of obedience and service to the Christian god and the white man (Churchill 2004). Rev. J. D. Don celebrated the pioneering of this model at Lovedale in the 1870s:

> I am deeply convinced that Lovedale possesses a great advantage in having the youths as boarders, living on the premises day and night, separated from adverse influences and subject to the rule of the institution for the whole term at a time. Otherwise the influence of even the best school is counteracted outside. (*Christian Express*, January 1, 1877)

The new African subject was constructed through the inscription of settler psychology, fear, guilt, and an inferiority complex, and the process depended on the deliberate disengagement and alienation—physical but also symbolic—of these children from their indigenous cultural anchors in this war on the African family. The prospective converts were sheltered paternalistically in the mission complex for intensive reschooling. Superintending the process at the Methodist evangelistic teacher-training institution of Nenguwo, Gray (1923, 51) emphasized that cognizance should be taken of the child's upbringing and home environment: "The background of his village life and his father's beliefs must be taken into consideration in drawing up the curriculum." A proactive curriculum was the only way to build up his soul "until he becomes strong enough to stand alone in the heathen environment." The grounding principle was that, as the spokesman of the Southern Rhodesia Missionary Conference told the Native Education

Commission, "When you educate the native you weaken tribal customs" (*Report* 1925, paras. 238–39).

A successful catechumen (one who would ideally graduate into a catechist) was one who had been thus alienated and turned against himself and his own people. In other words, as the Native Education Commission concluded, African acceptance of schooling was supposed to signify cultural surrender by a weaker "tribal system" to a "higher civilization." The Christian village was the ideal home for those seen as having conceded defeat. Thus, in 1926, the *ZMR* utilized the instructive metaphor of the Chishawasha Band to applaud the transformative power of the mission boarding school in growing its first generation of "new" Africans: "The boys who came to play in the band settled down on the estate, married and reared Catholic children." The birth and rearing of Catholic (not African!) children within the confines of the Christian villages would ideally complete the harmonious reordering of African society. Needless to say, the mission overestimated its power. Despite the certain physical and epistemological violence, many Africans approached the inevitable school with their own agenda, seeing it as a technology they could harness to survive and to challenge the same white overlordship that imposed it. The Burkinabe scholar and spiritual healer Malidoma Somé (1994, 54), who was himself kidnapped to the mission by French missionaries as a little boy, rightly observed that Africans began their greatest battle against this alien intrusion in earnest the day they signed the peace treaty with it.

Making catechumens involved attempts to erase African minds, turning them into blank slates onto which, as Morrison did with a hard straw on the backs of hapless children of Malawi, one could inscribe new truths of Europeanized Christianity and notions of European racial superiority and African inferiority. This reinscription was premised on the condemnation of the African home as a debased institution, no better than a pigsty for its pervasive animalism, as the crusading *Christian Express* (July 1, 1893) suggested:

> All around them was the great mass of heathenism. The air was full of heathen songs and sounds, and the vision of heathen sights and customs. The environments were entirely hostile to the growth of the Christian character. The fathers and mothers did not know how to save their children from the contamination of their surroundings. A worker in the slums of London says, "You cannot raise angels in pig-styes."

Familiar post-Enlightenment class prejudices against the European indigent were retooled through the crucible of race to justify the snatching away and alienating of susceptible young minds in the name of God and the engineering of Africans into subjects of empire. The sounds and sights of African "heathenism" were portrayed as just as unintelligible and revolting as the groans of the crawling body of the urban industrial outcast.

The aural Africa of the roving white missionary was at one level a projection of this ethnocentric mind; at another, it was a grafting of these preconceptions onto the realities of the African everyday. Missionaries' imaginations ran wild as they watched or, from a distance, listened to the frenzied acoustics of the "Dark Continent" on their itinerant treks and from their outposts, overnight camps, and stations. The acoustic village incessantly assaulted their senses and robbed them of sleep, or so they melodramatically claimed. The following archetypal anecdote, penned in western Zimbabwe and published in the January 1915 *ZMR*, imbues the missionary traveling register:

> I was camped for the night within half a mile of a large native kraal. It was in the middle of the rainy season. That year the rains were far below the average, and a dance was held that night to propitiate the evil spirits that were causing the drought. The dance started at sunset and lasted till sunrise, with continuous accompaniment of tomtoms. The night was sultry and sleep was fitful. Whenever I awoke I could hear the unceasing sounding of the drum; the yelling and stamping was always going on with the same vigour. There was one voice that could be clearly distinguished from the others. I heard it at practically every hour between sunset and sunrise. I was told the drummer is generally a specialist, and that the same performer goes on from the beginning to the end of the dance. A rough estimate gave for that night well over half a million beats of the tomtom.

This vested sojourner added in a wondering, almost sarcastic afterthought, "Really the power of endurance of the black people is astonishing. But do not ask them to show the same energy when they have to work for you." "Preaching the dignity of labor to these people," echoed a *ZMR* editorial in March 1932, "is like preaching kindness to animals." Later chapters explore how African performative cultures were co-opted to discipline colonial labor and attacked for disrupting it with equal vigor. And the *ngoma*—the so-called tom-tom—quickly became notorious as an instrument of torture to the missionary's visual and sensory rationality.

This was not merely a sensibility of the early cross-cultural encounter. Well into the colonial encounter, the "tom-tom" continued to transport European missionaries on primordial imaginative journeys into the colonizing self. In 1951, Ishe Mtarini of the Hlengwe people of Mwenezi invited two newly arrived Dumisa missionaries, the American couple Tillman and Gwen Houser, to a *shigubhu*. The young missionaries reluctantly went, feeling quite violated by the chief's insistence. Tillman recalled,

> I had a solid conservative Free Methodist religious background, which banned any attendance at a dance activity. . . . I was thinking, "How could a Free Methodist missionary possibly attend some heathen pagan function?". . . On the specified day we heard the drumbeats begin about eight in the morning.

> We waited until nine, and then walked toward the sound. Even some distance away we felt the pulsing sound in our chests. Ahead of us we could see a crowd of more than a hundred people standing in a huge circle. As we approached, the crowd gave way for us to see the dancing within the circle. The drum was a 55-gallon drum with the ends covered with cowhide. Men, some of my workers, were dressed in costumes of animal skin tied to their waists. They brandished spears of long sticks while dancing back and forth within the circle. One had a facemask made from the skin of a baboon. He danced right up to a frightened Gwen, shook a dead mouse in her face, and danced away. This was not what I thought was a "dance." (Houser 2007, 76)

Ostensibly granting the Housers a privileged vista to see in accord with the racialized dialectics of colonial visuality (Apter 2002, 572), the dancers quickly disrupted this framing of power. And could there be a more effective way to do that than by a defiant carnivalesque shoving of a dead mouse into the face of the wife of an impotent, rather reluctant missionary spectator? The Housers' sensibilities threatened to fail them not only at the sound of the reverberant, unfettered *ngomarungundu* (massive drum) and the unsettling ritual mockery of an African spectacle of power, but also at the sensation of the ground shifting under a conservative Protestant Christianity standing on notions of cultural superiority. In the United States, sulked Tillman, "a 'dance' was defined as a crowd of men and women holding each other in their arms while circling around in time to music of some kind." Vectors of Victorian narcissism, the missionaries were socialized to self-embrace; those who danced conducted "real dances" at tea parties to which "Africans were not invited" (Houser 2007, 76).

And those who could endure African performances subjected them to their own ethnocentric, hierarchizing canons. This was the functional catholicity of the European mission, a self-avowedly imperial and self-centered view of the world that Father Sykes advocated in a published "plea for imperialism" (*ZMR*, April 1909). Thus, Houser was confused in a truly Conradian sense, wondering whether "the prehistoric man was cursing us, praying to us, [or] welcoming us." How could he tell? (Conrad 1950, 105). The answer, namely that the *shigubhu* was organized both to welcome them into the community and to put them in their place, had to await Tillman's training in anthropology at the University of Oregon some ten years later (Houser 2007, 77). In retrospect, Houser was quite grateful he attended and saved himself "tragic embarrassment," as he would meet the same Hlengwe dancers again two years later when the government transported them to perform before the Queen of England and thousands of other spectators in the sports stadium in Gwelo during the Rhodes Centennial Celebration—about which more later.

Missionaries not only anticipated the alluring violence of the incessant "barbaric" dances on preaching tours, but often sought them out. Sister Josephine Bullen (2008, 22, 35) diarized at Empandeni on July 23, 1899, "About 4

PM Fr. Hartmann took us to visit Janke. . . . The natives had been told we were coming and began to dance and sing in quite a savage manner when we entered the kraal." They tried to police the more "repugnant" of the dances, discrediting the rituals associated with them as ineffective, thus generating spiritual tension as an evangelizing strategy. On October 15, Sister Josephine made another terse entry: "Last night [Father Hartmann] was out very late as some kraals were dancing and singing for rain." As a youngster in Mashonganyika, Lawrence Vambe (1972, 2) remembered villagers conducting the *mukwerera* rain ceremony whenever the rare drought threatened to extinguish the lives of both beast and man: "[The misfortunes] were regarded as total disasters brought about by the displeased spirits of avenging ancestors, who required immediate appeasement in the form of . . . prayers and spirit dances—often, at least in my experience, with dramatically positive results." It was this strong, transcendental relationship between the world of the living and the otherworldly realm of the ancestors, and especially the belief in the power of the latter to affect the affairs of the former, that terrified missionaries by challenging their esoteric gospel of a heavenly Jesus. Hence these ceremonies had to be condemned and extirpated as pure heathen evil.

Emphasizing "character development," the missionaries sought to transform African children into countercultural models for their people to emulate: deacons and agents of "disintegration and the complete reconstitution of Africa" (Wilson 1935, 33). The sheltered mission grounds and the public platform functioned as apprenticeship spaces that tested the children's readiness for deployment back to their own people to impart the new "civilized" ways. While many parents celebrated their children's attainment of new mission knowledge, others were dismayed to welcome back zombified cultural misfits whose cultural marrow the missionary witch had sucked dry. They welcomed back disobedient, contemptuous, and tragic vectors of social conflict. The missionaries taught them to despise the village and all that it represented, as Mushure recalled: "We learnt there and then told our parents that what they were doing was wrong. The white man's way was the right way, that's what we should follow, and we did exactly that. We no longer made sacrifices to our ancestors but to the Son, like the Fathers were teaching."[6]

Lungile Ngwenya, who, thanks to the mission, became Jane, grew up in the 1930s–40s and saw some children returning to their parents' homes to pitch tents rather than share their parents' houses, and bringing Primus stoves to cook only their own food. And they preached different standards when they became teachers: "Many of the teachers who taught us did not want their houses to be entered by people who came from homes where house floors were smeared with cow dung" (see chapter 10). Ngwenya understood that this was the white man's war to destroy *unhu hwemunhu*—African humanity. It was this alienated African that the Senegalese poet David Diop addressed in "The Renegade": "The thought of your grandmother's hut / Brings blushes to your face that is bleached / By years of humiliation and bad conscience." As deacons of the mission cultures, the children dramatized their alienation by pitching tents like itinerant missionaries, instigating social chaos. They had also become culturally itinerant, strangers who carried the mission's banner to reorient their communities' mores, including conceptions of everyday entertainment.

Around the hill mission of Chishawasha as elsewhere, the rituals of missionary Christianity and the "healthy entertainment" of the brass band supplanted the communal cultures of drumming, the strumming of *mbira,* the festive *jenaguru,* and the dances to welcome new brides, *chibhanduru.* The hegemonic sonic and ritual maps of the mission overwhelmed the African community's sonic universe, so that during the post-harvest *chirimo,* the resting and festive season,

> there were long religious processions, complete with band music, which covered the considerable distance from the church to the convent and back again to the church, ending up with the benediction service. There followed, as happened at Christmas, Easter and other feast days, a programme of musical entertainment by the band. . . . On these carnival-like occasions, the band filled the air with rousing marches, while a team of young boys gyrated in front of the instrumentalists. The throngs of cheering spectators, scattered all over the extensive school grounds, were treated to large mugs of tea and thick slices of rich brown bread made out of locally produced wheat. . . . And by the time all this was over, the sun was nearly setting and everybody went home feeling fully entertained as well as fully identified with the Church and God. (L. Vambe 1976, 39)

With the customary village dances condemned and largely muted in the precincts of the missions, it became logical for the communities' musical apprentices to apply and hone their musical skills in the mission bands in ways that poignantly tell the story of cultural displacement, enculturation, and enforced amnesia, which together account for the dearth of traditional musical cultures in some communities contiguous to mission stations.

Thus, the brass instruments of the mission band outshone the castigated "tom-toms" and "thumb pianos" (*mbira*) of "heathen" passions, consciously pressing the youngsters' minds to internalize the alienating aesthetic canons. And indeed, Chishawasha's best young musical geniuses became identified with the brass band, as Vambe recorded: "Quite the most brilliant of these . . . was Emmanuel Murwira. He could play every instrument, including the organ, as well as compose." Another was "the best known clown in all Chishawasha, Guido Chitengu, the drummer par excellence, who reduced everybody to fits of laughter with his extraordinary antics." Vambe recalled that these musicians would later form the nucleus of the renowned Rhodesian Police Band. More would take their skills to *marukesheni,* where they played the "western" instruments innovatively to craft a uniquely African urban popular music by the 1930s.

The coercive power of the mission threw youngsters like Chartwell Dutiro (2007) into an enduring dilemma. Growing up in Glendale outside Salisbury in the 1960s, Dutiro struggled to decide between two paths: the path of *mbira,* or that of the alluring Salvation Army Band. The brass instruments fascinated him without dislodging him from the ancestors' *matare,* the indigenous performative ethos: "I played the cornet in their youth band. I was meant to attend Sunday school, but regularly missed it because I spent Saturday nights playing *mbira.* That wasn't an instrument the missionaries wanted to promote. . . . Families were often caught between [the] two cultures" (1). His brother, Davies Masango, excelled on the brass instruments and was hired by the Police Marching Band. He captivated villagers when he brought a trumpet home, demonstrating the adoption of new tools that would take African musical creativity in whole new directions. Yet Dutiro was struck by the force of the underlying epistemic violence when the local *mudzviti* recruited him and fifteen other boys to form a "tribal trust land band" as part of a scheme by the Internal Affairs Department (the rechristened Native Affairs Department) "to make people happy" during the liberation war. They roved between *makipi* ("keeps," concentration camps) entertaining interned villagers. Glendale's Salvation Army Band, like its more famous counterparts at Chishawasha and Empandeni, became much more than an icon of authorized music; it became a symbol of African subjugation and co-

Transformed from creature fellows to fellow creatures: Chishawasha Mission Band.

Chishawasha on a feast day. "Pagans" look on from the fringes.

Singing from a book at Kutama Mission, the school famed for turning out products like Robert Mugabe.

optation, but also an opportunity for innovation. The twin processes of subjugation and co-optation always started with the remolding of the African child into a countermodel for the targeted community. The child was shamed and alienated at church and school for engaging in "pagan" performances at home, as young Nyamasvisva Tichaona Mafika (founder of the highly acclaimed Mawungira eNharira) was shamed for playing *mbira* with his grandfather, a *munyai* (spiritual messenger) in Zvimba (interview).

The brass band therefore became an index in missionary recrafting of the African (musical) being. To the youngsters, the band became a new authorized *dariro* for personal restyling. It retextured their iconicity, rearming them with the brass organ in the place of the condemned *ngoma, mbira,* and *hosho* (shakers), and it implicated the curious, witnessing, and cheering community (including the "pagans" peering from the margins). Mission hymns and brass percussion also sought to fill the void created by the silencing of indigenous instruments in communal rituals, resignifying intimate cultural practices by displacement. For example, starting with the funeral of Ishe Garande, "the first Shona chief to be baptized and buried within the mission precincts" at Chishawasha (*ZMR*, October 1905), the mission band displaced members of the community and usurped key ritual functions. During the funeral, the priest and the mission band commanded center stage, presiding over the ceremony and providing the music. Garande had been one of the fiercest fighters among those who attacked the Chishawasha Mission in the Chindunduma of 1896–97. But, broken militarily and disarmed spiritually, the chief departed from custom, reportedly "begg[ing] in his last will that the boys' band should play while he was making his way to enter heaven." In accordance with the chief's wish, "for some distance to and from church his body was escorted by the school band playing solemn music" (*Souvenir* 1990, 23).

Similarly, the burial of Paul Chidyausiku, a former guide to the colonial scout Frederick Selous and latterly the Paramount Chief Chinamhora of the Shawasha people, was attended with the same ritual and spectacle. As part of the postwar settlement, the chief had acceded to the mission's demand that all VaShawasha children be sent to the mission school. During his occasional visits to see them, he reportedly used to claim, "We are no longer pagans, for we have given you all our children. What more can we do? If I get sick I call you, and you will come and baptize me so that I may go to heaven." On his deathbed, the Chinamhora is said to have kept his word, declaring "in the presence of pagans that he was dying a Christian." He was duly baptized and given the "names of the three wise men: Balthassar, Gaspar and Melchior," and passed on shortly after (*ZMR*, October 1908). Again, his body became a blank slate upon which to inscribe a different regime of power, with church absolutions, parades, and musical processions asserting the new ritual order and gun salutations reminding everyone of the church's solid foundation in armed colonial force. A new arrival, Father Lickorish, was moved to inquire "what Chinamora [*sic*] had done to merit the great grace he received at the end of his life," and he was informed that "at considerable personal sacrifice and loss of prestige, he showed himself our friend, giving us his children to be educated as Christians, and thus setting the example to many others." This specularity became standard, replicated at the funerals of Zvimba, Kutama, and other "Christian chiefs" in the early 1920s (*ZMR*, January 1922).

These exhibitionist missionary rituals emphasized departure from *chivanhu*, African culture. Kapenzi (1979, 84) described one form of a traditional chiefly funeral, noting that for three days after a chief had passed, on the very rock or in the cave where he would be buried, a skillful drummer beat the drum to notify the entire community of the tragedy. For at least a week, all work was abandoned as villagers united in ceremonial mourning. Two weeks before the body of the chief was to be lowered into the dark cave, drums sounded all night in expressions of sympathy and concern. The late chief's close councilors took turns at the night watch, drumming to broadcast the chief's death. In Madzimbabwe cultures, to mourn is to cry, sing, and dance.

The church demanded that *vatendi* not only cease practicing, but also stay away from, these intricate "pagan" mortuary rituals. Hence the hurried and very public disposal of the Chinamhora's body the same morning of his passing (as if he were a social outcast or had died a ritually unclean death) became part of the mission's ritual reinscription, introducing a new, invented Christian tradition for African converts:

> [His] corpse was brought into the church, carried down from the hills and accompanied by hundreds of wailing men and women. . . . The procession to the grave was a notable one. After the cross-bearer and acolytes came 450 children, followed by the Chishawasha Band. After it, walked the Brothers and Sisters, the members of our Christian congregation, and finally the pagan men and women. The procession wended its way towards the hills. (*Souvenir* 1990, 25)

The missionaries' triumphal intervention in and subversion of the ritual transition of the deceased into new states of being cut out what Frances Davidson (1915, 341) called the troubling "feeling of unrest in the air[,] the wailing and dancing . . . for the spirits of the dead" that African funerals occasioned in "heathen kraals." Such events, agreed one Father Andrew, "brought home to one that which we all feel out here sometimes, the sense of spiritual evil" (Andrew 1933, 24).

To the missionaries, the song-driven funerary dirge and the customary *kudunura* (lamentation) were metaphors for evil that required eradication. Consequently, the new, exhibitionist Christian funerary procession represented a hierarchical reordering and revaluation of African society. The missionary community segregated itself from Africans in everyday interactions, in church seating (Houser 2007, 64), and even in death, with racially segregated cemeteries. While African polities subsisted, it was the first *vatendi* who suffered persecution as witches for spawning social havoc and upsetting society's spiritual order. But as the missions struck root, *vatendi* now turned on the "pagans," the new, mission-cultivated identity of demonization and shame. As Rev. Canon Lury (1956, 34) of the Catholic Church in Zanzibar noted, the word "heathen" or "pagan" has "a definitely derogatory meaning, and can never be used in polite conversation." Missionary discourse did not mean to be polite with Africans who contested its teachings. They were shamed and excluded even as they were kept within the outer circles of missionary recognition. Yet the church asserted its power not only by making social outcasts of such nonconforming Africans, but also by fostering new divisions and hatreds among *vatendi* following different denominations. For instance, Ishe Ndafunya Makoni observed how English Anglicans and German Catholics constituted themselves almost into distinct "nations" and came to the verge of war against each other in 1916.[7] Missionaries fostered these hatreds in the emergent African Christian identities, making shame and rivalry key tools of control. Represented by their recognizably different uniforms, the colonial school and church wielded these tools to great effect.

In independent African cultural contexts, the funeral of a *mambo* (king) or *ishe* (chief) was no matter for a hurried public spectacle involving children. Now, however, unadulterated chieftaincy had fallen with Chindunduma, reducing chiefs to virtual colonial servants merely discharging the edicts of the state. In the letter to the editor of the July 1, 1871, *Kaffir Express* quoted earlier, "A Colonist" had called for the establishment of a Native Affairs Department and articulated the grounds for turning chiefs into colonial functionaries. Through the assistance of missionaries, chiefs could be co-opted into veritable conduits of colonialism: "The Kaffir loves and adores his chief; and so long as he finds that his chief is not entirely ignored he is quite contented to be ruled by the white man. . . . A great deal can be done with the Kaffirs in civilizing them, if we can secure the services of their chiefs and headmen on our side." For this reason, it became symbolically important to secure legitimacy by asking the "permission" of the enfeebled chief before a mission station or school was established. At Chishawasha, Kuvhima Dzama, the Ishe Chinamhora, granted such permission to Rhodes and the Jesuits, recalled his grandson James Dambaza Chikerema (*How the British Stole Zimbabwe* 1984). Similarly, appropriating the dying body of a "Christian chief" was a calculated cultural *coup de grace,* according to these logics of indirect rule. The Native Affairs Department was therefore established in colonial Africa as a dual governing structure, intended both to repress the lurking specter of Chindunduma and to facilitate tax extraction.

While chieftainship represents both the political and the spiritual office in Madzimbabwe, *masvikiro,* spirit mediums, form the bedrock of the society's socio-spiritual health. Mwari's mediums, *masvikiro* are guardians of the African moral order and social harmony. That is why the colonists sought to eliminate them during the uprisings, with Father Richartz branding Kaodza Gumboreshumba, the medium of Kaguvi, the god of the Mashona, and denouncing Nyakasikana Charwe, the medium of Mbuya Nehanda, as "the celebrated witch and prophetess of Mazoe" (*ZMR*, November 1898). The missionaries—especially the Catholics and Anglicans—presided over the murders, claiming the moral right to bless the African soul by killing its recalcitrant body. To them, the murders were a spiritual victory of the white man and his religion over "superstition." Nehanda Nyakasikana Charwe, Kaguvi Kaodza Gumboreshumba, Chingaira Makoni, Muchecheterwa Chiwashira, and others were decapitated and their heads carted away as trophies for the Queen of England. As late as 1988, Catholic hagiographers still celebrated these executions as the crowning moment of the Catholic Church's "Zambesi Mission," and a personal triumph for Richartz, one of the invading Pioneer Column priests. In light of his colonial credentials, the hagiographers wrote in a centennial booklet,

> it was therefore appropriate that Fr. Richartz should have been the priest to visit the condemned leaders of the rising and help them to die well. Even Ambuya Nehanda at first listened to him quietly and with respect, though she refused instruction and baptism. Kaguvi, the chief leader, accepted instruction and baptism, and died well, asking Fr. Richartz to look after his family. (*Souvenir* 1990, 8)

The suggestion that Kaguvi Gumboreshumba, with a colonial noose hanging over his head, gave his children to the missionaries conveniently absolved the latter of their double crime. A Colored (biracial) woman, Bertha Ruth d'Almeida, saw Nehanda Charwe's and Kaguvi Gumboreshumba's children crying as they were brought to Chishawasha:

> The children . . . came crying to the mission. They were orphans. The white man had hanged all their family for preaching that white men were bad for the country. There were only seven children left—three boys and four girls. Nehanda's second daughter had refused to come to the mission. . . . But the eldest daughter, Makandipeyi, came. The sisters called her Mary-Ann. I used to wonder if she had her mother's powers, but if she did she never used them. Perhaps she was afraid of the danger after she saw her whole family hanged. But people used to come to visit her . . . [and] sit in a circle while she talked to them. I think she tried to keep the memory of her mother alive, because often they would cry. (*Sunday Mail*, February 6, 1983)

In accordance with Biehler's suggestion in 1897, the killing of the parents constituted a physical show of force to engineer a future that could only be sustained through destruction of the orphaned children's culture, hence the renaming, criminalization of identities, efforts to delete their memory and history, and indoctrination. Not only had the parents to be killed, their memory had to be reconstituted or deleted. This was the significance of Richartz's renaming the spirit medium Gumboreshumba "Dismas"—after the "good thief" crucified with Jesus of Nazareth—and the renaming of Makandipeyi and her fellow orphans into the Black Mary-Anns, Miriams, Epiphanias, and Janes that populated the missions.

Narrating his "preparing for death" those condemned in the western districts, Jesuit Father V. Nicot presented a picture of "thankful natives wondering how God brought them to Heaven by such merciful ways," finding redemption at the knot of the colonial noose (*ZMR*, November 1898). One of the men allegedly told him, "Umfundisi [teacher], I am glad you came to teach us how to die. When I had been some days in this prison, something told me in my heart that someone would come to help us to die well." What better foundations for self-legitimation and self-absolution for the "civilizing mission" than criminal heathens expressing gratitude for being sacrificed at the altar of colonialism in the name of a missionary god, after surrendering their children? To all this, Nicot haughtily sneered, "How quickly, when they are in this way near death, these natives realize the worthlessness of their false gods, of their 'Umlimos' of the caves, of their witchdoctors! One feels then that they, too, are made to know and to revere the one true God of Heaven, their Master and their Father." For Nicot, it was "a genuine consolation to be the instrument for bringing the grace of God to their souls." Part of the power of the colonial art of demonizing others inheres in the ability of the colonist to transfigure himself or herself into a victim of the "native." Through this story—to follow Lezra's (2014, 12) insight—Nicot denies, occludes, and sublimates the pain of the sacrificed Africans into the wound that he imagined he suffered prosecuting the "civilizing mission." And for that he deserves to be consoled; for was he not the victim? The church celebrated these executions and the postwar reprisals—burning the homes and food stores of the condemned, forced labor, rape, looting, and flogging—for finally not only breaking the older people's resistance to sending their children to the mission, but also throwing into disarray their "belief in superstition and witchcraft." This would continue to be the great hope and certitude of the mission, as the Rhodesia Mission Conference congratulated itself in 1917: "The religious basis of a great pagan people has been disturbed, the very foundation of animism shakes and crumbles" (Methodist Episcopal Church 1917, 18). It seems that "A Colonist" had been perceptively prophetic! Or perhaps not?

The Limits of Cultural Disarmament: Colonial *Ngozi*, African Refusal to Die

What were the limits of the colonial (and) evangelical mission's project of disarming and reengineering African being? In Madzimbabwe cosmologies, the death of the body does not end life, but transports it to *nyikadzimu*, the metaphysical realm of the spirits. And through rituals of *kurova guva,* the living call back home the spirits of their deceased ancestors to look over them. Similarly, murder is a crime with spiritual implications for the families of both the villain and the deceased. Restitution must be made; otherwise the deceased exacts retributive justice through *ngozi. Ngozi* is a foundational Madzimbabwe concept of transcendental being, inescapable accountability, and justice. It can wipe out the wrongdoer's whole clan, one individual after another, until the crime is atoned for.

We can define *ngozi* with Tafataona Mahoso (*Sunday Mail,* April 7, 2012) as a philosophical conception of the relationship between the individual soul and its *dzinza* (bloodline) and *nhaka* (heritage). Ngozi reveals the crime, its circumstances, and the villain, demanding redress:

> The soul of the departed relative recruits spirit possession, memory, telepathy, extrasensory perception, intuition, guilt and the confessional against erasure, against amnesia, against lies, against false alibis, against obsolescence. What the ngozi protects against . . . erasure are the circumstances in which the individual died or was killed; the bloodline (blood relations) of the individual; and all the possessions of the individual (nhaka) which belong to the bloodline and are the material basis for continuing the bloodline.

Murder is therefore an offence against not just the deceased, but the whole *dzinza.*

In Madzimbabwe cosmology, Nehanda is a national, founding matriarchal spirit whose history goes back thousands of years in Zimbabwean sociopolitical communities. Her spirit therefore commands the multiple bloodlines of Zimbabwe. Needless to say, the Nehanda spirit did not die with the murder of Charwe, her medium, in 1898. The colonists would contend with the *ngozi* of the murdered and dispossessed African patriarchs and matriarchs, whose memory and demand for restitution their progeny would invoke in story, song, ritual, and warcraft. As Mahoso explains, "the key purpose of ngozi is the continuity and continuation of the interrupted bloodline of that deceased individual." The Nehanda spirit is celebrated "because it is the spirit of a national ancestor taking the entire colonized Zimbabwe as its lost assets." In this sense, therefore, the 1896–97 Chimurenga was a holy war. This is why the colonial church and state were terrified by spirit mediums, the possessed bodies of African memory that defy Cartesian, western linear time and notions of individual justice and rights over (stolen) property. This is also why the colonial episteme sought to create new African identities by rendering African children orphaned, ahistorical, and disempowered, severed and alienated from their bloodlines and from the memory and history of their parents and ancestors.

The colonists were terrified by the reality of this unconquered, spiritually transfigured African being, rooted in what Mahoso describes as African living law. That is exactly why Rhodes was haunted by the specter of M'limo of Malindadzimu. In 1915, the Superintendent of Natives at Salisbury captured the persistent anxiety over the immanence of another Mwari-inspired Chimurenga when he wrote, "I do not wish to pose as an alarmist (but) those well acquainted with the natives of this territory know how easily their superstitions can be worked on by a bold and clever witchdoctor," adding that "if the Mlimo of the Matopos and Nyanda [Nehanda] were to persuade them to rise, they would, I believe, do so."[8] Never mind the demonization; the colonists certainly understood the power and grasped the truth of African living law. Similarly, as the settler "Responsible Government" was replacing the BSAC administration in 1923, rumors that Mwari had ordered people to stock grain in the mountains triggered settler panic (Daneel 1970, 34).

For the same reasons, the colonial intelligence system kept watch on movements to and from Matombo, and constantly worried about *masvikiro,* Mwari's messengers who presided over various national endeavors, including warfare, farming, and the observation of *chisi,* the sacred weekday. In 1907, the *ZMR* condemned one particular *svikiro,* an elderly woman:

> In the Spring of this year she gave out that the Umlimo was very angry because people had begun hoeing in their fields without asking his permission to do so, and that the locusts were going to eat up all their crops in consequence. A little later she said that they must propitiate the spirit by offerings of beer, corn, goats and money, and that if they wished to get any crops this year they must get seed-corn which had been specially doctored by him; further that nobody must work in the fields on Saturday [*chisi*]—they were to work on Sunday instead. (*ZMR,* April 1907)

These cultural precepts maintained spiritual and ecological harmony and fostered the people's sense of security. The colonial state and church were exasperated by them, with the *ZMR* expostulating, "These stupid people believe the hag, and many have been the offerings made to the Umlimo. Many, too, now never work on Saturdays, but desecrate the Sunday instead." Colonial counterinsurgency consequently targeted the "witchdoctor" and kept an ear on the ground for the "tom-tom" announcing *mapira* (spirit possession ceremonies) and other condemned "pagan" rituals.

The colonial regime recognized that Africans' laying down their arms in 1897 did not necessarily mean their defeat, let alone absolute disarmament. In a few decades, they would recall Mukwati, Nehanda, Kaguvi, Chaminuka, Chiwashira, Umlugulu, and other ancestor-leaders, invoking their memory as a crucial usable past as they rearmed for another assault on the colonists. Until then, however, they mostly articulated their resistances covertly in hidden transcripts, while many entered the mission church and school to reappropriate the sanctioned spaces and to tap the new witchcraft in order to reequip and refashion their embattled being. Meanwhile, politically and spiritually wounded and orphaned, the African family had to contend with the missionary "(step)fathers" and the Native Commissioner "chiefs." The family of Kasingadomwe (The one who shall not be named), as the children now called their patriarch Gumboreshumba, were scattered by his killing, reuniting only after generations (*Mbira Dza Vadzimu* 1978). Other African families were similarly broken and scattered, abandoning the names of their "rebel" fathers and crafting new identities of refuge. This is how the mission helped to simultaneously instigate African social disorganization and crisis and position itself as a sanctuary for African children. In so doing, it built African evangelization on the foundations of epistemicidal violence and criminal humanitarianism. As a social laboratory, then, the mission station sought to elaborate its new African personality redesigned on the negation and erasure of *unhu*, African humanity. This colonial alienation and African responses to it defined culture as a theater of critical epistemological struggles in colonized Madzimbabwe.

2 Purging the "Heathen" Song, Mis/Grafting the Missionary Hymn

You remember that missionary hymn we used to sing at home: "They reach their dusky hands to you; for bread of life they cry." What do you think Sister Taylor they do?

—*Evangelical Visitor,* March 3, 1930

I HAVE READ THE missionary effort to redesign African being through schooling and the lens of the brass band. The school brass band is, however, only part of the story of the evangelical musical odyssey. The first part of this chapter explores the mission's efforts to graft the more conventional missionary idiom, the hymn, onto the African musical psyche. The mission employed the now familiar *modus operandi:* assaulting the hymn's imagined antithesis, African song. The second part examines how this missionary ethnocentric cultural policy threw the mission church into crisis by midcentury, when some second-generation African Christian converts and a small coterie of mainly expatriate missionaries intensely interrogated the missionary demonization of African musical cultures and the arbitrary grafting of alien musical registers onto them. Ironically, when the church imperiled itself in this way and its survival was at stake, it nervously turned to the same African song, and to related aspects of indigenous cultures, in a process of selective ritual appropriation and cooptation to salvage itself. By locating the politics, the agency, and the limits of this reformation, this chapter problematizes a rather fashionable portrait of a Christian church, especially a liberal Catholic church, receptive to African cultures by the 1940s.

Mis/Grafting the Missionary Hymn

Reverend John B. Radasi was a Zulu missionary who founded Bembesi Mission Station in Matabeleland in 1903. As a young boy, Radasi went to America with a group of musicians, and there he converted to Christianity. He recrossed the Atlantic, traveling on to Edinburgh, where he enrolled as a student of theology. Eventually he was posted back to the "mission field" in Southern Africa, choosing Matabeleland. Soon after his deployment, Radasi (1966, 5) expressed his impressions of "the field" in a letter to a friend: "The Matabeles are still uncivilized, but they seem to be a nice and kind people and willing to learn."

Radasi was a music crusader. In copious letters to his superiors in Scotland, he chronicled his efforts to teach locals hymns to replace their "heathen" songs. In his very first letter, he explained that he was delighted to find "several Psalms in metre in the Wesleyan native hymnbooks. . . . There is altogether nine Psalms—more than I expected to find—and I am using them only" (1966, 8, 14). He sent the psalms to Lovedale to be rendered into "Kaffir verse" and printed in a separate hymnbook for his church's use, writing persistently for over a decade to check on the slow progress of the project until Revs. John Knox Bokwe and William Kobe Ntsikana took on the project and printed the psalms in tonic sol-fa notation for him for a fee.

Bokwe was the famous arranger of "Ulo Tixo Mkulu" (Thou great God), the "first Christian hymn composed by an African," Kobe's father, Ntsikana, about 1820. Ntsikana had become one of the first Christian converts among the Xhosa after coming into contact with Revs. John van der Kemp and Joseph Williams of the London Missionary Society. Bokwe recounts the story that on his way from an initiation ceremony, an "abakhwetha dance," Ntsikana was seized by the Holy Spirit, saw some visions, dashed to a stream, and "washed off the clay from his body." He abandoned the "heathen dances" and became a Christian. By 1876, the Lovedale Press had printed volumes in tonic sol-fa of not only Ntsikana's hymns, but also compositions by other Xhosas, Zulus, and men of other ethnic groups, publishing them in "every Christian Kaffir hymnbook in South[ern] Africa." The British school system introduced these hymns in the African curriculum, and European pastors taught them to Africans as part of their efforts to "stamp out" "pagan" song customs (Kirby 1959, 38). The myth of Ntsikana's Damascene conversion and his inspired confessional hymns constituted a powerful part of the Lovedale legacy that helped drive wider evangelization, including Radasi's work.

Among his congregants, Radasi insisted, in accordance with the Scottish Presbyterian fundamentalist doctrine, on singing "the Psalms of David only," which they did "sitting down," standing up only to say prayers. His church proscribed all other hymns, songs, musical instruments of any kind, and all dancing (Radasi 1966, 30, 60). To the Scots, dancing and playing instruments risked mirroring the "heathen dances" they strived "to their best to stamp out." While African songs tended to be animated, the psalms appealed to the Scots partly because of their somber mood. This somberness would serve the church's designs well, as it claimed in its report on foreign missions in 1914:

> The translation is a piece of good work; Psalms XVI and XXII are outstanding examples of idiomatic and euphonic Kaffir. . . . In these days of sorrow and desolation, the church is learning anew what a treasure it has in the Book of

> Psalms. The Kaffir Church and people may have days before them when they will also find that no book expresses their feelings like it. (Radasi 1966, 86)

The church suggested that the sorrow and desolation of the 1914 war called for solemn consolation, which could be found only in the psalms' inspired and infallible words of truth, counsel, and promise. They taught the colonized Africans to mourn the travails of the European war, in addition to their own "sins."

Like the Free Scots, another Matabeleland mission body, the Brethren in Christ Church (BICC), similarly forbade dancing, the playing of musical instruments, and conspicuous dressing by its *vatendi,* even during weddings (Urban-Mead 2008). The BICC emphasized plainness in dress, song, comportment, and worship. As Charles Baker, an elder in the United States, explained, congregational *a cappella* singing was "more pleasing to the Lord than the most charming music that was ever produced by any harp, or musical instrument" (*Evangelical Visitor,* February 15, 1898). Another elder claimed that the human voice, cultivated in the fear of God and used to his glory, is of divine origin, while "the instrument is man's invention or origin . . . good for enthusing the flesh while the voice has the power to enthuse the spirit" (*Evangelical Visitor,* February 15, 1892). Africans' rich array of instruments, including *mbira, ngoma, marimba, mabhosvo* and *hwamanda* (trumpets), *zvigufe* (flutes), *zvipendani* (string bows), *hosho* (shakers), and *magavhu* (leg shakers made of dried pods), could therefore not be played by converts. Most missionaries condemned African musical cultures, often assaulting performers in the community and driving the rituals and the contexts that produced them underground.

The church barred its members from participating in indigenous weddings. These involved singing, dancing, and family elders conferring with the ancestors to bless and protect not only the newlyweds but also the families brought together through the marriage. The church sought to replace these ceremonies with church weddings during which attendees sang only Christian songs. These proscriptions were universal among both the Catholic and Protestant mission churches. Wendy Urban-Mead observed that the fundamentalist BICC missionaries also objected to dancing, for two principal reasons: that it stimulated sexual desire, and that it was closely associated with ancestor veneration and spirit possession. These objections were consistent with the church's founding doctrines in North America, which, as one Sel noted in a letter to the *Evangelical Visitor* (July 1, 1902), regarded dancing, card playing, gambling, horse racing, theater, and similar entertainments as "devices of Satan." Sel ventured that a "dancing Christian," especially a "dancing Methodist," could not be a spiritual Christian. He saw little difference between dancing and copulation: "Beyond the thrill of music and poetry of motion, [dancing] has a sex reference." To the BICC, the Methodists were not Christian enough.

The missionaries recast their doctrinal positions in Africa through the myth of Africa as the "Dark Continent" of licentiousness. Sexually symbolic musical dances such as *mbende* were performed in appropriate cultural contexts: at weddings and initiation ceremonies and in welcoming back hunters and warriors. BICC Sister Frances Davidson denounced the dancing that she saw at Mapane in 1905 as "wild orgies"; and for her colleague Adda Engle, the dances were her first encounter with "the work of darkness" (Urban-Mead 2010, 32). Similarly, one Miss Hallward (*Mashonaland Quarterly* 66, 1908, 19) wrote that she and her colleagues loathed the drum because of its associations with the "heathen past," and also because it excited people. At its Native Conference of 1916, the BICC unequivocally expressed disappointment at the persistent breaking of its rules; wedding gatherings continued singing "improper" songs and dancing deep into the night in the villages, frustrating the church's proscriptions. Some converts learned the dances in town and practiced them for weeks, in preparation for huge wedding celebrations that often attracted as many as five hundred guests. The conference reaffirmed its directive that "native teachers . . . report to their respective missionaries any who disobey this injunction [to stop the revelries]" (Urban-Mead 2008, 231). The BICC crusaded against these "night dances" that "caused longing of the flesh" into the 1950s.

In addition to deploying overseers to supervise proceedings, the BICC held bridegrooms responsible for infractions at their weddings. Moreover, under its 1944 Native Wedding regulations, the church arrogated to itself the prerogative to approve wedding guests in order to screen out "heathens." The church thus not only intruded into African homes to police the converts' daily social relations and demeanor, but also interfered with and dislocated the African family in critical ways. Recounting the novelty of a group marriage ceremony at Mwenzo Mission in Malawi, Reverend Morrison (1969, 85) recorded that the father of one of the brides, Mary, "being a heathen," stayed away for fear of "darken[ing] the church door," reflecting not only the semantic and epistemic equation of the African race with sin, but also the church's fracturing of Africans' social order. As Henry Weman (1960, 194) wrote rather theatrically after observing weddings among the Zulu, "A wedding is a great event in the everyday life of the African. He goes to a wedding as a great feast, dressed in all his finery; joy at the festal occasion shines from his face." The church tried to transform the wedding (and marriage) from a process with deep sociocultural implications into an event just for the conjugal couple. That is how the Jesuits tried to grow its "Christian villages" as counterinstitutions ranged against the African homestead. They required those who married in church to leave their family home and build a new one in the newly designated "Christian villages," physically and socially abandoning their condemned communities. As one Jesuit Father Sykes intimated in the *Zambesi Mission Record* (1902, 57), the physical separation symbolized the necessary spiritual and moral separation of *vatendi* from their old environment and a necessary protection against the pull of traditional life.

In this way, the missionary church taught youngsters to denounce the authority of their fathers, to forsake their cultural heritages, to run away to the mission to "marry properly" (Bullen 2008, 64), and then to resettle in the sequestered Christian village. Marrying properly meant monogamous unions conducted in church as the wedding couple's personal affair, consecrated by the new father—the missionary—and chaperoned by hymn-crooning congregants in place of relatives ritually blessing the newlyweds in mutual, socially vested consanguinary processes of growing the clan. Sister Josephine Bullen (64, 81) contrasted "marrying properly" with what she called the "undignified merry-making" and "wife buying" ceremony that she recorded at Gwandu's village in western Zimbabwe:

> The women rushed out, all very merry, and planted themselves in the road before us and began to dance, slowly advancing as we advanced, all the time singing and striking the ground with their long poles. After a few minutes, they stopped, asked us if we liked it and divided to let us pass through the middle. One or two of the women had rows upon rows of dried pods round their legs which when they danced made a sort of music.

The sisters tarried to watch, struggling to repress their enchantment. These wedding dances provided a complete contrast to the solemn mysteries presided over by the priest at the church, where the drums, wedding songs, and *magavhu* were silenced, where the intergenerational and extended family bonds, feasting, and libations to ancestors were banished; where the omnipotent priest, the adoptive spiritual father, presided over his adopted African children.

The mission did not limit its reach to its *vatendi,* often tasking children to report on their non-Christian or otherwise nonconforming parents. Thus, as young children in the 1950s, Stella Rambisai Chiweshe and her friends were "instructed to run to report their parents and neighbors as Satan's people" to the priest at St. Michael's Catholic Mission in Mhondoro whenever they saw them playing *ngoma, mbira,* and *hosho*—the signature instruments of their entertainment and spirituality (Chiweshe, interview). Years later, Chiweshe would answer the call of her ancestor Kaguvi Gumboreshumba to play *mbira* for him, and she soon realized that she was one of those "people of Satan" against whom her priests had warned. And her tortuous journeys to learn to play *mbira* are a good measure of the impact of the missionary crusades. Chiweshe had to travel long distances from Masembura, where she then lived, looking for someone to teach her. So drastic was the missionary impact that "no one continued to play *mbira* in Masembura." She took the bus, hunting for a potential tutor in distant places, but she met only ridicule from strangers and cruel gossip back in her village. Fortunately, her uncle Flavian Maveto still played the instrument in Mhondoro, and quite against the gender conventions of the time, he agreed to teach her, a girl. Her peripatetic searches at last bore fruit, and the rediscovery of *mbira* immediately dissolved the knot of pain that had eaten away at her chest for years. Through *mbira* song as cord and optic, Chiweshe could now summon the ancestors—hers and other people's—during *mapira* ceremonies.

However, even very late in the colonial period Chiweshe still had to contend with the persistent criminalization of African cultures. Thus, she recalled how, in about 1963, the *mudzviti* for Bindura sent a Native Messenger to Masembura to warn people that anyone found with any traditional instrument or apparel was going to be arrested: "We took everything—*mbira,* sound gourds, ritual canes, and cloths for the spirits—and we buried them in a big pit that we dug in the middle of the field." (This proscription also targeted the skin hats that Africans then wore as symbols of African cultural sovereignty, which I will discuss later.) Chiweshe would later muster the courage to recover her *mbira* set, but not until algae had destroyed almost everything. We shall see later how the missionaries worked very closely with the colonial state in these campaigns against African cultural sovereignty.

The missionaries were quite aware of the limits of their designs, however. The stubborn reality of African constitutive cultures could not be easily snuffed out. As Langston Takawira Mahoso (1979, 67) observed, after a few decades of Christendom African converts were no longer too eager to report each other to the overbearing missionaries. Many Africans did not simply self-immolate at the missionaries' altar of cultural prejudice. Scholarship on African independent churches shows that it was partly on the grounds of missionaries' ethnocentrism that Africans increasingly broke away from the white-missionary-dominated churches, beginning in the early twentieth century. Disaffection had simmered for a long time. In the March 3, 1871, *Kaffir Express,* one missionary recorded Africans' reservations about "the mournful foreign rituals: the ceaseless ring of the Church bell, the sermons often long and wearisome, the wails of assembled multitudes, which are often called songs of praise, but which ought rather to be called songs of sorrow, the petitions and readings of the Bible, the family and secret devotions that are all a penalty imposed on the Jew because he crucified Jesus Christ." These Africans did not think they should share the burden of what they saw as the Jew's *ngozi,* avenging spirit, which was not theirs to bear. They did not sympathize with "the Jew's beseeching" other nations, "from sea to sea," to share the pain of his *ngozi.* They bemoaned "this thing [that] is robbing us of our nationality and fast converting us into foreigners." To many Africans, the notion of conversion was tantamount to cultural alienation.

Thus, while many would convert or syncretize the new cultures, others refused to concede. And the missionary ridiculed and demonized them for their stance:

> If [the kaffir] embraces the Gospel he is not to countenance circumcision with its festivities and its joy. No matter its vile abominations, and for the fact that

> it is often the first school of thieving and impurity. The Gospel forbids him to be happy according to the customs of his country. In a year of plenty, when the nation is rejoicing and waxing fat, he is not to be privileged in the autumn season to make a man of his son, and watch him from kraal to kraal girded in his palm dress dancing the white boys' dance to the song of the women, while the band repeatedly breaks forth in measured numbers predicting the future of the lad. Is he to sacrifice all this joy simply for the sake of being a Christian? Would he be such a fool? Never!

These objections, the author argued, wielded a mysterious power over "the heathen mind," discussed as they were "in secret, in huts after nightfall by red painted barbarians seated round the blazing fire, beside the cattle kraal by day when there is none to refute them."

The homestead court, the *dare,* this missionary confessed, remained a hard-to-penetrate zone of cultural refuge and a platform for anticolonial counterinsurgency. In the words of Inés Hernández-Avila (2003, 56), zones of refuge are places where "knowledge has been historically guarded, exercised and sustained." They represent safe physical and psychological spaces where indigenous cultural matrices continue to find expression even in the face of the determined project of colonial erasure and substitution. At the *dare,* the home and its knowledges were safeguarded, daily agendas plotted, and challenges resolved; there, children were schooled in their own people's cultural mores for societal self-reproduction, and every family prayed to Mwari through the ancestors. The *dare* and the home were privileged cultural spaces and memoryscapes that defined African sovereign being. They were therefore not open to strangers who bore a gospel of ruination; hence missionaries waged a fierce battle to annihilate the *dare*'s moral, spiritual, judicial, and aesthetic power.

Narrating his Christmas visit to Kutama and Murombedzi missions in 1915, Jesuit priest C. Daignault wrote that he helped to feed the children to strengthen them against the temptations of the kraals. After eating, the children marched, sang, and danced to the accompaniment of their teacher's cornet, "ending with 'God Save the King'" and the distribution of sweets: "All went home in the afternoon, the boys returning to sleep at the school." He noted with much relief, "It was gratifying to see that at the end of the day all were perfectly sober, since there was plenty of beer-drinking going on all day at their kraal, and the temptation to indulge must have been very strong" (*ZMR,* April 1915). At Murombedzi, the mission's impact was strong, thanks to the local teacher-catechist: "I noticed a marked improvement in the children, due to the guidance of their teacher Patrick." Daignault was moved when the children prayed during Mass, pronouncing their singing "edifying, albeit distracting." He was ambivalent because "they had no harmonium and nobody to teach them how to sing, so each one sings to his own tune, note and pitch." To the missionary, the sonic disharmony mirrored the obstinate social "disorder" of the villages.

The missionaries brought hymns written in four-part harmony, and they strived to ensure that Africans sang them correctly. Catholic and some Protestant missions also promoted the playing of novel wind instruments, particularly the harmonium, the brass drum, and the cornet. Most of the songs were colonial ditties or otherwise thoroughly imbued with western culture, and the missionaries insisted on their wholesale transplantation. This transplanting of a western musical canon remained a point of dissonance, as Catholic priest Father Brenno wrote from Monte Cassino in the July 1916 issue of the *Zambesi Mission Record:*

> The Mass of St. Aloysius was sung. I am no musician . . . but in my opinion the singing was a little too slow, though the clear and perfect pronunciation of the Latin made up for the slowness. It is difficult to get the natives to pronounce Latin words correctly, and the correct pronunciation in the *Gloria, Credo, Sanctus,* and *Agnus Dei* amply proved what infinite pains had been taken in teaching the children.

As Brenno's diffident assessment implied, the transformative value of this meticulous drilling of European cultures into the consciousness of African students in the name of Christianity remained rather dubious. Missionaries were troubled by "the native" capability to "transform" either way. The recrudescent and avenging spirit of "savagery," as they discovered to their horror, did not spare even their model, the evangelist-teacher. Doing his rounds in the Zambezi Valley, J. H. Morrison (1969, 69) dramatized the image of the lurking demons of heathenism in a racially inflected anecdote about "one-eyed Shem":

> We spent the night at his village. He met us, neatly dressed in a white duck suit, and put his scholars through a very credible exhibition. The loss of one eye was more than made up by the terrible intensity of the other, heightened by a squint. If you dared to look in the direction of the blind eye you found the other glaring at you across the bridge of the nose in the most disconcerting way. In the evening our *ulendo* boys ["native helpers"] played a game of *mpila,* in which Shem joined with enthusiasm. The game consists in tossing a ball among the players, with an extraordinary amount of hand-clapping and ornamental leaping. Shem was one of the showiest players. He seemed literally to follow the ball through the air, wriggling in every limp. At length, finding his duck suit a hindrance, he stripped without ceremony, and stood garbed in a dirty black loincloth and the tattered remains of what had once been a striped cotton jersey. It was a painful transformation. . . . Shem now looked the wildest savage of the lot, and no stretch of the imagination could have conceived him as a schoolmaster.

Weman (1960, 115) contemplated the African child being reborn by taking the "decisive step from the kraal to the mission." There he received the mandatory thorough ablution for bodily filth, the baptismal cleansing for spiritual dirt after *kureurura* (confession of sins), the signatory new name, and instruction in "civilized etiquette," recitation of the Creed, and how to sing like a white person. Sekai Nzenza, daughter of a schoolmaster, was one such child at the Anglicans' St. Columbus School in Buhera. She vividly recalled this protocol of Christian rebirth: "When you know the Creed [by heart], you can be baptised, then you can change your name from the one your parents gave you to a learned and Christian one like Demetrius, Cleopatra or Dorcas." Sekai noted that nobody quite knew what these names meant, "but they were 'English' names. . . . Anything English was Christian" and therefore "civilized" (Nzenza 1988, 10). The inevitable shirt that followed, added Weman, was a befitting outward sign of the new dignity, a symbol of the radical change. The Jesuits explained the power of this symbolism with reference to baptism and communion during the Feast of All Saints at Empandeni in 1907:

> There were twelve baptisms and eight first communions. Of the baptized ten were schoolchildren—six boys and four girls—and two adults. The sisters had made special suits and dresses of white to be won by these children on the day of their spiritual birth, and they looked very nice in their snow-white robes, the symbol of their baptismal regeneration. The sign produced a good effect on the bystanders, of whom there were a good many present. (*ZMR*, October 1907)

However, this transformative imaginary could be quite an illusion, as Johnson feared. Looking at Shem engrossed in *mpila*, he visualized the antinomic disguise and fragility of a grafted "civilization" and worried that "there may be some who can peel off the veneer of their education as Shem peeled off his white ducks and revert to their native barbarism." Evoked through the embodied performance of an unlikely schoolmaster who was little more than frenzied limbs and a rolling eye, the physical and metaphorical capability for spectacular recrudescence came to life in a particularly troubling way for the missionary. Missionaries expected African teachers and their students to be the "front trench men bearing against the enemy," in Johnson's words. But conversion had regressed them into perpetual "babies in faith and knowledge," "vulnerable to the powerful draught of ancestral superstition and to native custom and amusement."

By the 1940s, this crusading missionary attack on African cultures had come under direct challenge by young African converts and some liberal-minded missionaries. They demanded that the church cease this assault and instead co-opt African musical cultures for liturgical purposes. Thus, the turn of the half-century opened a new age of cultural dissidence and demand for reform that destabilized the conservative foundations of the crusading mission church.

Dissident Voices: Belatedly Debating African Music

In a book that earned him deportation by the Rhodesian regime, Ralph Dodge (1960, 48), a rebel American Methodist bishop, wrote that the Christian missionary church in Africa in the 1950s was a church under fire. It came under severe criticism from within, mostly by younger African Christians who charged that the church was in league with, and worked as an agent of, the colonial state in the continued oppression of Africans. The church's condemnation of African cultures was an index of this oppression. In 1940, Thompson Samkange, a leading African Methodist minister, argued before the Native Conference Executive that the church should be indigenized, meaning that it should not only have African leadership, but should also be reconciled with African cultures: "Certain customs in the church at present are foreign and difficult for the African to understand, it would be better if some customs which are associated with spirit worship are introduced into the Church" (Ranger 1993, 334).[1]

Another Zimbabwean wrote to Bishop Dodge from India complaining about music specifically:

> At my home school, where I was a teacher and its headmaster, I was surprised and sorry to find that parents, including my own, discouraged the use of the drum to accompany singing. The reason given was because the drum was used to accompany songs of tribal worship in the past, therefore it must go; it is heathen in this Christian era! . . . They hated the slightest sound of a drum, even on wedding days. I cannot think of a more suitable musical instrument for such occasions. (Dodge 1960, 15, 17)

Sekai Nzenza shared this critique. Disappointed by the mirage of white civilization she had pursued to its "cradle," England, she reminisced, "When the Europeans taught me to pray and to sing, they taught me to do it the European way. When they tried to sing my way, my African way, they made fun of my real way of worship" (Nzenza 1988, 25). She felt the pain deeply at a very personal level. The problem was not merely that the European hymnal idiom, creed, and curriculum were inappropriate; they were tools deployed to destroy the African mind. She understood the damage much later:

> I realize how irreparable damage the missionaries did to me, working hand in glove with the colonial system. All my education . . . came from the missionaries, for which I am most grateful. But what they did to my mind will not be compared with the education they gave me. They sucked my brains dry. The religion they gave me ate me up and made me an unthinking, unimaginative, scared, guilty, and inferior person. (120)

These sentiments, particularly the biting critique of the mission's music policy, found a vibrant platform in the newsletter of the African Music Society (AMS), an organization of European enthusiasts, collectors, and preservationists of African music, led by Hugh Tracey and others. The topic spurred heated conversations and frenetic experimentation to redeem the imperiled church. Ironically, it was in African song that the mission saw its hope for salvation.

Writing from the Congo, Rev. R. P. Peeters triggered the debate when he ventured that "no art, of any country or any people, is perfect or exclusive." He argued that preferences are legitimate but summary disapproval is not, because "the beauty of art may shine with a thousand facets of form, movement, colour and sound" (March 1949, 9). Peeters contended that these facts were true of both secular and sacred art in Europe, and thus asked, "Why should sacred art be looked on differently" in Africa? He accused the Catholic Church of erring by failing to recognize the religious essence of African song: "If they sing from their souls they will pray easily and with fervour. Why should their own singing not be capable of raising them spiritually?" Peeters's argument represented a spirit of reform within the Catholic movement, which, after decades of deprecation, increasingly began to open up to the desirability of employing African music for liturgical services in order to save the marooned church, and apparently to also realign it with the fast-changing political environment.

This new stance was received rather hesitantly by older Christians, including Africans. For instance, also writing from the Congo in the same issue of the AMS's newsletter, one M. l'Abbe Idohou charged that the idea of African songs in church was ridiculous. Cushioning his position with the disclaimer that the music under discussion was the music of his country, which he understood and rarely listened to "without being moved to the depths of my being and sometimes even to tears," Idohou went on to dismiss the music as embryonic and monotonous. Therefore, he reasoned, it was "not capable of elevating the spirit and the heart." Idohou claimed to speak for educated Africans, the so-called *évolues:*

> Its monotonous rhythm is distasteful to cultured men and to progressive people accustomed to the variety of musics which the church uses to reinforce its teaching. It does not attract educated Natives because they judge it inferior and disparage it; I have seen them smile at it. We must take note of their opinion, because their numbers are increasing. (11–12)

To Idohou, African music belonged outside the church walls. There, "it can amuse as well as teach; it can make you laugh, jump, dance." Despite the evolutionary premises of his argument, Idohou vowed, "I will never have indigenous music inside my church."

At Kikongoi in Zanzibar, Africans reportedly walked out on a priest who tried to bring Shambala music into church. Similarly, congregants frowned upon Reverend Lury's attempt to use a drumbeat to give rhythm to singing during a Palm Sunday procession at Korogwe, Tanzania. He quickly abandoned the idea (1956, 34). From Southern Sudan, one Father Filiberto Giorgetti had declared (again in the March 1949 AMS newsletter), "Although I am a European, I am strongly for African music in Africa." But he was frustrated whenever he "attempted to persuade these young Azande 'monkeys' not to despise their music but to improve it." He pointed out that "the Azande educated in schools are the first to discard their African tunes for the less beautiful common English folk-songs they cannot even reproduce well" (9).

In the next issue (July 1950), S. M. Katana responded to Idohou from Uganda, employing the evolutionary argument more positively. He pointed out that he, like Idohou, loved the music of his country, but "unlike him I prefer having the music of my country in a Christian Church." This in spite of the fact that "at present, the mere utterance of 'African Music' causes images of 'Primitive instruments: bottles, bells, castanets, drums, beating of hands and feet,' and sensations of 'the same rhythm and shake.'" Katana argued that the rich and colorful music of Africa was rapidly evolving, just as European music had also evolved over time. Katana based his valuation not simply on aesthetic perceptions, but also on the spiritual significance of the music. He elaborated,

> My personal experience in singing tribal songs is that each song arouses feelings connected with the words and intentions for which it is sung. . . . In either singing or listening to such songs, one strongly feels and experiences the moods for which they are intended. Why should he not feel them if they were intended for the worship of Our Lord? . . . We should worship Our Lord in our very native tones, in our characteristic ways in which He created us.

To Katana, rather than celebrating cultural alienation, Africans had to reclaim their confidence and pride in their own languages in order to develop as a people, because "the music of a race remains the music of that race at any stage of its development" (42–43).

The feeling was strong that African music could only develop and be adopted for the church if it was steeped in its indigenous roots. Philip Gbeho (1954, 82), from Achimota College, Ghana, echoed Katana's argument by "seriously attack[ing] the progenitors of the idea that our music is primitive, fit only for the devil." Gbeho demanded that missionaries should stop preaching that gospel and erecting an "iron curtain" between the educated African and his music, "else there will be a conflict between us and they will regret it in the end." He argued that the effect of "the missionary prohibition of the music that is the centre of our culture was that today we have a vast majority of educated Africans who have not the slightest idea of their own music and culture." Gbeho fought this prejudice not just at home but also in the metropole, where his "musically one-track-minded fellow students and teachers at college in London often wondered why a competent student in western music should spend so much time discussing the 'tom-tom.'"

Josiah S. Tlou (1975, 198) was a schoolmaster and a graduate of Rhodesia's Morgenster Mission. By his own account, he epitomized the educated African convert who lived a conflicted lifestyle, suspended between his indigenous beliefs and *chirungu*—the European ways he strained to accommodate. When the idea of introducing African musical instruments was broached in his Lutheran church, Tlou remembered older churchmen, both African and European, shooting down any such notion, arguing that bringing in such instruments was tantamount to introducing "pagan" practices into Christianity. He agreed with the position then. The proponents of reform had argued that the church that baptized and accepted individuals who decided that they wanted to become Christians should certainly accept instruments, which had neither soul nor mind of their own, and that these instruments could be adapted to the church's purpose. The outcome was a compromise, with the instruments gradually introduced for some church services.

Looking at this and related incidents in retrospect, Tlou later understood that the church's refusal to "revitalize and reincorporate into our Christian belief system those of our cultural traits which are worthwhile" was one deep scar of the spiritual violence the mission had inflicted on Africans. It was partly testimony to the depth of this spiritual scar that, as Reverend Lury (1956, 34) observed, Africans still wished to make a complete break with their "heathen" past, for which they had been condemned viciously for decades. There was also a persistent anxiety that African instruments, dance movements, and "gyrations," which smacked too much of "heathen" ceremonial, could easily erode "the control and discipline connected with the solemn religious ceremonial" of the missionary church (Carrol 1956, 46). This concern instigated repeated papal directives to the missions to incorporate indigenous music in the church.

In 1955, Pope Pius XII repeated for the third time a directive that he had first issued in 1936 and then reissued again in 1949. He ordered,

> Let messengers of the Gospel in pagan lands freely promote . . . this love of religious chant which men committed to their care cherish; but in such a way that these people may replace their national religious songs . . . with similar sacred Christian hymns, by which the truths of the faith, the life of Christ our Lord, the praises of the Virgin Mary and of the Saints, may be known in language and melodies familiar to them. (*Newsletter of the African Music Society* 1956, 47)

This injunction caused "an equal measure of surprise both within and outside the Roman Church . . . [as] no missionary had dreamed that such far reaching adaptation and adoption within the framework of the official liturgy was possible" (Bekkum 1957, 93). The "surprise" at this very conservative decree demonstrates the depth of the missionary ethnocentrism. The decree simply encouraged a different approach toward the same end—the replacement of national religious songs with Christian songs. It did not forbid the continued deprecation of African musical cultures. Thus, reviewing music education and practice in Rhodesian schools and churches in the late 1950s, Weman noted the persistence of "such a strong desire to break completely with all old customs and practices that native music continued to be automatically rejected as 'heathen.'" In fact, he concluded, "folk music, its song and instruments," were still treated as dangerous and firmly excluded from the Christian scheme of things (1960, 116).

Nonetheless, one of the immediate effects of the reissue of the directive in 1955 was that, at least on the literati platforms, it promoted a more tolerant perception among some of "the monkeys who smiled at their own music." Among those already sympathetic, it added impetus to the vociferous calls to shift from merely translating European hymns into the various African languages to actually promoting African-composed hymns. Before considering the church's response to these calls to co-opt African music, it is essential to understand African perspectives on the hymns. Did Africans gain wholesome replacements for their condemned musical "sins?"

Discordant Hymns, "Baptizing Heathen Song"

The fires that scorched the mission church did not spare the hymns, including the tonic sol-fa notation that structured them in the schools. The chief criticisms were, first, that the European technical structures of the notation seldom agreed with African linguistic rules and, second, that the songs lost meaning when transliterated into African languages. The overall effect was that the hymns became distorted, lost their meaning, and became virtually unsingable. Their stanza form, metric patterns of stressed syllables, and four-part melodic structures froze African tonal musical expression into a straitjacket (Carrol 1956, 47). The question had changed from "How shall we sing the Lord's song in a strange land?" to "[How shall we sing] the Lord's song in a muddled version of the mother tongue to tunes that don't fit?" (McHarg 1958, 50). James McHarg was responsible for drafting the music syllabi in Southern Rhodesia's African schools, and he was convinced that "the answer cannot be brought into the church until it has been worked out in the school." Yet in these laboratories of evangelization, Africans reportedly "massacred" the hymns, singing in "ridiculously twisted and inverted accents" (46). Weman keenly observed these struggles:

> At first, the skill at which the melodies are sung following the Tonic Sol-fa system is remarkable; even in the lowest classes, there are children who are capable of singing the simpler kind of melody direct from the printed page. Their skill, however, finishes there. When the text is added, both the teacher and the pupils experience the limitations of the system. It is in fact difficult to co-ordinate text and melody, and the teacher must possess a great store of patience in order to be able to bridge the gulf. (1960, 117)

The overreliance on sol-fa meant the music remained foreign and that Africans were actively schooled into musical illiteracy. It also alienated them from

Christianity; as Johan K. Louw (1956, 43) noted, "the foreignness of the music we use in worship is a very important contributant factor in making the Christian religion to be something Western in the mind of many an African." James McHarg reported (1958, 49) A. M. Jones's disappointment with European hymn singing in Northern Rhodesia: "Father Jones examined a thousand European hymn tunes and found only three which could be put directly to African use, these having a rhythmic structure which ended in a weak accent." He went on to advise, "If the African church is to achieve sincerity in worship and be moved by the power of song in the vernacular, the tunes have to be found in indigenous music." The translation of European hymnbooks into African languages spawned significant errors in the songs' style, accentuation, and meaning, which, because of long usage, Africans and Europeans alike came to accept as normal. Referencing the critique by people like Jones, Weman (1960, 144) bemoaned the consequences of this transplantation of European hymns into the African church:

> We hear beautiful tunes murdered—and we blame the African: we sing hymns with the metre all wrong and actually come to accept them as normal things. We go on making hymns with the wrong rhythm in every line: we set them to tunes of which we are fond, but which the native cannot sing.

Percival Kirby (1959, 38) observed that the negative effect was felt not only on the music, but also on the various African languages in which the hymns were rendered: "The forcing of Bantu words into the Procrustean bed of European hymn forms led to a degradation of the language, which was at first bitterly resented by thoughtful converts." Yet continued usage of these "white men's native songs" apparently normalized the violations.

When Africans sang these meaningless and unsingable hymns nonetheless, they had either to create their own meanings or to simply repeat the hymns in all their alien mysteriousness. Asked about the meaning of a particular hymn, one catechumen in Southern Rhodesia was perturbed: "But I never understood that these hymns were supposed to have any meaning!" (Louw 1956, 43). Similarly, in West Africa, E. G. Parrinder (1956, 37) reported,

> The hymns and canticles have been translated, or rather transliterated, into the different African languages without any attempt being made at finding a poetical or musical form native to the language in question. The hymns of Wesley and Whittier have been turned almost word for word into Yoruba, Twi, Baoule, and a hundred other native tongues. They have been sung to the tunes of Sankey, Barnby, and the rest, which have no kinship with traditional African music. The tragic result has been that these hymns are utter nonsense!

The hymns also lacked sensuality, as one Zimbabwean secondary school female student pointed out: "We do not feel these things when we sing them, but we feel our own African songs" (Parrinder 1956, 37). And, as some of the missionaries quickly learned, their fondly held songs about "Africans extending their dusky hands for the bread of life" did not make sense either, as Africans sustained their worldly lives with *sadza* and other quite different staples. The Anglican priest Archford Musodza (2008, 333), of the Harare diocese, recently commented on, among others, the hymn "In the Bleak Mid-Winter," which the church took from the English hymnbook *Hymns Ancient and Modern* and translated literally into Shona as "Kare Kare Chando Chakachena Kwazvo," to illustrate how the mission church has remained "out of touch with the Shona people who [live] in a different geographical landscape that is not prone to snow." This superficiality and foreignness in idiom and tune, then, failed to stir Africans spiritually. Dodge (1960, 52) argued that "the hymns of Wesley and Watts" were meaningful to Europeans and Americans, and the latter could also find meaning in "Negro spirituals." But all these lacked emotional meaning for Africans, because they reflected neither their personal experience nor their own culture. J. K. Louw pointed out that foisting these alien hymns and idioms onto Africans had the effect of making Jesus a European, rather than a universal, savior.

Even more seriously, some Africans ominously identified the mission of such a Europeanized Jesus in shining armor with the familiar near-genocidal violence they had suffered at the hands of his priests. A student in the 1940s, Jane Lungile Ngwenya (see chapter 10) struggled with such hymns as "Wauya Mucheki"—still popularly sung today—which promise eternal brimstone to sinners, that is, all non-Christian Africans:

Wauya mucheki mukuru	Lo and behold, comes the gory reaper
Kuzotora vatsvene vake	To take his faithful adherents
Vakaipa vose	All the sinners
Vachashaya pokuvanda	Shall find nowhere to hide.

The hymn promised Africans an even more intense and eternal suffering than they endured at the hands of the worldly European settlers and church! Ngwenya recalled the psychological violence they suffered while they sang "It Is Well with My Soul," "Swing Low," and the national anthem, "God Bless the Queen": "We sang those songs at schools standing still. You would not move even when a pesky fly bothered you. I don't despise the churches, but it was the church that was used to really destroy us." Moreover, because most of these songs were in English, or translated from English while retaining their foreign tunes, they had to be sung in contrived, stilted European voices, not the natural expressive African singing voice. Ngwenya remembered that children were taught "to sing like 'Missis' [the proverbial white woman]." Yet appreciating African music on its own terms might have made Christianity more resonant. Gbeho (1954, 82) wrote that Africans naturally danced for worship, "hence our music is always associated with religion." Had the church allowed African music to flourish,

"Christianity would have meant a far more serious thing to the African than a mere social conversion." To most Africans, whose welfare depended on the learned behaviors imposed by church and school, conversion simply implied social conformity.

All this criticism made the call to bring African music within the church walls logical. But these were the same pagan chants and demonic amusements targeted by the missionary crusades! Two possibilities were suggested: first, the promotion of new hymns by African composers, and second, the appropriation of preexisting African ritual songs for the church. Some missionaries and settlers had considered the second option quite early on, after encountering resistance to their efforts to supplant African cultures. Thus, in the March 3, 1871, *Kaffir Express,* one missionary had urged the church to compromise with "the kaffir's peculiar customs," if only because the "kaffir was roughly and hastily formed . . . neither for ornament nor for beauty," and could therefore not be easily swayed from his "heathen" ways. Another writer, who signed himself "Umlungu" ("White man"), elaborated this analysis in the same issue:

> We must bear in mind, while we try to win the Kaffir over from his uncivilized state, and endeavour to bring him under the influence of religion and civilized habits, that we entirely deprived him of all the amusements to which he was before accustomed—amusements in dance and song into which he entered body and soul, and that we supply him with no substitutes for these amusements. The raw Kaffirs . . . are passionately fond of singing and dancing.

Giving Africans Bibles, psalms, and hymns—which were never meant for amusement—not only deprived "the Kaffirs" of their national customs, argued Umlungu, but also converted them into dull, idle, melancholic, and discontented drunkards. It often became easy for them, he opined, to "fall back to the happy, joyous life of their former selves." Umlungu believed in empathetic appropriation, rather than confrontation. He professed a genuine appreciation of the beauty of African singing and dancing:

> Watch the real enjoyment of both men and women at their dances, and listen to the rich and beautiful harmony of their voices as they make the hills echo with their dance-songs, rude tho' they may be. See the spirit that is inspired into the fagged abakweta at their dances, as the beautifully clear voices of the women with the rich voices of the men, join the really stirring chorus of some favourite song. Listen to the music of their voices at their night dance, when the men have to go [through] the severe exercise of the intlombe dance. Can anyone then deny that our Kaffir young men and women (and even older men and women) do not look back to all this with longing and melancholy hearts—and begin to suspect that the heathenish life with its joys and amusements is preferable to the dull and quiet life of Civilization and Christianity into which we have brought them[?]

Umlungu urged missionaries and settler society to transcend their dislike of these "objectionable, uncivilized amusements" and harness them as weapons to achieve the goal of "civilizing the Kaffir." He encouraged African students at Lovedale and similar institutions to "bestir themselves and show us what they could do" by composing "Kaffir songs" for Christian purposes. Many colonists, suggested Umlungu, were willing to come forward with pecuniary inducements to encourage such good work.

Apparently no mere idealist, Umlungu not only mailed this letter to the editor of the crusading *Kaffir Express,* but also enclosed a portion of an *umbongo,* Xhosa sung poetry, which "(besides many others) was composed and recited, or rather chanted, in a rich, clear voice by a young Kaffir named Tshota at the circumcision dances of Nonqane, a son of Kreli." The journal's editor happily published Umlungu's "sensible" letter, but regretted that the "Umbongo—or Circumcision Dance Song—[was] not fitted to our purpose." He also argued that young men faced so many inducements to forsake their education and leave their employment for circumcision ceremonies "that we can't afford to place an additional one before them by throwing the halo of song and romance about the practice." He pointed to a case where "all the young lads have lately left a mission station and the missionary's care to have this rite performed," forsaking years of mission instruction. Furthermore, the editor reminded Umlungu that circumcision was "a great barrier to the progress of civilization and Christianity." Africans often wondered at the missionaries' contradicting the Bible on such matters as circumcision and polygamy.

While this early suggestion had failed to win support, selective appropriation presented itself not just as a possibility but as an avenue that promised to salvage the mission from the grave criticism of estranged Africans. S. Douglas Gray (1923, 46) recorded that Methodists pondered long and hard on the possibility of "select[ing] . . . such customs as are not inimical to the growth of the Christian character, and the building upon them of the teaching of Jesus." Their ideas never wandered too far from the orthodox. Gray mused, "The ideal is surely that whenever a tribal custom is condemned and made taboo for the Christian, some better thing should be substituted." For decades, the missionaries hesitated and fell back on the *tabula rasa* approach that loathed the linking of "Christian life and the outworkings of Animism," braving the erosion of the church by Ethiopianism rather than countenance cultural syncretism. It was only in the 1940s–50s that this idea was pragmatically adopted as a means to save the church from sure collapse.

The preferred model for cooptation was the African American—or, more precisely, the slavery—idiom, as one Catholic missionary implied in the AMS newsletter: "Can we in Africa not attain that which the Protestant missionaries have done with the Negroes of America? Are we incapable of christianizing in our turn the music of the Natives?" (March 1949, 14). The idea was that African suffering under colonialism could be exploited to bring them closer to God, as enslavement had allegedly achieved with African Americans. Far from looking at African music in its own light, the idea was to harness it for functionalist purposes in ways that demonstrate Césaire's critique of the equation of colonialism with "civilization"—a false equation modeled on the originary Euro-American lie equating enslavement with "Christianization." By way of elaboration, the missionary suggested that new melodies could be created "scientifically," making them "as artistic as European hymns" while following specific indigenous techniques, always within the parameters of "true sacred music."

This approach would also involve appropriating African sacred music and "baptizing" it for the church. After all, argued Weman (1960, 54), this was the genealogy of the European Christian hymn as the church emerged from ancient synagogue traditions: "This is clear from the continued use of the Psalter. . . . That the church did not dispense with the old laws of tonality is also proven by the living tradition preserved in our modes, which still have Greek names." The latter also underwent some form of "purification" process. The same was true of hundreds of hymns sung in the contemporary church; they were appropriations of European secular songs. Quoting F. Smith, Weman contended that the important thing was that "once the external considerations have been lost or put aside, any music that is intrinsically artistic can qualify for 'baptism' in the one, true Church." In fact, controlled adaptation was a key strategy, which some missionary organizations utilized to minimize resistance to conversion. As Heise (1967, 23) noted, such missionary organizations submitted their innovations within the framework of indigenous institutions and practices: initiation rites, religious ceremonies, local songs, myths, and festivals. In this way, selective appropriation or adaptation could easily be channeled into new creative directions.

Consequently, people like Rev. Johan K. Louw (1956, 44), a teacher in Nyasaland, did not waste time, but started working to convince African musicians to emulate the spontaneity of Nyanja praise poets when they dance or mourn or praise a chief or a hero; African Christians should similarly "praise God spontaneously, or to come to Him in time of distress, or express any other normal religious experience in song." He believed that when a true African Christian musician "is brought to disregard any form of church music that he may have known in the past and breaks forth praising God in the musical medium that lies closest to his heart, half the battle will have been won." Louw sent African students to tap the same founts that had nourished the making of sacred music for generations in their communities. The only obstacle Louw found himself facing was Africans' reluctance to "baptize" preexisting sacred music. His students advised him that "this music had to be something new since all music of the past had its own associations and meaning and could not just be transferred into a new experience." To Louw, this seemed a fairly logical position because, he mused, the Christian with a new experience had to give expression to that experience in the musical language of his own soul. Louw's students composed songs based on folktales, myths, legends, local dirges, Bible stories, and everyday events in the communities. The songs revolved mainly around such subjects as personal loss and bereavement, which Louw adjudged a good start (51).

In Southern Sudan, Father Giorgetti experimented with the Azande's sacred drumming and dancing with accordion music. He staged a Christmas show depicting "the consternation created in hell by the announcement of the birth of the Saviour and of the joy of the Azande and other tribes who come to pay homage to the child Jesus Christ" (Louw and Louw 1956, 75). On a different occasion, the dance was converted into a ballet and performed on the feast of Corpus Christi, accompanied by a band and the singing of a Eucharistic hymn. Unsurprisingly, while these experiments received wide acclaim, they did not appeal to everyone. One J. F. A. Swartz, who regarded himself as an enthusiast of African music, argued that, like tenth-century European music, African traditional music had very little value, as it was a "little more than a wail and a howl" (Swartz 1956, 33). But perhaps a more serious challenge were the Africans who cried, "Never back to the kraal again!" After generations of demonization, many converts were not too keen to be reminded of their "heathen" backgrounds as they sought to make sense of their new lives as Christians (Weman 1960, 170).

Weman conducted experiments in South Africa and Zimbabwe as bold as Father Giorgetti's among the Azande. He took his lessons directly from African students who had been drilled in tonic sol-fa. He began by watching them at the ubiquitous "musical evenings," where soloists, groups, and *makwaya* (choirs) performed for prizes in organized school and village competitions. Such events were sometimes presided over by the Inspector of Music in South Africa and by colonial administrators and Paramount Chiefs in both countries. The musical evening was a platform for competing musical conventions, where emergent mission cultures clashed or hybridized with traditional performative forms. Watching one such performance in Durban, Weman noted that the general public, both black and white, received the European songs—the school staple—politely enough, "but interest waned as the evening progressed. . . . However, as soon as the same choir broke with convention and produced a native song with its accompanying movement and dance, interest . . . quickened." He concluded, "That choir had made immediate contact with the public and everyone listened eagerly." The lesson was driven home. Even at the missions, African cultures were barely below the surface, roiling under the oppressive weight of the identities of shame.

In Zimbabwe, at Chegato "kraal" school, Weman discovered that students had greater scope to perform their own local songs away from the proscriptive gaze of the missionaries. He listened keenly to the choir, which, "after a good deal of procrastination, got to its own repertoire." He was fascinated as he watched their dancing and "the fluent movement of the parts, and the fine musical line in 'Pamatarirano,' a high class polyphony sung in four-part counterpoint, coming from the heart of the people." The students went on to sing "Mari Yangu Yaperera Muchitima" (I squandered all my money in the train), a contemporary secular ditty referencing the everyday misadventures of train rides and pleasurable urban consumption. He imagined that such songs could form the foundation for capturing African songs for Christ.

Similarly, at Musume School, Weman had students introduce *ngoma* to some of the more common hymns. This was revolutionary, as the drum had shared with *mbira* so much of the missionary buffeting. He recorded that the drums had a splendid effect upon the level of attendance at evening prayers, as "curious neighbours came from the nearby kraals to take part. What was for the African a new drumming technique was introduced for Kiwele's refrain, which soon echoed round the district." Even more daringly, the students performed—on the *mbira dzavadzimu* set—such songs as "Wadane N'anga" (He who has invited the traditional healer) and "Terera Ngoma" (Listen to the drum). "Wadane N'anga" is a traditional *mhande* (dance) piece that celebrates the prowess of the healer as restorer and guardian of society's physiological and spiritual order, while "Terera Ngoma" is an initiation song, sung as boys cast off their youth (often together with their foreskins) to become men.

Weman had first heard the latter song at a Remba circumcision school, and described it thus:

> The violence with which the song is delivered, the ecstatic upward trend, lifting a semi-tone at a time as the song progresses, the sounds forced from tensed throats—all these combine to give the overwhelming impression that something unusual is in progress. When this school is over, and the young people are allowed to return to their huts in the village, the spirit of rejoicing takes control. Dance follows dance, and the celebrations go on all day, and perhaps all night as well. (81)

This was the school, the indigenous knowledge that missionary evangelism had tried to destroy—without much success. Now the mission tried to appropriate its indices, its expressive song and drum, to salvage itself. The mission church, especially the Catholic Church, enriched itself on African songs and drumbeats, including the familiar rhythm, the colloquial "Fata Murungu," which proclaimed the paradox of the white father of black congregants. Clement Masakure's grandfather remembered "Fata Murungu" as originally a royal piece played in eastern Zimbabwe before the Catholics co-opted it (Clement Masakure, pers. comm.). But, as Africans remarked then, "Asi ngoma ndiyo ndiyo" (The beat is but the same). Nothing much had changed (Jabulani Ziwenga, pers. comm.). Even among the Ethiopian churches, as Hubert Bucher complained as late as 1980, the African church displayed superficial "semblances of Christianity" while intrinsically "remain[ing] tied to the traditional [African] cosmology" (Bucher 1980, 14). The line between cooptation and indigenization was very tenuous, as the stubborn language of familiarity suggested. Some Africans correctly read the missionary cooptation of their indigenous registers backward, seeing it as the domestication of the church.

Working with the Methodists in Zimbabwe from 1961, Robert Kauffman had Africans arrange traditional tunes for the church. His approach largely consisted of taking existing tunes and superimposing new texts on them. One of the people with whom Kauffman worked was the late Dumisani Abraham Maraire, who had studied indigenous music at the Kwanongoma College of Music and later on attended the University of Washington in the 1960s–70s, during which period he pioneered the export of *mbira* music to the United States. Maraire composed quite a few tunes on the *mbira* that, in the view of J. Lenherr (1967, 75), showed great imagination and technical skill. Similarly, a Catholic catechist in Bikita, Simon Mashoko, employed *mbira* in his proselytizing excursions. Mashoko also did the unthinkable: he not only brought the voice of the ancestors—*mbira dzavadzimu*—into the Catholic Church but extended the experiment, subsequently building his own independent church that centered on indigenous principles (Zantzinger 1999).

Kauffman's experimentation drew on the model of Vabvuvi, a Methodist laymen's singing group formed in 1940 as a male version of Ruwadzano, a pioneer women's group that had been founded eight years earlier. As Kauffman (1960, 31) observed, both groups were highly evangelistic and had high ethical standards. Members had to serve two years as novices, help recruit new church members, and even start new churches. Their evangelization style consisted of extemporaneous meetings during which they frequently burst into purely African-style songs (although some had been derived from the parent Methodist organization). These songs had made them popular throughout Zimbabwe, particularly in the African independent churches that adopted them. What is also striking about Vabvuvi's style of worship was the freedom to transcend the church walls, reclaiming the alienated, unruly commons "in the great dramatic style of the pagan religions," as Reverend Carrol (1956, 47) observed of similar independent churches among the Yoruba. Reconciling with alienated indigenous spirituality meant reclaiming the demonized voices, idioms, and styles of worship and the sacral landscapes. The Ethiopian movement had long transcended the disciplining church building by congregating under trees, on hilltops, and by riverbanks, spaces the missionary church tried but failed to command. Such spaces constituted not only dangerous margins to the imposed Eurocentric hegemony, but also indigenous infrastructures of spirituality that the European missionary church could never hope to command or control, hence it lost the battle to the rebel Ethiopianists.

The efforts to encourage educated Africans to write indigenous hymns also bore a bounteous but curious fruit, *makwaya*. Innovative Zimbabwean teachers and their students wedded indigenous tunes and texts to the four-part harmonic structure of the hymns. As Jones observed in the AMS newsletter (July 1950, 10–11), *makwaya* (sing. *kwaya*) consisted of young singers who proceeded in a column four abreast, often under the direction of a leader, singing action songs. The "modernist" singing style was strongly influenced by European church singing in form, and by indigenous music in style. The songs' shortcoming, measured by the European hymnodal canon, was that they were based on too few chords in root position, and they were therefore musically too repetitive to fulfill the mission church's liturgical purposes. As Jones described them,

> *The songs are danced;* the tunes are strongly *metrical;* and the nature of the dancing makes them much more metrical in the usual European sense than ordinary village dance songs. . . . While the tune is still unquestionably African, the structure of it has been influenced by European music.

To Jones, *makwaya* were a legitimate outcome of the impact of European musical cultures on Africans. He imagined them as a natural step toward the development of African hymns, complete with the purged rhythm. He wrote, "We only have to watch ma-choir to be convinced that these new harmonies are so thrilling to the African that he becomes actually mildly intoxicated by them."

Makwaya took schools by storm in the 1930s–40s. At the Anglican St. Augustine's High School in Penhalonga, four hundred students participated in a competition to compose indigenous songs for the church. The ones adjudged the best were all composed in *makwaya* style, and they soon spread across the country. The *makwaya* phenomenon taught the missionaries keen on developing African hymns that the notion of "the (musical) African" was much more complex than they had imagined. Concerning the experiment at St. Augustine's, Jones concluded,

> It would appear therefore, that we are now to cater for two classes of Christian. The ordinary villager, who is best served by hymns in his own idiom, that is hymns of the type of village songs; and the African who has been recently to school, who needs hymns in the new idiom of the ma-choir songs with the harmonies inseparable from that idiom. (12)

The psychological hangover of this *makwaya* intoxication remained with Nathan Shamuyarira, a graduate of the Methodist Waddilove Training Institution, to the end of his life. *Makwaya* singing was a high point of social life in the rural schools of Chihota where he taught at Chivizhe School. Together with his fellow-teacher and friend Chivanda Kennedy Manyika, whom he adjudged one of the greatest *makwaya* singers of the time, they organized interschool competitions and toured villages for weekly shows.

However, the expectation that the fledgling *makwaya* would be a toddling step in the development of genuinely African hymns largely evaporated by the beginning of the 1950s, as reservations about indigenous musical cultures persisted.

In his historical assessment of the fate of *mbira* and the church, Anglican priest Archford Musodza wrote, "Although in some denominations such as the Roman Catholic Church this instrument is being used, no attempt has been made in the Anglican Church to use it" (2008, 287). *Ngoma* and *hwamanda* fared no better across the denominations. Anglican Bishop Peter Hatendi (quoted in Musodza 2008, 287) explained the problem as stemming from the lack of concerted or organized support for musical indigenization after the 1940s.[2] But a second reason for this stagnation, more baffling to the African originators of *makwaya,* was the fact that the missionaries soon began to charge that their concerts were spawning immorality, and stepped up to quash them in familiar fashion (Shamuyarira, interview, 2011; Manyika, interview). The next chapter explores this nexus between *makwaya* and the discourse of immorality. What is clear here, however, is that missionaries' belated efforts to nurture African hymns for the church clashed with both the persistent demonization of African cultures and the innovative registers of African self-fashioning that refused to serve narrow Christian missionary ends. *Makwaya* had very little, if anything, to do with the church's evangelical agenda, and for that they suffered.

To conclude, it is important to underline that the missionary assault on African musical cultures had a deep and conflictual impact. On the one hand, the ethnocentric European missionary ideology did manage to produce a new kind of African, who felt culturally inferior and ashamed of the cultures and past of his or her own people. On the other, the mission's epistemicide produced a cultural crisis, which threatened the mission church's own future in Africa. Ironically, it was to African song and cultures that the mission church turned, using selective appropriation to salvage itself from the prospect of certain ruin. The search for new musical pathways out of this crisis helped foster African innovation and produce such new genres as the energetic *makwaya,* which generated a third, hybridized, and often subversive space between the orthodox missionary hymns and the condemned African traditional performative forms. What might this history mean for African music and cultural historiography? Scholarly interest in Christian music—"gospel"—has become fashionable and is growing (Chitando 2002; Gwekwerere 2010). However, this interest has thus far managed to build only a presentist historiography, largely focused on analyzing and—like older church historiography that documented the "growth" of the church in Africa—celebrating the recent boom in gospel music without mapping its tortured genealogies or defining what the genre really is. This critique is important because gospel music today, like the church itself, remains ambiguous, simultaneously seeking to reconcile with and to perpetuate the colonial alienation of African humanity, on whose forms it has come to partially depend since the troubled 1940s.

3 "Too Many Don'ts"

Reinforcing, Disrupting the Criminalization of African Musical Cultures

The Native Department, therefore, assisted by missionaries, is decidedly the only safe stepping-stone for us in dealing with the natives, and if we despise that stepping-stone, all our efforts in dealing with the present objectionable native customs and amusements will ultimately recoil upon ourselves.

—"A Colonist," letter to *Kaffir Express*, July 1, 1871

I have seldom been more shocked than in conversation with Protestant missionaries. They have absolutely filthy minds. They cannot see anything in negro manifestations except illicit copulation. . . . Dances are only an excuse for the orgies they inevitably end in; any negro meeting was an orgy.

—Geoffrey Gorer, *Africa Dances*

"THAT NIGHT I sang and danced as I had never done before. I just let myself go and really had a wonderful time. I was surprised when it was dawn. . . . The concert had ended and we walked back home, tired, sleepy and happy." These are the words of Stanlake Samkange (1975, 13), son of Rev. Thompson Samkange, reminiscing about his first scintillating experience of a *konzati* (concert, pl. *makonzati*) at Madzima School in Zvimba sometime in the early 1930s. It was in response to a *konzati* like this one and related "night dances" that, in June 1930, the Southern Rhodesia Native Christian Missionary Conference—of which Stanlake's father was Secretary and a "directing force" (Ranger 1993, 318)—passed a resolution, with the backing of its white superior, the Southern Rhodesia Missionary Conference, requesting the government to "provide a means whereby the so-called dances or tea meetings held at night by irresponsible persons can be eliminated in the outlying districts or kraals" of the country.[1] The missionaries charged that these "night dances" fostered beer drinking and promiscuity among young girls. They doubted the government fully understood this "evil," and demanded investigations. The government obliged, and the Premier, Howard Unwin Moffat (who was himself the son of a missionary), tasked the Chief

Native Commissioner and his Native Affairs Department (NAD) officers with making a full probe.[2]

The investigations produced conflicting results, with some Native Commissioners (NCs) confirming, and others disputing, the existence or nature of the purported evil. Still others were puzzled by the vagueness of the resolution even as they proceeded to give their own observations and opinions, or report what they had already done to extirpate the evil. Taken together and read in the context of the deepening colonial domination of African society, the reports reveal intensifying intergenerational, class, and gender tensions that often pitted African elders (both Christian and non-Christian) and their uneasy allies in the colonial state against African youths. All these tensions were articulated through the ill-defined register of "night dancing."

The discourse generated through these reports is important for at least three reasons. First, it reinforces the significance of the alliance of church and state in efforts to reengineer, control, and discipline African being. Second, it underlines the impact of missionaries, demonstrating how some of the first generation of African mission Christians had already internalized and begun to bolster foreign cultural prejudices against their own indigenous life worlds. And third, it illustrates the power of song and dance as instruments of self-fashioning and resistance to the internalized, pathologizing inferiority complexes. Through the musical dance, young Africans, especially teachers and their students, were able to generate and stage their power in ways that interrogated and threatened to undermine the gerontocratic structures of rural colonial politics through which capital reproduced and sought to exploit subjugated African being. The chapter illustrates, therefore, how the musical dance was a performative crucible within which younger Africans could interrogate power and articulate competing moral and political orders and disorders in a context where the state forcefully intervened into the intimate realms of African lives, regimenting and circumscribing their aspirations. Ultimately, the instructive facts that the probe was instigated by the African fraction of the mission church, and that the alleged villains, young African teachers and students, were the key products of the mission, shows the conflictual impact of missionary witchcraft on African societies.

The NAD's investigation shed some light but also spawned confusion in official circles over the meaning of "night dancing." Further, it also demonstrated the anxieties of a colonial state-church hegemon that was increasingly concerned about the potential repercussions of its overdetermined alienation of the colonial subject. I utilize the reports generated by this investigation within a broader context of colonial conversations about African being to understand the internal processes and anxieties of colonial knowledge production and subject making through the dancing African body. The vague phrase "night dances"—a blank slate—authorized unfettered colonial inscription and interpretation of both the phenomenon and the general conceptions of rural and peri-urban African being on the margins of the colonial polity. In other words, because nighttime was the temporal locus for most African recreational and ritual musical performances, the investigators struggled to identify the form of the dances in question while the nocturnal metaphor allowed them to contemplate and ascribe to them all manner of social and political sinfulness. For these reasons, what constituted an evil night dance was almost anyone's guess. This vagueness simultaneously constrained and enabled policymaking and state action against Africans. I assess the phenomenon primarily through the Native Commissioners' reports but also by listening to the unmediated African voice as it can be gleaned through interviews and contemporaneous African writing. Yet it should be remembered that the NCs' reports represent both internal colonial dialogue and mediated African voices; they constitute a digested mush of African views and voices, culled and processed through the colonial crucible of African messengers, interpreters, clerks, chiefs, and headmen, re/presented and sanctioned by the *mudzviti,* the Native Commissioner.

In his report, the *mudzviti* for Gutu reported that night dances were prevalent in his district, having come to his notice in 1927.[3] He attributed the phenomenon to village schoolteachers and their students, who threw parties they called "kwayira"—*makwaya. Makwaya* were itinerant communal performances. The *mudzviti* gave a vivid description of the social organization of the dances:

> They pay a round of visits from kraal to kraal choosing those inmates of kraals who they consider are well to do in stock and grain. They assemble in front of the owner's hut and dance and sing until the owner gives them a present—a beast, a sheep, a goat or grain, unless he objects and drives them away, which seldom happens.

Close friends Nathan Shamuyarira and Chivanda Kennedy Manyika—who called each other by the nickname "Shrinko"—were pioneers of these *makwaya.* They helped organize them in the reserve schools of Chihota during their schooling and teaching days there in the 1930s–40s. They both agreed with the *mudzviti*'s description of the format of these roving *ngoma* or *madandaro,* traveling concert parties, which took them away from home for days on end almost every week. They staged the dances at selected schools beginning Saturday night, mostly during the holidays but also in term-time. Representatives of different schools competed at these traveling *ngoma,* with choirs taking the stage in turn and the champions getting prizes. Winning students and their teachers took their prizes and a share of the money raised back to their schools, where they prepared meals and then, as the NC for Gutu reported, "the party foregathers and dancing and singing again take place."

African teachers organized these youth-centered dances, which borrowed the four-part hymnodal format and recast it in indigenous expressive *ngoma* styles, including festive singing, dancing, and feasting. *Makonzati* approximated particularly the traditional *mashangamukamuka*, in which youths made collective post-harvest forays into the fields to gather any remaining crops, out of which they prepared food for their own communal feasting. Parents helped by also providing meats and vegetables. Born out of the quandary and re-creative tensions that bedeviled the latter-day mission church, *makonzati* also appropriated the school as a new *dariro* on which to stage the cultural innovation that mediated influences of both the village and the mission. The school enabled the teachers and students to innovatively extend their everyday cultural practices within the rubric of traditional participatory work and consumption, song, dance, and youthful festivity.

In Mzingwane, the only night dance that the NC reported was the infrequent school *konzati* that a local mission teacher organized. At this *konzati*, the NC noted, the organizers charged entrance fees of sixpence for men and threepence for women, and accepted donations on the same scale for encores, with the fiesta starting at 7 PM and ending at dawn, about 5 AM.[4] This organizational structure reinforced youthful self-expression, socialization, accumulation, consumption, and self-help. Monetary proceeds were sometimes channeled toward building classroom blocks and teachers' houses.

Norman Zikhali participated in these *makonzati* as a student at Nkwazi in Tsholotsho District in the 1940s (interview). His teachers, including the headmaster, Matshovisizithende Ncube, and a Mr. Mfene, a South African, composed the songs and conducted the singing. They staged the performances in makeshift enclosures at the appointed school, where students converged from dozens of others:

> We would make a shed. You cut tree branches and thatch grass and make a sizable enclosure to protect the children from the elements, and therein the choirs would compete. And a goat and a cockerel would be ready as prizes. The goat, and sometimes a cow, went to the choir or school that took first position.

The enclosure also enabled the organizers to control crowds and levy the entrance fees. Good performances were highly appreciated, with audiences tossing money—*kukanda mari*—to keep the best choirs on stage. As Zikhali explains, the money meant, "'That's nice, go on and sing again and again.' And your money piles up, beating the other choirs."

Stanlake Samkange enjoyed his first *konzati* as a Mariga student, hosted by a neighboring school, Madzima:

> We left Mariga at sunset as part of the local choir. This allowed us to be admitted free of charge, otherwise we would have had to pay at the door. I was very anxious to attend one of these concerts because I had heard so much about them. About three hours after leaving Mariga we were near Madzima School.

> We began to sing one of those songs which not only praised our school, Mariga, but also eulogized and lionized our teacher, the evangelist Magedi. The concert was held in a large grass enclosure near the school. From the large fires already burning we could tell that several choirs had already arrived and the concert was in progress. (Samkange 1975, 102)

Each choir boasted its greatness in *rumbo rwekuvhundutsira*—a self-adulatory song—as it approached the *dariro*. Chivanda Kennedy Manyika remembered how the Chivizhe choir, which he and Shamuyarira led, sang,

Tazouya	We have come
Tazouya	We have come
Isu vana vekwaChivizhe	We the children of Chivizhe
Vana vekwaChivizhe	The children of Chivizhe.

Choirs strived to outdo each other to get on and stay *mudariro*, on the stage, with the MC guiding the proceedings, receiving monies, and keeping order. Recalled Samkange,

> [The MC] invited people to come forward and asked for any choir to sing at the cost of a tickey, i.e., three pennies, while the other recorded the pennies. Somebody went forward, placed a tickey on the table and asked that Mariga should sing. Whereupon the MC shouted "Hear ye! Hear ye! Mr. Dutiro, great son of Chipata says: 'What is money? What is a tickey? We, at our home, say a tickey is peanuts, and with this tickey I say Mariga should sing!" Clap your

Chivanda Kennedy Manyika conducting his Vungu School Choir, c. 1930s. Courtesy of Chivanda Kennedy Manyika.

Chivanda and Rahab Manyika, Gweru, 2012. Courtesy of the author.

Reminiscing about *makonzati*: Dorothy and Nathan Shamuyarira, Harare, 2011. Courtesy of the author.

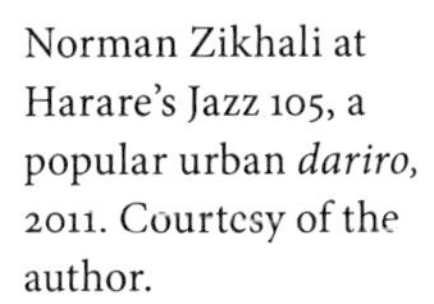

Norman Zikhali at Harare's Jazz 105, a popular urban *dariro*, 2011. Courtesy of the author.

> hands! And Mariga Choir began singing and dancing, advancing and retreating; making such slow progress towards the table as would have shamed a chameleon. (102)

Mariga owned the *dariro* for a few precious minutes, crooning and strutting before Mgugu shouted them off as "rubbish," backing his opinion by placing his *mukono* of sixpence on the table to replace them with Chikaka. Audiences cheered and joined in the next round of singing and dancing, repeating the routine until dawn forced a halt to the fun with everyone still intoxicated with the festivities.

The economics of *makonzati* were significant to an African youth excluded by the alienating gerontocratic alliance of African and colonial patriarchy that also extracted their labor and income. *Makonzati* presented opportunities for unregulated mobility and for independent accumulation, consumption, and self-construction, generative processes that disrupted the structures of control and appropriation at a time when the colonial economy's labor demands dislocated the African family, thrusting youths into the labor migrancy that became the new rite of passage. In this context, colonial officialdom framed "night dancing" as youthful disorder and rebelliousness. Unlike *mashangamukamuka* or other youthful moonlight fiestas, which reinforced intergenerational pleasurable socialization within controlled home environments, the money economy and the school platform disengaged them from close dependence on parental support and oversight in ways that foregrounded generational independence or, in the eyes of the elders, straying. Where the sonic codes of the village *ngoma* and *mbira* had ordered their socialization, the alienating *makonzati dariro* spawned disorder.

An appreciation of "night dancing" as delinquency can be gained from elders' complaints. In his report, which conveniently veiled his own colonial mandate, the NC for Gutu maintained, "The elders of the kraals are very much opposed to this practice, as they lose the services of their children."[5] By the 1920s, the underdevelopment of the African economy and the corollary engineering of African men into migrant laborers had resulted in the breakdown of the authority of African patriarchs, who lost their ability to control children, wives, junior siblings, and other dependents (Grier 1994, 29). White settler farmers, miners, and missionaries depended on African patriarchs to furnish them steady supplies of the unfree labor of their children in line with the precolonial structures of power relations that, ironically, colonial capitalism simultaneously undermined. Colonial capitalism preyed on these structures of African familial authority, turning the elders into despots, but emasculated ones holding only a delegated authority. For example, asked by the South African Native Affairs Commission in 1903 how Rhodesian farmers recruited labor under the labor tenancy system, one farmer elaborated the usefulness of an intact "tribal system" for colonial accumulation:

> When I say "head of kraal," it may be only one man living in that kraal. As a rule, where there are several living in a kraal, they have always one man . . . and that is the man they look up to, and the man the Government here generally takes as having authority over that kraal and the people in it. (Grier 1994, 36).

"Night dancing" disrupted these structures of intergenerational authority, control, labor mobilization, appropriation, and discipline.

As a metaphor for the capacity to independently earn and spend money (and time), a form of freedom, the "night dance" subverted the colonial labor imagination of the African body. This is because, according to Rhodesia's labor laws, juveniles could not legally contract themselves out to work, but required the authority of their guardians, who would sign the labor certificates on their behalf and be accountable for any misdemeanors they might commit. Independent accumulation and consumption—through both "night dancing" and unmediated labor contracting—challenged this insistence on tight control and the socialization of African children as (future) acquiescent laborers. This became a serious difficulty in the 1920s when "hordes of piccanins" ran away from parental control to seek work in the new centers of production, generating a vexed discourse of counterinsurgency on juvenile desertion, insubordination, insolence, drinking, and promiscuity—problems the state tried to tackle through the Native Juveniles Employment Act (NJEA) of 1926, among other effects.

As per the 1925 recommendation of the Commission on Native Education, the NJEA empowered the Native Commissioner to act "*in loco parentis* to such juveniles." The office of the *mudzviti* thus intervened in juvenile labor matters by issuing *chitikinyani,* the identity paper that young men were required to carry. The piece of legislation authorized him to whip, fine, imprison, or otherwise discipline youngsters adjudged delinquent. Together with the Masters and Servants Act and related laws, it sought to reinforce statutory and parental authority over African youths for the benefit of the colonial state and capital. This bolstering of colonial order legitimized ultra-cheap African child labor, crippled youth aspirations, and fostered conflict between African elders and their children. The hysteria over the so-called night dances was in large part an expression of this tension these acts attempted to manage.

For Shamuyarira, for instance, who entered teaching so young that he was still carrying *chitikinyani* in lieu of *chitupa,* the adult pass, organizing *makonzati* provided him a side income to supplement his £1 10s. monthly salary as a junior teacher (interview, July 2011). *Chitikinyani* not only materially stymied his socioeconomic aspirations as a "native teacher." As a marker of his status as a "native," it stripped him of his humanity by limiting his mobility and thus hindering, even arresting, his development into an adult, in spite of his education. *Chitikinyani,* like *chitupa,* formed the text and tag of the colonial state's violation of African right to autonomous personhood, perpetrated and personified by the superintending, self-important *mudzviti.* Shamuyarira had turned fifteen when his father took him to the *mudzviti*'s office to get *chitupa,* in accordance with the new colonial rites of passage. The visit was a lesson in the self-conceit and power of this official. When they presented themselves, after removing their shoes and hats and being deliberately kept waiting, Shamuyarira was stunned when the *mudzviti* humiliated his terrified evangelist father, demanding to know why "it" had come to his office (Shamuyarira 1965, 33). This colonial enactment of power—this reaffirmation of the animalization of Africans, of his own father—never left the younger Shamuyarira's mind. He was issued *chitikinyani:* a tag of infantilization that crippled him and constantly reminded him of his denied potentialities, adulthood, and autonomy. *Makonzati* were therefore much more than just entertainment to Shamuyarira and his colleagues; they were a performative, rebellious crafting of alternative spaces for self-fashioning and self-expression, which were denied them on the formal economic and political platforms. *Makonzati* were a *dariro* on which to explore the possibilities for independently crafting a generational mandate away from the fetters of his emasculated and unwillingly complicit father.

While it is clear that most of the dances that took place at schools were in the highly formalistic *makwaya* format, those staged in more marginal arenas (such as farm and mine compounds) and in African villages were less legible to the colonial state. In that context, the didactic designation "night dances" allowed most of the NCs and missionaries to pass judgment on the moral ills for which, as Gorer wrote, they considered the dances only an alibi. In the *ZMR* as early as 1908, Father Edward Biehler of Chishawasha proffered what to him was the last word on African dances, categorizing them into two groups: the "harmless," performed largely for amusement, and the "superstitious," performed for the spirits at night only, and during which beer was often drunk. The "superstitious" dances, the NC for Gokwe concurred, were associated with unmitigated drunkenness: "Anyone reaching the kraal early in the morning is struck by the dissipated appearance of the inhabitants, even old women and mothers with children on their backs reeling from the effects of drink."[6]

Beer drinking was certainly an important component of African leisure and ritual cultures. Sekai Nzenza's father doubled as schoolmaster and evangelist at a local school in midcentury Zimbabwe, and neither of these two responsibilities dissuaded him from his people's beer:

> Most Saturdays my father came home drunk singing and speaking in English. We used to sit and listen to him talking to us in English and we would all giggle and imitate him. He never missed the word *educated* and *linguistic* when he talked. . . . On Sunday mornings [he] would not be able to get up and ride his bicycle the twenty miles to go to lead the service at his school. (Nzenza 1988, 11)

As the congregants waited for Sekai's father in vain under a tree as the day grew hotter, "men and women would be talking of the last harvest and where the beer party was that Sunday." "Soon after the service," Sekai recalled rather dramatically, "[they] went off to drink beer." Predictably, his white superiors cautioned and then dismissed the drunkard evangelist. The psychologies of racialized drinking did not escape Sekai's young mind. To the missionaries, African beer was "made by filthy women who belonged to the Devil . . . [who] was using them to stop the spread of the gospel. It was alright to drink wine from France or England because it was pure, had gone through good hands, and came from fresh grapes."

Beyond the bigoted psychologies, missionaries' sensibilities were also rooted in more selfish interests. Dependent on coerced African labor, like the NCs, mine owners, and other labor users and agents, they took a vested interest in Africans' physiological condition. Night dances and beer drinking were antithetical to colonialism's imagination of African being as ultra-cheap labor. The festive night dance therefore symbolized moral recalcitrance in a double sense: spiritual depravity and the spurning of the "civilizing" doctrine of the "dignity of labor" that demanded a clear temporal break between leisure and work from a people whose beer culture was closely tied to work parties. Colonists looked at these night revelries through Africans' economic condition, which either facilitated or frustrated the economics of colonial extraction.

African self-sufficiency militated against the colonial design of turning them into machinery for colonial profit. Thus, the labor factor tended to be at the forefront whenever colonial functionaries and missionaries attacked African rural entertainment cultures. For example, Jesuit missionaries at Empandeni welcomed a locust infestation in 1899 as a fortuitous agency for the "civilizing mission." Sister Josephine Bullen (2008, 26) explained in her diary that while "Father Prestage objects to locusts as when they lay their eggs here it means suffering for the people, [o]ther Jesuits hoped they would come as the natives are much more docile when they are rather short of food and they have no beer to drink all day long." So, while colonial discourse tended to emphasize the social effects of these dances and Africans' supposed immoral conduct during them, the subtext was a far less humane or spiritual concern—the imagination of Africans as laboring subjects.

Nonetheless, the potent intersection of dance, beer, and sex was guaranteed to spawn poignant moral tales for those who claimed concern for the African traditional moral order. Assuming that posture, the *mudzviti* for Gokwe wrote, "If one should happen upon the revels at night when they are in full swing, one will more than likely observe in the veld in the neighbourhood of the dance, men and women in compromising positions." Girls, but also wives of absent husbands, postulated the NC, often conceived "children of the grass" by unidentified men in this way.[7] The concern was shared by the Assistant NC for

Bindura, who had no doubt that the organizers of these "extremely popular" entertainments "invite[d] the attendance of a few girls of immoral character who mingle[d] among the dancers and afterwards receive[d] a share in the profits." Moreover, he added, the offer of free admittance to even more girls and the provision of beer added to the attraction of the dances, generating an environment of "general lewdness of speech and gesture." He called the dances "tea dances," and blamed them on the revolutionary impact of the colonial economy on African society. "Prostitution is increasing to an almost alarming extent with the extension of European occupation. The distribution of labour results in an enormous preponderance of males in some centres, with a corresponding preponderance of females at the kraals."[8]

The logic is that the money economy threw the settler farms, the mining areas, and the margins of industrial centers into new moral economic terrains of production and consumption that spawned gendered anarchy. Such terrains conceivably provided opportunities for adventurous women who followed these itineraries of rearticulated African society to socialize with minimal restraint. The Commission on Native Education made the same observations in 1925 (para. 664), identifying European "civilization," including the missionary factor, as the root of the debasement of African social order:

> It should be stated that the partial collapse of tribal and parental control and the increased freedom of Native women and girls, resulting partly from missionary effort, partly from legal enactment and partly from the general intrusion of European ideas, are held by several witnesses to be responsible for an increase of immorality.

The reconfigured African family, as the emergence of new centers of production and consumption, reshaped youth socialization. *Makonzati* provided new loci for juvenile mobility, consumption, and sexuality. Thus, the Madzima School *konzati* not only unleashed young Samkange's imagination on the dance floor but also led him along new paths with girls. With the *konzati* over, he walked home with Keresiya, a Mariga girl:

> Keresiya had first attracted my attention at my cousin's wedding. She was of medium height, was a little plump, had a beautiful baby-like face, large bright eyes, grade one milk-white teeth and a pair of seductive dimples on each cheek. She had full erect breasts, nice big buttocks and enticing thighs. We walked together. Some boys ran about trying to touch the girls' breasts while the girls, not unexpectedly, did everything to foil their attempts. . . . It seemed to be accepted by both boys and girls that any young man could fondle the breasts of any girl . . . if he could catch her off guard. (Samkange 1965, 103)

Samkange wrote that he held Keresiya's warm, soft hands as his imagination ran wild, without saying to what horizons.

Since they were secreted away from the more sheltered home atmosphere, it is not surprising that these school dances elicited such moral panics. They were a slippage from the homestead over which elders had nominal control. Nzenza's (1988, 24) reminiscences of *dembe* and other village youth dances she enjoyed as a young girl provide a contrasting perspective on the more sheltered socialization:

> In the full moon Aunt Jemima would take us all to the nearest village where the dance was. Dancing and singing and playing drums were all part of growing up. As soon as the elders retired to bed, we used to start our night with lots of games and this used to go on till late or till dawn. Some big boys and girls got to know each other during these hectic nights and some got married later. It was all well organized and each house took turns to have the gathering for the night.

These were fun-filled dances that involved the playful "choosing of partners" to such songs as "Sarura Wako Kadeya Deya Ane Ndoro Chena" (Choose your own partner; mine is beautiful and black) and to lyrics like "Ndinotsvaga wangu / musuki wendiro / anodzichenesa / semwedzi muchena" (I am looking for my own love, the washer of plates who makes them as clean as the full moon). Sekai described the games: "One boy would sing and pace up and down, describing his partner. And when he gets to her, he embraces her and carries her away. The girl would sing and do likewise" (24). During this culturally authorized socialization, young men and women flaunted their youthful dancing energies and skills as they negotiated their way into adulthood through *madanha nemavingu,* rich socially licensed and age-appropriate registers of romantic play and praise poetry.

This protective home environment and cultural register minimized juvenile scandal and ensured the reproduction of social order and cohesion by encouraging youngsters to marry *vematongo,* partners from known families of good reputation. Yet the earth had already been hit by the sledgehammer: earned status, particularly that attained through education, was beginning to supplant a good family name alone as a marker of respectability. Songs that teased unschooled young men signified this new social barometer of youthful aspirations as early as the 1930s. Manyika recalled girls singing,

Mukomana akanyenga pamusha pedu	The boy who proposed at our home
Ngaabve aenda kuchikoro	He has got to go to school
Mushure memazuva masere	Otherwise, after only eight days
Tinomusiya pachena.	We will reject him.

Girls increasingly desired educated boys as husbands in a society increasingly wired into the matrix of industrial labor and capitalist consumption.

Likewise, the new contagion economy allegedly tested the virtues of traditional village life as young girls and even married women faced the temptations of easy and sweat-free lifestyles. In the view of the Assistant NC for Bindura, "The virtuous girl is condemned to the drab routine of kraal life while her less virtuous sister leads a life of ease and comparative luxury, dances and pretty frocks, without so far [as] I can see jeopardizing her prospects of marriage to any considerable extent."[9] These town and mine joys, he suggested, "must have [their] contaminating effect on kraal life." Thus, the town and the mine, like the school, became key foundations of new moral economies and sites for the reshaping of gendered identities and social status.

Yet beyond spawning new foundations for African musical dances, the colonial economy also preyed on and fueled them. Thus, the Sinoia NC suggested that the popularity of these dances could be gauged from the fact that "the storekeepers now stock the ballet skirts—'mbikisa' [*sic*], 'scotch', e.t.c., for the occasions."[10] The skimpy *mbikiza* and *skochi* conceivably hypersexualized the dances that the NC reported were popular among both indigenous and "alien natives" in the Zvimba Reserve and its neighbors. The NC also suggested that, rather than a byproduct, "illicit sexual indulgence, generally speaking, is one of [the dances'] objects." His colleague in nearby Bindura concurred, averring, "While I agree as to the evils of these 'tea dances,' it seems to me that it is not so much a case of the dances resulting in loose habits as of loose habits resulting in the dances."[11] For this reason, he concluded, "the root of the evil was not going to be eradicated by the elimination of the dances." The NCs took little care either to identify the particular offending dances or to furnish evidence to back their theory that the colonial economy simply provided an outlet for innate urges toward immorality. According to Manyika and his wife (interview), it was fly-by-night dances like *pfonda* and *sinjonjo,* with their suggestive bodily gestures and rolled-up skirts, that triggered immorality. The two dances, added Shamuyarira (interview, 2011), caught the imagination of African youths but quickly lost favor after parents disapproved of them. The colonial officials' tendency toward blanket condemnation was useful; it authorized the policing of African personhood, rather than just the perceived conduits of its contested expression.

Policing African Morality

Fortuitously, this countrywide probe into "night dances" coincided with the state's moves to tighten its Kaffir Beer Ordinance of 1911, by which it banned African brewing, trading, and consumption of beer in the cities and towns, giving the municipality-run beer halls a monopoly. The Liquor Act of 1898 had already criminalized African consumption of distilled ("European") alcohol. The popular association of "night dances" with drinking and immorality implied that Africans at these dances were engaging in not only immoral activities, but also criminality. Similarly, the suggestion that "irresponsible persons" organized these gatherings implied political, rather than merely social, immorality. And the camouflage of darkness conceivably gave free rein to all sorts of carnal thirsts and political mischief. Thus, most of the Native Commissioners who favored a legislative approach to resolving the "evils" of night dancing advocated controlling beer, the organizational scapegoat for the imagined multiple immoralities. Most of the NCs agreed that drinking was an evil that was intimately tied to the dances, but some disagreed with the legislative approach because it would be difficult to enforce or for fear that it would stoke resistance.

The *mudzviti* for Gwanda pointed out that policing the dances would be almost impossible because of not only their irregular occurrence but also the thin and scattered nature of African settlement in the district. The best that could be done to check "this evil practice," he believed, would be to "take every opportunity to impress on all natives the evils that could result in these night dances and the penalties under the Kaffir Beer Ordinance for the sale of beer, and for attending the beer assemblies after sunset."[12] Similarly, the NC for Marandellas laid the blame squarely on the "established and lucrative" beer business in the reserves and on the farms.[13] The problem, by this logic, was the illicit beer economy that thrived in the districts. Prostitution was a mere corollary that, as the Marandellas NC put it, "always follows in the train of such business." If beer were a central feature of the "night dances," prosecuting offenders under the Kaffir Beer Ordinance would be an indirect way to curb the dances and reinforce state beer monopolies. The NC for Inyati testified to the (potential) effect of this law, but worried that beer was provided surreptitiously and drunk secretly in order to avoid prosecution under the Kaffir Beer Ordinance, making it very difficult "to trap the offenders."[14] The admission fees some proprietors charged for the dances covered the cost of the beer. It was therefore difficult to prosecute those accused of providing beer at the parties.

While the chorus condemned the "night dances" and demanded their elimination, a notable number of NCs either defended them or otherwise interrogated the prevailing official wisdom. The NC for Hartley, for instance, opined that "dancing as indulged in by natives at outlying kraals is quite harmless," and that beer was seldom provided at such occasions.[15] He understood that the dances were a reflection of the general social and behavioral transformation "in these days of greater freedom and almost entire absence of parental, tribal or any other control." It was a sign of social freedom, a trickle-down replication of the "big dinners, tea meetings and concerts [that] appear to have become the fashion in the locations [racialized African ghettoes]." He had in mind what aspiring middle-class Africans called "tea parties," where beer drinking was not the primary goal, and when it was consumed, the purpose of such consumption seemed a noble one. From the location, the dance traveled to the reserve:

> I believe that a similar entertainment has lately been introduced by native teachers to the schools in the reserve, 3d is charged as entrance fee, and 3d for tea and bread or cake; anyone calling upon another to amuse the company

> with a song or dance must pay 3d to the funds, the money is said to be used for school purposes.

African evangelist-teachers at schools like Nenguwo and Epworth coordinated the concerts, raising money that often balanced school budgets (Summers 2002, 161). In such cases, the missionaries often seemed to be upset by the fact that, instead of being staged for Christian purposes and for self-help, the gatherings were a form of popular entertainment.

A number of the NCs were, then, correct in tying the origins of the "tea meetings" to the influence of missionaries, thus effectively challenging the whole point of the probe. From Plumtree, the NC wrote the Chief Native Commissioner (CNC), "I have to inform you that the evil complained of is increasing with civilizing influences for which the missionaries were largely responsible." The *mudzviti* called for police help to prevent the sale of beer and, more importantly, he suggested that the NCs hold special gatherings with chiefs, headmen, and leading "natives" to impress upon them the need to exercise their restraining influence on their communities.[16] In Mtoko, in the east, the NC took a more conciliatory attitude toward the dances, and an even more uncharitable one toward the church's resolution. He reported that he had attended hundreds of these so-called night dances and in no single instance had he found beer present. He defended the gatherings and accused the Native Missionary Conference of exaggerating the evilness of the dances: "Those attending have always conducted themselves in an exemplary manner, and I have never noticed anything immoral or anything to which exception could be taken."[17]

However, the NC conceded that beer was consumed sometimes, such as after a funeral or *nhimbe*, a work party. Indeed, dancing and drinking continued after dark if any beer was left over. "But," he argued, "I wish to emphasize that night dances do not necessarily include beer-drinking. Indeed, beer-drinking at night dances is the exception and not the common practice." The NC disapproved of repressive legislation, arguing that the dances were innocuous but essential to Africans: "I am opposed to legislative measures being introduced to prevent night dances. It is the one great recreation and enjoyment natives have at their homes, and there is no more evil in them than there is in European dances." Moreover, he was equally concerned that a negative approach to "native administration" could easily stir resistance. He mused, "Natives are already so bound down by legislation that one wonders sometimes how much more of it they will submit to." In this case, he was apparently referring to traditional dances that took place in the home as an aspect of the work, funerary, and other cultures that missionaries targeted for assault. He saw no problem with these dances.

The Native Education Commission had heard similar hesitations five years earlier, when some of its informants rejected the notion of "civilizing natives by legislation," specifically concerning perceived female immorality. One NC had told the commission that "further legislation would only lead to swelling the police court rolls and filling the prisons" and would reduce "the prestige of the Government." For one thing, Africans would not appreciate such laws. Second, and more importantly, the laws would be unenforceable, exposing the weakness of the state (para. 670). The commission also drew on the wisdom of the late Theophilus Shepstone, Natal's Director of Native Affairs, who had argued that "altering certain Native customs by law was like trying to straighten the hind legs of the grasshopper by legislation." The commission's own verdict was quite contrary to insinuations by some NCs that moral laxity was an innate African attribute: "The moral looseness has already increased among Native women and young girls as a result of our breaking down Native restraints more quickly than we could replace them" (para. 671). Promiscuity was a "modern," colonial disease.

This was the irony of the missionaries' call for state action against the dances and tea meetings. Richard Parry (1999, 58) has described the "tea meetings" as large social or religious gatherings where only nonalcoholic beverages were drunk. The gatherings were usually held under the auspices of a white religious body, often the Wesleyan Church, even though Africans themselves generally organized them. In this form, tea meetings or tea parties were therefore an essentially colonial phenomenon that reaffirmed the values of white settler and missionary society. Africans flaunted the adoptive, "progressive," and orderly polite socialization, as seen in an advertisement placed in the May 3, 1918, *Rhodesia Herald* by immigrant black South Africans:

> We are asked to state that a tea meeting under the auspices of the Union Natives Association will be held tonight at 7.30 in the Native Canteen, Salisbury Location (by kind permission of the Mayor of Salisbury) for the purpose of raising funds in support of the Prince of Wales and the Belgian Relief Funds. It is hoped that employers in Salisbury will be kind enough to allow their native employees to leave their employment, on this occasion, in time to allow them to attend.

In a context where white culture was promoted as modernity, both "black settlers" who had helped European colonists and accompanied them from South Africa and their local counterparts who aspired to middle-class status within the new colonial system appropriated this and other elements of white culture as part of their search for inclusion and respectability. Moreover, as I discuss later, these aspirant elites also associated with white missionaries (and often municipal officials) to seek refuge against frequent crude racist attacks by settlers who resented their demand for white privileges and status on the basis of their education. They exploited this "protection" to organize around social and political causes; they employed the idiom of the tea party to raise funds for self-help, as one missionary recorded:

> Recently I attended a native tea meeting, at which more than £12 was raised by this very poor congregation. Their way of doing it was characteristic and amusing. They paid two shillings to sit down to tea. Then someone would pay three shillings for such and such a man to be required to get up again and leave the table. The man thus assailed would pay 3s. 6d. for leave to sit down again. There was a special table at which six could sit, paying an extra shilling each for the privilege. They had just got seated when a man paid seven shillings to clear them out, and they paid another eight shillings to sit on, and so it went on. They arrange all this themselves, and this is their way of giving to the cause. One man had a tin of syrup. He said he would pay two shillings to pour it over another man's head who had got himself up well in a large collar, etc.; this man paid three shillings to be let off, the first man four shillings again to do it . . . and oh! (*Rhodesia Herald*, May 3, 1907)

This playful recasting of the tea meeting—particularly the "bidding" that the NC for Mzingwane condemned as the root of the evil of "night dancing"—reduced the patron missionary to a bemused, legitimating figurehead. In this way, "educated" Africans (but also commoners, as I show later) brokered this performative form, tea meetings (together with *makwaya*), and propagated it to the urban locations and, to a limited degree, to the village school.

This cultural diffusion and innovativeness deployed the musical idiom to great effect, as the Native Education Commission observed at the schools: "Singing is loved by the Natives and some missions teach it well." The Commissioners recorded,

> Excellent concerts are given at several schools, a very keen spirit being exhibited. The preparation for such concerts is in itself both educative and recreative. Action songs were a special feature with one mission body. A small book of action songs had been prepared in the native tongue and distributed to their third-class schools. Thus a fine wholesome recreation was provided for great numbers of children. (para. 386)

According to the evidence presented to the commission, action songs—*makwaya*—were catching on in village schools where "advancing civilization" had created an apparent recreational vacuum by "displac[ing] the arts of war, hunting and so forth." The commission noted that certain missions had a plan for teachers to instruct each other in teaching methods, especially in music. Many village schoolteachers allegedly lacked musical skills, so that, in their schools, "there is little distinction between singing and shouting." "Where there are several schools within a reasonable radius a better-class school with a good Native teacher is set up in the centre of the group" (para. 381). Teachers from the neighboring schools then visited the central school on weekends or holidays for training, and the better teacher visited them to survey their work. African teachers used this itinerant schooling model as a vector for their *makwaya* performances in the villages, independently extending their performative space beyond the mission, and their repertoire beyond the authorized hymn.

Looking at this history of tea parties and *makwaya*, which were closely tied to the mission school and the church, some NCs were puzzled as to why the missionaries did not simply snuff out their own veldfire, if it now offended them. The NC for Mtoko asked, "If the missionaries do not like them, [why] do they not instruct their native teachers to discontinue them?"[18] He suggested that African missionaries themselves were supposed to exert a positive moral influence on their flock, rather than demand that the government legislate morality, which he argued would be a "perfectly useless" exercise. The NC for Range and Enkeldoorn recommended that the missionaries themselves should check the evil by "sterner methods," since the offenders were mostly young converts.[19] The NC for Mrewa thought it was illogical for the mission to call on the state to rescue it from problems of its own making. More importantly, he charged that the Native Christian Conference's resolution was deliberately misleading and aimed to curry favor with the state:

> We have no such things as Tea Meetings at outlying Kraals, except at Mission Centres, and the resolution cannot possibly refer to them as they would be composed of Christian natives; but we do have "Night Dances" and I cannot agree that these dances held at outlying Kraals are so great an evil as we would be made to believe by the wording of the resolution.[20]

Apparently, NCs for Mrewa and Mtoko lacked sympathy for missionaries' constant battles against "native" converts who "backslid into a life of drinking, fornication and dancing," battles that were already raging by the 1920s. Their neighbor in Marandellas was more charitable to this missionary quandary, which he articulated as follows: "My own observations do not confirm that the Christian faith professed by so many natives has taken root to the extent of influencing their conduct. They readily appear to resort to so-called pagan practices when opportunity offers."[21] He was therefore not surprised that "Christian natives" struggled to bring their influence to bear on their own people and to "take active measures to prevent their womenfolk from attending such gatherings." In the words of the NC for Range and Enkeldoorn, these Africans were merely "apeing the European missionary," as they might be expected to, without inner conviction. This condescending critique of the "educated" or "semi-educated mission boy," allegedly spoilt by the well-meaning but often misguided missionary, was typical of white settlers.

In some areas, the gerontocratic axis of rural politics—missionaries, government-appointed chiefs and headmen, and Native Commissioners—had already taken "sterner measures" and snuffed out the dances. In Mzingwane District, Chiefs Ntola and Petshengu had already proscribed the dances on the grounds that "darkness facilitates immorality." As a result, when the CNC asked him to investigate in 1930, the NC reported that the dances had become infrequent in his district.[22] Another chief in the same area, Mtshede, had agreed that the dances were tied to the increase in immorality, but questioned the orthodox explanation of causality: "Whether it is light or dark, these people will indulge in immorality if they wish to." The NC shared his chief's viewpoint, noting that, in spite of the supervisory oversight by the mission teacher who had organized the one recent dance in the area, sexual encounters still took place. He observed, "As far as I can ascertain at this concert, the choir boys and girls were not allowed to leave the concert hall, but patrons were not so restricted naturally, and the veld was there for those who desired to indulge in courting." Thus, the NC shared Chief Mtshede's doubts about the causal connection between sexual immorality and the so-called night dances, suggesting that immorality was just as likely to occur at this sort of dance as at any other function, at night or during daytime. To him, money was the evil: "I surmise the system of bidding in cash for encores, etc. at Native concerts is responsible." While the notion of "night dances" evoked the image of morally depraved and debased dancing orgies in the corrupt minds of most officials, the designation was not that simple and straightforward to everyone. This ambivalence made the African Christians' call for general proscriptive action difficult.

However, the ambivalence did not stop Chiefs Ntola and Petshengu from harnessing the coercive instruments of the state, including the police, to crush the dances. Moreover, in spite of his personal doubts, the NC promised Chief Ntola the full backing of the 1927 Native Affairs Act to stamp out such activities.[23] Among numerous other repressive clauses, sections 51 and 53 of the act demanded that "all natives shall promptly obey and comply with any lawful or reasonable order, request or direction of any headman, chief or Native Commissioner" without question, or risk heavy fines or jail time for insolence, contempt, and undermining the authority of these officers of the government.[24] Without elaborating, the NC for Mazoe told the CNC that, at the request of African elders, he had similarly suppressed a dance introduced from Mozambique in 1929,[25] a possible reference to the erotic *pfonda*.

In Sinoia, the heavy hand of Chief Chirau and his colleagues, together with the Catholic Mission at Kutama, also resolved the matter, as the NC pointed out: "The Natives do not indulge in these affairs in the areas under Chiefs Chirao [*sic*], Magonde, and Bepura; nor in the immediate neighbourhood of Kutama Mission." In Sinoia town and its precincts, the night dances used to happen irregularly, but they had latterly been crushed as Sinoia legislated against "immorality," or at least its overt public expression. The district employed national legislation and enacted its own statutes to suppress the "evil," as the NC explained: "Besides the use of the provisions for prescribed areas under the Kaffir Beer Ordinance, we have brought into force a bye-law against all noisy meetings."[26]

Mission schools told parents in writing that students were required to abstain from all traditional religious ceremonies, including "night dances" (Stanlake 1903, 67). This rule banned all forms of traditional performances, which usually took place at night. The NC for Sinoia reported that in the area around Kutama Mission, "the orderly conditions are to be ascribed to the authority of the missionaries. In the [neighboring] areas, tribal and parental authority still exists."[27] Therefore, in Sinoia as in Mzingwane, the combined force of the African patriarchs, the paternalistic missionary, and *mudzviti* ostensibly triumphed over condemned African musical dances.

Similarly, as Shamuyarira recalled (interview, July 2011), the American Waddilove Methodists (Nenguwo), acting in alliance with the government, suppressed their dances in Chihota:

> Our *makonzati* were suppressed by the government, which was responding to pressure from the missionaries who were saying, "They are increasing prostitution; they are increasing bad behavior among young people; they are sleeping in the bush," and so on and so forth. Missionaries were very ruthless on this. . . . One weekend we just heard that *makonzati* are no longer allowed because it is said that you are misbehaving.

In fact, the performances were not summarily banned in Chihota. Instead, Shamuyarira and his colleagues were asked to conduct them during the day. This was difficult, because daytime performances conflicted with school and work regimens, destabilized the temporal aesthetics of the musical *dariro,* and demanded too much effort to keep them going. Explained Shamuyarira, "School ended at twelve noon, and we had to walk from Chivizhe to whatever school was hosting the *konzati.* Sometimes we would get there at 3 PM, and then start performing, then come back to Chivizhe before going to our homes." They held two or three of these daytime concerts before they lost the energy to trudge between the distant schools and home. State and missionary interference thus undermined the dances. As already hinted, some missionaries expressed plausible-sounding concerns about African (im)morality in order to extirpate these dances. As Summers (2002, 17) wrote, many African teachers abused their positions of power and distance to take liberties with young women at the schools. *Makonzati,* which were held away from parental control and under the cover of night, would certainly provide splendid opportunities for such privileged indulgence.

However, it was central missions like Kutama, Murombedzi, Chishawasha, St. Michael's Mhondoro, and Waddilove that seemed most successful in enforcing these prohibitions. In villages distant from mission stations, as the evangelist J. Chihombori told Peaden (1970, 12), parents disingenuously accepted the mission prohibitions against traditional dancing. Moreover, Peaden argues that non-Christian parents regarded the proscriptions of their children's participation in cultural ceremonies as only postponing the day when they would take their place within the traditional structures of their societies. He also observed that in areas where missionaries could not consistently raid with their purgatory whip, it was not humanly possible to send schoolchildren to bed when crowds had gathered to sing and dance. Instead, he notes, "they would sit in on the proceedings and observe all that was going on, but would not participate." But Peaden misunderstands what participation in family ceremonies means. Sitting in the sacred ritual spaces and observing the proceedings was a form of participation, albeit a passive one. The power of the African transgenerational spirit is such that one does not necessarily need to be taught how to play, or to be asked to play. For example, Chartwell Dutiro (2007, 2) believes his ancestors called him to play traditional instruments for them. He wrote, "I remember a special drum that sat in our hut when I was young, and I once woke up in the middle of the night and played a rhythm on it that I didn't know but that others did. I played for ten minutes, and woke up my brothers." He would go on playing *mbira* in ceremonies on Saturday nights, and miss Sunday school as a result. Students who drowsed in class or skipped school altogether roused the suspicion of the missionary, and often invited his whip.

It is also noteworthy that while most missions sought to violently suppress African cultural dances, particularly those of a spiritual nature, they looked more ambivalently on Europeanized forms, such as tea parties, *makwaya,* and *michato* (wedding celebrations). To reiterate, tea parties and *makwaya* were largely youth affairs, run by young African male teachers and students in the rural districts. The youths' involvement in this alternative leisure economy tended to antagonize and undermine the authority of African elders, who frowned upon the dances not only for their purported immorality, but also because they took away their children and the fruits of their labor. In fact, by drawing the children away from home for days on end, the itinerant *makwaya* conceivably affected not only work programs, but also the in-home traditional ceremonies in which both parents and children took part in transgenerational bonds of performativity. Thus, caught up in the webs of colonial patriarchal control and resentful of missionaries' attacks on their traditional cultures, African elders could only murmur about the exact nature of the control that they lost over their children. African elders and missionaries harbored mutual suspicion over cultural matters. The NC for Range and Enkeldoorn wrote, "Chiefs, headmen and parents . . . complain that they no longer exercise authority over their children and that the controlling forces are missionaries and kraal school teachers."[28] I have also suggested that the alliance of missionaries and African teachers was ambivalent, designed to turn African youngsters into obedient disciples, while the youngsters largely harbored their own agendas that were often quite antagonistic to the missionary evangelical scheme.

Three decades after the introduction of mission-run schools, African teachers had fashioned themselves into competing but marginalized alternative models of "modern" African personhood. Coming from the margins of rural politics dominated by the alliance between African chiefs and the NAD, they effectively deployed their acquired educational witchcraft to challenge this gerontocratic authority and to interrogate their missionary patrons. As "scholars," they were held in awe in their communities. The NC for Gutu was informed that the reason why African elders did not complain about the night dances was that "they were afraid of offending the teachers."[29] The teachers utilized western cultural capital to fashion novel, powerful identities and to demand respect and treatment befitting their special status. Perhaps this was part of what the colonial state, through the Native Affairs Act, loosely defined and sought to stamp out as "native insolence and contemptuous behavior." And yet, with the support of their missionary patrons, the teachers resented the superintendence of chiefs and headmen as stipulated in the act.

The Secretary of the Southern Rhodesian Missionary Conference, Latimer P. Hardiker, sketched out this tension in 1928 in a critique of the Native Affairs Act:

> The native teachers objected strongly to being placed under the authority of pagan chiefs who are so often jealousy [*sic*] of them simply because they, the teachers, are the advocates of progress. . . . It is neither direct rule nor indirect rule. If the intention was to restore tribal authority, it is doomed to failure. We have no great, powerful chiefs in Southern Rhodesia. We have no native king with his councilors and court but only petty chiefs who have already lost authority. To make these men constables, the paid agents of the European government is not restoring tribal authority in any real sense. Moreover, it is foolish to demand of chiefs and headmen that they shall, under heavy penalties be compelled to arrest the members of their own families. (O'Callaghan 1977, 147)

The missionaries and African teachers believed that "conflict is inevitable" if "authority over educated and progressive natives is to be placed in the hands of uneducated, pagan chiefs." Conflict and tension can be located in the colonial state's backing of the now emasculated, hand-picked "traditional" elites—the chiefs and headmen—over new, self-made competing models of progress, the teachers. Missionaries played *agent provocateur* with their divisive images of chiefs as backward pagans and teachers as progressive Christians. The latter internalized the usable discourse. Yet intergenerational and cross-class African relationships were more complicated than these colonial and missionary interests suggested. Moreover, some of these social positions were not mutually exclusive in an era in which some "new chiefs" had been to school themselves.

While the colonial state sought to infantilize them, African teachers were often viewed with much respect, not just fear, by students and their parents. Songs were composed to lionize them, such as "VaMuzondo," which glorified Nichodemus Muzondo, a village head, headmaster, and the founder of Mumhurwi School in Chikwaka in the 1920s. Similarly, Chivizhe students exalted Manyika, their perennial award-winning choirmaster, as "Jongwe guru," the rooster:

Ndiani jongwe guru?	Who is the big rooster?
Ndiani jongwe guru?	Who is the big rooster?
Manyika, Manyika	Manyika, Manyika
Manyika jongwe guru!	Manyika the big rooster! (Manyika, interview)

Roosters rule, or at least they claim to; they do not impotently submit to competing authority. Thus, in Gutu, teachers refused to ferry water for the dip tanks, adjudging the task demeaning. Similarly, they defied the structures of rural politics to dabble in nationalist politics, getting involved with the Southern Rhodesia Native Association against the wishes of the *mudzviti*. Revs. Samkange and Esau Nemapare, the patriarchal figureheads and models of educated African Christian adulthood, helped found the Southern Rhodesia Bantu Voice Association, a movement that engaged in politics under the linguistic cover of constitutionalism, campaigning for "equal rights for all civilized men." Chivanda Manyika did likewise in Gweru, eventually becoming an organizer and underground operative for the National Democratic Party (K. G. D. Manyika, n.d.).

Through the medium of these contentious dances, therefore, teachers were able to negotiate social space for themselves in ways that variously upset both traditional political structures and colonial tenets about "native" etiquette. Their transgressive self-fashioning spiced up the politics of "native insolence," which were beginning to rouse the ire of the *mudzviti* in the districts (Shutt, forthcoming). Manyika would be repeatedly expelled from his teaching job on suspicions of dabbling in politics under cover of these *makonzati*. Yet this political mischief was not limited to outlying districts. In the cities, politicians organized or took advantage of concerts at the municipal recreational halls to engage in political organizing in the backrooms, and formed dancing clubs to raise money to fund political activities (Nkala, interview).

Teachers sometimes also charmed colonial officials in poignant a(nta)gonistic dances with power. One teacher thanked God for bringing the whites to Zimbabwe:

Toita sei nenyika yeRudhizha	What shall we do with Rhodesia?
Toita sei nenyika yeRudhizha	What shall we do with Rhodesia?
Mwari akaita akatumira vachena	Thank God for sending the whites
Mandevere, aida kutonga	The Ndebele wanted to rule,
Mazezuru, aida kutonga	The Zezuru wanted to rule,
VaManyika, vaida kutonga	The Manyika wanted to rule,
Mwari akaita akatumira vachena	God served us well by sending the whites.
(Manyika, interview)	

Neither missionaries nor Native Commissioners would quarrel with this song, which conveyed African gratitude to God for bringing whites to rule and stem alleged "tribal carnages" amongst the contending Ndebele, Zezuru, and Manyika. Interschool concerts propagated this *Pax Britannica* narrative, which was the staple of colonial "native" education, and it became quite (un)popular around the country. Jane Lungile Ngwenya believes this was a cunning corruption of a song that whites regarded as subversive, in which Africans denounced colonial rule (2012 interview; see also chapter 10).

When a dip tank supervisor was posted to Chikwaka in 1933, Nichodemus Muzondo welcomed him with song. Manyika and his fellow students practiced the song before approaching the white man's tent, waxing lyrical about his white beauty:

Tokwazisa kunamambo	We greet you, king
Tokwazisa isu varanda venyu	We, your slaves, greet you
Tauya nerufaro pano	We come here in happiness
Ane meso anoenda-enda	He has eyes that rove about
Ane mhuno inenge mutswi	He has a pestle-like nose
Ane vhudzi rinenge shinda	His hair is like wool
Ane meno anenge mukaka	His teeth are like milk
Tauya nemufaro pano.	We come in happiness here.
(Manyika, interview)	

Popularized during *makonzati,* such apparently obsequious songs sought to charm the white overlords who presided over the structures of rural politics. Was Muzondo, the powerful community head and schoolmaster, genuinely grateful to the white authorities who gave him *tsvimbo mbiri*—two scepters of power? Or did he seek to deploy the magic of praise poetry to appease the white lord and urge him to moderate his known agenda of forced labor extraction and cattle culling? The possibility of critical subtexts can only be speculated about.

In his sharp reading of the Native Christian Conference resolution, the NC for Mzingwane seemed conscious of possible subterfuges and tensions, which were at once intergenerational and political. He suggested that, "reading between the lines of the resolution contained in the circular letter under reply, it would appear the movers are concerned as to the irresponsible persons who organize the dances or tea meetings."[30] "Native teacher" and "irresponsible person" read as near synonyms in the emergent official discourse of counterinsurgency. The state often saw African teachers as dubious carriers of subversive ideas, which, in this case, conceivably exploited the mission-inspired idioms of the tea party and the *konzati.*

It is not surprising, then, that the state had kept an eye on such events even before the missionaries complained in 1930. For instance, as in Chihota, the *mudzviti* for Nyamandlovu banned young people from holding dances at night. He informed the CNC, "The ordinary dance or 'tea meeting' closes at sunset." These dances were mobile, which means that they had potential to outrange local district authority. The state was quite aware of this, and it duly sought to plug the hole. So the *mudzviti* added, "On one occasion some natives came from

Bulawayo and held a 'tea meeting.' As the consumption of Kaffir beer was suspected, however, any further meetings of this nature by strange natives were prohibited."[31] In any event, section 42 (1) of the Native Affairs Act criminalized the unauthorized presence of "strange natives" (those outside their own districts) without the consent of the NC. If there was any undercurrent beneath this hubbub over intergenerational and social morality, it was that this colonial nervousness betrayed official anxiety over "political immorality" by "wily natives." The state was battling the shadow of Garveyism and the challenges of the Industrial and Commercial Workers' Union (ICU), a fiery pan-regional labor and political movement, at this time.

Another dance that presented difficulty for both the missionaries and the state was *muchato,* the festive Christian wedding dance. This was the apparition of Range and Enkeldoorn, as the NC explained: "The principal dances are those celebrating Christian marriages. The practice is to dance one day and night at the bride's and two days and nights at the bridegroom's kraal."[32] According to missionary designs, Christian marriages were supposed to be solemn exhibitions of converts' break with the demonized African traditions of "undignified heathen feasts and revelry." Yet many African converts resisted this wholesale missionary demonization and erasure, often recasting received Christian rites into preexisting practices to innovate and enrich their own registers. To Africans, weddings were a critical rite of passage, and were accordingly celebrated through public singing and dancing festivities in familial circles. Stanlake Samkange's (1975, 100–101) account of one wedding at Mariga demonstrates the persistence of indigenous cultures of marriage. Non-Christians patiently waited out the mysteries of the altar to whisk the couple away, serenading them on the way back to the village to consecrate them as husband and wife all over again in the best way they knew how:

> When the bridal party emerged from the church . . . we all sang all the way to our village where a large crowd, that grew bigger as the day grew older, awaited us. . . . As soon as we arrived at our village, our aunts began to sing songs extolling the virtues of the bride while disparaging the qualities of the bridegroom. Many VaShawasha present took up the cudgels on behalf of the bridegroom and, for a time, there was a good-natured, mudslinging, disparaging contest between the two groups, to the great amusement of all present. . . . In the meantime food and beer, both sweet and strong, were being served. . . . Students sang and danced school songs while older ones took to dancing, and sang African traditional songs with drums. Spectators drifted to whatever group caught their fancy.

The story of *jerusarema* dance, below, illustrates the same logic of African inculturation of new ritual idioms, sometimes to camouflage their own tenacious indigenous practices. That was one way to performatively beat the strident evangelical and settler cultural ethnocentrism.

Thus, while the NC for Range and Enkeldoorn pledged to constantly bring up the matter of these transgressive Christian marriage dances in meetings with "natives" and to make every endeavor to mitigate "the evil," he complained that "in the past, when efforts were made to check the trend, one was often accused of interfering with liberty and retarding advancement and progress."[33] Africans appropriated and redeployed the discourse of progress and liberty, as represented by certain Europeanized cultural practices, as a useful shield against colonial assault. Indeed, the people targeted by the Native Christian Conference's resolution might have enjoyed the extent to which it confused the NC for Shabani, who, echoing his Mtoko and Mrewa counterparts, reported that he saw neither any obvious sign of immorality at the dances nor any causal link between the dances and immorality. He feared that the conference's resolution "might reasonably be considered to savour an incubation of autocracy likely to create ill-feeling amongst its heathen brethren, who it must be admitted have few forms of amusement."[34]

While the "night dances" organized by teachers elicited suspicion from both the state and missionaries, state officials tended to look upon those taking place in the more marginal districts as genuinely innocent or inconsequential. Thus, the NC for Mrewa granted that the "night dances" in outlying parts of his district were harmless and quite an ancient institution amongst the "natives," one that long predated the advent of missionaries. Like his counterpart in Mtoko, he opposed state intervention on the grounds of personal experience: "I have seen and attended many of them amongst the Abafungwi on the outskirts of Civilisation to semi-civilised dances at and near Mrewa, and I have seen nothing to which I am prepared to take exception." He pointed out that he did not see any beer-drinking at the dances, and would be saddened by any steps to suppress or, "as the resolution says, 'to eliminate them.'"[35]

If there is a case to be made for Native Commissioners supporting African cultures, the argument might rest on such problematic cases as this one. The case is still improbable, however. It should be observed that such stances tended to be predicated on a perceptive sense of statecraft that "liberal" colonial discourse passed as "native interest." After all, the *mudzviti*'s mandate was to prevent another Chindunduma. That was precisely the meaning of *hudzviti*—the enforcement of the regime of imposed colonial law, coercive extraction, and order, all thriving on the criminalization of African being. Yet *hudzviti* was undoubtedly a difficult undertaking, requiring this violence to be balanced with "negotiation" in dealing with Africans. Thus, to perceptive officials like the NC for Mrewa, banning African dances amounted to a callous violation of this critical balance and an invitation to trouble:

> This is again one of those "don'ts" which otherwise well meaning people, without a true idea of the consequences, would try to foist upon the native; there is nothing more wrong with the Native Night Dances than there is at the Show

> Dance at the Meikles [Hotel], or a Saturday Night Dance at the Grand [Hotel]. Too many "don'ts" make life irksome to the native, and is liable to do more harm than good; we have quite sufficient of them in our present native legislation and should be careful how we add to the number. Do away with Night Dancing and what is to take its place? Something worse.

The Native Affairs Act was one piece of "'don't' law" that made any directive by an authority figure—from *mudzviti* down to the village headman—a word of law to be obeyed without question.

What the ostensibly open-minded *mudzviti* did not mention was the bruising war against *mbende*, a sensuous dance in which pairs of men and women advance on each other twisting, thrusting their legs, and jiggling their pelvises to a staccato of drumming, singing, and clapping of hands and wooden boards. From their advent, missionaries persecuted this dance, which was popular among the Zezuru people of Murehwa, as lascivious and morally repugnant. Africans held on to it, clothing it with a Christianized name, *jerusarema,* a disguise that, although it fell short of hoodwinking the missionaries, still helped ensure the dance's survival with little fundamental modification over the generations. The Native Education Commission heard testimonies against *jerusarema* when it collected evidence on music in the schools in the early 1920s, but its informants, and thus the commission itself, seem to have misunderstood the dance's origins and thus misconstrued what was happening:

> Some [schools] have taken simple native dances and set them to harmless rhymes. "The Jerusalem Dance," however, came in for a good deal of criticism. It is not a dance taught at the missions, but *one the young Natives have apparently invented* for themselves and have adapted school tunes as the accompaniment. Native teachers said it should be stopped. (para. 391; italics mine.)

Manyika and his wife—both teachers at this time—argued that "*jerusarema* was clean. It was a traditional dance adults staged for entertainment during *kurova guva* and related ceremonies. It was not essentially a youth dance" (Manyika and Manyika, interview). What they adjudged immoral, instead, was *pfonda:*

> *Pfonda* was an immoral dance that had been introduced by immigrants. The dancing styles were sexual, as was the dressing. You would see girls rolling up their skirts until they became virtually half-dressed. And such dances were of course popular with weak characters—some men and also some married women who were allowed to do that by their husbands. I went to one such dance to punish participating students. And I found them naked, taking occasional forays into the bushes. Parents wielded the stick to preserve *unhu hwavo*—their ethos—against this moral corruption.

The criminalization of *mbende* dealt it a sort of generational setback as its performance became largely restricted to adults at home. Chivanda Manyika

(Manyika and Manyika, interview) observed that, "From about 1935, jerusarema and *ngororombe* (a reed music dance) were being slowly abandoned, particularly by the school-going youths." *Mbende* was equally pummeled on the urban stage that reified other local traditional dances into colonial spectacles or into "authenticity" conduits of "native administration" (see chapter 5). The *Bantu Mirror* reported in Salisbury on April 15, 1944,

> The Mazezuru, accompanied by the rhythm of the drum danced themselves to exhaustion. This dance, it is stated, is peculiarly popular among Africans of the Mrewa District which, although tribal, did not present a pleasant entertainment, especially in connection with women participants.

Mbende's survival was therefore purely a result of the resilience of its practitioners, who found it culturally significant and valued it both as entertainment and as a fertility and war dance. In 1930, the NCs congratulated themselves for "cleansing" the dance, giving it an innocuous form.

The NCs for Mtoko and Mrewa were clearly frustrated with the Native Christian Conference resolution's failure to unambiguously identify the offending dances. The resolution, and hence some of the reports from the NCs, lumped African traditional dances into the ill-defined category of "night dances" that were allegedly associated with immorality and beer drinking. In any case, most African dances were anathema to the crusading orthodox missionaries. However, if the Christians also had these traditional dances in mind, their arguments failed to convince some of the colonial administrators, representatives of a secular regime whose principal interest was the making of the colonial state.

And thanks to the ambiguity, in some districts the investigation deteriorated into a census of African dances. The NC for Chipinga [Chipinge], Peter Nielson, pointed out that Africans in his district danced *chinyambera, muchato, chingondo,* and *chibububu*. He explained that *chinyambera* was usually staged by moonlight during the first fruits season, as a communal thanksgiving for anticipated harvests. *Chingondo* was a dance that migrant Sena (Mozambican) communities performed, also mostly at night, invoking the spirits of their guardian ancestors for blessings. Some of the participants spoke in tongues, in the fashion of apostolic sects, during this spirit possession ceremony. *Chibububu,* on the other hand, was a contemporary rearticulation of the moral economics of gendered labor. The NC explained that the latter was the most common night dance, "held in welcome of those who have returned safely from work in the Johannesburg mines 'with the money for the government.'" The returnees strutted about like roosters to the tumultuous cheers of young "hens" (women), or swaggered in erect postures, mimicking convoys of the *stimela*—train carriages—that conveyed them to and from those distant hunting (under)grounds.

Most reports indicated that *muchato* was held "only by the more or less educated natives at the time of the marriage by Christian rites or before the Native Commissioner of their girls," in a fashion akin to European peasant weddings.[36] Reporting to the NC for Chipinga, the Assistant NC for Melsetter observed that the latter ceremony also invariably involved old men and women at open sites generally close to the kraal.[37] Concluding his conciliatory report, the Chipinga NC suggested that if the old people argued that these dances sometimes offered young people opportunities for illicit lovemaking, he would accept that as an "expression of the opinion of the old polygamistic diehards."[38] The insinuation was that intergenerational tensions and jealousies were to be expected in a context where young men no longer depended on their patriarchs' goodwill to raise *roora* (bride wealth), and could now therefore compete for wives with their formerly privileged patron elders.

In fact, the resort to migrant labor as the new mode of making men in these districts contiguous to the mines of Joni threatened to subvert patriarchal authority in a very real sense. To the colonial state, maintaining traditional patriarchal authority was only a concern insofar as it facilitated "native administration" and the mobilization of youth labor. Tax money was the key objective here; and, happily for the NCs, that need seemed well served, if the popularity of *chibububu* was any measure. The important issue, then, suggested the Assistant NC for Melsetter, was to police beer drinking by these returnees. In 1930 he wrote, "Chiefs, headmen and heads of kraals have been repeatedly warned not to hold beer drinks at night." He had last warned them the year before. Having succeeded in engineering labor and tax money, it seems clear that the state was turning its attention to extracting and controlling the fruits of that labor. After all, together with suppressing the omnipresent ghost of Chindunduma, this was the *mudzviti*'s chief mandate.

"Night Dancing" and "Native" Policymaking

How did this discourse of night dancing shape "native" policymaking? The Chief Native Commissioner forwarded the collated reports, together with his own summary and recommendations, to the Premier and the Minister of Native Affairs, Howard Moffat. The CNC noted that seventeen Native Commissioners and Assistant Native Commissioners had indicated that the dances were either not prevalent or harmless, while the rest confirmed the Native Christian Missionary Conference's position.[39] Concerning the purported sinfulness of the "night dances" and "tea meetings," the CNC deduced that the evil was social, and directed that it should therefore be combated through social endeavor, restraint, and discipline by the missions and their "native" teachers. Despite history and existing policy, colonial orthodoxy consigned social evils to the province of social, not criminal, control.

This conclusion was in line with several NCs' observations that "it is the educated Natives who popularise the sort of dance or meeting in question." The CNC also considered the tying of these performances to beer drinking problematic. He was persuaded that in the cases where beer was consumed, it was obtained as part of the social transactions, and not always by sale. Such transactions, he hoped, could be prevented by amending the existing Kaffir Beer Ordinance—that is, through the supposedly undesirable criminalization. With regard to the unseemly power of African teachers, which allegedly spawned intergenerational chaos, the CNC recommended that the government "direct a trend of policy to restore or support parental authority" in line with the newfound wisdom of reinforcing "the tribal system" as a way of solving the social ills of "civilization." Overall, the self-contradicting CNC rather ambivalently discouraged direct inhibition through legislation, "*save, perhaps, in Townships and other European areas where byelaws may be passed by local authorities as has been done at Sinoia.*" The root of his ambivalence, it seems, was that the "night dances" were largely a nonurban issue and therefore did not radically threaten the seat of white power. The Premier agreed with these recommendations and decided against a blanket legislative prohibition of "night dances" at the national level.[40] He preferred and endorsed targeted legislation to control African beer consumption, local bylaws, and social control by missionaries and African patriarchs.

It is important to reinforce a few points here. I have observed that "night dancing" and "tea partying" emerged as enigmas and a headache for missionaries, the colonial state, and some African patriarchs. An analysis of the discourse this problem generated has shown that the phenomenon was as much an existential problem as it was a register by which the uneasy gerontocratic axis of Native Commissioners, African elders, and first-generation African missionaries expressed its various intersecting fears and anxieties in the face of challenges by restive African youngsters. Equally, I have shown that, in the hands of these ambitious youngsters (especially those who were rural teachers), "night dancing" emerged as a vista for fashioning dissident identities out of suppressed desires and potentialities for upward political and socioeconomic mobility. Therefore, deployed by the regime of colonial order and discipline, the "night dance" can be understood as a metaphor for multiple "native immoralities," social, economic, and political, and as a text of this regime's struggles to read and stem the multitextured generational subaltern insurgencies. In many ways, therefore, state and church action—the *ad hoc* policing and nervous legislating—amounted to shooting arrows in the dark, and some of these ricocheted badly, particularly on the church, as both this probe and the midcentury mission crisis illustrate. The church that bred the first generation of African Christians, many of whom were apparently overzealous, also produced its first rebels among the lot.

To buttress this point, this chapter must end where it started, in the Samkange household. The role that Reverend Samkange may have played in passing the 1930 resolution against night dances is not clear. Neither does his son, Stanlake, who was thrilled breathless by his first *konzati,* say whether or not his "respectable" parents knew or approved of it. What is intriguing, however, is that by the 1940s, Reverend Samkange had stood up as a defender of African cultural sovereignty against the deepening colonial criminalization of African being. That sovereignty included the right to dance. Thus, in August 1944, the Education Inspector, A. R. Mather, whom Ranger (1993, 337–38) describes as a dour American Seventh-Day Adventist, wrote to instruct Reverend Samkange, then a superintendent of dozens of reserve schools in Shurugwi, to ban all-night concerts at the schools. Samkange refused and instead questioned the premises of the missionary criminalization of African morality. He sent Mather an audacious letter:

> Since I have been in the Ministry, I have never tried a case where the immorality took place at a concert. . . . It is said that Concerts should be prohibited and that anybody holding a Concert be prosecuted. I feel it would be an injustice. Africans have night dances as well as Europeans. . . . [The] concert is the only social entertainment which the Christian Africans have as all native dances have been condemned as HEATHEN. . . . If those missionaries were to enforce their views upon those who think differently from them, they will have to prove it to some of us. I do not think it is fair to think that Africans though not quite civilised would organise a social entertainment which they know would result in moral lapses of their children.

This was a father's intrepid defense of his son, directly or indirectly. But it was perhaps a belated defense against an enduring assault. Wearied by unrelenting white paternalist overlordship of the African church and school, and emboldened by the Methodist conference in Tambaram, India, which had been attended by Africans and "natives" from other countries in 1939, Samkange had become a radical Black Methodist missionary and politician. Samkange—like Ndabaningi Sithole—constantly clashed with his white patrons, including the Dadaya Mission schoolmaster Garfield Todd, who was soon to become Prime Minister, over his growing agitation for African cultural, ecumenical, and educational autonomy.[41] Samkange was the founding president of the Southern Rhodesia Bantu Congress (1943) and a member of the Rhodesia Native Association; in 1945 he helped these and other early nationalist organizations unite as the African National Council (ANC), setting the structures of contemporary mass nationalist politics from the relative safety of the mission church (Mhoze Chikowero 2011). His son Stanlake served as Secretary of the ANC, as would Stanlake's brother Sketchley in successor parties.

This father-son(s) partnership in pursuit of African rights and dignity, including the defense of *makonzati* and African forms of worship, cautions against overstating colonialism's power to poison African intergenerational bonds, even as their images remained somewhat entrapped by the western discourse within which they operated. Thus, even though in 1944 Samkange reinforced colonialism's premises by regurgitating the idea that Africans were "not quite civilized," he was clearly beginning to articulate a discourse of African cultural sovereignty and political self-liberation—*kuzvisunungura*. Similarly, even though he might have belonged to the first generation of African mission Christians, his (belated?) dramatic defense of *makonzati* illustrates the limits of the arbitrary powers of the gerontocratic structures of rural colonial politics and missionary censure. Reverend Samkange's stance becomes even more significant in light of the fact—explored in the closing chapters of this book—that the African nationalist movement deployed musical dances to camouflage guerrilla mobilization for the Second Chimurenga in the 1960s–70s. Traveler and writer Geoffrey Gorer (1935, 289) noted this resistance when he wrote, "Africans used to dance until their families and clans were destroyed, until the constantly gnawing anxiety about taxes and military service and distant work clouded their lives." They danced "until missionaries forbade dancing as heathenish, and administrators stopped dancing because it disturbed their sleep or prevented people working, until they lost the physical strength necessary for the dance." Yet this repression could never be total because, as Gorer added, Africans "still dance[d] in small villages where there [was] no administrator, no missionary, no white man." Yet even more significantly, the concerted interdiction soon produced a(nta)gonistic dances of subversion and war, both in authorized spaces and on the margins of colonial geographies of power.

4 Architectures of Control

African Urban Re/Creation

> It has become a commonplace saying in Western countries that "Whoever captures the leisure time of the people, gets the people."
>
> —Ray E. Phillips, *The Bantu in the City*

THE WISDOM THAT Reverend Phillips cites in the epigraph above summarizes the history of colonial state and capitalist investment of money, time, and energy in African urban entertainment in white settler Southern Rhodesia and most of Southern Africa. By the 1930s, the weight of colonial expropriation and enclosure had begun to squeeze and dismember the African family in the rural reserves, further dislocating young men into "native locations"—*marukesheni* (sing. *rukesheni*)—the sequestered racial ghettoes where they lived as seekers of alternative subsistence in the urban economy. From the mission schools, "mission boys" also took their education, adopted European cultural capital, and new musical literacy to the ghettoes. Together with the streams of conscript *nthandizi* (migrant labor) from Malawi, Zambia, and Mozambique, these itineraries of preponderantly male migrants constituted the African early colonial urban experience in the *rukesheni*. Their stories, desires, and self-expression weaved the tapestries of what Joyce Jenje-Makwenda (2004) celebrated as Zimbabwean "early township culture." Before examining the township culture, it is important to understand the sociopolitical maps and designs of this *rukesheni* leisure culture, born of racial criminalization and expropriation. How did the *rukesheni*'s design as a colonial kraal, an architecture of socioeconomic engineering, racialized spatial confinement, subject making, and sociopolitical control affect African modes of self-crafting?

Like the mission station, *komboni* (mine or farm compound) and *ruzevha* (rural "native reserve"), the *rukesheni* was a colonial kraal designed to extract, control, confine, and regulate the colonized. Writing on colonial Nigeria, Andrew Apter (2002, 571) observed that "the key transformation of African culture under European eyes occurred through formalized closure." The Rhodesian state regulated African urban self-crafting largely through the Native Social Welfare policy, a euphemism for racialized and depoliticizing recreation, sponsored by the state and by capitalist interests. The *rukesheni* was designed to structure African leisure through formalized architectures: halls, regimens of programs and bookings, user fees, limited seating, approved etiquette, separation of performers from audiences, competitions, adjudication by settlers, awards, supervision, and the constant threat of punishment for transgressions. This chapter locates subversion of and resistance to this enclosure or kraaling, that is, power, at the intersection of policy and performance and argues that the music that Africans performed in and outside of these urban kraals was inescapably steeped in official agendas and practices of "native administration," colonial spectacles, and African engagement therewith. African "early urban culture" was not an autonomous domain, but an outcome of these colonial structures and African innovative agency.

Dis/Locations, Re/Assemblages: Native Social Welfare as Sociopolitical Engineering

The African "urban influx" quickly stoked settler fears that the "natives" were going to "swamp" them, occasioning both "influx control" and the tightening of urban racial residential segregation. Influx control, that is, regulations on African urban presence, was justified on the grounds of racial difference. And cultural performance animated this difference. Rhodesia's policy on Africans in the cities was reductively framed through the Native Social Welfare policy, which consisted largely of controlling and superintending African presence and leisure activities. After work hours and during weekends, a large proportion of the preponderantly male migrant workers entertained themselves by drumming, singing, dancing, and playing the guitar and pennywhistle, as well as by playing soccer, boxing, and enjoying related sports in the open commons. The focus here is primarily on music and dance. While reigning settler opinion deprecated African "modern" musical performances—viewing the category ambivalently as an epitome of "detribalization" (the dangerous specter of Africans abandoning their cultures and mimicking European ways)—urban authorities, industrialists, and white liberals sought to utilize it to engineer a desirable African urbanity. One way to do so was to "kraal" African performativity in "native recreation halls" and similar infrastructures. Africans had also lobbied for entertainment facilities to be created in the segregated "native locations," which were set up away from the city and white residential areas.

This is how Zimbabwean township culture became synonymous with Mai Musodzi Hall and Stodart Hall in Harare, and Stanley Hall and McDonald Hall in Bulawayo. Mai Musodzi and Stanley were built earliest, in 1935 and 1936, respectively, following the model of the Bantu Men's Social Center in Joburg and the Bantu Social Center in Durban, both set up a decade earlier. One Reverend

Fredrick Bridgman founded the Bantu Men's Social Center in 1924 with the support of the municipalities, the police, and Rand mining houses. Its stated objective was "to get Natives under wholesome influences during their spare time [to] counteract the tendency for them to stroll about the streets on Saturdays and Sundays when they fall into temptation through the influence of agitators." The officials adjudged that the pervasive gospel of the dignity of labor was insufficient to fully manage African urbanity; that "it is not enough to teach the Natives to work effectively. They must also be taught to play healthfully" (Badenhorst and Rogerson 1986, 200). The same logic informed urban "native social welfare" across the Limpopo River.

In Southern Rhodesia as down south, the city councils utilized money donated by industrialists and also obtained from the ubiquitous "Kaffir Beer Fund" (earned by the municipalities through their monopoly on the sale of "traditional" beer to Africans) to build these halls in the locations. The logic of urbanization on the cheap meant that the state used the Kaffir Beer Fund to support projects connected with urban Africans, spending as little of the money raised from white taxpayers on Africans as possible. Native social welfare therefore amounted to a double measure designed to confine Africans socially and politically in the name of entertainment at minimal or no financial cost to white settlers. Of course industry had a vested interest in contented African laborers. The political significance of this concession is clear from the fact that as late as 1944, Prime Minister Godfrey Huggins was still warning the municipalities of the consequences of delaying the implementation of the Land Apportionment Act (1930), which forbade African ownership of urban property: "Every day the possibility of the African acquiring property in the township increases."[1] Both the central government and the municipalities actively discouraged African urban settlement even as the need for "stabilized labor" increased with the boom in industrialization during and after the war. The building of African recreational facilities in the cities was therefore a matter of pragmatic "native" management. The facilities were designed as infrastructures of control.

The construction of Mai Musodzi and Stanley Halls illustrates not only colonial resistance to African settled urban presence, but also the significance of the emergent idea that "native" welfare could be a necessary palliative to functionalize that exclusionary policy. In 1935 the Bulawayo Town Clerk wrote the Internal Affairs Ministry asking for £300 to augment the £600 Beit Railway Trust pledge for the construction of a recreation hall, similar to the one built in Harare for Bulawayo Africans at an estimated total cost of £1,200. The council was prepared to match the government's donation.[2] Money was eventually found, thanks to the Kaffir Beer Fund, and the hall was constructed in 1936, but apart from expressing "every sympathy" with the project, the government had offered no money because, as CNC C. L. Carbutt reported, it was not the function of the government to contribute toward the cost of such a building in a municipal area. He advised Bulawayo to follow Salisbury's example: "On the initiative of the local Native Welfare Society, a recreation hall has been constructed in the Salisbury Location at the expense of the Salisbury Municipal Council."[3]

Salisbury Location's Recreation Hall was built in 1935. It was later rechristened Mai Musodzi Hall in honor of Musodzi Ayema, an African social worker appointed a Member of the British Empire (MBE) for nursing convalescent soldiers during the First World War and for her pioneer work in the Red Cross and Homecraft Clubs (Jenje-Makwenda 2004, 57). Born Musodzi Chibhaga in 1885, she survived Chindunduma, the 1896–97 anticolonial war in which her father's sister, Nyakasikana Charwe (the medium of the ancestral spirit of Mbuya Nehanda), played a leading role. Taken to the Catholic Chishawasha Mission with her aunt Charwe's children and other children of captive African families, Musodzi was baptized Elizabeth in 1907 before moving to town as, in the words of her great-grandson Leonard Chabuka, an influential woman agent of the gospel (Ruzivo 2005, 4). She then married Frank Kashimbo Ayema, who was the son of Lewanika, the Northern Rhodesian Paramount Chief, and who had been Colonel Hartley's "pioneer" escort to Southern Rhodesia. Mai Musodzi's grandsons, Chris Chabuka and Francis Joseph Ayema, became prominent Harare musicians, playing at Mai Musodzi Hall with De Black Evening Follies (*African Parade*, November 1953; Simemeza, interview). Joseph Ayema's name, like that of his fellow teacher-musician John Madzima, is immortalized as a street name in Mbare, the historical location and for decades the sole home for urban Africans in the Southern Rhodesian capital. As the African population outgrew the capacity of Mai Musodzi, Stodart was added, as was McDonald Hall in Bulawayo's Makokoba Location, both named after superintendents of the two "locations."

Together with the ubiquitous beer hall and soccer stadium, the recreation hall was an enduring architecture of African *rukesheni* urbanity for a people who were regarded as merely sojourning in the "white man's town" to serve the white settler economy. "Native administration" was firmly anchored in managing the social problems stemming from inequitable provision of amenities, low wages, and political disenfranchisement. Recreation centers like Mai Musodzi and Stanley Square were meant to serve that limited purpose. In this light, therefore, E. S. Gargett's (1973, 2) argument that "native social welfare" sought to help "the African" to transform "from displaced peasant to settled townsman" is hyperbole. Gargett was one of Rhodesia's longstanding social engineers. His job consisted of capturing and confining a people whom officialdom considered "to be in the city but . . . not of it" (Gargett 1977, 14), allowing them to vent their "excess energies" in these authorized spaces to prevent "disorder" or political intrigue.

Conceived under the guise of entertainment, this policy sought to serve capital by sustaining the exploitative migrant labor system, rather than facilitating

In honor of Mai Musodzi Elizabeth Chibhaga: one of the first recreational spaces for Africans in the "Native Locations." All images in this chapter are courtesy of the author.

Africans repurposed recreation halls for political activity, renaming Stanley Hall Lumumba Hall. Bulawayo, 2012.

Now an unrestricted beer hall, Happy Valley was the first hotel for "better-class Africans" in Bulawayo. Photo taken in 2012.

anything like transition. As John Rex (1974) observed decades ago, the location was never meant for African settlement, but as a reserve of displaced ultra-cheap African labor for the benefit of the white economy. African presence in, and movement in and out of, *marukesheni* were therefore tightly governed by a battery of pass laws that, as T. D. Shopo (1977, 207) incisively argued, were not simply instruments of racial discrimination but also forms of extraeconomic coercion that placed Africans in a position of powerlessness and exploitability.

The "native social welfare" philosophy was a crucial lever of the ideology of separate development, officially initiated by the arch-segregationist Prime Minister Godfrey Huggins, who ruled Southern Rhodesia from 1933 to 1953. It became the spine of his paternalist Federation of the Rhodesias and Nyasaland (1953–63), which he infamously conceived of as "a horse and its rider," and it outlived him as the cultural underbelly of Ian Smith's rabidly racialist rebel settler regime (1965–78). The settler understanding of "native social welfare" as separate development enabled Smith to defend racial legislation when it was increasingly called into question in the era of African revolutionary struggle by arguing that the "whole body of so-called racially discriminatory legislation . . . in fact protects the customary social life of the African against unwanted and unwelcome intrusions of European influence" (Palley 1970, 20). Huggins had laid out this false alibi in 1934, when he told the Legislative Assembly, "I shall do all I can to develop the native, if I'm allowed to protect my own race in our own areas, if I'm not, I will not do anything."[4] Separate development did not mean doing nothing, but quite the opposite, as Huggins himself explained bluntly seven years later. In the white reserves, he argued, "the African has to conform to white requirements. . . . He is not obliged to go to the white town; he can earn outside the town what for him is a good living, if he does not like the restriction in the towns" (Devittie 1976, 6).

Huggins conceded the need for urban African accommodation only from 1945, when it had become the most pragmatic way to promote the development of "his own race" by "stabilizing native labor" to serve the growing needs of industry.[5] Thus conceived, Huggins's and his successors' urban "native policy" revolved around the creation and maintenance of white geographies of power: controlling African presence to preserve white security, to minimize the risk of labor unrest, and to circumscribe political activity, all crucial protections of settler privilege. To socialize Africans into "their place," the settler government gave the Native Affairs Department (NAD) a broad mandate to oversee the "education of natives and any other work designed primarily to further the agricultural, industrial, physical and social advancement of Africans" (Devittie 1976, 6). The NAD overzealously superintended African subjection to colonial development.

Colonial ideologues framed "native social welfare" as a white man's burden, geared to aid what Gargett (1973, 1) characterized as the "immense social change: the vast and sudden transference of people from a rural subsistence economy to an urban industrial economy, from traditional to modern living." This was marketed as a burden to "civilize," shorthanded in the constant vocabulary of change that cloaked colonialism with its thin messianic robe. Rev. Percy Ibbotson, the founder and Organizing Secretary of the Federation of African Welfare Societies (FAWS), articulated the liberal soothing function: "The presence of substantial African [populations] in the urban and semi-urban areas involving the breakdown of many tribal customs and restraints placed upon the Europeans grave responsibilities from which there can be no reasonable escape."[6] White people "upset the social and economic conditions of [African] life . . . therefore, it is our duty to assist in a solution of the difficulties which have arisen" (Ibbotson 1942, 71). The solution was white trusteeship of Africans and cultivation of their contentment with their condition and loyalty to the rapacious regime, hence the unending, self-serving race relations welfare projects. This criminal welfarism sought to exact ideological conformity and ingratiation as its price, that is, it sought to control (Steinberg 2007, 61).

Reviewing two decades of "native social welfare" in 1955, Gargett (1973, 3) signaled the politics of sociopolitical engineering at play by arguing that, to the public, the municipalities appeared as sources of inexhaustible facilities, with the result that "welfare operated in an atmosphere of the 'providers' and the 'provided-for.'" Gargett averred, with no sense of irony, that "the former had to figure out what might be good for the latter—and a good deal of effort went into persuading people to use facilities which they did not comprehend and had not been conscious of needing." Thus, colonial cultural policy depended on inducement as a weapon for coercive agency:

> Some of the inducements were quite blatant. Youth club members were rewarded with free soft drinks, or passes to film shows; women's clubs offered materials at wholesale prices on easy terms; competitions and prizes marked every activity—women sewed frantically to win pots and kettles; children ran furiously to win shirts and belts; boxers fought for 7/6d divided between the winner and the loser; tempting cheques were offered to those who improved their homes or gardens.

Colonial welfarism cultivated wants for the purposes of governance, to soften domination. As Ibbotson wrote in 1942, "the origin of the Social Welfare movement in Southern Rhodesia was not found in any request from Africans for help and guidance," but from among Europeans "who had a sympathetic outlook on Native questions" (71). These "sympathetic" Europeans superintended African competitions as adjudicators, awarding prizes supplied by the city councils, industrialists, and other consumers of underpaid African labor.

Managing African urbanity was critical for the colonial project. In view of this, the municipalities recruited white officers from overseas and South Africa to discharge this mandate. In the late 1940s, Salisbury hired five new British officers to work under A. C. Davis, charging them "to cheer up the African townships—to prevent or arrest the disintegrative forces of town life . . . to provide decent, gay, attractive and constructive recreation as an alternative to beer-swilling and fornication" (Gargett 1973, 3). Similarly, in 1949 Bulawayo hired Hugh Ashton to apply his "native welfare" expertise, gained in Joburg and Lesotho, to "lighten up and give color to the locations."[7] The duties of the paternalist Welfare Officer seemed unbounded. Davis, the Welfare Officer for Harare (formerly called the Native Location; now Mbare), also "act[ed] as Father Confessor, guide and confidant to the community" upon his arrival from England (*Parade*, February 1954). In the administrative construction of colonial society into some sort of hierarchized family, the Welfare Officer acted as a missionary father, rearing the infantilized races of empire to leave behind their purported (self-)destructive behaviors like "fornication" and criminalized beer swilling. Ashton told Mark Ncube in 1994, "We wanted people to be happy and develop, encouraging the places to be happy, comfortable, beautiful. . . . In South Africa and Zimbabwe, the townships were terrible places." The state and capital kraaled Africans into these terrible places and bought their contentment with the industrial system at minimal financial and political cost.

This self-interested welfarist intervention was premised on, and reinforced, the falsifying image of the location as a site of African self-induced dislocation and colonial stabilization in a process of agent deletion, masking its creation as an institution of intensive labor extraction and racialized containment. Colonial social welfarism thus played an important socializing role, which is quite discernible behind functionaries' apologia, such as Gargett's (1973, 4):

> This is easy to criticize in retrospect, but it was very understandable in the circumstances of the time. In all the confusion of early urban settlement, when neither the people nor the workers really knew what was expected of them, and the population was growing by ten thousand a year, there was little realism about the theories of self-help and self-determination. The inducements may have been morally indefensible, but at least they effected an introduction; they opened up communication between "us" and "them" and without communication there could have been no development.

Politics, not morality, formed the backbone of colonial economics, and, needless to say, it thrived on the destruction, rather than fostering, of African self-determination. For this reason, sponsored, controlled entertainment sought not only to soothe Africans into contentment but also to transfigure and mask the coercive agency of colonial domination by occluding the causal link between settler development and African underdevelopment.

Recounting the emergence of "organized" African boxing in Bulawayo, the municipality chronicled how the sport used to be "dry hands" and dangerous, taking mostly the form of "faction fights," with Kalanga yard workers sparring against other ethnic groups. These fights would often get out of control, with axes being brought out, prompting the intervention of mounted police: "That was when the Bulawayo Municipality's Mr. Taylor set up a boxing ring at Stanley Square, where Zezurus fought against the Manyika and the Kalanga, etc, to cultivate inter-ethnic co-existence and respect, putting up 3 pounds 6 pence prize money for the winner" (Bulawayo Municipality 2000, 15). The *Bantu Mirror* echoed this narrative of *masiye pambili,* colonialism's self-proclaimed, disciplining forward march: "For many years the Makalanga Dancers and bare fisted boxers used to meet in the veld at Mbombera outside the location . . . but recently they have been using the Stanley Hall Square on the instruction of the authorities" (*Bantu Mirror,* February 24, 1945). The boxers were compelled to wear gloves. Thus, it was in the context of "tribal faction fighting," unbridled illicit imbibing of liquor, and other forms of "disorderly" and menacing socialization that the state established boxing rings, community halls, and more beer halls as "outlets for physical energy," that is, disciplining leisure. The battle was waged over performative space, with the state seeking to confine artists into enclosures and away from arenas designed to be empty. The logic of performative power, explained Ngugi wa Thiong'o (1997, 28), is that the artist strives for openness while the state strives for confinement, hence the open space "is perceived by the state as the most dangerous area because it is the most vital." Open spaces can produce unmediated performances and elide the distinction between play and politics.

The Industrial and Commercial Workers Union (ICU) represented the sort of specter the state saw in the open spaces. As the constant police harassment, arrests, and intimidation of the ICU activists suggest, the crowd that the state and capitalists designated a social evil and intervened to "help" through welfarist programs did represent a political threat. Formed by Malawian migrant Clements Kadalie in Cape Town in 1919, the ICU set urban crowds afire, with its leaders addressing thousands at rallies where attendant police officers menacingly recorded proceedings. At a rally in Makokoba in 1929, its Bulawayo leader, Masotsha Ndlovu, told the crowd, "It is a wonder that you are not all thieves. You get 30 shillings per month and out of this you pay 18 shillings rent, leaving 12 shillings. How do you live?" (Ranger 1970, 158). The combined effects of increasing African dependency on waged labor, the steady reduction in real income since the early 1920s, and the tightening color bar in employment deepened Africans' poverty and piqued their anger. Ranger's estimates suggest that, for instance, in 1903, 31.4 percent of the African population had been dependent on wage income. By 1920, the figure had spiked to 80 percent, thanks to colonial destruction of the African rural economies. The end-of-decade economic depression brought more reservations of jobs for whites, retroactively codified through the Industrial Conciliation Act (1934), which swept away Africans' minimal job benefits, subsistence wages, rights, and protections by redefining them as laborers rather than employees. This radicalized the "I-See-You!" as the ICU styled itself.

African disenfranchisement was a problem of power, which could only be resolved politically. Ndlovu defined the root of African urban politics at another rally in January 1930:

> What is wrong with the Mayor and the Town Council? We are citizens of this location but we have no privileges. . . . We will not let the council or the government rest. We must have rights in this location . . . our own councilors, inspectors, and guards. There are 7000 in this location with no voice. . . . We are a suffering class. (Ranger 1970, 158)

This was no province for police action alone. Beyond the harassment and deportation of ICU leaders like Robert Sambo and Clements Kadalie (Kadalie 1970), Ndlovu recalled how the city council moved in, with one councilor collecting money to fund football and other sports: "If you competed in a bicycle race and won, you were given a new bicycle. People then began not to attend meetings. They were now fascinated by the new entertainment. . . . That weakened the ICU as I used to wait alone under the tree without any people coming."[8]

Young Lawrence Vambe (1976, 98–99) participated in these "native social welfare" events when his Chishawasha Band was invited to provide musical entertainment. "Like many of the Africans in the huge crowds of mixed races who turned up, I was not aware of the political intention behind these events, so conspicuously supported by those in power. I enjoyed them enormously." Years later, Vambe reflected, "Just as the Government had foreseen, the general effect of these organized activities was to make the public meetings of the I.C.U. less attractive, except to the most politically minded." That was how the tree—representing the open infrastructure of African political self-organizing—was figuratively stumped. And that is why Ndlovu "seriously detested" state-funded entertainment: "I knew that was killing us."[9]

Before he discovered nationalism, Maurice Nyagumbo was a migrant hotel worker in South Africa, where he attained wide acclaim as a ballroom dancer in the 1940s. He patronized ballroom dances while his colleagues attended the South African Communist Party (SACP) and African National Congress (ANC) meetings. So engrossed was he that he welcomed the apartheid regime's banning of the former:

> In the May [1953] elections, the Nationalist Party was returned to power; and, as predicted, the Communist Party was banned. It was a bad thing for my friends, but to me it was a great relief as it was now possible to go into dancing in a big way without interference. The party had been banned just at the right time. We were preparing for a very big ballroom competition which was to be held in August the same year and was adjudicated by Victor Sylvester of England. (Nyagumbo 1982, 80)

Not even offers of scholarships to the USSR could coax him from his hobby:

> I used to argue that the situation in South Africa did not affect Rhodesian Africans who, I believed, were suffering more hardships than those faced by Africans in South Africa. This argument I used as a means to stop anyone who tried to persuade me to join the ANC. I did not want anything that could detract [*sic*] me from ballroom dancing. (82)

Sponsored entertainment psychologically bewitched the colonized. Like Ndlovu in Bulawayo, Eddie Roux, the leader of the SACP, struggled to mobilize distracted activists: "It is very difficult organizing them for serious effort to oppose their oppressors. Sport and games absorb a lot of the thinking of the people. Sunday sports attract so many people that we cannot get a hearing on Sunday" (Phillips 1937, 311). The "dignity of labor" took care of them after Sunday.

Meanwhile, the establishment celebrated this "healthy leisure for Africans." The *Star* (April 26, 1948) crowed about how the various African "tribes" "shook the Wemmer Grounds" in a day of sporting events and "tribal dances" that "unwittingly presented a strong argument" for more sporting facilities:

> From 2000 to 3000 spectators were present and about 360 took part in the athletics and boxing events, and about 1000 in the tribal dances that wound up the day. Several hundred Zulus from Johannesburg's flats and business houses shook the Wemmer Grounds. Some even showed a glimpse of their uniforms beneath their feathers. Then came the Chopis with their xylophones and shields, and finally the Shangaans with their drums.

A large part of that "argument" was the effect of the gathering on social control; the paper emphasized that "THERE WAS NO POLICE CONTROL OF THE CROWDS" yet "there was no disorder, no arguments, no fights."

However, in Makokoba, Ndlovu and African politics did not remain under the deserted tree for long. Some Africans soon subverted the state-sanctioned sites of overlapping leisure and politics, turning them into independent spaces. Hugh Ashton recalled that in 1949, "the African Welfare Society used to run football. But they had a row and the council said it wanted to take it over but the footballers said they wanted to run their own football."[10] The colonial use of recreation paid for by the Kaffir Beer Fund to nurture "orderly" and disciplined entertainment was informed by familiar historical schemes of social control for proletarians back in Britain. The *mudzviti* for Belingwe had proposed this idea to his superior, the Chief Native Commissioner, in 1910:

> The hands old or young in every [British] community were enthusiastic "supporters" of some local football team whose Saturday afternoon matches furnish a topic of interest for the remainder of the week. Here [in Rhodesia] the labourer's principal recreations are connected with beer and women, leading frequently to the Public Court and the risk of being smitten with one or other

> of the venereal diseases which are so insidiously sapping the strength of the native population. . . . The native is intensely imitative, often vain, and always clannish and all these are qualities which would further "sport"—a parochial spirit of sport if you like—but one which would forge ties of interest and *esprit de corps* between the labourer and his workplace. A patch of ground, a set of goal posts and a football would not figure largely in the expenditure of a big mine. (Van Onselen 1976, 190–91)

The discovery that African drinking could be harnessed for both profit and social control allowed every town and big mine to have its own beer hall, recreation hall, stadium, and square.

At the apex of African urbanization in the 1930s, missionaries and other "sympathetic" Europeans stepped up to establish and run "native welfare societies" with the help of "responsible" Africans. Educated Africans deemed responsible, such as the prominent musicians Kenneth Mattaka, Moses Mpahlo (of De Black Evening Follies), Joshua Nkomo (Ashton's former student in South Africa), and Mai Musodzi (Nehanda Charwe's niece), worked as welfare assistants under white Welfare Officers who presided over a wide array of sports, musical activities, Boy Scout and Girl Guide training, and instruction in "house and garden hygiene." They helped with job applications, the leasing of halls, the vetting of "films for Africans," organizing intertown and interterritorial competitions, and the maintenance of order. Whites adjudicated the competitions, awarding prizes supplied by the city councils and industrialists.

As well as providing infrastructure and administration, the state also involved itself in programming. For example, in 1941, W. S. Stodart, the *katsekera* (Superintendent) of Harare Location, briefed the mayor about a concert in Mbare by the British South African Police Band, which he adjudged "exceedingly popular and successful entertainment [which] was appreciated by an audience of over 200 Africans."[11] Inspired by this success, the Native Welfare Officer agreed with the police and the municipality to stage twelve such performances in the Salisbury Public Gardens and twelve more in the Native Location every month, with all expenses (including payment for the band, its trainer, and its instruments) paid from the handy Kaffir Beer Fund. The Bulawayo Welfare Office replicated the program soon after, inviting tenders for instruments and a suitable band trainer. Similarly, the NAD formed a Native Brass Band for Salisbury to entertain location residents, which remained active into the 1960s.[12] Wielding guitars, trumpets, and drum sets in place of guns, dogs, and truncheons, colonial administrators effectively implicated the colonized in their own policing via the entertainment rubric.

At the same time, state officials closely superintended independent African recreation. For instance, in 1951 the Salisbury Native Administration reported that

> five troupes of entertainers hold regular concerts in the Recreation Hall. These are styled "De Black Evening Follies," "The Bantu Actors," "King Cole," "The

> Merry Makers," "The Merry Bluebirds," and "The Boogie Woogie Songsters." Their shows are popular and are well attended. The Bantu Actors made two tours of Northern Rhodesia and the Congo during the year and De Black Evening Follies visited Bulawayo in December 1950.[13]

The NAD and its partners funded some of these groups and activities. In its 1949 annual report, the NAD announced that it was eliminating support for the Salisbury and District Dancing Club, which was one of the most flourishing and therefore now required less assistance: "Dances are held every Friday evening and a monthly competition is judged by various interested Europeans invited for the purpose," with crowds of African spectators paying for the entertainment.[14]

These reports emphasized the popularity of the various shows, as measured by the "masses" of African spectators. Although brass or concert band performances, like soccer and boxing matches, directly involved only a limited number of performers, their accessibility to large crowds meant that audience members were full participants in the proceedings. The colonial architects created and exploited mob psychology in order to cultivate sociopolitical compliance.

These benefactors of African entertainment were quite aware of the developing new class sensibilities in African society, and they had to manage them. In 1948, the Salisbury Municipality's Welfare Office founded the Bantu Social and Cultural Centre (BSCC) to organize recreational activities for the "better educated natives of Harare."[15] The club helped reinforce these educated Africans' sense of class identity, because "there is nothing that builds a sense of oneness more than singing," as *Parade* commented six years later. Groups like the City Quads and De Black Evening Follies belonged to this club and "performed to their best whenever they were called upon to help the club." As it was exclusive, the BSCC provided the middle class with space to "waltz, jive and rock and roll, setting free their animal energies . . . in an atmosphere free from the rough boys . . . without risking their dignity" (*Parade,* April 1954). The dying colonial state sponsored not just tribalism through entertainment; it also reinforced class sensibilities by investing in a class buffer against the African masses.

Under the chairmanship of Enoch Dumbutshena—an "educated African" who always appended his powerful credentials "B.A., B.Ed." to his signature—the club was the domain of journalists, clerks, nurses, and teachers. But it should be noted that it not only sheltered these men's and women's precious "dignity" while they reveled, it also provided them momentary respite from the gloom that characterized their everyday lives and threatened to blur the all-important class distinctions they bore on their very persons like a talisman. One patron made his class aspirations clear when he told *Parade* (April 1954), "Most of us live in very squalid conditions owing to poverty and poor housing, and it is refreshing to be able, now and again, to get out of this depressing environment." In Bulawayo in the early 1950s, Jerry Vera, proprietor of the appositely named Happy Valley

Hotel, the first black-run hotel (perched at the edge of Makokoba), and Mrs. M. Quick worked in the Welfare Office organizing all entertainment under the supervision of J. M. Banefield.

In addition to the entertainment programs at Stanley Square, the Bulawayo Welfare Office also provided a library to keep African men and women busy and to prevent juveniles from "run[ning] into mischief" (*Parade*, October 1954). Africans were encouraged by these developments, and they demanded more. But the logic of colonial investment was not responsive to popular needs. Ashton recalled criticism from members of the African Advisory Board: "Because one of the first things we developed was a beer garden. They would say, 'Why not schools?' In those days the school was not our responsibility. We produced offices, and beer halls and libraries and things."[16] Schools would entail settled African urban family life, which was contrary to Rhodesian urbanization policy. Testifying before the Jackson Commission in 1930, the Bulawayo town engineer laid bare the immorality of location urbanism when he reported, "There is not a single decent building in the Location, except the Superintendent's office and the brewery."[17] The provision of recreation halls, beer halls, libraries, and "nice parks" was meant to cultivate Africans' contentment with their dislocation. And the NAD could apparently measure such contentment, awarding prizes not only to dancing champions and the well-dressed, but also to the "best-behaved natives." This was how the state conceptualized the middle-class social space, a platform where it could help cultivate a limited fraction of African society into unthreatening models of African progress—defining the latter by political moderation and adaptation to "superior western" cultural standards.

Such state patronage became anathema in the eyes of radicalizing African nationalists. The proprietor of the Happy Valley Hotel, Jerry Vera, found that Nyagumbo, a newly patriotic returnee from Joni, and other nationalists avoided his hotel, labeling him a quisling. Other moderates—such as Dumbutshena, who allegedly refused to lead the ANC because he was afraid of losing his job as a journalist—were also so labeled (Nyagumbo 1982, 105).

The NAD and other architects of urban African sociopolitical engineering celebrated the socially ambitious and politically moderate fraction of African society. In June 1954, for example, *Parade* hailed "the African's rapid change from tribal rural life to urbanization and the modern economy." The celebratory note was punctuated by vulgarly patronizing self-interest: "The African has adapted himself to the complicated western system very well and that says much about his intelligence and adaptability. Today he is a fully fledged unit in the Rhodesian industrial machine." As we shall see, this sort of African being was not simply a laborer; this imagined male-gendered being had also become an important consumer of industrial products. By their self-evaluation, the administrators of "natives" had done a wonderful job.

The constant presence of industrialists at African recreational activities is therefore quite logical. They provided the models for, cosponsored, and adjudicated this process of African "transition." A May 1954 *Parade* report on a Harare fashion show is illustrative:

> The success of the show was equally dependent on European businessmen and others interested in African Affairs as on other factors. Realizing the economic value of the African in business, various firms readily offered valuable prizes which included wrist watches, jewellery, trousers, hats, shoes and gramophones. Some of the firms were Messrs. Moffat Radio, Hoppy's of Charter Road, The Music Shop, Nagarji and Sons, H. N. Patel, E. Saleji and H. Hari and Son. The judges were, for the ladies Mrs. Arnold, Mrs. Griffiths and Mrs. Heally and for the men Mr. J. D. Smith, Mr. Heally and Mr. Griffiths.

The men ended the fashion show with a rendition of "Ishe Komborera Africa" (God bless Africa), "the unofficial African national anthem" composed by South African teacher and musician Enoch Sontonga in 1897, ostensibly marking their progress as "successful" Africans. As we shall see in chapter 9, the white patrons of African "progress" were quick to condemn their underlings when they sang the same song in the wrong places. "Native social welfare" was also tightly wedded to socializing Africans in the ghettoes and policing their mobility within the racialized urban geographies. Locations were therefore doubly articulated sites of racialized im/mobilization, and thus powered subaltern transgression and subversion.

Dis/Location of Power: Segregated and Transgressive Leisure

Sponsored "native" leisure presented limited scope for interracial interaction. In keeping with Rhodesian custom and the "native social welfare" design, white patronage was largely limited to the warders: the capitalists and administrative officials. Muchemwa Mutyambizi recalled, "The only whites who came to our shows were those who intended to invite us, and those who came to judge our competitions, dressing and ballroom" (interview, Mutyambizi family). Asked why whites judged their shows, he explained that fellow Africans would make "biased judgments potentially favoring their relatives. Some of us then believed that a white person had justice." Yet as Muchemwa's brother, Mutizwa, further qualified the statement, this was a clearly parochial idea of justice bordering on not only interiorized African inferiority, but also capitalist self-promotion: "The white person adjudicating would likely be a factory owner with the knowledge of the quality of the garment one would be wearing. So, in that case, he would make an informed judgment." Mutizwa recalled, "There were popular trousers called Montana, and if those wearing Montana were winning, it was likely that everyone would buy Montana . . . the trousers that win."

Capitalists praised Africans' adopted dressing conventions as "vindicating fully the African's taste for good clothes and wisdom in choosing the right garment for the right occasion" (*Parade,* May 1954). Commerce capitalized on popular musicians' self-construction as models of African modernity. In fact, the music scene in early colonial urban Africa stands out for its artists' flaunting of "western" jackets, ties, and top hats (worn on *seda,* parted hair) for the men, and starched petticoats and flowing butterfly dresses on boom shoes for the ladies. Zimbabweans of those generations never tire of emphasizing that they "really knew how to dress!" Keen to offload the costs of production and reproduction onto the African family, industry happily marched hand in hand with the regime of law and order in cultivating a domesticated, limited African urbanity.

"Native social welfare" was about socializing Africans into authorized spaces. Africans had to live in the locations and they had to entertain themselves there, away from the "white" areas—the city center and suburbs. Until they bravely invaded these spaces, violating the *cordons sanitaires* in the "freedom sitting" movement of the 1950s, they could not normally patronize city hotels, restaurants, or nightclubs. Leisure in Rhodesia, as in other white settler colonies, was strictly segregated. Yet by its nature, music had the power to challenge these geographies.

Within the confines of the limited interracial interaction, a few individual whites went out of their way to defy the colonial racial conventions. One such individual was Eileen Haddon, a member of the Interracial Association who edited the *Central African Examiner,* a newspaper popular with African elites during the Federal era (1953–63). Haddon and her liberal-minded white colleagues saw the Federation of the Rhodesias and Nyasaland as offering an opportunity to cultivate racial partnership beyond that of a horse and its rider, in Prime Minister Huggins's formulation. Together with Pat Travers, a Colored (biracial) musician-activist, Haddon organized multiracial concerts with groups like Travers's Arcadia Rhythm Lads, the City Quads, and De Black Evening Follies (Jenje-Makwenda 2004, 23). As Travers told Jenje-Makwenda, he used music as both a tool to bring people together and a weapon to fight oppression. As a Colored, he could "pass" the racial bar easily. Thus, when requested to perform in hotels, Travers often brought along Black fellow artists. And because of his popularity, hoteliers compromised and allowed them to perform.

Some whites invited African musicians to entertain them in private home parties. Muchemwa remembered performing at these with August Machona Musarurwa's Cold Storage Band. Whites would deposit money at their workplace to hire them to play at birthday parties for white children: "We would go there and play until 11 or 12 midnight. At night we played right inside their houses, but in their gardens during daytime." They also ventured into white residential areas to play for pennies, as Mutizwa recalled (Mutyambizi family, interview):

> During Christmas holidays, we would wake up and go to their flats to play our pennywhistles. They came out holding their glasses because they knew

that "these people are begging." They watched and threw down money on us from their balconies, when they had gotten drunk and were making fun of us, because they were the people who had money. From there, some would then ask us to "come and play for me at my place while I relax."

Many musicians thus deployed their art to test the racial mapping of social space and to break down racial laws and conventions.

Yet when exceptions were made and Africans performed in white public spaces, their presence only highlighted and confirmed the rule, as their treatment often reminded them. They went there strictly to entertain whites, but they could not freely interact with them. Ignatius Nyamayaro, a former member of the Harare Mambos and St. Paul's Band, told a *Herald* reporter (November 21, 2007), "We performed at Skyline Motel, among other [venues] . . . playing for whites." The segregation was palpable: "To be honest, we could not mix with them after and during the shows. They did not like us, but they liked the music we played—which was the greatest challenge we faced during the colonial days."

While many Rhodesian homes and social clubs used the ubiquitous meal bell to communicate with their armies of African servants and to announce meals in the "real English style," some had their cooks play them music at table. Recalled one (former) Rhodesian, Dan Skipworth-Michell, in a Facebook group discussion,

> [Many used] a dinner gong. . . . It announced all meals at the Holiday Association at Inyanga Village, tea at the Highlands Park Hotel and, I think, meals in the Salisbury and Bulawayo Clubs. The waiters usually wore tall red fez and white starched uniforms. They sometimes played a fantastic Marimba with a rhythm that only Africans have. . . . It was amazing what a waiter could elude from a xylophone or a monotone gong. . . . It was just exuberance and a "feeling" for the rhythm! You could always tell; those with a sunny disposition played, those without just "rang."[18]

From there, some of the waiter-musicians got invitations to perform in the more private home settings. Skipworth-Michell told me in a follow-up Facebook interview, "In the latter years of Rhodesia the Marimba bands made a good living playing at 'white' weddings—they were popular!"

Thus, some whites' love for African music spawned the transgression of convention. Yet it also fostered the dramatization of both the ritualization and the policing of racial segregation. Abel Sithole and his Cool Four often transgressed the racial frontiers in the 1950s, and they experienced the fundamentals of this intimate segregation:

> At times we performed in whites-only venues, like Carlton Hotel here in Bulawayo. When we were there we were segregated against and made to sit at the backyard. They used to do strip tease at that hotel, and during such sessions

> we would be bundled out into the corridor or to the backyard where they disposed of their ash so that we don't see a nude white person. And we would be called back when the woman teaser was through. They liked our music, not us. And it was impossible for blacks to sit in there and eat together with whites. (Sithole, interview)

Such testing of the limits of racial partnership often elicited the attention of the highest offices. In 1958, the federal Attorney General inquired whether the *Citizen* newspaper could be sued for sedition for reporting that white girls had danced with African boys at a multiracial dance held at St. Augustine's School in Penhalonga. The Attorney General adjudged the article seditious because whites would become hostile at the thought of such intimacy, and Africans could read such a reaction as proof that whites did not support racial partnership. The article was provocative enough for the chaperone of the girls to declare in a statement to the Attorney General that "at no time did any European girls dance Rock and Roll with an African." She told the investigating authorities that she even went to the school before the dance to watch the African students demonstrate the "dinky two-step" and rock and roll. No one was sued.[19] Race and sex were two potent tools in white settler ideologies of power. And music could at the same time powerfully reinforce the sexualization of racialized space and challenge the criminalization of social interaction. Rhodesia tried hard to police the sacrilegious convergence of leisure, race, and sex. Entertainment spaces dramatized the potential for, and therefore the policing of, such social sacrilege.

When debate emerged in the 1950s over the need to accommodate visiting foreign Blacks and "emancipated" Africans—so-called "honorary whites" with Standard 6 education—the Rhodesian officials ran out of ideas. The Director of Native Affairs agonized over this question in a memo to Salisbury city authorities:

> With regard to the right to use amenities in any hotel, the great practical difficulty is the identification of, and the making of distinction between classes of Africans. This is a subject that has for some time been a particular hobby horse of mine, in which connection I have advocated the introduction of a statute of emancipation which could be the means of avoiding a whole series of permits and exemptions presently required by our statute law. One always comes back to the practical question, however, as to how to ensure that the (European) man in the street could recognize an emancipated African. I have no more ingenuity than to try to get over this hurdle by suggesting the issue of a button-hole badge for the purpose, but this is not really a reliable proposal.[20]

The changing times, signaled by the perennial headache of class, troubled Rhodesian racial conventions. And when difficult decisions had to be made, the artificial hedge of white privilege could always be thrown up to balk African freedom. Thus, the NAD Director suggested that, as in the Ridgeway Hotel in Lusaka, Zambia, "economics and the ability to pay will govern the situation. . . . Undoubtedly, the *bona fides* of professed multi-racialism would be tested by Africans when a hotel was first declared to be such, but this would not recur very often if the tariff was right." Where the letter of the law had become bothersome, Rhodesia's apartheid political economy could levy "white tariffs" to price Africans out and indefinitely protect the "islands of white."

Bob Bardolia, an Indian businessman, defied convention and built the Bhika Brothers' Hotel—which Africans called kwaKarimapondo, a commentary on how the businessman "farmed pounds"—outside Salisbury Location in the 1950s. Together with the Federal Hotel, this became one of the first spaces outside the ghettoes where African musicians and spectators could escape the hedges of race (*African Daily News*, November 17, 1956).[21] However, police soon harassed Karimapondo out of business, slowing down the desegregation of the physical and psychological maps of public leisure.

This sketching out of the architectures of Rhodesian urban recreation has demonstrated the vested interest that drove the state, capital, the missionaries, and colonial social science to involve themselves with African leisure, shrouded as it was in the rubric of "native social welfare." This analysis shifts the paradigm in the debate about whether the Rhodesian state suppressed or promoted indigenous musical performance. The point, further elaborated in the next two chapters, is that the colonial state sought to co-opt (certain forms of) African musical cultures in order to reinforce its own structures of power and governance. The question should therefore be reframed: why did the colonial state and white liberals involve themselves with African music? Available evidence—mostly confessional voices from the official archive—points at sociopolitical engineering and away from philanthropy. The agenda was to reinforce the status quo through the confinement of African urbanity. The outcomes of the hegemonic design can only be fully diagnosed by examining African engagement with this kraaling through the actual performances that took place within, but also beyond, the kraals.

5 The "Tribal Dance" as a Colonial Alibi

Ethnomusicology and the Tribalization of African Being

If a man does not keep pace with his companions, perhaps it is because he hears a different drummer.

—Henry David Thoreau (quoted in H. Tracey, "Musical Appreciation")

As soon as one culture begins to talk about preservation, it means that it has already turned the other culture into an endangered species.

—Malidoma Somé, *Of Water and the Spirit*

Texts and Contexts

On April 19, 1944, the *African Weekly* reported the prevalence of African weekend musical drumming and dancing in open spaces in the Salisbury Location:

> It is interesting to visit the Native Location on Sunday afternoon. Sunday appears to have become the day of tribal activities. One finds almost every tribe busy organising itself. One hears drums beating everywhere in the Location. It is pleasing to watch these tribal dances and, no doubt, from the point of view of physical training, to those who take part, they must be beneficial. Apart from this point, these dances keep the Bantu public occupied and, as a result, the number of crimes committed by Africans on this day is small.

These dances had swept towns and big mining settlements by the 1930s. They emerged spontaneously as Africans reconstituted their broken communities and passed time after the working week. The state and capital quickly stepped in, superintending them in "tribal dancing" competitions they sponsored under the Native Social Welfare program. Colonial officials and industrialists hailed the dances for distracting Africans from disruptive behaviors like fighting, drinking, and stealing. But they also promoted the dances for their utility in constituting templates of intra-African difference and collective African distance from whites; their imagined belonging to "tribes" rather than the nation; and their reinforcement of Africans' sense of migrancy, loyalty to the state as the supreme political authority, and respect for the "dignity of labor."

This chapter examines the functionality of these ethnomusicological ideas in capturing, stultifying, and promoting these performances as "native administration." As Mahmood Mamdani (2012, 2–3) has aptly observed, "native," like "tribe," "does not designate a condition that is original and authentic." Instead, "the native is the creation of the colonial state: colonized, the native is pinned down, localized, thrown out of civilization as an outcast, confined to custom, and then defined as its product." "Tribal dances" were a vivid text of this colonial vernacularization of African urban expressive cultures into this usable discourse that colonial ideologues surreptitiously deployed as an alibi for apartheid rule. The colonial state conceived "tribal dancing" as a performative instrument for articulating a self-justifying discourse of conquest and domination in a process that produced the African "Other" as a lesser, "tribal" being with no claim to "modern" rights. Fashioned from preexisting and emergent African *ngoma* and *madandaro,* the "tribal dances" were an aspect of the colonial "traditions" that colonists and Africans cocreated in reactionary ways at the moment of colonization. The colonial state harnessed them into a cultural technology of domination. To Africans, they were an attempt to reconstitute indigenous leisure forms in the urban context, and had the potential to simultaneously reinforce and subvert colonial domination.

(Re-)creating African "Authenticity," Performing Colonial Difference

Powered by the colonial canon of "native authenticity," the "tribal dance" amplified not only intra-African "tribal" differences, but also collective African cultural distance from settlers. Colonial social engineers promoted and marshaled the public (re-)creation and staging of this difference to craft African subjectivity as "native administration." The deployment of "tribal" performance to re-create tribalism as a tool for settler governance was most useful in the urban terrain, where dozens of so-called tribes from all over the region entertained not only themselves but also hordes of curious white tourists who marveled at the dance spectacles (Badenhorst and Mather 1997). Marshaled by capital and the various state arms, sport and recreation both antinomically amplified and disciplined intra-African differences into the useful register of "tribalism," colonial order, the regimen of industrial time and urban governance.

In his study of the Rhodesian *chibharo* (forced) labor regime, Charles Van Onselen (1976, 187) observed that in response to white miners' cultural separatism, expressed through privileged and exclusive social gatherings and mine dances, poorly paid African workers resorted to a "more popular, cheaper and more familiar pastime . . . tribal dancing." At Wangi Kolia (Hwange), management introduced rudimentary sporting, bioscope, and other entertainment facilities "to complement its comprehensive system of labor surveillance," and the entertainments reportedly "proved popular amongst the natives" (Phimister 1994,

75). Thus, recreation, and particularly the "tribal dance," became a pervasive instrument to interiorize subordination to regimes of colonial labor and social control. Similarly, in the cities the NAD, the municipalities, and their partners steadfastly promoted "tribal dancing" as a solution to African restiveness, with the disciplining effect of sponsored recreation replacing or complementing instruments of direct force.

It was in this context that in 1949 the Salisbury Municipality expressed satisfaction with "tribal dancing," which was "very popular . . . tak[ing] place at weekends in the open spaces of the townships."[1] Five years later, it recorded that an "estimated . . . 15 000 spectators saw members of the Shangaan Tribe win the Annual Tribal Dancing competition for the Coronation Shield, in Harari." The Makaranga and the Sena came second and third, respectively.[2] Significantly, the colonial administrators sought to promote and project these activities as fragments with which Africans could be encouraged to reconstruct their identities, imagined as "tribal," subordinate, apolitical, and traditional, and as threatened by "civilization." For this reason, colonial administrators were preoccupied with and anxious about the (in)authenticity of the dances. The Director of Native Administration lamented "that many of the so-called tribal dances performed by the various groups had European characteristics. The Shangaans were the only ones with any kind of traditional dress and musical instruments."[3] This assimilation of "civilized" European characteristics can be read profitably with Homi Bhabha (2001, 15) as an excellent exemplar of the power of mimicry, which, articulating itself through resemblance, threatened to obliterate difference, the cornerstone of colonial authority. The anomalous countergaze of the disciplined displaced the colonizer's surveillance optic, horribly turning the observer into the observed. The administrator expected the dancing colonized body to confirm colonial notions of primitive authenticity, which would reaffirm colonial authority over both the people and their cultures, now imagined as both endangered, and requiring conservation, by the same force—a triumphal Europe. The report gave no sense of what the performers were actually singing, reducing the performances to "a natural, almost non-linguistic level" (Thomas 1994, 30), a colonial imagination of the "authentic, frenzied tribal." That the particular urban context did influence ever-changing African forms of contemporary self-expression did not fit the colonial ideology of tribalism. Instead, it signaled its feared inversion, "detribalization"—the specter of the colonized shedding their primitive identities and becoming (like) "us."

The primitivist discourse was deployed to reinforce colonial authority. Here, the opposite happened, throwing into crisis the self-arrogated prerogative of the colonist or the anthropologist to "decide what is authentic and, by extension, what is worth paying attention to, saving, or stealing" (Root 1996, 21). It is not surprising, then, that these officials reproached "native culture" that refused to be imprisoned in preconceived "tribal" boxes or, in Fabian's (1990, 757) words, that refused to deliver "bare bosoms and frightening fetishes." Even "a glimpse of their uniforms beneath their feathers," as the *Star* voyeuristically reported on one Joburg "inter-tribal dance" (April 26, 1948), troubled this colonial notion of "tribal" authenticity. Such exasperation and fascination betrayed the fact that these performances signified something beyond their musicality. Colonial functionaries looked at "inauthentic" "tribal" dances and, as if gazing into a distorted mirror, saw in them the prevalent "evils of detribalization"—symbolized by the "European" musical instruments, costumes, and dance routines substituted for indigenous ones—staring back at them and threatening to unleash "chaos" in the city. Chaos meant "cheeky natives" claiming equality and the privileges of "civilization."

The terrifying resemblance threatened colonialism's certitudes. It suggested that the "native" might steal the soul of the colonizer through mimicking the latter's body, posture, and comportment, thereby gaining "native" knowledge of the European. Of course, it was such claims, that is, politics, that colonial officials contemptuously condemned as "chaos" and "disorder" when they were articulated conventionally outside of the licensed, quasi-normal mask of authorized dance. Thus, dance forms and costumes constituted critical signs in the performative dialogue, which the state sought to control as a tool to construct colonial space, inscribe "tribal" identities onto colonized bodies, and animate a self-legitimating colonizing discourse. The latter thrived on the accentuation, not erosion, of cultural difference. Noncompliance—and, even more significantly, disingenuous compliance—subverted the state's agenda by producing competing, unauthorized discourses on authorized platforms. This discursive semiotics of power can easily be missed in celebratory histories of the colonial state's preservation and promotion of indigenous music.

Ethnomusicology and the Primitivizing Crusade: Hugh Tracey in Context

It is through this prism of struggles to control and manipulate indigenous cultures—in other words, through questions of power, appropriation, and representation—that the works of early ethnomusicologists like Hugh Tracey, Percival Kirby, and other self-proclaimed "experts in primitive music" must be examined. I will concentrate primarily on Tracey, whose copious writings and archival efforts were concentrated on Southern Africa. Tracey not only made a career of "collecting" and recording "tribal" music across the continent, he also worked with the ubiquitous NAD in both Southern Rhodesia and South Africa. In the 1920s, he recorded legends, stories, and songs he heard sung by "boys" and villagers by firelight and "in the tobacco fields of Southern Rhodesia" (Tracey 1933; Tracy 1973, 3). In 1929, he led fourteen Karanga musicians down to South Africa, where he pressed their songs and his earlier collections onto discs with the visiting Columbia Recording Company. CBS's John Hammond would shortly play some of these recordings at Carnegie Hall. By 1933, Tracey had recorded or "collected" over a thousand "tribal" songs from Southern Rhodesia and beyond, thanks to a Carnegie grant Harold Jowitt, the Director of Native Development, had obtained for him "to study the background of the music of Southern Rhodesia" (Tracey 1933).

Tracey explained his and his colleagues' interest in "native" music as driven by their belief that "far from being just quaint and savage, the musical arts of Africa provide a channel, a veritable fiord into the hearts of African spiritualities which may yet provide a key to their distinctive character." Just so, colonial social scientists acted as self-appointed interpreters and producers of meaning in the cultures that they appropriated in accordance with a preconceived template and objective—researching "natives" in order to better dominate them. It was this same objective that authorized one Greta Falk to urge the editor of *Parade* (September 1954) to preserve any publications on "African custom or folklore and songs so that eventually they may be published in a book for the study of those who have Africa's welfare at heart." Such a book, she reasoned, would be of "inestimable value to future administrators and scientists in Africa"; it would be "an undying testimony of the ability of the African to lay aside the ancient inhibitions, a proof that the goat is no longer wild, but has learnt to give birth in the herd." "Claiming to protect authenticity against the threat of progress," wrote Mamdani (2012, 30), "the settler defined and pinned the native."

The British had perfected this *modus operandi* in their colonization of India through its languages, customs, and related attributes: "These vast amounts of knowledge were transformed into textual forms such as encyclopedias and extensive archives that were deployed by the colonial state in fixing, bounding, and settling India" (Cohn 1996, 8). Until that elusive goal was achieved with some determinacy, "the native" existed as a perennial question, even a problem. Falk is suggesting with Malinowski (1959, 12; see also Mudimbe 1988, 30) that, armed with this knowledge, the anthropologist can readily manage the disciplinary shift from the "study of beings and things retarded, gradual, and backward," to the recording of how the "savage" becomes an active participant in modern civilization. This is a mutual, double move: the codified knowledge of the fast-disappearing Southern African "savage" (like the Tasmanian, Red Indian, and Pacific Islander savages) rescues the threatened discipline—anthropology—and ushers in a new "anthropology of the changing, detribalized native" in even more urgent service of colonial policy (Malinowski 1959). This is how research became a dirty word in colonial practice; it was deeply embedded in, and served, imperial and colonial objectives (Smith 1999, 3).

The political economy of colonialism had long struggled to tether and kraal the colonized in the "location," the "reserve," and the "compound" in the manner of the goat—that most nonsensical little animal. Thus researched and objectified by dehumanizing colonial pseudoscience, alleged African animality was not expected to change radically; its capacity for "progress" was measured by its domesticability, that is, its willingness to conform to colonial designs. Consequently, its threatening excesses could now be curbed through administration enabled by this customization and codification of the conquered knowledge. Wielding a corpus of "tribal custom," colonial scientists and administrators could now confidently appropriate elements of African cultures and deploy them to perpetuate their preconceived ideological agenda. This is how colonial knowledge of the "native" translated into power, as "governmentality" (Thomas 1994, 40; Foucault 1979, 194). Africans were urged to take pride in their indigenous cultures, because, whether romanticized as "traditional" or authorized as "modernizing," such cultures epitomized a valorized African difference that licensed the reigning paradigms of colonial rule.

To the colonizer, domesticated difference is manageable difference because its animality is affirmed, knowable, and predictable. Falk's zoological register therefore represents triumphalist colonialism confirming its self-fulfilling hegemonic prophecies. It is colonialism unlocking its own puzzle: representative superior western and inferior "native" identities have been hierarchized on the pyramid of race and culture, and apartheid colonialism no longer requires justification because the "tribal system" has been fully functionalized as its alibi. Canonized into the self-authorizing intellectual technologies, colonial knowledge can now replicate itself into the copious collections, studies, and writings by "experts" like Tracey, which exalt the colonized's cultural ingenuity and decry his inauthenticity, while masking its own political functions and economic gain. Tracey's (1970) ethnographic *Chopi Musicians: Their Music, Poetry, and Instruments* represents his ultimate agenda and labor. The book entirely ignores Southern Africans' musical cultures of self-liberation while celebrating their artistic creativity, which he still sought to "preserve" this late in the colonial era. This is the effect of the "special mix of learned attention and the imperial enclosure" and silencing that Said (1993, 207) saw as the key connection between culture and imperialism. As a trope for "primitivity," the "tribal system" disqualified African claims on the modern polity, exposing perhaps the real, unsaid agenda of the "civilizing mission"—the de-civilization of Africans. Writing "at" the colonized in these ways produced "tribes," and, as Fabian and Root have argued, that was hardly distinguishable from shooting at them. The notions of "tribes" and "tribal systems" were lethal shots in Rhodesian "native" policy. Needless to say, this argument is not limited to urban policy, bearing in mind Thomas's (1994, 153) eloquent observation of the "direct contradiction between any [talk about the] preservation of [rural] tribal structures and life, and the demands of white farmers and mine owners of labor, which colonial administrators effectively represented."

It is on such contradictions that the "civilizing mission," governance by violence and deception, thrived. Nonetheless, the liminality of the urban terrain comes out clearly in the social evolutionary framing of the "native" threat to colonial authority and privilege.

In 1933, the *mudzviti* for Marandellas, W. Posselt, expressed concern about the growing "necessity for the provision of waifs and strays," suggesting that the government should take responsibility for their welfare (Devittie 1976, 8). But the Prime Minister dismissed the idea because under "native custom the liability for their old people is recognized and cheerfully undertaken by the natives." And in the case of children, "there are always those anxious to take them over, as whether they are boys or girls they are recognized as an asset rather than as a liability as is unfortunately the case with Europeans." Similarly, the Bulawayo Superintendent of Natives drew the CNC's attention to the need for old age relief for Africans, but the latter advised that the solution to the problem lay in strengthening the "tribal system." This "customary fact" justified colonial capitalism's offloading its productive and reproductive costs onto the disinherited African family. Needless to say, "poor whitism" scandalized the colonial state to no end. To culturally fortify the citadel of "separate development," legitimize colonial ideology, and delegitimize, silence, and dismiss Africans' existential concerns and claims on the state, the latter invested in and invoked the idea of the "tribal system." That is how, as Cohn (1987, 283–84) argued, "the conquest of India was a conquest of knowledge. . . . The vast social world that was India had [been] classified, categorized and bounded before it [was] hierarchized." In Rhodesia as elsewhere, "tribal" cages served colonial governance well.

Efforts to strengthen the "tribal system," or, more accurately, "tribal" consciousness, varied. Sponsoring the performance of cultural difference was a powerful one. This was the context in which, for decades, Tracey and others found ready support from the state, western institutions, and international capital, including record companies such as Gallo—which was "looking for romantic talent which must be as good as the calypso singers of the Caribbean" (Tracey 1933, 53)—to research and resuscitate African interest in "their own" music and cultures. Record companies sought to mine the cultural difference objectified in "traditional" music, while the colonial state cultivated it to feed its exclusionary ideologies. Tracey enunciated this logic most eloquently when he posited (even as late as the revolutionary 1960s) that the study of the "African personality" was of "first-class" importance to the colonial project. The best avenue for such study was music:

> The world knows itself largely through its artists, its composers, and writers, those who are leading in the symbolic arts. Hans Cory, the doyen of the anthropologists in Tanganyika, always maintained that the royal road to the understanding of African people was first to study their songs, because in those songs

> you find a reflection of the whole of their social organization, their opinion of themselves, their opinion of their womenfolk, their ideas about religion, their attitude toward children, towards social discipline and so on. It is all there. I have often had occasion to agree with Hans Cory on that. (Tracey 1961, 155)

Anthropological wisdom closeted African society in traditional, unchanging custom as it carefully suppressed the mention of contemporary politics in African cultures. And Tracey agreed more than merely "often" with Cory; these primitivist ideas formed the foundation not only of Tracey's own conception of African music, but of an orthodox disciplinary approach to what Martin Stokes (1994, 2) called "remote tribal" peoples. It is for this reason that Stokes was titillated by A. Seeger's reductive depiction of the Amazonian Suyá community as "an orchestra, its village . . . a concert hall, and its year a song." Such studies, focusing on an allegedly dying past precariously lingering in the present, were presented as historical. But colonial knowledge was never sure-footed and total in the face of contestation. It remained dubious; hence the perennial inquiry. There was no singular, affirmed, essential "African personality," and so anthropologists resorted to truncated elements of African cultures, including "tribal" song and dance, in the hope of pinning it down. It was in this light that Tracey captured African music as a salvageable icon of the African "past"—the locus of "true" African identity for colonialism—and housed it, appropriately, at the International Library of African Music (ILAM), which he set up in 1954 and which is now affiliated with Rhodes University.

Thanks to recording technology, Tracey was able to appropriate the works that "thousands of African folk musicians, singers . . . and instrumentalists" performed for him "without monetary reward of any kind but with genuine satisfaction at being able to hear themselves for the first time through the . . . medium of electric recording" (Tracey 1933, 5). Those who for generations have benefited economically from this largesse are aware of the massive theft and employ a wonderfully anthropological self-justification to ward off potential criticism. The ILAM website hesitates momentarily over whether it is morally obliged to compensate the owners of these songs, but quickly deploys the same anthropological alibi: the owners and their descendants can be neither identified nor traced, because the singers are deceased and their works are "tribal"—they belong to no one (except, of course, the ethnomusicologists and their descendants)! Noel Lobley (2010) has recently traced these songs to the families of the musicians.

Paradoxically spurring but also impeding this movement to "salvage" and resuscitate interest in African traditional music, complained Tracey, was the settlers' "little interest" in such music, coupled with the view that "recordings of tribal music, however good, [had no] commercial value." Tracey correctly attributed the apparent lack of interest in African indigenous music to the ethnocentrism of missionaries, "beginning with the Livingstone era," who, on the one hand, condemned indigenous music and religious practices as demonic and, on the other, associated greater status and participation in industry and the civil service with conversion to Christianity. This, he averred, opened the door to the imitation of the foreign European in dress, social habits, and ambitions. With the advent of gramophone records, films, and radio programs, "imitations of imitations proliferated, largely because improvisation and strongly nodal or 'out of tune' performances were not only tolerated, but encouraged [and] imagined to be the best foreign tradition" (Tracey 1933, 155).

Tracey (1966–67, 96) also condemned Africans as unreflexive mimickers who became trapped by the missionaries' ethnocentric prejudice and their own "inability to evaluate aesthetically," thus undermining their own "security" within the ideal society their colonial masters envisioned. Tracey was quite self-consciously stifling questions of power, with which he was unabashedly complicit. He saw Africans as Aesop's "dog who lost his bone grasping for the one in his reflection." "The present generation," he charged, "grasping for the blessings of civilization, is losing much of what was good in the primitive state." The inevitability of cultural extinction that Tracey implied here licensed modern technology's cannibalistic power to disembody and fossilize, through a "more permanent recording[,] . . . the pleasant and quaint and essentially Native [songs], untouched by any outside influence"; no longer would their survival be dependent on "the forgetful offspring of ancient Africans." Tracey's aestheticized primitivism and self-interest hardly veiled the racism of the shared settler idiom. By casting Africans as no more than recipients of execrable elements of the colonizing self, he reaffirmed the "colonizing structure responsible for producing marginal societies, cultures, and human beings" under the false guise of saving Africans from themselves (Mudimbe 1988, 4). The ideal colonial society, which Rhodesia and similar neo-Europes approximated, was a "two nations" society (R. Gray 1960). That was no mutual project, as colonial survival depended on cannibalizing African autonomy. Conceding to sponsored, unchanging "tribal" identities implied conceding to colonial capture.

Bhabha (2001, 118) correctly argued that the visibility—and hence, one might add, the terrifying power—of mimicry is always produced at the site of interdiction. I argue later that these (urban) Africans to whom Tracey denied independent consciousness did not simply imitate, but rather appropriated, aspects of "western" cultural forms as usable tools for undoing their marginalization. Thus culturally reequipped, they were able to literally perform modernity, critique its discordant colonial inflection by blurring valorized cultural differences, and refashion themselves beyond the colonial identity ascribed to them as "primitive natives"—a foundational category and imperial cultural *raison d'être* for their disenfranchisement.

In light of this existential engagement, it is surprising that Tracey expected his "anticivilizational" objectification of African music to elicit African pride. He reproached Africans for (allegedly) misguidedly destroying their own authentic cultures, advising that "non-African music performed by Africans should be removed from protected cultural occupations and allowed to find its own level through the box office" (Tracey 1966–67, 53). This was the context of the Rhodesian (and South African) radio broadcasts of "tribal" music—a key lever for apartheid sociopolitical engineering. Tracey's advice to reject the possibility of sameness or hybridity and his ideological insistence on tribalism emphasized the legislative functions of anthropology: its power to define, categorize, dis/approve, appropriate, proscribe, marginalize, or destroy. As Thomas notes with reference to the settler celebration of Maori spirituality, such primitivist constructivism theoretically marginalized most Africans, who had to "negotiate identities in urban contexts, with non-traditional social relations, institutions, jobs and so on" (Thomas 1994, 186). Needless to say, such African agency testifies to both the assailability of the anthropological construction of the identity of the "other" and the capacity of Africans to self-fashion. The flourishing of African "township" guitar music and culture had nothing to do with purported colonial "cultural protection," but was due to African cultural versatility, resistance, appropriation, and innovativeness.

Interrogating Valorized Colonial Difference

The preservationist crusade did not go unchallenged. While equally lamenting the destructive impact of western commercial music on African indigenous creativity, Alain Daniélou (1969, 19) criticized western specialists' study of African music as premised on "grave errors of conception," particularly an obfuscation of questions of race and culture:

> The idea that a form of expression in sound is associated with a particular species may be valid for the different genera of birds, but not for man. There is no doubt that race affects certain features of sensibility, that, for instance, a Finn will tend to create musical forms different from those of a Spaniard. But culture, by its very nature, oversteps such boundaries.

Deploying traditional performances to mobilize for the liberation struggle, nationalists would proffer a more radical critique. The Zimbabwe African People's Union (ZAPU) attacked the racist premises and objectives of the "tribalization" projects, particularly the harnessing of cultural differences to fortify the deceptive notion of separate development (*Zimbabwe Review*, 1969). The history of Southern Africa abundantly illustrates how the overstepping of cultural fault lines threatened to undermine the colonial project. Daniélou (1969, 21) also observed that the term "ethnomusicology" itself implied a predetermined standpoint, a search above all for the "primitive." This, together with notions of "tribes," he further argued, completely falsified the value of art and culture. Because of these faulty premises, he averred,

> what is recorded as primitive folklore is in most cases merely a threadbare form of an antiquated song that has lost its real musical context. There is a programme of the ORTF (French Radio and Television Organization) that telephones each morning the post office workers, typists [and] butchers in the provinces and asks them to sing a song. The result is usually a song by Gilbert Becaud or Silvie Vartan indifferently mauled that in fact corresponds, in comparison with the original, to what ethnologists and folklorists too often reverently collect in the villages.

Many of Tracey's transcriptions bear out Daniélou's point, particularly the "preten[sion] to notate forms whose system of reference one does not know," and "then pretentiously [teach] vague melodic outlines, as erroneous as they are mediocre, all the while imagining that one is 'saving national folklore.'" Daniélou might well have been commenting on some of Tracey's works, such as the 1929 article in which he catalogued some "historical" songs sung by the "Makalanga . . . and by the people of Cherumanzu [*sic*]," in which singers lamented "the horrors perpetrated in . . . tribal wars, singing as if they were an eye witness." Tracey prefaced his article with a disclaimer that he was an amateur in the music and the languages of the musicians. That, however, did not prevent him from freely translating and interpreting the songs. Here is one example of such arbitrariness:

CHORUS: *Heha heha heha, hoho, heha hereha, heha hehea, Kutsa ngoma ngore (we Joba).*	Heha heha, etc., Sound all the drums (the drums of Joba).
SOLO: *Wakomana wa enda kwa Marange*	(the home of the rain doctor).
CHORUS: *Ndichakutengere hore*	(I will buy you a rain cloud).

"This war song is the song of the women, who are bewailing the ravages of war upon their food supplies," explained Tracey (1929, 96), "blaming, in that last phrase, their enemies with the cry, 'nai Marungu.'" The unintelligible "nai Marungu" reads like it ought to be "nhai murungu" (tell me, white man) or "nhai varungu" (tell me, white men), in which case it might well have been a question addressed to Tracey himself in the context of recording. Even if this song was a war song, there is no discounting the possibility that the singers might have been referencing a different war altogether—most likely the recent and very significant anticolonial 1896–97 Chindunduma, which the singers might have witnessed, or even participated in! Tracey's transcription produces nothing linguistically intelligible or historically sensible. This confusion is a defining feature of many of the songs he transcribed and categorized as "historical, mystical or appertaining to witchcraft, laments, love songs, war and hunting songs, primitively humorous ones, and those sung as dance accompaniments" (Tracey 1933). Clearly, Tracey indulged in tribally jaundiced listening, implying through juxtaposition that rational, "civilized" songs do not thematize witchcraft, mysteries, "tribal war," hunting, "primitive humor," or simply inarticulate lamentations.

Charles Hamm (1995) noted Tracey's leading role in the "Bantustanization" of African music in South Africa. As a director of one of the South African Broadcasting Corporation's "Bantu" radio stations in the late 1940s, Tracey helped freeze African music into finite "tribal musics" in line with, and in the service of, the apartheid regime. Tracey also personally designed the Joburg Crown Mines' three-thousand-seat semicircular dancing arena, part of mining capital's efforts to "retribalize" and control African laborers through the promotion of "tribal" dancing (Badenhorst and Mather 1997, 484). Similarly, as already noted, corporations and the Southern Rhodesian government commissioned him to study African music in the 1930s. It is not surprising, then, that the government's policies mirrored his blueprint, describing Africans as "so heterogeneous, so unlike each other from tribe to tribe, that what holds for one tribe with great musical ability may be quite the reverse with their neighbouring tribe with little or no musical sense of any significance" (Tracey 1933, 5).

Moreover, a closer reading of his life history suggests that Tracey was significantly implicated in the Southern African colonial political economy, beyond his role as a state apparatchik. His statement that some of the "tribal" songs he recorded came from "boys" in Rhodesia's tobacco fields anecdotally suggests both his sociopolitical location in Rhodesia's racialized power structures and a conscious attempt to deflect his readers' attention from the existential, historical significance of those two tropes: the colonized bodies of African men and the Rhodesian farm as sites of settler socioeconomic dispossession, domination, and violent extraction. Such a deflection was in tandem with the depoliticizing function of the "tribalization" crusade. Tracey and his brother Leonard were Rhodesian farmers who expropriated the land and the subjugated labor of African men, infantilizing and exploiting them as "boys."[4] This point helps better contextualize Tracey's approach to African music. By controlling the colonized Africans' cultural expression, Tracey helped deliver them to capital and empire while amassing a fortune for himself and his family. To him, Africans' labor and cultures were both gold mines.

If Tracey eventually became intellectually and culturally competent to listen to African music, he chose to hear the "tribal drum" over the contemporary (political) concerns of African laborers. Consider, for example, the protagonist of the folk song "Chemutengure" that Africans sang to "lighten work," *kurerutsa ndima*, or during *mapira*, ancestral ceremonies. In one version, the protagonist decries the slave wages he earns on the settler farm, "sufficient only to pay colonial taxes" (Maraire and Mujuru 2003). He complains about the public mockery he endures on account of his ever-wet pants soaked in *dova*, morning dew, as he drives the white man's trekker wagon for a pittance. His interlocutors unhelpfully suggest that the poor man might use some of the wagon grease for body lotion, and that his neglected, impoverished wife might help herself to the same grease in lieu of *dovi,* peanut butter. This song is a lighthearted commentary on the grave matter of the colonial destruction of the African family and economy, which drove Africans to work for their colonizers for slave wages.

Thomas (1994, 180) discussed the authoritative white protagonist (colonist or writer) whose role in a colonial situation is to record the truth of an extinguished culture. Tracey would fit this description, except that he was much more than a self-constructing, far-sighted humanist: he was a vested Rhodesian settler, colonial intellectual, and cultural engineer. This might help explain why, for instance, in his quest to capture the "primitive" (which he pursued into the 1970s), he silenced independently conceptualized (authentic) indigenous musical voices that powered the African quest for self-liberation. To reiterate my argument, the insistence on primitivist tropes fulfilled the colonizing discourse's objective of depoliticizing African being. The state employed the same tropes in commercially promoted colonial spectacles like Rufaro Week and Neshamwari Tribal Dance Festivals, spectacles that sought to stem the rising nationalist tide and reinforce beleaguered colonial rule late in the colonial century.

Festivals of Founding: Staging and Contesting Empire

During King George VI's visit in 1934, W. R. Benzies, Matabeleland's Superintendent of Natives circulated a memo to all Native Commissioners asking for "tribal dancers" to be sent to Bulawayo two days in advance to rehearse for the planned imperial spectacle. Characteristically arrogating to himself the authority to invent tradition, the Superintendent stipulated that the dancers "should bring their native dancing costumes, and none of the dancers should appear in tattered European costumes," *marengenya.*[5] Correct "native" dancing costumes would presumably include such things as reeds, local beads, bark cloths, the skins and tails of small animals, feathers, and fur. These, in the colonial imagination, not only reinforced the contrast with "civilized" dressing conventions but also resonated with the voyeuristic notions of "native nakedness" and "savagery," colonial tropes of "tribal" authenticity.

Empirically misleading, such imag(in)ing can be read in two ways: as an elision of the capitalist transformation of the African everyday emblematized by factory clothes—itself informed by the colonial hunger to savor the "primitive"—or as a contrastive tool to index the ambivalent fruits of the "civilizing mission" in a context where some Europeans still disproved of "cheeky natives" who wore "European" clothes. However read, this invocation of "native" un/clothing metaphorically referenced colonial imaginations of "native culture." The point, of course, is that colonial authority thrived on ritualized difference. At the end of the proceedings, the gathered "native" leaders presented King George with a leopard kaross—a potent gesture signifying submission and loyalty to imperial authority. In African cultures, leopard and lion skins symbolize the king's or spirit medium's sacrality, authority, and legitimacy, which is why commoners are expected to surrender them to such figures after a hunt. Ritualized conferment of such items represents investiture, submission, or tribute to the superior authority. One thus honored usually reciprocates in the manner of a magnanimous superior, animating a cultural semiotics of power in so doing. African "loyalty" to empire was often reciprocally recognized and codified in medals and badges of "honor" at such festivals.

Royal visitors to the colonies usually toured major population centers, where they met African leaders chaperoned by the NC, the self-styled *nkosi* ("Great White Chief"). According to the workings of colonial protocol, it was the prerogative of the *nkosi* to invite African leaders and present them to the visitors, usually amidst much pomp and in the presence of African crowds that dutifully lined roads to welcome the visitors (*Native Mirror,* October 1934). Such ceremonies constituted carefully choreographed and controlled imperial spectacles. As Jasper Savanhu, hiding behind a symbolically anonymous moniker, "African Journalist," wrote of the 1953 visit by Queen Elizabeth and Princess Margaret for the Rhodes Centenary Exhibition (RCE), "The leading Africans who were selected for presentation to the British Queen and Princess Margaret were mostly those whose leadership lay in what they had done or were doing to advance their people. The militant, vocal type of leader was left in the background" (*African Parade,* November 1953).[6]

Official rhetoric constituted a veneer over this discourse of divisive control and domination, identifying loyalty to colonialism as progress and criminalization of dissent as barbarism. Addressing Africans gathered to welcome King George at Ndola (Northern Rhodesia) during the trip in 1934, M. J. L. Keith, the District Commissioner, extolled African subordination:

> I should like to assure [Africans] that it will not be one of the least of His Majesty's joys today that his jubilee is celebrated by millions of loyal Africans. I am glad to see that Chief Chiwala has joined us today. He lived . . . in the days of slavery and barbarism and can perhaps more than any of us appreciate the benefits that the King's rule has brought to central Africa. (*Native Mirror,* October 1934)

This imperial self-adulation and praising of African "loyalty" constituted a rather unsophisticated justification of conquest "well beyond the [military] encounter" (Ouden 2007, 104). Ouden rightly argues that conquest is also an ideological project that is normalized by discourse. Because the fragile ideology cannot be self-sustaining, it requires constant reassertion and reauthorization. Clearly, therefore, Keith's rhetorical contrasting of "savagery" with "civilization" can be located squarely among the discursive attempts to mask colonial predation and, to reinforce Aimé Césaire's (1972, 3) critique, to suppress the African reading of the *Pax Britannica* as nothing more than enslavement and barbarism.

The *Mirror* reported that, after mission and other African choirs "gave good renderings of native songs" and "God Bless the King," the NC presented several of the gathered chiefs with silver jubilee medals, "which they were told were a great honour." To reiterate, the sharp contrast between officials' self-congratulatory rhetoric and the silence of the politically neutered "chiefs"—analogous to the way that those considered loyal were visually exhibited, while dissidents were subjugated and rendered invisible—is instructive in deciphering the practical functions of the perpetuated discourse of conquest. This discourse is authorized by violence, which always lurked close to the surface. This is how, argues Root (1996), art can operate as an alibi for cannibal power. It is able to gild ugly social and historical facts with the patina of taste and beauty, and thus elicit lofty sentiments while obscuring the conditions under which these same lofty sentiments are made possible. Africa had been conquered; its people could now be controlled and the external trappings of their cultures and aesthetics safely consumed. Stokes's (1994, 8) argument that "the violence which enforces dominant categorizations is seldom far away from musical performances" is borne out in these ritual performances of colonial power and domination through the co-opted agency of African culture. The RCE, staged in Bulawayo in July and August 1953, was a poignant ritual exhibition of imperial domination that also illustrated African contestation of imperial spectacle.

The Rhodes Centenary Exhibition, 1953

Leslie Witz's (2003, 129) study of South Africa's Jan van Riebeeck Tercentenary Festival of 1952 illustrates how colonists staged founding festivals as performances of public history and identities, depicting European civilization and its alleged benefits to "grateful natives," a point the Ndola District Commissioner emphasized in 1934. The exhibition of Chief Chiwala at King George's reception, typical of the way Africans were generally displayed in subservient roles, was a performative legitimation and reinforcement of colonial power.

Preparing for the RCE in 1953, the Southern Rhodesia NAD engaged African troupes and individual artists "from all over Central and Southern Africa" to perform in the "African village" section of the exhibition park that Hugh Ashton and J. F. Holleman, a South African anthropologist, had helped to "curate" (Shutt and King 2005, 369). However, illustrating how such staged shows of supposed unity-in-difference remained contestable, many of the invited African performers and participants spurned the invitation, leaving the NAD to report contemptuously,

> Offers were made whereupon certain of these troupes, particularly from Northern Rhodesia, proposed to visit if members of their tribal groups would assist by providing additional men and women to join in choruses and other subsidiary parts. In an endeavour to facilitate matters, the Department tried

> to obtain the cooperation of representatives of these groups but so nervous were they of the gauleiters who had put out a "boycott the exhibition" order that fearing ostracism for having contributed in any way to anything connected with the exhibition, they chose instead to make lame excuses and to absolve themselves from responsibility in the matter and the opportunity was lost.[7]

A Mr. Price from the department had consulted the Bulawayo African Advisory Board (a politically ineffectual African organization) on April 22, 1953, to ask it to urge local entertainers and spectators to participate in the festival. As Simon Muzenda recollected, Price had told the incredulous board that the festival would be supported by "seventeen colonial governments south of the Sudan," whose participation was meant to "show the world the progress and developments that were taking place in those countries as a result of the cooperation between the two different races" (Bhebe 2004, 92). After voicing reservations about celebrating their colonization, board members adjourned the meeting to the next day, planning to discuss details then. Subsequently, African leaders met at Stanley Square and resolved to urge people to boycott the festival. Muzenda, who was by this time cutting his leadership teeth in the nationalist movement, would boycott not only the festival itself, but also the April 23 board meeting; significantly, that was the only meeting he missed during his tenure on the board. The Matabele Home Society also refused to send "tribal dancers" (Ranger 1999, 211), questioning the Rhodesians' right to appropriate and represent Ndebele cultural symbolism. Esther Lezra (2014, 9) coined the term "monstrification" to describe the irony of colonists labeling dissenting colonized monsters. A "gauleiter" was a Nazi provincial leader in Germany, and the Rhodesians clearly found the term useful in their prose of counterinsurgency that depicted African nationalist leaders as authoritarian monsters bearing down on "simple natives."

However, this critical stance did not represent a particularly unified African political consciousness. As Allison Shutt and Tony King show, African opinion remained divided, with many middle-class Africans, including Lawrence Vambe, Mike Hove, and J. Z. Gumede, not only attending the RCE but also celebrating the "African village" exhibit erected to represent African life. Similarly, not only did many African singers and dancing groups—including the Jazz Revellers, Dorothy Masuku,[8] the Bulawayo Golden Crooners, De Black Evening Follies, and South Africa's Manhattan Brothers—participate, the Follies and the Manhattan Brothers also cosponsored the "Miss Mzilikazi" beauty contest, which Masuku, a beauty queen as well as a singer, won (*Parade,* November 1953; Masuku, interview). Some of the performers were handsomely remunerated, with the Manhattan Brothers donating a large proportion of their prize money toward building Nyatsime College to further African education.

The exhibition was problematic in many ways. The beauty pageant, for instance, might be read as an instantiation of phallic colonialism, especially in light of the celebration of Rhodes as the uncrowned King of Rhodesia by virtue of, among other things, his politically significant taking of several of Lobengula's sons for personal servants. Thomas (1994, 100) makes the important point that "gender is . . . a crucial dimension of difference that often encodes or valorizes other differences such as those based in 'race' or geographical location." By evoking a nineteenth-century Freudian representation of Africa as a licentious and docile female "Other" to be conquered and dominated (Kisiang'ani 2002), the "Miss Mzilikazi" trope feminized the founding Ndebele King and, despite Rhodes's homosexuality, reinforced the myth of a virile Rhode(si)an conquest. With the "savage" dissected and proven effeminate, "she" could now be safely venerated! Nothing embodied masculine settler valor more than the trouncing of the "blood-thirsty" Ndebele King, "chased out of town like a goat!" (*Rhodesia Herald,* July 22, 1893). Encapsulated in the Rhode(si)an ideal, these projectionist, self-referential tropes, reenactments, and celebrations of conquest and occupation reinscribed settler virility and "native" effeminacy. The image of the cooperative eunuch "chief" and the courtly "tribal" dancers prostrating themselves to a superior European authority reenacted the crucible of conquest and institution of the *Pax Britannica* as progress. African culture—or "barbarism"—provided a foil with which to wrap the discourse.

The "modern" African bands that performed at the RCE represented African adoptive conceptions of "progress" and "cosmopolitanism," which the exhibition blazoned as testimony to the benefits of the "civilizing mission" some middle-class Africans hoped the newly instituted Federation would consummate. This semiotics of colonial self-legitimation had no space for monstrified "gauleiters" like Muzenda who questioned these rituals of colonialism and undermined the new order, "civilization." Yet the system's desire for approval by the colonized opened cracks that some Africans exploited for personal benefit. To Masuku, the "African village" was a windfall. She boasted, "The African Village was a centre of attraction and I made big money during the celebrations—I was well-paid" (*Parade,* May 1959). This simulacrum of what Mungazi (1983, 6) described as a "primitive, stone-age African society" in the heart of the colonial city—where, to their own amazement, some Africans played *mbira,* danced "tribal" dances, and cooked and ate *sadza* (Sithole, interview)—is intriguing. By abstracting, objectifying, and reincorporating elements of a culture it had fragmented, the Rhodesian state sought to elide, or to recode and sanitize, the ugly truths of its own origins while constructing an alibi for its apartheid governance in the white mind.

Colonial Bulawayo was founded on the ashes of the Ndebele capital and the ruins of African houses that the city had pulled down in "urban renewal" programs. In its colonial representation, to borrow Te Runanga o Ngati Awa's apt words, the "African village" had changed from a "living" meeting space, which the people used, to an ethnological curiosity for strange people to look at in the wrong way and in the wrong place (quoted in L. Smith 1999, 52). This intersection of commodified cultures and colonial violence teases out the multivalent strands that conspired and competed to depoliticize and recode African cultural performance in the service of a colonizing ideology. Because the ultimate focus was the colonizing self, represented in Rhodes (Britain's imperial destiny personified), such performances allowed colonialists "to conquer people [and] at the same time feel good about it" (Root 1996, 163). Moreover, the specular nature of this exploitation of cultural difference meant that "instead of seeing the native as a bridge toward syncretic possibility, it use[d] him as a mirror that reflect[ed] the colonialist's self-image" (JanMohamed 1985, 66). Some Africans' boycotting of the RCE signaled their suspicions of the ill-fated Federation's notion of "racial partnership," Britain's desperate attempt at a supposed new inclusiveness that Prime Minister Huggins, in his characteristic bluntness, designated "a horse and its rider"—with Africans being the horse and whites the rider. Seven years later, Dorothy Masuku, August Musarurwa, the Jairos Jiri Choir, and the African American jazz maestro Louis Armstrong would refuse to record and sing white-composed songs promoting the Federation.[9] The usual suspects—the nationalist demagogues—had intimidated the artists, the state helpfully explained.

"Tribal Dances," Nationalist Masquerades?

The state's harnessing of "tribal dances" for ideological purposes escalated in the second half of the century in response to intensifying nationalist flames. In 1974, under the auspices of its Rufaro brand of beer, the Salisbury Municipality's Liquor Department inaugurated an annual Rufaro Show Week to promote the "African image" through music and dancing.[10] The inaugural carnival at Mbare's Rufaro Stadium lined up "Drama by the 'Makadota Family' [*sic*], shows by the BSAP Band, Tribal Dancing, Marimba Band, Football final, Pop music, B. A. A. Tribal dancing, Shangaan Dancers, Pop music, SA pop group, fights, money distribution, [and] final Miss Rufaro contest."[11] The "tribal dance" had not only persisted as the dominant motif of colonial African cultural policy, it had also solidified as the emblem of ascribed "African identity." In addition, the municipality also organized the Rufaro Tribal Dancing Festival and the Neshamwari Music Festival, exclusively "traditional" music and dance competitions whose finals were also staged at Rufaro Stadium.[12] According to Basil Chidyamatamba, the Organizer and Performing Arts Coordinator of the Salisbury City Council's Community Services Department, no fewer than fifteen "tribes" were taking part in these "traditional tribal dancing" festivals by the late 1970s, among which he enumerated the following groups and/or genres: "the Muganda, Angoni, Mafue-Goteka, Ngororombe, Jerusarema, Chinyambera, Karanga-Mbakumba, Nyao-Gure, Shangaan-Muchongoyo and other Traditional folks" (*Herald*, November 6, 1978).

The object of the festivals had not changed; they remained an attempt to confine and surveil. Some of the groups had staged street parades, leading the state to intervene—purportedly to protect residents offended by the performances or the tumult they generated. For example, some Gule WaMkulu Nyau dancing groups caught both the administrative and the anthropological eye of Harare's *katsekera*, J. P. Courtney, prompting him to write the Ministry of Internal Affairs in 1972:

> You will be aware that I'm attempting to research Nyau Dancing *with a view to formulating some form of control*. There have been complaints from residents who do not subscribe to the spiritual beliefs of the participants. African dancing and drumming has [*sic*] been interests of mine since I first came to Africa. One of the distressing things is that *with the onset of civilization many of these dances and the old songs and drum refrains are becoming lost*. I'm slowly making headway with the leaders of the Nyau cult and I hope I am building up mutual trust. At a later date I wish to attend a full scale dance. It struck me that it would be of value to record parts of the dance on film and tape.[13]

African performative self-organization signified the deeper import of the dances, beyond the colonial tribalizing designs. At the same time, the *katsekera*'s statement is a powerful colonial confession that blends cannibalistic fascination with nonwestern cultures as objects of study (and consumption) and the disciplining agenda of colonial knowledge into a potent imperial antinomy, the "violence of understanding." Contrary to the claims that "culture" was being used to improve race relations, the history of colonialism bears evidence that, as Todorov put it, destruction becomes possible precisely because of that understanding, a dreadful concatenation whereby grasping leads to taking and taking to destruction (quoted in Ouden 2007, 111). Naturally, the colonial state feared not only the "native," but also its own ignorance, symbolized by its paranoia about the open space, as Ngugi wa Thiong'o (1997, 26) observed:

> It was not sure of what was being done out there, in the open spaces, in the plains, in the forested valleys and mountains. It was even less sure of people dancing in the streets, in market squares, in churchyards and burial spaces. And what did those drumbeats in the dark of the night really mean? What did they portend?

To gesture an answer to Ngugi through Sartre's words (in his preface to Fanon 1968, 19), the settler suspected that those drumbeats in the dark portended the "natives'" painfully contracted muscles. Perhaps they were no longer dancing merely to relax them, but already miming secretly "the refusal they cannot utter and the murders they dare not commit." To reiterate, then, the urge to destroy, wholly or partially, through domestication or ethnographic espionage and superintendence emerged from colonial nervousness and fear, rather than from strength and self-confidence. The targeted groups were aware not only of this domineering, nervous gaze, but also of the administrators' increasing suspicion that "tribal dances" were becoming a (locus for) nationalist masquerade. Anthropological documentation and representation lay at the heart of the antinomic colonial agenda to both salvage and destroy. To those targeted as subjects or objects, the inscriptive audio-visual technology could not have been in more insidious hands. As the *mudzviti* was in the rural districts, the *katsekera* was the everyday face of the colonial violation of Africans in the cities. Thus, recording devices constituted potent tools and symbols of what Andrew Apter (2002, 566) called the optic violence of colonial appropriation. They were an extension of the colonist's will to see in both space and time; they enabled espionage, surveillance, inscription, control, and repression, reinforcing the cannibal power of the colonist that the *katsekera* embodied. The incarnation of the colonist as researcher self-evidently betrayed the value of knowledge imperialism.

In addition to its social scientist functionaries, the state also closely partnered with industrial capital, which had a vested interest in disciplined but rootless African urbanity. The mine labor barons of the region, particularly Joburg's Witwatersrand Native Labour Association (WENELA), occasionally sent "tribal dancing" troupes to Rhodesia for the Neshamwari Festival and others, in regional campaigns designed to mollify migrant laborers (Badenhorst and Mather 1997, 485). In 1975, it dispatched a Xhosa group to tour Salisbury's African beer halls in Mufakose, Kambuzuma, Rugare, Mabvuku, and Mbare, but with a strict prohibition on visiting the nationalist and politically volatile Highfield.[14] WENELA was wary of African nationalists' militant opposition to "the racist Rhodesian regime's exchange of (African) slave labour for foreign currency" with the South African apartheid regime (*Zimbabwe Review,* February 8, 1975).[15] More importantly, the nationalists were critical of the colonial conceptualization of African being through the so-called tribal dances, and they were cultivating indigenous performances themselves in an effort to breathe life into the liberation struggles. By the 1970s, then, the nature of cultural performance as an ideological battleground had turned full circle. WENELA and its partners realized that its "tribal dancing" public relations stunts might backfire in Highfield.

In this atmosphere, even the state's paternalistic relationship with the various dancing troupes was ruffled. For example, in October 1968, Chidyamatamba, chairman of the fifty-one-member Salisbury African Choral Society, submitted his group's constitution to Morris, the Director of African Administration, for approval, as was required under the battery of antiterrorism laws, and he took the opportunity to communicate his group's "unanimous decision" to request that Morris be their patron.[16] The Director declined the honor, heeding the Townships Officer's advice that accepting the request might

> cause considerable embarrassment in the future should this society start drifting into the political field, which is always a possibility. Besides this, I think

> it is bad, in principle, that you, as the Director of African Administration, should seek out one particular Society, upon which to bestow your blessing by becoming its patron, when there are others possibly offering a better service to the community, who may resent this.[17]

This was the closest the state came to admitting the limits or failure of its "tribalization" project. Said (1989, 223) marvelously interpreted the rude awakening: "The subaltern and the constitutively different suddenly achieved disruptive articulation exactly where in European culture silence and compliance could previously be depended on to quiet them down." The depoliticizing agenda was shattered; the Africans who were performing supposed "tribal dances" were not gyrating back into some imagined "tribal" past, but ritually performing and calling into being a different future of African nationalist self-rule.

Chidyamatamba, a great fan of classical music, often conducted the Salisbury African Choir and "tinker[ed] to himself at the piano" (*Rhodesia Herald*, January 26, 1975). Because of his lived knowledge and institutional training and the privileged status he had attained, he represented those organic intellectuals whom the state mandated to capture and organize "the people" on its behalf through their cultures—a role he would continue to play after the attainment of independence, marshaling artistic activity in the service of the post-colonial state's efforts to create a socialist state through the arts.[18] He was also the municipality's Performing Arts Organizer and Coordinator and, thus, the public African face of the city's cultural programs. The Director's patronage might have provided his group with some sense of security in an atmosphere where *rukesheni* dwellers faced escalating harassment by both state agents and radicalizing African political activists. Emerging struggles to harness the power of not just music in general, but "traditional" performative culture in particular, for contending political ends must have compounded Chidyamatamba's and his colleagues' vulnerability. While the state had employed the notion of "tribal authenticity" to justify its apartheid policies, nationalists were appealing to the same vernacularized episteme, cleansing it of or underplaying its "tribal" connotations, then revaluing it into a forceful, historicizing counterdiscourse for mobilizing mass participation in the nationalist project. As Ranger (1988, 16) observed, administrative attempts to capture tradition could not hope to compete with the ongoing, profound imaginative nationalist reworking of indigenous culture.

The state recruited prominent African personalities in conspicuous positions in hopes of legitimizing its entertainment programs and masking the political significance of its superintendence. The Salisbury Municipality confessed as much when, in 1949, it tried to reassure Africans that it did not wish to control their entertainment, but wanted rather to work with them in a relationship defined by indefinite tutelage:

> The department assured the local population that far from wishing to control sport, it is anxious that their clubs and other recreational bodies should carry as great a share as possible in the organization of recreation and that every assistance will be given to those who fall in with this idea. This is one aspect of native administration where a start can be made, without serious risk of repercussions, in giving the African a small share of responsibility for organizing his own affairs, and the readiness of the majority of those Africans concerned to accept this can be regarded as a healthy sign.[19]

Thus, recreation presented some limited openings to those Africans with ambitions for social mobility or otherwise keen to work for their own communities against the currency of colonial exclusion. This helps explain the heavy involvement of Africans in sports, music, and other recreational or "welfare" programs. Such subordinate participation simultaneously underpinned and threatened the colonial project.

This hegemonic scheme informed the Rufaro Festival, at which the legendary footballer George Shaya and the radio stars Wellington Mbofana and James Makamba judged the Miss Rufaro contest. Interestingly, these popular African personalities all distanced themselves from the "tribal" dancing segments of the show in a move that apparently betrayed their "modernist" class sensibilities.[20] Nevertheless, in spite of the apparent conjoined political and commercial intents, these activities greatly helped to boost interest in and the performance of Zimbabwean traditional music and dance genres in the towns, where, according to Chidyamatamba, they had largely been shunned. When he joined the municipality in 1965,

> traditional dancing groups were rarely heard of. Today they number 34. The Karanga dance mbakumba, the Ndau dance the muchongoyo, the Zezuru dance the shangara and the jerusarema. . . . Western music had a lot of influence with these [urban] kids. . . . But with the introduction of adult traditional groups they realized that it was part of their culture. Now they have started learning it in the schools as well as in the clubs. It's very important because some of these kids are born in the city and don't have the chance to see the music of the rural areas. (*Rhodesia Herald*, January 26, 1975)

While not entirely incorrect, Chidyamatamba's explanation for the general lack of interest in "traditional" performances not only overstates the rural-urban divide (Chitando 2002, 87), but also underplays the significance of African political consciousness, which turned ambitious youngsters away from these tribalizing dances. Many were wary of being represented and constructed as "primitives." They were well aware of the designs of colonial "native" policy; hence, as I illustrate in the next chapter, the politics of culture actually fired their passion for "modernity" in a process of self-fashioning that strained to outrange the oppressive, ascriptive underclass colonial identities. This is what Kenneth Mattaka, a mission-educated artist, signaled when he told me, "Traditional music didn't fit with the educational line and Christianity." It was this tension between the reified notions of "tradition" and "modernity" that, on the one hand, the colonial state and its partners like Hugh Tracey and, on the other, African nationalists had to contend with in their efforts to harness indigenous performance for rival political projects, whether explicit or camouflaged. These were useful, creative identities—exploitable and self-liberatory.

Urban colonial authorities and capital harnessed anthropological instruments to wage a concerted crusade to atomize African musical dances in order to animate a primitivist, colonizing discourse. The colonial state, its social scientist functionaries, and capital hoped that Africans could be encouraged to "tribal-dance" their way back into idealized rural identities in accord with apartheid development and urbanization policies. Such policies would save the state the burdens and costs of African urbanization and reinforce racial geographies of power that fed on colonial difference. Moreover, the ethnomusicologists' "preservationist" crusades were deeply implicated in the state's social engineering agenda and commercial interests. This is all clearly implied in Tracey's imperious and ethnocentric objectification of African music as "quaint," "savage," and "primitive," and in his stated research objectives, including his quest to discover the "African personality" through the music that he "collected." Overall, Rhodesian cultural policies toward Africans can only be understood fully if viewed as part of its larger apartheid colonial project that sought to control Africans intellectually, socially, and economically. This understanding is possible only through a robust rereading and reinterpretation of the ethnomusicological archive, methodologies, and discourses, which have hitherto been read at face value as unproblematic knowledge or as indicative of colonial fostering of indigenous culture. In the hands of the Rhodesian state and its ethnologist architects, culture was an important ideological lever to ensure that Africans continued to "hear a different drummer," to apply Thoreau's crude anthropological wisdom. Yet the power of the colonizing discourse was never total; it remained fractious, fictional, and contestable.

6 *Chimanjemanje*
Performing and Contesting Colonial Modernity

> The songs that live in our ears and are often on our lips are the songs which we heard sung by those who shouted while we groaned and lamented. They sang of their history, which was the history of our degradation. They recited their triumphs, which contained the records of our humiliation. To our great misfortune, we learned their prejudices and their passions, and thought we had their aspirations and their power.
>
> —Edward Wilmot Blyden, *Christianity, Islam and the Negro Race*

NOT VERY LONG ago, wrote Jean-Paul Sartre (in his preface to Fanon 1968, 7), "the Earth counted two billion inhabitants, that is, five hundred million men, and one billion five hundred million natives. The former possessed the [v]erb, the latter borrowed it." This was the "Golden Age" of empire, which, however, "came to an end: the mouths opened, unassisted." European colonizing discourses justified the despoliation of Africans on the grounds of cultural difference, namely, that Africans were illiterate, precapitalist "heathens." Among other responses, Africans selectively appropriated this colonizing discourse, and repurposed and redeployed it to unmake their marginalization. Here, complicating Sartre's thesis, I explore how Africans appropriated, redeployed, and rearticulated western cultural capital to refashion their own identities and reclaim space in an urbanizing colonial environment that alienated them.

Many African students were graduating from the few mission schools as literati-musicians by the 1930s. Their basic literacy and drilling in the hymns and brass bands equipped them to invest their creative energies in the world of education, commerce, and Christianity, the three pillars of western modernity, out of which they crafted *chimanjemanje* (or *smanjemanje*), "new cultures of today." Many of these "modernizing" Africans internalized the cultural self-contempt their colonizers inflicted on them and sought to cast the authorizing register of *chimanjemanje* as an empowering polar opposite of their *chinyakare*—traditional, passé, and therefore shameful cultures. These scholars' public mediation and reinterpretation of western "civilization" at the *dariro,* the "communal assembly" (Mokoena 2009), produced a rich dialogue of self-fashioning that tended to simultaneously affirm and disrupt the *raison d'être* of the discordant colonial modernity that colonists deployed to disenfranchise them.

These African self-fashioning efforts were ranged against a racially politicized urban environment. An appreciation of this environment is therefore vital for understanding the dialectics of African cultural politics. In 1918–19, an African messenger at the Rhodesia Native Labor Bureau placed the following advertisement in Rhodesian newspapers:

> Ladies and gentlemen of African blood, residing in and outside Salisbury and in its suburbs: Hereby you are all informed that I am giving a great and grand tea meeting and dance on October 2 at Salisbury Location. Having obtained permission to use the location canteen building, the meeting will take place therein, and I trust that there shall be a big attendance at this meeting. I wish to tell you that all proceedings thereof shall be purely for the Red Cross Fund. This being the case, I am confident that you will do all in your power to assist in making it a big success. All natives and coloured people are invited. Come and drink a nice cup of tea. Come and listen to melodious music specially arranged for the great occasion. Come and take a round in this smart dance. A great number of ladies from outside districts are expected, and I am sure the dance will be the first and finest ever given at Salisbury. You cannot afford to miss this excellent entertainment, the first given in Mashonaland.

The Jesuit *Zambesi Mission Record* (*ZMR*) reprinted the ad (July 1919) and read it as illustrative of the "patriotism," the "most astonishing and unexpected spirit of generosity and sacrifice of natives of this country," who were allegedly otherwise "very reluctant to give away anything." Its begrudging commendation quickly morphed into light-hearted banter about the "very amusing" literary self-styling of these unlikely patriots, the "educated natives." The paper commented with undisguised mirth, "When natives essay to write a letter in English the result is often very curious, the ideas, and the manner in which they are expressed, being such as could occur to a native only." The editor suggested that African self-expression, even in a language that might have hidden African identity, unmistakably gave itself away.

For the settler press, this "native" self-representation was not a laughing matter, but an outrageous political claim. Back on December 15, 1904, the *Rhodesia Herald*'s weekly edition had denounced these "black pests," warning whites that if they did not wish to see their "whole political power wrested" from them, they had to take "extreme measures to curb the growing influence of the 'kaffir.'" The newspaper also denounced the missionaries, especially the Wesleyans—personified by the nonconformist Rev. John White—as "black coated brigades" who reneged on their duty to supervise their "social pets" so as to ensure that the offending "terminology" of this emergent "kaffir" discourse did not escape their observation and censure. The editor resented that his paper should be used to cultivate "such foolish mimicry." Whites were "ladies and gents," not the "kaffirs," sneered the editor as he stridently warned against "the policy of putting false notions into the kaffir mind[, which] is vested with grave danger to the white community." The fear emanated from disproportionate colonial demographics: "The kafir population is increasing far more rapidly than the white, and . . . endeavoring to inculcate into their minds ideas that they are entitled to equal rights and privileges with the white is a policy to be denounced in the strongest possible terms."

One Eric W. Pope spoke for many when he wrote in the *Rhodesia Herald* (February 15, 1918), "There are, I own, gentlemen amongst them, but they are not the town and mission boys but the native who wears skins and limbo and who calls a white man 'Inkosi' or 'M'lungu' and means it."[1] Perceiving aspirant African elite self-making as politically devious and insurgent, settler vigilantes decried African harnessing of the mask of the tea dance and the language of "civilization," seeing these trappings as surreptitious weapons for making claims on the state. Racial politics were inflamed by the black man's intolerable political claims, which Achebe (1978, 8) elaborated on: "It is the laying of this claim which frighten[ed] and at the same time fascinate[d] [some whites], 'the thought of their humanity—like yours . . . Ugly.'" Urban Africans deployed these politics of culture to regenerate a despoiled self and reclaim space.

The Family Metaphor: (Re)Constituting African Communities

The Southern African urban "location" emerged as a reassemblage of local and disenfranchised transterritorial labor seekers, tying Salisbury's Mbare and Bulawayo's Makokoba with the township networks of Northern Rhodesia's Copperbelt and South Africa's ghettoes through mobility and cultural creativity. It was within these regional cultural continuums that the literati crafted their identities as global. Defying the colonial system that insistently constructed them as "not yet" modern (Chakrabarty 2000, 8), many "educated Africans" struggled to prove their worth and capacity for "civilization" by redeploying an adoptive discourse of "progress." Propagated by a small, aspiring middle class, this register presented itself as apolitical and unthreatening, emphasizing "modern" entertainment, European manners, organized sports, and self-improvement through education, Christianity, and labor—the blossoming seedlings of the missionary enterprise.

My artist-interlocutors represent the various characteristics that defined colonial African urbanity by the 1920s. Kenneth Mattaka personified the first tier of Africans who seized the mission hymn, and Euro-American music and musical styles funneled through the mission, imported sheet music, the gramophone, and, later on, the wireless (radio), as technologies to articulate pertinent issues of changing African realities and desires. Mattaka and most early twentieth-century singers belonged to the first generation of mission graduates, whom the missionaries had trained to help purvey the gospel of "modernity" to their people. Through their influence, Abel Sinametsi Sithole was able to steep himself in the mission culture by association, thanks to his two trainee teacher-brothers at Mt. Selinda. And, like many other important figures in early urban Zimbabwean music, he also greatly benefited from Mattaka's "professorial" mentoring. Lina, Kenneth Mattaka's wife and the daughter of a respectable pastor, personifies the "modern girl" (Weinbaum, Thomas, et al. 2008) who strived to attain status and express herself through both education and the "protected" environment of "progressive" male guardians.

The flip side of this respectable womanhood was the complex domain of Dorothy Masuku, who, in typical "wicked" fashion (Hodgson and McCurdy 2001), both capitalized on and transgressed the Victorian and traditional African patriarchal gender conventions to boldly express herself beyond the mere adoptive repertoires of colonial modernity that few questioned. This was a collegial, intricately connected network of entertainers who, up to the 1960s, learned from, shared with, and mentored each other, making a distinct, although loosely bound, creative community. Their individual and collective endeavors to sing with and mentor each other, and to employ music to articulate communal issues, reshaped African life in the locations, the dung heaps of colonial urbanity. These are stories of African agency and struggles to reconstitute destabilized selves, families, and communities. The stories map a collective refusal to succumb to subaltern silence even though, too often, the quest for modernity meant "borrowing the colonizer's verb" for self-expression, learning the colonizer's prejudices and passions, and misunderstanding them as modernity.

The Mattakas: Patriarch and Matriarch of Zimbabwean Township Music

Kenneth Mattaka was born in colonial Malawi in 1915, "a short time from 1890,"[2] as he put it; he had some schooling at village schools and as a boarder at the Church of Scotland Mission before taking the *nthandizi* (labor migrancy) road to colonial Zimbabwe with his family in the early 1920s. Here, young Mattaka enrolled in the Jesuits' St. Paul's Musami School in Murehwa before transferring to the newly opened Domboshava Government School, one of Herbert Kegwin's experiments with the American Tuskegee Institute industrial schooling model for blacks. At Domboshava, Mattaka came under the influence of "progressive" African teachers, including degreed South Africans. Under their instruction, he honed his literary and musical skills, reading scripture and singing English and Zulu songs, mainly choral ballads, church hymns, and African American spirituals. He also learned leatherwork, printing, and agriculture, technical skills that would prove invaluable in the world of industrial labor and entertainment.

Mattaka sang in the school choir that featured prominently during prize giving and term closing days. With his friends S. Dzviti, Pamisa, Sibitso, and E. Kawadza, Mattaka formed the Domboshava Old Boys' Choir and performed in the evenings and on weekends at school before venturing into the community by the late 1920s (*African Parade,* May 1959). Like the Chishawasha Band members, these mission boys were hero-worshipped when they returned to their homes for holidays. They demonstrated their new singing skills to their parents, siblings, and communities "to show that we are coming from school; we are changing; we are being taught. We sang at weddings those songs that we were taught at school." They shined—*kushaina*—delivering English speeches full of "jawbreakers" to their illiterate yet highly appreciative audiences at communal assemblies. Speaking "complicated" English that no one understood added to one's "educated" mystique.

Being a student had become a status symbol. Nathan Shamuyarira (1965, 115) remembered two boys from Chihota who went to Waddilove Training Institution (Nenguwo) in 1933 and returned "totally different persons." They came back clean, well-fed, and respectful, and above all, able to utter a few words in English. This significantly reshaped villagers' perception of school:

> To be a "student". . . became a mark of honour for both the students and their parents, even if they were just studying Standard 2. We youngsters used to group round the students, just to hear them speak English. At concerts and weddings one of the most exciting items came when everyone stopped to listen to English being spoken by the students. No one in the audience understood a word, but they simply marveled at the intelligence and high learning of the young boys.

Singing "school songs" and speaking English soon became staple features of weddings and concerts. Stanlake Samkange (1975, 101) recalls how, at a wedding in Zvimba, the Master of Ceremonies, an evangelist named Moses Magedi, halted the choir and ushered the students onto the *dariro* to speak English:

> Hear me! Mothers and fathers, brothers and sisters all here assembled. You know we have young men here who have recently returned from big schools. Much money has been spent on these young men. Let's hear our money's worth. I call upon Gore from Waddilove, the school where they eat "Mghutshu," stumped mealies, to speak English to us.

Samkange's Waddilove competed with Mattaka's Domboshava, delivering impressive speeches by famous African Americans like Booker T. Washington—the ideological architect of their schooling model—to reflect their learning in the same ways that *makwaya* also vied with each other, shaming the stiff-tongued into hiding. In addition to demonstrating their erudition through speech and song, the students also performed "modernity" and sophistication by dressing flamboyantly and eating in an "English" style, sitting on the *dariro* to demonstrate their dexterous handling of forks and knives as they dined on chicken and rice.

However, these mission values and mechanics of constructing a colonial elite identity diverged little from the indigenous processes of making men, particularly the cultivation of oratorical skills and etiquette. This valued traditional quality separated *varume chaivo,* real men who resolved communal matters in the great circle of wisdom, the *dare,* from the goat-skinners on the margins of the proceedings. This was the indigenous professorial space that brought up Lawrence Vambe before he went to Chishawasha Mission. He recalled listening with deep admiration to elders marshaling issues with skill:

> [Participants] recounted the sequence of events and put their point of view without hesitation, as if they were reading from a book. They never stopped to search for words. . . . They modulated their voices from time to time, stressing certain words and phrases, so that the effect of their delivery was musical, like the declaiming of poetry. (L. Vambe 1976, 4)

A speaker who stammered frequently would be assumed to be lying, struggling to find words to patch up the lies. Similarly, students who stammered or failed to translate a sentence on the *dariro* indicted their school for "missing some words" (Shamuyarira 1965, 115). Put differently, the colonial school further nurtured, rather than killing, the griot (Zeleza 1997, 145). Africans sought to utilize their preexisting technologies to domesticate "education" into the communal agenda, reequipping youngsters to carry the intergenerational mandate to ensure societal self-reproduction. Writers like Norbert Mafumhe Mutasa, the author of the 1978 classic Shona novel *Mapatya,* honed their art by reading to the village, as his son recalled (*Herald,* April 30, 2014):

> A devoted follower of the Shona tradition, [Mutasa] would invite the whole village to a public reading of one of his books either before or after it is published. Mutasa would kill a beast and brew beer for his listeners who included the young and oldest villagers. Then he would read out (without a loud speaker) his book to the whole village and the audience response was always amazing as his audience would relate to some of the characters and events in the stories.

Thus, beyond breaking barriers of marginalization, the literati demystified and tamed colonialism and its school by both performing and transposing the white man's magic through their own technologies and spaces. Where the mission believed it was redeploying cadets to "civilize" villagers, the latter often welcomed back *hombarume,* great hunters who brought back bounty for the community to savor. This is how, musically, Mattaka and his friends came back to publicly unpack the mysteries of the white world, navigating them through song, dance, oration, and "etiquette."

Mattaka's colleagues graduated and joined the British South Africa Police (BSAP). The BSAP boasted numerous marching bands, an opportunity for the boys to employ their musical skills learned at the mission. Many musicians who later become prominent, including legendary saxophonists Isaac Musekiwa (who helped reshape rhumba in the Congo) and August Machona Musarurwa, honed their skills in a police band (Karanga, August 2012 interview). Mattaka took a post as a messenger and office orderly with the *Herald* in Salisbury and reconstituted his band with another coterie of mission boys: Masere, Ernest Gwaze, Samuel Gotora, and Elisha "Chabata" Kasim, all Waddilove graduates (*African Parade*, May 1959). They toured and performed at company Christmas parties.

Mattaka and his colleagues credited the mission for grooming them into Zimbabwe's (self-proclaimed) "first professional entertainers," a status they had attained by the 1930s. By then they had also taken a new name, Expensive Bantus, courtesy of their Mhangura fans, who deemed their act expensive. They justified their unprecedented one-shilling gate charge "because we had that badge that we were coming from college . . . doing tap-dancing and other clever gestures that matched the songs, and we were better organized than the many general acts." They became crowd favorites whenever they took the stage. They would change their name three more times, first to Bantu Actors, then briefly to Expensive Brothers, before maturing into the Mattaka Family. Each of these contours of identity fashioning signposted key moments not just in Mattaka's own musical career, but also in the broader transfigurations of African cultural self-consciousness. Calling themselves Bantu Actors reflected, in part, a more complex repertoire of stage works that included not only singing but also dramatic acts like devouring loaves of bread, sketches, and stunts like (supposedly) swallowing razor blades. This repertoire got them on television in the 1940s, when the Native Affairs Department (NAD) sponsored them to stage its "films for Africans." Their next name, Expensive Brothers, marked the consuming desire for modernity. Giving a sense of how this desire became a collective self-consciousness, Bill Saidi (pers. comm.) recalled how he and his colleagues "chided [the group] for the 'Bantus' and they changed their name to 'The Expensive Brothers,' even as they sang songs in Shona and English." Apartheid philosophy had soiled the term "Bantu," making it sound unsophisticated to these "modernizing" youngsters.

Mattaka met his future wife, Lina, the daughter of Northern Rhodesian-born hotel-worker-turned-pastor Reverend Marumo, on tour. This was in 1944 at Stanley Hall in Makokoba. Here, as at Mai Musodzi in Mbare, African men performed music, watched films, and played sports. Women came mainly to do domestic crafts—literally crafting their futures as respectable housewives to educated mission boys. Lina was born in 1922 and educated up to Standard 4 at the Wesleyan Nyamandlovu School and at the American Methodist Episcopal School in Makokoba. Failing to get into nursing, she took to domestic work in white people's homes to help raise her younger siblings after her mother's untimely death. She had grown up singing in church and had often accompanied her father on his evangelizing missions around Southern Africa. These trails opened her horizons for a future as a professional entertainer. Together with Rona Mthetwa and one Sipambaniso, she worked at Stanley Hall cooking for patrons and sewing curtains and costumes for Scout Rovers under the patronage of a white missionary woman, Mrs. Lewis.

Lina also befriended two other pioneering songsters at Stanley Hall: Christine Dube and Julia (Juliet) Mutyambizi Moyo, who toured between Makokoba and Mbare to perform. Julia performed with the Home Lilies and the Shanty City Kids in the 1940s, the latter group organized by her brothers, Henry Muchemwa Mutyambizi and Alexander Mutizwa Mutyambizi (Mutyambizi family, interview). Similarly, Lina and her colleagues formed their own women-only choral group, the Bantu Glee Singers, which groomed her into the "Soprano Queen" who stole the touring Mattaka's heart in 1944. Their marriage transformed the Mattakas into a family band, the Mattaka Family. But the Mattaka Family was much more than a band; it became the metaphor that shaped the country's music for the next generation.

A few years later, the Mattakas became a nuclear family band, adding their son Edison "Nunusi," a wizard on the piano, and their daughter Bertha. Moreover, the Mattakas practically became surrogate parents, providing shelter and guidance to virtually every aspiring young musician in the country who happened to pass through Salisbury, Gwelo, or Bulawayo, where the Mattakas successively settled. For most Africans at this time, colonial towns were only differently constituted *marimuka,* wildernesses, rife with not only promise but also risk, just as the traditional hunter's jungle harbored predators. Multitudes of young men and women who deserted the impoverished *maruzevha* ("native reserves") had to contend with the criminalization of urban Africans, the multitude of influx controls, and the new and strange scourge of homelessness. In this context, therefore, the Mattaka home retained the African clan model to provide mentorship and comfort to countless youngsters out to try their luck in urban show business. An adaptable concept of African family was thus instrumental in both physically and culturally relocating and reembedding a society fragmented and dislocated by colonial capitalist vice. Moses "Fancy" Mpahlo Mafusire and his colleagues in De Black Evening Follies and those in the Epworth Theatrical Strutters, and also Safirio Madzikatire, Susan Chenjerai, Dorothy Masuku, Kembo Ncube, Abel Sithole, and Thomas Mapfumo, were among the musicians the Mattakas sheltered or groomed at some point in their careers.

Like mother and son: Lina Mattaka and Abel Sinametsi Sithole, Bulawayo, 2012. All images in this chapter are courtesy of the author unless otherwise noted.

Herbert Simemeza, former member of the Epworth Theatrical Strutters, Harare, 2011.

Wining, dining, and jazzing at Jazz 105 in Harare in 2011. Friday Mbirimi (holding guitar), William Kashiri (far left), Lovejoy Mbirimi (second from left), and an unidentified friend.

Kembo Ncube belting out "Skokiaan" on harmonica, while Abel Sinametsi Sithole listens. Bulawayo, 2012.

The Mattakas held strictly to a repertoire of Christian hymns undergirded by Western folk music, but that did not restrict the artistic creativity of their brood of adopted children. For example, they groomed Mapfumo and his Black Dots, young men who, they told me, "were so involved with these traditional things" during the fledgling stages of a resurgent Zimbabwean indigenous musical consciousness. Mattaka recalled that Mapfumo and his friends

> came to demonstrate their acts, dancing *jerusarema,* etc., with Thomas asking for ideas about organizing things as a leader. He came to stay with us and we toured the Salisbury-area farms with him, so that he could get ideas about how to organize. And we performed with him at the Art Gallery [in Salisbury] when it had just opened, about 1951. We taught him how to approach people, etc., and when he was satisfied, he left and organized a new group for himself.

This is how, to quote Martin Stokes (1994, 3), "the musical event . . . evokes and organizes collective memories and present experiences of place with an intensity, power and simplicity unmatched by any other social activity." The Mattaka Family became a metaphor for reconstitutive African "extended" families, communities, and platforms that enabled youngsters to build careers and craft viable lifestyles out of a disruptive colonial modernity. And their home was a veritable refuge: "There was no time that anybody came to Harare and did not pass through our house. We looked after many of the groups. Those who went to form their own groups came back whenever they faced any problems, and rejoined us," reminisced Lina. The band became a refuge in two senses: those who stumbled in their solo careers rejoined the Mattaka band, and those needing shelter were housed and tutored under the Mattaka roof.

Dorothy Masuku, winner of the Miss Mzilikazi Beauty Pageant, Bulawayo, 1953. Courtesy of *Parade Magazine.*

Abel Sithole, of the Bulawayo Golden Rhythm Crooners, also belonged to this brood. Sithole was born in 1934, and his family could not afford to send him to school like his brothers; he had to sell newspapers to help his mother, a domestic servant, feed the family. However, he looked up to his two brothers at Mt. Selinda: "When they came home on holidays, they had us sing at home as a family as they did at school. We sang the songs they had learned at school." In this way, Africans like Mattaka and Sithole's brothers who had been socialized in the mission school environment became lay educators in their communities. This point helps explain the cultural context of education in early colonial Zimbabwe. After their initial resistance, Africans had by the 1930s begun to appreciate that, despite its design to subordinate them, colonial education could be repurposed into a useful compass for navigating the new order. Following the mission template, they used music to propagate the gospel of education. They turned song into a vector of much more than it was designed to carry, as Yvonne Vera would say.

Classroom without Walls: Staging the Gospel of Education

The sophistication that students weaved around *makonzati, michato,* and oratorical erudition turned the *dariro* into a classroom without walls. There, these mission-educated artists tutored each other and conspicuously demonstrated their literacy to admiring audiences. The *dariro* allowed the musicians and their audiences to collectively perform their aspirations and craft their imagined identities, as performers made eloquent speeches and marshaled musical scores to the admiration of celebrating crowds. The *dariro* enabled Mattaka to perform a "civilized" African identity. He articulated his philosophy of education and performance to me: "When I took that book and read and practiced it, whites saw us as capable. You would see them clapping their hands . . . admiring that." Mattaka fully appreciated the significance of "singing to the white man" as a way of gaining his approval in a society circumscribed by racial legislation and discriminatory custom. His inspiration was South Africa's Griffiths Matsiela, whose Darktown Strutters were hailed as "the only Bantu [group that] filled the Durban and Maritzburg town halls with an appreciative audience of Europeans." Significantly, Matsiela abandoned teaching to become a full-time musician (Ballantine 1991, 131).

The Darktown Strutters stirred imaginations when they toured colonial Zimbabwe in 1936. The *Bantu Mirror* (March 14, 1936) enthused,

> Bulawayo people, viz., Europeans, Natives and Asiatics, have been extremely fortunate of late in having had a unique visit from a troupe of almost peerless singing [*sic*] and actors from Johannesburg under the celebrated elocutionist Mr. G. Matsiela. They performed remarkably well at several platforms in Bulawayo. . . . The Bulawayo Community has, hitherto, seen nothing so pleasant and so entertaining as they saw being performed by these "strutters." So . . . would it be wrong to advise some of the active members of the teaching profession at Bulawayo who were privileged to see them perform, to take a cue from them and train a few boys to sing and act in the same fashion? Is such a beautiful thing not worth attempting "Matitja-ako-Bulawayo" ["boys of Bulawayo"]?

Bradford Mnyanda, a Bulawayo socialite working for the NAD, facilitated the Strutters' tour, for which he duly earned praise from the *Mirror,* the department's mouthpiece. The group's influence was contagious. According to Bill Saidi (pers. comm.), a contemporary journalist and musician, Kenneth Mattaka's group took the name Bantu Actors to reflect the new emphasis on stage gestures, or "styles," especially after the tour by the Darktown Strutters, whose tap-dancing moves "Mattaka did not hesitate to mimic." South Africa, a conduit to the larger, pan-African Black Atlantic, had become a rich fountain of innovation, and performers paid homage to it. Saidi told me,

> The most well known singing group of our time was the Mills Brothers, an African American quartet composed of brothers, although after one of them died, the father took his place. This group made hundreds of records, including "Paper Doll," "Across the Alley from the Alamo," and "You'll Never Miss the Water." De Black Evening Follies sang these songs without changing anything—the language or the notes. Before that, the Bantu Actors had done the same. But the influence of South Africa's Manhattan Brothers was the most dominant on us all. They sang what they called "jive," which we copied.

Zimbabwean bands closely followed and copied the American music scene, and, like their more immediate South African models and co-innovators, chose names that referenced the abstract global modernity anchored in the Black Atlantic imagination. This was the world of the Brown Darkies, the Epworth Theatrical Strutters, the Dark City Sisters, the Gay Gaieties, the Capital City Dixies, and the Modern Brothers.

Similarly, adopting the "styles" and songs popularized by Mattaka's group, Saidi teamed up with his cousins, Faith and Reuben Dauti, and their uncle, Chase Mhango. Another uncle, Canisius Mhango, dubbed them the Milton Brothers, "almost a copycat of the Mills Brothers" (despite the presence of Faith, a woman). The shared palpable fascination with Black Atlantic sensibilities, which was flaunted in vernacularized names, languages, performative forms, and clothing fashions, constituted a solidarity that Tsitsi Jaji (2014) conceptualized as a particular African stereomodernity. The groups saw indigenous languages as incapable of capturing this *passion moderniste.* "We did not specialize in songs in Shona and Ndebele, at least initially. Only later did we do songs in the mother tongues," explained Saidi. For many, "later" did not arrive until the nationalist deployment of indigenous cultures as weapons in the escalating liberation struggle of the 1960s–70s.

Many African "children of the missions" deeply criticized the "civilizing mission." To Mattaka, however, colonialism was an unmixed blessing, because at its advent, Africans were still "primitive, wearing *nhembe* [animal skins], while others did not even bathe." This affirmative view of colonial modernity and discourse shaped his creative philosophy. Mattaka was a self-professed mission deacon who not only witnessed but also lived out "the evolutionary trajectory from the primitive to the modern, the oral to the written, the traditional to the progressive" (Peterson 2000, 11). The intermediary position mandated people like him to disseminate a broadly conceived education to their less fortunate fellows in order to redeem them from the "thralldom of darkness and barbarism." A faithful student, he maintained that "it was education that opened people to change," and that "it was in the schools that we saw vast differences between modern life and our own ways." His efforts to bring the school to the people were complemented by liberal-minded whites, missionaries, and self-proclaimed philanthropists. Mattaka pointed out, "Most of the whites we knew were very happy to see Africans developing. They gave us good support." One of these was a Harare Social Welfare Officer, H. C. Finkle, who was also the Secretary for Native Education, a key architect of the policy that sought to educate Africans to be servants to whites (Finkle 1962, 9; Bhebe 2004, 10–11). Concerned not with the policy's pitfalls but with the benefits they saw accruing to those who consorted with its officials, Mattaka and his colleagues prized such well-placed interlocutors for their ability to offer small concessions in a racialist bureaucracy.

Mission literati like Mattaka took the hybridized mission and the African *dariro* model of interactive performance and reproduced it on the urban music stage. As Mattaka put it, "We came with that knowledge to also teach others."

> Some uneducated youngsters . . . joined us in Harare and stayed with us. . . . Over time, no one could point out that they had not been to school. We combined everything in music. When we instructed them in reading music, the brain followed the musical progression and became alert and intelligent. Music made them appreciate education. And they could converse with educated people. While we relaxed, we talked about education—and read stories from all sorts of books. . . . They learned that way.

The musicians were able to construct orality and literature as complementary expressive forms, one helping to foster the other in a mutual process of identity fashioning. These collegial musical elaborations and literary adumbrations of new selves, both on a public *dariro* and in a welcoming home, gave form and soul to the African community that these performers desired, enabling them to not merely imagine but actually experience it.

Technically savvy, Mattaka drew on his education and printing experience to champion literacy amongst his colleagues. The band bought a typewriter and duplicator, which enabled them to type their songs and reproduce posters, pamphlets, and flyers to promote their performances, which had grown beyond just singing. One 1970s poster in Mattaka's memorabilia chest advertised:

> Variety Show: by "Professor" K. M. Mattaka, a professional entertainer and film actor. A member of the International Brotherhood of Magicians; assisted

> by his wife, a dynamic old singer, film/stage actress. Programme: tap-dancing, singing and stage comedy, educational and historical—by the backbone of the once famous Harare Bantu Actors; will swallow razors.

In his twilight, the patriarch of Zimbabwean township music had accepted the accolade of "professor" from his fans and legion of apprentices, who honored him for "giving them brighter scopes . . . not only through singing, but also through typing and printing." Domboshava's Tuskegee doctrine of technical work served Mattaka well.

Although she largely resided in her husband's professorial shadow, Lina, like a true matriarch, would help anybody who came looking for assistance in her husband's absence, even leading their coterie of apprentices on tours around the country on her own. Over the years, together with groups like De Black Evening Follies, the Mattaka Family dominated the entertainment charts, "appearing on TV as the country's best entertainers, especially at Christmas," as the NAD reported in its administrative annual in 1952:

> The two groups most worthy of mention are De Black Evening Follies and the Bantu Actors [the Mattaka Family]. During the year, both have given many excellent performances. As a result of arrangements made by Miss. B. Tredgold, of St. Michael's Mission, Runyararo, these parties combined to give performances for European audiences in the Cathedral Hall, in aid of the Runyararo Nursery School. The Black Evening Follies also took part in a film produced by Films of Africa Ltd, Gatooma. The Bantu Actors, under contract with Lever Brothers for 14 weeks, toured Southern and Northern Rhodesia. Although this was an advertising campaign from which Lever Brothers will undoubtedly derive some material benefit, the actual shows, consisting of English and African songs, a Quiz and film show—were enjoyed immensely by all who saw them. 14 shows were given in Salisbury, 10 in the Recreational Hall.[3]

The use of song to promote literacy was an unsurprising strategy; teachers were at the forefront of the African musical self-fashioning. They not only conducted choirs at schools; many of them also formed or worked with popular bands in their communities. Examples include a trio of legendary footballers at the Chitsere School (Harare), John Madzima, Jonathan Chieza, and Samuel Mhlanga, "perhaps the best pianist of the time," who, as one of the many "Mattaka children," taught young Edison Mattaka to master the instrument at the tender age of six. The alphabetically named A. B. C. Rusike, a journalist and a teacher at Bulawayo's Mzilikazi School, and Ticha Zikhali, of St. Columbus School, formed and led the Boogie Woogie Songsters and the Brown Darkies, respectively. Teachers also frequently attached themselves and their students to the Mattaka Family for tours throughout the country and the region.

Successively styling themselves the Shelton Brothers, the Crazy Kids, and the Broadway Quartet, Friday Mbirimi and his colleagues (Simangaliso Tutani,

William Chigoma, and others) grew up listening to and imitating groups like the Waverly Brothers at Chitsere School and his father's and uncle's De Black Evening Follies from the 1950s. Although his father was a policeman, Friday followed his uncle Jonah Mbirimi into teaching, becoming the founding headmaster of Epworth Mission in the 1970s (Mbirimi, interview). This tradition of combined musicianship and teaching was hailed in songs like "Kudzidza Kwakanaka" (Education is good), a 1950s composition by the Epworth Theatrical Strutters, another group that boasted teachers in its membership. Education was good because, in a line that Mavis Moyo, a former Mzingwane student and retired radio announcer, told me she remembered singing, "It brought us from darkness into the light." My interviewees repeatedly told me that every school had a teacher or two who taught or performed music in those years. Many of these teachers, like their students, sang with the luminous Mattaka Family at some point, and Mattaka and his colleagues "taught them music, not only because it helped them in their teaching, but when they could do those songs, they looked brighter in the classroom."

Touring South African and U.S. artists complemented this moral and financial investment in African education. Thus, the South African Manhattan Brothers and Louis Armstrong staged shows in 1953 and 1960, respectively, donating proceeds to the Nyatsime College Fund, an African initiative that built the boarding school in Chitungwiza (Sithole, interview). These efforts had the full support of African leaders such as Jasper Savanhu, who escorted the Manhattan Brothers on their countrywide tour. Savanhu was one of the few African members of the Federal Parliament in the 1950s. His fellow parliamentarian, Schotting Chingate, led the Gamma Sigma Club, which promoted musicians and hosted Christmas parties for "educated" Africans. Victoria, Schotting's wife, was a nurse and singer with the nurses' group, the Gay Gaieties, which was co-led by Grace Mandishona (Mandishona, interview). Schotting invited his middle-class colleagues to watch performances by his wife's group. The respectable social standing of the nurse-musicians and their promotion by Victoria's MP husband helped dispel the "cheap lady" stigma that haunted most female musicians. As Grace's brother, Gibson, averred, it was this social power that enabled his sister's group to challenge the then male-dominated music circles.

Driven by the reigning spirit of community development, Harare's City Quads built a nursery school in the 1950s, putting the idea of self-help into practice in their own communities (Jenje-Makwenda 2004, 51). Similarly, *Parade* (November 1953) reported of De Black Evening Follies,

> In 1952, an invitation came to them from certain Europeans to stage a show in aid of St. Nicholas African Nursery School, under the Anglican Church in Harare. The entertainment was a joint effort of the Follies, the King Cole Brothers and the Modern African Stars, all of Salisbury. Since then they have

> given entertainments in aid of charitable institutions and sporting and other organizations throughout the Colony. Nothing succeeds success. The Follies also promoted beauty contests at the main centres of the country at which youth and beauty of Mashonaland demonstrated their charms. . . . For the first time beauty contests were introduced in Southern Rhodesia and since then several have been sponsored by the same company in Salisbury, Gwelo, Bulawayo and Umtali.

Through music, Africans built proud, functional communities.

Education had come to represent one of the very few avenues of possible escape from the enclosures of colonialism. Consequently, in their fight for schools, Africans demanded curricula that emphasized academic subjects, especially English (Summers 1997). Through education, the lucky few escaped the drudgery of physical labor to become teachers, interpreters, nurses, and other professionals. (Mattaka was first a messenger at the *Herald* and then a salesman with various manufacturing companies.) They constituted a small but influential class of colonial subjects with strong desires for upward mobility. Education also equipped some of them to engage colonial certitudes as critical partners and to fashion their own destinies within their otherwise circumscribed environments. The trap was that colonial education and culture constituted key levers of a Eurocentric episteme, which, because of their middling roles and aspirations, many internalized or failed to interrogate. What seemed important to Mattaka, for instance, was the ability to interpret and represent the new world through music and the ability to converse in English; by doing these, he performed both progress and symbolic claims on an exclusionary modernity. This, wrote Bill Saidi (*African Parade,* May 1959), was why Mattaka's songs centered largely on education, morals, and tradition.

The flag-bearer of his generation, Mattaka did not engage colonial injustice. It is tempting to approach Mattaka's music as a "public transcript" Scott (1990), a typical subordinate's singing to power in the latter's own register of domination or in (deceptively) deferential tones, hoping to gain whatever limited benefits he could while masking a "hidden transcript"—more critical, more subversive, or less deferential perspectives on power. However, the politics of survival meant that most immigrants conceptualized colonialism differently than did its primary targets: the indigenes.

The hours I spent listening to Mattaka's ideas as expressed in songs, interviews, and private conversations failed to hint at that possible hidden transcript. What the majority of Africans called colonialism Mattaka defended as development, because "whites came not to take, but to develop." To proud and rather uncharitable locals, it was a dirty Malawian thing to trudge along the *nthandizi* railway line for months to work for the settlers, and to stand on their side in labor and political struggles, as most— but certainly not all—labor migrants did (L.

Vambe 1976). In songs and also in private conversation many years later, Mattaka nostalgically upheld colonialism as a "civilizing mission" and, borrowing colonial terminology, denounced the liberation struggle as hooliganism.

The same ironies marked Mattaka's idea of tradition, in Saidi's schematization of his music. The tradition that Mattaka sang was not African, but rather European, consisting of quaint folk songs and madrigals. These the Mattaka Family imported and restaged: "We took any song that when we rendered it in our own voices, people would admire us, that as people who were coming from schools, we were being taught: songs like 'Good Morning, My Lady . . . come over the brook, come kiss me.'" He explained, "These were songs sung at picnics when one is admiring the beauty of the world, watching fluttering and singing birds; and also *ngoma dzanaCaluza*" (discussed below). Mattaka's desire to be modern pushed his imagination to interiorize an abstract, mythologized Renaissance European world of picnics and musical cheer, an image of a western culture Rhodesians never tired of referencing. They faithfully performed these songs *a cappella* or accompanied them on mouth organs, pianos, concertinas, and other "mission" instruments.

Looking south across the Limpopo, Mattaka and his colleagues tapped into the tradition of *ngoma dzanaCaluza,* songs by late nineteenth- and twentieth-century singers whom Loren Kruger (1994) designated "new Africans": R. V. Selope, Madie Hall Xuma and her husband, Dr. A. B. Xuma (who was president of the African National Congress in the 1940s), the brothers Herbert and Rolfes Dhlomo, and Reuben T. Caluza, whom David Coplan (1985, 70) called the most important composer of Zulu choral music. These were educated men and women who, following the shared Black Atlantic model, vigorously pursued the cultural route to a Europeanized "civilization." This pursuit meant appropriating and parading European music as cultural capital for self-redemption in the eyes of European audiences. These influential political and cultural leaders composed songs clamoring for schools so that they could reach the same levels of development as their African American brothers and sisters—Paul Robeson, Florence Mills, Turner Layton, James P. Johnstone, and other "descendants of a race that has been under worse oppression" but still rose to become models of what Black people could achieve, given the chance (Ballantine 1991, 131). The 1890 tour of South Africa by Orpheus McAdoo's Virginia Jubilee Singers—an acclaimed epitome of Black self-redemption—bolstered this African American iconography (Erlmann 1994, 165).

Education, self-help, and race consciousness were conceptualized musically and staged publicly. Mattaka and his colleagues shared and reproduced the "new African" discography, which decried black people's "life in the dark"—*kurarama murima*—and exalted the redemptive power of education to bring them *chiedza,* light. Zimbabweans knew that opportunities for education were relatively better in Joni (Johannesburg). Thus, at twenty-five, the would-be nationalist leader Joshua Nkomo (1984, 29) gave up his unsatisfying job driving a truck and embarked on what he called a journey "to see the world" in 1942: "I wanted to qualify as a carpentry instructor . . . and there was no imaginable way for a Southern Rhodesian African to get such a qualification in his own country. . . . I set my heart on going to Adams College in South Africa." His compatriots, Simon Muzenda, Robert Mugabe, and others, would follow suit from the late 1940s. Thus, the discourse of education for social mobility that musicians thematized was a common dream. However, because of his unquestioning faith in the "civilizing mission," Mattaka steered clear of Caluza's politically engaged works.

Most of the Zimbabwe township musicians limited their careers to performing covers of European and American songs. A corrupt and dishonest recording industry conspired with this fascination with the incoming to hamper the development of independent recording careers. Mattaka left hardly any recorded works. By the 1960s, argues Turino (2000, 129), musicians were recording their works to build public profiles and to legitimize themselves in both their own eyes and those of their followers. This capitalist truism did not inform Mattaka's thinking; he did not want industry to commercialize his music. His was a well-calculated strategic decision premised on a different mindset that would resonate with today's generation of piracy-buffeted artists:

> When we started performing, we gave ourselves a rule that "We are live performers. Therefore, if we have our songs recorded and bought on the street, they will become common and familiar and no one will come to our shows." So we said, "No one will have our songs in their house; they must come to see us on stage." For as long as we lived, we didn't want to be dispensable. People must be keen to see us, rather than say, "Ah, I have their songs in my house; I bought their songs." That is why, against advice to the contrary, we chose to be permanent live entertainers.

The highly exploitative record companies—which gave no contracts to artists—did not help matters, particularly in Africa. South Africa's Miriam Makeba (2004, 42) captured this: "Even when our records were selling, we did not know much. We were just happy to be recording. . . . We never even knew what happened to our recordings or where they would end up after we left the studio." The result was many people shared the fate of Makeba's compatriot Solomon Linda, who, despite having composed the 1939 hit "Mbube" that earned millions for American recording companies, "walk[ed] next to his shoes"; he was so impoverished that his shoes literally fell off his feet. The Gallo, Troubadour, and His Master's Voice recording companies partitioned the regional market.

For Mattaka and his friends, live shows widened their appeal beyond their own creative limits. Entertainment meant staying at the frontline of the market to interpret imported material to fans as soon as it became available. He explained,

"Whenever we heard a beautiful song, we would sing it, following the original as much as possible after buying the record and a copy of the sheet music—sometimes ordering it from London. . . . [We would] fit in the gestures so that people would see that we are expressing the mood of the song: tap-dancing, moving up and down, using our hands, body postures, and facial expressions."

I have argued that the claims to "civilization" that structured Africans' *chimanjemanje* sensibilities often stirred political uneasiness and threatened to erode the shores of "native policy," which was designed to concede rights only very gradually and piecemeal. Artists deployed mimicry as an a(nta)gonistic performative play with power and colonial identities, and it was on the *dariro* that Africans most loudly rejected their construction as backward "tribes" by colonial social engineers. This power of play threatened settler privilege. With the whole mainstream African urban culture constructed around this assimilationist play with colonial culture, the state secretly worried that the masquerade might easily become reality. In 1955, the Ministry of Internal Affairs called a policy meeting and expressed concern that

> in this country we have inevitably brought with us the musical traditions and tastes of Western Europe and Western civilization, of which the musician has always been a recognized and essential element of society. In Rhodesia we have as it were started at the wrong end. The gramophone and later the radio were in existence before it was possible to give thought to the claims of the musician, but there is every reason to fear that the system of importing and relaying recorded music, and the paradox of music without the musician, will be perpetuated. It appears to us that so long as our Radio authority continues the policy of purchasing the recorded products of musicians living elsewhere, so long will the musical life of the community be retarded and possibly stifled.[4]

The art of mimicry enabled popular participation in the performance of "modernity," and for many that meant contesting colonial exclosure.

Education, even superficially conceived of as the ability to speak English, was one element in the fashioning of *chimanjemanje.* A seductive local engagement with vampire capitalism, *chimanjemanje* flaunted assimilationist, materially sophisticated lifestyles and mass consumption that tested colonial boundaries. Timothy Burke's (1996) masterful narrative of the penetration of industrial commodities into Zimbabwe teases out a reading of African stories beyond capital, that is, a Europe (and America) in Africa. This is because commodification did not remain a prowling capitalist behemoth that came from elsewhere; locals wrestled to domesticate, interpret, mediate, and reorder it into their own project of self-fashioning. This story can be enriched by unraveling how Africans embedded commodification into their own registers of song and dance, the sideways gaze on the street corner, the significant sweeping gait of the "revo" bell-bottom, the top hat, and the women's bleached-out "Fanta faces" and "Coke legs" of Mbare,

Makokoba, Alexandra, and Sophiatown. African artists' interventionist, adoptive, and repurposive agency crafted this *chimanjemanje* culture that swept early twentieth-century Southern Africa. It was the artists who modeled, performed, and vocalized what it meant to consume with swagger, *kushaina*. They brought the gospel of industrial "civilization," which sought to create "rational" African being, into the locations, compounds, and villages—and they so retextured it that even their benefactors, the missionaries, became exasperated and decried all this "native" vanity.

"Christian" Progress Fighting Ignorance: Artist-Agents of Commerce

Industrial commodities constituted tangible symbols of the *chimanjemanje* long imagined in song. As a philosophy, "civilizing commerce" was foundational in missionary evangelization, as David Livingstone (1857, 28) proclaimed:

> Sending the Gospel to the heathen must . . . include much more than is implied in the usual picture of a missionary, namely, a man going about with a Bible under his arm. The promotion of commerce ought to be specially attended to, as this, more speedily than anything else, demolishes that sense of isolation which heathenism engenders, and makes the tribes feel themselves mutually dependent on, and mutually beneficial to, each other. . . . Those laws which still prevent free commercial intercourse among the civilized nations seem to be nothing else but the remains of our own heathenism. . . . Neither civilization nor Christianity can be promoted alone. In fact, they are inseparable.

Livingstone's "native" deacons carried on this gospel, diagnostically connecting Africa's "condition" to "ignorance" and prescribing Christian enlightenment and commerce as liberation. The problem was epistemic, pitting an Africa of darkness against a Europe that bore light. This is why, in his contrapuntal song "Maroro," Mattaka mocked belief in the power of charms as retrogressive:

Ndakaenda kuMaroro	I went to Maroro
Kunotora muti	To get a charm
Muti wemaraki	A lucky charm
Unopa urombe	That causes bad luck
Zango remuchiuno	A charm around the waist
Rimwe zango remuruoko.	Another charm around the arm.

Maroro is the mythical lode of charms in popular Zimbabwean lore, "somewhere" in Chipinge. Mattaka sang this whenever missionaries invited him to minister to parishioners through song, usually coupling it with another that exalted the power of Jesus' name.

Echoing the missionary crusade against "witch doctors," Mattaka denounced Africans' belief in the power of charms, urging them to turn to Christ. He saw this as the only way to "save many people [who] were being conned by bogus healers in the towns":

Ririko zita raTenzi	There is the Lord's name
Rakanaka kwazvo	Which is a good name
Rinonyaradza maKristu	Which comforts Christians
Rinodzinga kutya.	It banishes all fear.

These songs emphasize the power of Jesus' name in defeating the fears and superstitions that Christianity posited as the defining tenets of African cosmology, and which it held brought Africans poverty and misfortune, *urombe.* Thus represented, the Christian faith entailed education, freedom from "superstition," and, by extension, increased opportunities for material well-being. Africans, the logic went, could find not only spiritual but also economic salvation through Christian morality, not by adorning themselves with "heathen" charms.

In the era of limited recording and broadcasting, this music had to reach audiences live. Thus, the Mattaka Family lived on a tight schedule touring farms, mines, and small towns to sing to workers. Companies like the cotton ginners David Whitehead, and others like Linton Tobacco, Lever Brothers, and his former employer the *Herald,* invited them to perform at Christmas parties and similar special occasions. Richard Costain, a Kariba Dam contractor, brought them to perform for the thousands of laborers at the dam site. Daily, farmers and miners in the precincts of Salisbury hauled them in open lorries to perform for £5 10d per show. For a fee that small, Mattaka often trimmed his troupe to his wife and children only. Contracts from community halls, farms, and mines, rather than record labels, built his fame.

So central was live entertainment in this period that large firms began to hire entertainers on a full-time basis. Thus, Kembo Ncube, a comedian and musician, became a *mushambadzi,* an itinerant entertainer doing road shows for various companies. He reminisced in an interview about how

> cars used to come here, shop owners coming to pick me up to promote their merchandise or to open new outlets. I worked for BAT for nineteen years, and opened TM shops, Lever Brothers, doing pick-a-box, etc. They knew I was a sharp comedian. We traveled everywhere: Nyanga, Bindura, Serowe, Gaborone, Francistown, etc.

Born in 1922 in Chirumhanzu, Ncube traveled across the Southern African musical network, working as a waiter at Joburg's Sea Point Hotel and as a musician and comedian with groups like the Manhattan Brothers at the Bantu Social Centre before the 1940s. Frustrated by South Africa's pass laws, he returned home not only to work at the frontline of pioneer commercial capital but also to map the wider recreational scene revolving around music, boxing, and soccer, developing the sort of social capital that business found useful.

Ncube staked his claim to the status of "indigenous intellectual" with songs like "Bulawayo Guy." He sang, "I am a Bulawayo guy / Who sings to entertain people / So that Bulawayo may have *morari.*"[5] The grimness of *rukesheni* (*elokishini* in Ndebele), the "native location," increased the need for entertainment or, as Ncube implied, the need to raise people's morale and lift them from the pervasive sense of hopelessness. Africans' tenacity and innovativeness led them to take initiative in building their own communities, as *Parade* reported in November 1953 of De Black Evening Follies: "It is ten years since a small band of young people formed a troupe of artistes, their object being to bring a ray of happiness and cheer into the often dull lives of our people as well as boost African music in the colony." Musicians were key agents of transformation and barometers of social health, agents that commercial interests exploited.

The state-owned Dairy Marketing Board (DMB) commissioned Masuku, whom they praised as "Africa's leading recording star," and the Follies to market their products. One of their singles was the famous "milk song" that reminded audiences that "after you have been 'jiving' and 'rocking and rolling' you need refreshment" from the DMB's flavored fresh milk. Then listeners were urged to "take six empty milk bottles to any DMB depot in the Townships" to redeem them for free records (*African Parade,* August 1959). In its great march, capital tied the enjoyment of music to the consumption of industrial products, making the marketing of the two different commodities mutually reinforcing. In the same way, the Cold Storage Commission (CSC) hired August Machona Musarurwa as a resident entertainer in its workers' compound in Bulawayo, where he formed the Cold Storage Band together with the Mutyambizi brothers in the 1940s (Mutyambizi family, interview).

More intriguingly, the figure of Musarurwa partaking of distilled alcohol graced late 1950s popular media, representing statutory concession that "certified" Africans—"honorary whites"—might now enjoy "European" liquor. Musarurwa personified African struggles against the criminalization of alcohol. He had flagrantly flouted the laws and also composed the popular song "Skokiaan," which articulated Africans' defiant production and consumption of criminalized home brews. Together with Dorothy Masuku, young female entertainers like Faith Dauti, Mattaka's daughter Bertha, and Miriam Mlambo, who had been a nurse before becoming a radio presenter, personified the femininity of commodification. Their voices on the radio and their images in popular magazines and newspapers became associated with such "beauty" products as Bu-Tone and Ambi, skin bleachers that blessed "modern" *elokishini* women with "Fanta faces" and "Coke legs."

These commercial roles allowed the artists to pitch themselves simultaneously as fashionable beauties and as entertainers while also popularizing industrial consumption and imported aesthetics, the *chimanjemanje* ideals they shared with their fans. These were *vashambadzi,* agents and models who drove, animated, and infused meaning into things from the stores, *zvekumagirosa.* So invested were they in these roles that Musarurwa opened his own trading store in his rural township in Zvimba, leading the township itself to be named after him: KwaGosi, "August's" (Musarurwa, interview). These artists therefore personified not only "Lifebuoy men and Lux women," to use Timothy Burke's phrase, but also the defiant "ladies and gents" who fashioned subversive identities and economies on the tide of capitalist consumptionism and in the face of a fretful, gatekeeping settler society and an alienating colonial political economy. Commercial sales jobs filled their pockets in ways musical shows alone would never do. Above their regular weekly wage, many also earned additional incomes entertaining fellow workers in the compounds, "bush allowances" when they toured to promote merchandise, and advertising royalties. Pauline Banda recalled that they never had to buy soap, toothpaste, cooking oil, and similar groceries because her father, Kembo Ncube, brought home all the samples he took on his advertising road shows. Indeed, these stars' creativity ameliorated their ironic "messengers-and-nannies-by-the-day-and-celebrities-by-night" tag (*Port Elizabeth Herald,* February 22, 2006).

This was the context in which Mattaka returned to the familiar world of industrial employment. In 1966, Gweru's Bata Shoe Company advertised a sales job for someone with a musical background. Armed with a salesmanship certificate and decades of musicianship, Mattaka grabbed the opportunity and left Salisbury. At Bata—the flagship of Gweru's industry—Mattaka utilized his popular image as an entertainer to market shoes all over the country, retracing his old itineraries but this time hoisted by the gospel of healthy feet, hygiene, and good animal husbandry—a corporate agenda carefully grafted onto his iconic status in popular culture. Thus, in the late 1960s and early '70s, Mattaka and his band visited schools and villages as Bata sales promoters and industrial agents, "lecturing and showing people what we could compose" and what Bata could make. They especially targeted agricultural shows and field days, demonstrating the various processes involved in shoemaking, from tanning the hides to designing the shoes. The idea was "to show them that shoes come from cowhides . . . [and] to make them appreciate the importance of looking after their cattle properly, with healthy skins."

They gave lectures at schools, singing, doing conjuring and other magic tricks, and "twisting minds" through stunts that included swallowing razor blades. Industry presented Mattaka as a star-studded performer, as another poster in his tin trunk proclaimed in 1971:

> Magic, magic, magic, by Mattaka, the oldest entertainer, from 1936–71, non-stop. See him live in the Bata Shoes for Healthy Feet. Stage entertainer, actor, magician, tap-dancer and TV star!

To initiate students into shoe culture and bolster his message, Mattaka conducted quiz shows awarding shoes as prizes. In this way, the companies harnessed entertainers as cultural agents, using their music, drama, and other localized performance idioms to reach into the communities in a somewhat subtle but effective manner that captured wide audiences and kept them entertained while patiently nurturing them into dependable markets. This was a careful approach that required an understanding of these potential markets before they could be ideologically remolded. Socialized through missionary education to admire Europe (as per Livingstone's intent), Africans like Mattaka became vital purveyors of capitalist modernization to the villages, to people this gospel constructed as primitive and unwashed (Burke 1996, 54). As *Parade* affirmed (June 1954), the industrial products constituted tangible symbols of cleanliness and were "amenities of civilization." To these apostles of capitalism, the absence of such products in the targeted communities confirmed that African lifestyles were undesirable and needed to be transformed.

Mattaka was a steadfast believer. He looked back to his boyhood and insisted,

> I will tell you something: those whites came with high western standards, when we still wore *nhembe* and others didn't even bathe. . . . And there were big shops, some which served whites only. . . . Decent; you see? Some people were reckless . . . in those days. At Domboshawa there, some people who later became MPs, they were walking naked, wearing tattered shorts. Some had only one item of clothing, or two, relying on the uniform. And even that uniform, for some, was filthy.

To his wife, African privation meant only material difference, not indignity. Colonialism inscribed and read evil into that difference. Three decades later, Mattaka the salesman worked religiously to stem this "evil": "I used to move around . . . working for Bata; school children wore no shoes. We gave them free pairs, those who got quizzes correct, and we taught them the importance of shoes, which they learned, gradually." The commodification crusades gestured at the possibility of capitalist self-fulfillment while symbolically deferring its attainment by anchoring the rewards of insertion into the capitalist culture on a narrow conception of education. The school and church were key portals for the penetration of this capitalist culture and the production and disciplining of the consuming, confessing African body.

In *Provincializing Europe* (2000), Dipesh Chakrabarty argues that the histories of popular music and commercial capital are mutually reinforcing, not least for their disrespect for territorial boundedness. Historically, African being tended to define itself relationally through mobility, a fact that bred the cultural commonalities that bind Southern Africa today. The colonial state pitched its sovereignty within the Berlin regime of boundaries, mediating (simultaneously curtailing and accentuating) these mobilities. The regional matrices of migrant labor and uneven development impelled continued cross-cultural pollination as individuals traversed the region's new circuits of work and pleasure. By the 1930s, pan-regional political organizing helped to tighten this conversation into trans-territorial solidarities. This meant that *chimanjemanje* identities and repertoires tied together Mbare, Makokoba, Alexandra, and Sophiatown.

Transterritorial Circuits

Perhaps more important than the mission songs that Sithole learned from his mission "scholar" brothers in the 1940s were the gramophone and records they also brought home (Sithole, interview). Armed with a guitar and a suitcase of these imported records, any aspiring young musician felt surefooted on the musical odyssey. Thomas Mapfumo and his younger brothers William and Lancelot dramatically illustrated the value of this equipment by recounting to me the tragedy that befell them when their expensive yellow suitcase filled with records fell off the roof of a hitchhiked car on the road to Mutanga Nightclub in Musana in the 1950s. They retraced the road to no avail, keeping their patrons waiting for a no-show band! Chipinge-born Sithole's adopted hometown, Bulawayo, was an important cultural node and crossroads for the regional and international musical transactions that built these cultural materialities.

Sithole's call to musicianship literally drew him away from home. Braving the stern hand of his mother, he habitually stole away in the afternoons to join the crowds that chased after and sang along with the popular bands that did rounds to advertise their evening shows at Stanley Hall. With his friend Naison Nkhata, Sithole slipped past the guards who screened out juveniles and watched the shows from the back benches. He participated in youth talent contests, winning £5 once, with which he bought his mother a set of enamel teacups that earned her tacit approval for his chosen career. Sithole watched one-man bands, *omasiganda*, including Sabelo Mathe, George Sibanda, Josaya Hadebe, and Kanda Mandela, and saxophone players like the City Esquires, Patrick and Richard Makoni's Black and White Band, as well as "the old man, Mattaka, and his Bantu Actors." Mattaka not only inspired him but later took him into the comfort of his home like a son. Like his age-mates, Sithole also spent a fortune building a collection of records by foreign artists, which he "listened to intently and imitated."

The popularity of the rather naive propaganda musical film *African Jim* (*Jim Comes to Joburg*) (1949) solidified the romanticized rural-urban migrant imaginary African youngsters constructed through these suitcases full of records. Sithole remembered the character of Jim, a Zulu migrant job seeker in Joburg who, after blundering into endless trouble because of his clumsy rural demeanor, eventually finds a cleaning job at a nightclub where Dolly Rathebe, a contemporary of Dorothy Masuku, is the star performer. Listening to the seductive music as he mops floors, Jim becomes captivated by the singing, slips away from his duties, and joins in the fun with broom still in hand, immediately hitting gold both musically and romantically with Dolly. For people already hooked on the mysteries of Sophiatown, the rags-to-riches narrative of Jim confirmed the belief that Joburg was the place to be; anybody could hit its golden streets running. Sithole had seen young men trekking south to burrow gold and diamonds from the belly of the earth and returning to "change money and throw it at people." This Joburg of gold—eGoli—lured many young men and women across the Limpopo. Sithole, his musician brother, his sister, and—not to be left behind—his father all hit the golden trail in the 1950s.

In Joburg, Sithole reunited with his brother, who had partnered with the budding jazz saxophonist Hugh Masekela while he settled into the Zimbabwean Ndau diaspora that dominated Joburg's carpentry business. Sithole was quickly devastated, however, when his father asked him to take his pregnant sister back home. It was not until the 1960s that he would reconnect with his Sophiatown buddies—now as exiled guerrillas vocalizing the raging fires of the liberation wars. The unfortunate incident that cut short Sithole's Joburg tenure metaphorically represented one important dimension of the fabled city that unsettled many parents: eGoli was sin city, where the young and the bold discovered independence and dangerous freedom. It invited a moral hysteria about young women's sexuality, boosting and frustrating dreams. Masuku rode these gendered panics to claim regional superstardom.

Dorothy Masuku: "Ndizulazula eGoli"

Masuku, "Auntie Dotty," a "wicked" woman who took the Sophiatown music circuit by storm in the early 1950s, embodies what might be imagined as a pan-regional Southern African identity. Born in Bulawayo in 1935 to a Zambian father and a South African mother, Masuku went to school in her city of birth and then moved to Salisbury before some nuns sent her to Joni for further education; she ultimately graduated with an enviable Form 2 certificate (*African Parade,* April 1959). Masuku hit the Joburg music scene after an assignment to work on cadavers unnerved her out of nursing school, the quintessential gateway to "modern" African womanhood in a Southern Africa of the job color bar.

Leading the creative curve, Masuku discarded the conventional "copyrights" (western covers) in her early career to tell her stories through her own compositions. She shrewdly fought and co-opted into her service Sophiatown's violent gangsters to catapult herself to the top of what Chitauro, Dube, and Gunner (1994, 119) describe as "a community of women singers who were part of the vibrant black urban culture of the 50s which had Sophiatown as its hub but spread much further afield and was linked through record sales, radio and concert tours to urban centres such as Salisbury and Bulawayo and other towns of the Northern Rhodesian copperbelt." Masuku's "sisters" in this transnational musical sorority included the Zimbabweans Faith Dauti and Susan Chenjerai, and Joni's Miriam "Mama Africa" Makeba, Dolly Rathebe (the singing sensation of

"Jim Comes to Joburg"), Letta Mbulu, Thoko Thomo, Susan Gabashane, Thandi Klaasen, and Sophie Mgcina. Some of these songstresses, especially Makeba and the jazz crooner Hugh Masekela, rose to fame partly by doing renditions of Masuku's compositions. Makeba (2004, 42) noted in her autobiography, "[Masuku] wrote, sang and taught me many beautiful songs that I sang many times throughout my career." As Coplan (1985, 146) observed, Masuku helped make the 1950s something of a golden age for female singers: "By the end of the 1940s Sophiatown's Dolly Rathebe and Bulawayo's Dorothy Masuku were more popular than most male vocal quartets." Indeed, the 1950s were "a time of the feminization of fashion as well as the feminization of dance" (Ranger 2010, 178). Masuku and her friends were the models for such fashions, and composers of the songs that choreographed the dances.

But to climb that pedestal, Masuku had to conquer the vices of eGoli's misogynistic and xenophobic entertainment circles. She told *Parade* (April 1959) how inhospitably the city had welcomed her during her debut at Alexandra's King's Theatre: "When I got on to the stage, the house was nice and fat, but as soon as it was learned that I was a Rhodesian, there were some booes and shouts of Kilimane!—a derogatory term by which our black brethren in the Union sometimes call us we who come from across the Limpopo River." But she refused to be intimidated, claiming space in her audiences' hearts by enchanting the assembled "eminent stars of jazz who had thought it funny when they heard that Dorothy is going to sing tonight" with her "Ndizulazula eGoli." She jubilantly told *Parade*, "That song was to be heard whistled, hummed and sung in the streets by people as they returned to their homes that night."

From that bold start, Masuku toured extensively with the African Inkspots, the Manhattan Brothers, the Woodpeckers, and the Harlem Swingsters, among others, "leaving audiences spellbound" and propelling herself to the "highest [rung] on the steps of the music ladder in Africa" through socially and politically conscious compositions that weaved African traditional expressive styles into the *smanjemanje* "jive" idiom. She was soon overwhelmed with requests to feature in every troupe. But like her friends—Miriam Makeba and others—she was plunged by her rapid success into the underworld of zoot-suited and slang-spitting *matsotsi*, gangsters. Some of the felonious characters allegedly attempted to assassinate her at a party in Sophiatown, accusing her of being a proud "English lady" who despised "Afrikaans." Clearly, Masuku was out of her depths with the (Afrikaans-inflected) *tsotsitaal* language of Joni's *lumpenproletariat* subculture. Fortunately, being the "wicked" girl that she was, she had anticipated such trouble and hedged herself with her own "boys," who sternly warned the troublemakers that "if Dotty was born to sing, she'll sing throughout the length and breadth of this country and eventually abroad" (*Parade*, April 1979). These travails and triumphs constituted rites of passage for Masuku, because, as Coplan

(1985, 163) noted, "Gangs that supported one band often tried to suppress others, and many shows turned into violent confrontations as *tsotsis* attacking the musicians were met with others rising to their defence. Gangsters often pressed their friendship on popular musicians as a means of enhancing their own prestige. Female vocalists were particularly vulnerable." Most of Masuku's "sisters" suffered the "protection" of these *klevas,* including routine kidnappings, stabbings, and assaults. It was understood that "every gangster had to have a glamorous girl and every performer had to have a gangster (whether you liked him or not)" (Makeba 2004, 32). In 1957, Makeba barely escaped with her life after one of many attempts to abduct her by these gangsters "who liked to terrorize women artists" while she performed with the Manhattan Brothers at the Bantu Men's Social Center. The fracas degenerated into an intergang shootout, prompting her to quit the Manhattans for Masekela's Woodpeckers (Masekela and Cheers 2004, 92). A younger boyfriend among her band of lovers, Masekela was often reduced to a helpless witness to these terror assaults on Makeba, leaving him in no doubt that "being Makeba's boyfriend was not necessarily going to be a joyride."

Masuku was also caught in this vortex of intergroup rivalries, including that between the archrivals the African Inkspots and the Manhattan Brothers, and that similarly accentuated her vulnerability. Blessed with the looks that had won her the Miss Mzilikazi beauty crown in Bulawayo in 1953, she quickly emerged as a star in the region's show business. On her maiden Cape Town tour with the Harlem Swingsters, she caused a furor by snatching "the man to talk about in town" from under the noses of his "three score and five other girlfriends." She narrativized the social havoc she had triggered in her hit "Pata Pata" (Touch touch), which Makeba, Masekela, and recently, Oliver Mtukudzi and the Afro Tenors all rerecorded. This and other songs, such as "Khauleza," not only helped to launch and propel the careers of artists like Makeba and Masekela; they also helped to spur the new jazz craze, *kwela,* a pennywhistle pioneered by, *inter alia,* Spokes Mashiyane and Lemmy "Special" Mabaso.

"Pata Pata" signified the commotion these ladies of style stirred up as they swayed along the pavements of eGoli, dazzling men into extending their "admiring hands" to *pata-pata* them (Chitauro, Dube, and Gunner 1994, 123). Coplan (1985, 158) captured the sensuous *kwela* semiotics as a dance genre: "This was an individualized, sexually suggestive form of jive dancing for young people in which partners alternately touched each other all over the body with their hands, in time with the rhythm. The dancers often shouted the word *kwela* (Zulu: 'climb on,' 'get up') as an inducement for others to join in." This is the sense amplified by Mtukudzi's rendition of the song. Popular creative figures like Masuku introduced new urban performative poetics and set trends. In fact, beyond the overemphasized sexual innuendos, the *kwela* performative register was deeply implicated in the more complex gendered political economy of the underclass *shebeen* (illicit alcohol) subculture. Framing Musarurwa's hit composition "Skokiaan" and the "wicked" women's urban folk song "Aya Mahobho Andakakuchengetera," *kwela* was a deeply coded metaphor of Africans' engagement with the brutal colonial criminalization of their urbanity and of their underground survival economies, including beer brewing and street hawking. As Vera (2000, 6) wrote, "Kwela [Shona: Kwira] means to *climb into* the waiting police jeeps," but refusing to let go of the word.

This reading signals an entirely different semiotics: police brutality and audacious, mocking refusal to concede to brutality. *Kwela* was therefore mimicry of the banal violence that anti-illicit-liquor police and municipal police squads unleashed on *elokishini* female brewers and street hawkers as they force-marched them into jeeps to exact fines and other punishments. The women clasped the word and infused it with powerful creative currency so that, in the performance, the simulated "touching all over the body" parodied the invasive body searches. Africans' use of the word as a creative genre, then, represented "their ability to pull a word 'back from the police jeep'" (Vera 2000, 6; Samuelson 2007, 26). Nonetheless, the textual footprints of subcultural art defy clinical formulas, as Vera observed: "Kwela include[d] the harmonies one can name, and misname." In any case, it is this ability to deploy tropes of a violent and pleasurable everyday to spin critical counterdiscourses that defined people like Masuku as "dangerous," more than their seductive femininity or bohemian lifestyles.

Unlike the conformist *chimanjemanje* of Mattaka's oeuvre, Masuku's subversive creativity was fired by a defiant pan-African political consciousness. In 1958, the apartheid Afrikaner government kicked her out of the country after she composed "Dr. Malan," a song that resonated with the defiance campaigns in attacking the government's tyrannical, racist laws. She would defiantly etch herself into the annals of Southern Africa's guerrilla artist history by extolling Patrice Lumumba in a follow-up song, "Lumumba." Lumumba, the Congolese pan-African hero after whom Masuku named her own son, represented the dawn of a new post-colonial Africa, an antithesis to the entrenching white settler regimes of the region. Masuku returned to colonial Zimbabwe, and after two years of trouble with the government, headed off to England, where she was at one time marginally involved with the touring South African jazz opera *King Kong* (*Parade,* January 1961). By this time, Masuku's songs were being "sold [at home] and [in London] with a speed that defie[d] all past African records," authoritatively declared *Parade,* which proclaimed her Southern Rhodesia's "ambassador, just like Louis 'Satchmo' Armstrong for the Americans." Within the touted *chimanjemanje* imaginary, nothing could be more symbolic of success than performing for the BBC and ITV in London, and touring North America. Masuku was quite conscious of this significance, as she boasted in *Parade* in March 1965:

> I have done shows on Channel 2 of the BBC and have appeared in some nightclubs in the West End of London. . . . In a few weeks' time I shall appear on "Ready, Steady, Go!" the big show produced by ITV, and that's the day—the crowning moment of showbiz for me! Everyone who matters goes on to "RSG." The Beatles, Rolling Stones, everybody who matters.

In the self-framing rubric of *chimanjemanje,* Masuku now mattered. And her road to success did not depend on the stereotyping, exoticizing red-light district of the racially overdetermined entertainment circuits of European capitals: "I have turned down some offers because I don't want to appear in shows where there are strip-teasers."

While she belonged to the second generation of contemporary African urban musicians, whose claim to fame was the displacement of spiritual and intellectual themes by a more sensual performative aesthetic, Masuku had the *locus standi* to boldly redefine independence and freedom beyond the youthful excesses of the shoulder quivers, hip jerks, and other bodily shaking and twisting that gave *tsaba tsaba,* for example, its notoriety in the eyes of older generations. At home, she fought the battles of the underclass urban female, egging on the "*shebeen* queens," female backyard brewers, in their defiance of alcohol laws and police harassment in songs like "Khauleza!" Tackling the apartheid beast and openly engaging in the everyday battles of the disenfranchised demanded uncommon courage in an era when record companies colluded with the state to silence artists. Explained Makeba (2004, 42),

> There were a few black people, so-called "talent scouts," who worked for record labels. Their job would be to report us if we dared sing anything considered seditious. We could not sing anything political, which meant we could rarely sing anything directly saying what was really happening to us in our lives. It took artists like Dorothy Masuka, who was bravely singing *Khauleza*—saying, "Hurry mama, Hurry mama, Hurry up and hide because the police are coming!"

Thus, while moral gatekeepers (like "Pendlindaba," the letter writer in the May 1959 issue of *Parade)* appealed to the government to do something "to curb the jazz of the rock 'n roll, kwela and jive type [to protect] our children's character and brains," Masuku's "sextual/textual politics" (Khan 2008, 146) creatively utilized these aporic tensions to inform a complex, politically conscious African agency that directly engaged the realities of its colonized being.

Masuku trod where pioneers feared to go. Although Mattaka toured the region as far as the Congo, he gave South Africa a wide berth, repulsed by the country's "sinful" image. He explained to me, "You know what used to happen? People offered us their children and we didn't accept them unless they were of good moral standing. And especially girls . . . we never accepted girls, particularly those who were independent. But for those who were staying with their parents, we'd require the parents' permission—to instill discipline. Discipline—that's very important." Molded by strict missionary paternalism that emphasized "character formation" (Duncan 2006), Mattaka eschewed irreverent female boldness: "We refused naughty children in the group, working only with decent children, like Susan Chenjerai. The naughty ones went to the tea parties, or *mahobho* parties, to dance, where people sold beer to make money." In Sophiatown, as Masekela once quipped, "every third house was a *shebeen*!" Its matriarch, the Shebeen Queen, personified defiance of colonial urban authority and the adoptive African middle-class notions about respectability. Her place was where class, race, and gender collided in particularly creative ways. At such criminalized cultural crossroads, defying the tyrannies of patriarchal control and confronting statutory discipline, music with a protest sensibility emerged with force.

Thus, the rather ambiguous line between performing colonial modernity and contesting it seems discernible between Mattaka and Masuku. To Mattaka, tea parties were a dangerous mix of decadent westernization and ghetto culture. He avoided places "where people danced touching each other," choosing instead to "entertain educated, church people." His repertoire was stridently embedded in the prevailing Victorian ideals of respectability, defined by education, Christian morality, and matrimony. On his disciplined *dariro*, such values were reflected in the classical separation of audiences from performers, such that Mattaka's smartly dressed "boys would stand up to do their mesmerizing steps, clapping hands and tap-dancing to produce enchanting sounds" while the audiences sat and watched in silence, applauding appreciatively only at the end of each act of the "variety concert shows." Such performative discipline replicated the polite, domestic moral and social order that defined the respectable nuclear household on the European model. The sanction against the "wicked" female performer was due to her perceived threat to this imposed gendered order. For this reason, Julia Moyo watched her dream of making it big in Joni wilt after her mother refused her permission to leave, vowing, "If you go, I will smash this calabash on the ground; you will not get there alive" (Mutyambizi family, interview).

Julia told me that she had made her mark after being invited to perform at the Bulawayo Municipality's Large City Hall. Dressed up in hired clothes and wearing make-up provided by the municipality for the occasion, she had sung so beautifully "many people thought she was from South Africa, only realizing that she was from Mzilikazi's V Square after reading the story in the newspapers the next morning." To her, that misidentification was a stamp of approval, certifying that she, too, fitted into the glitter of eGoli. Similarly, reporting Masuku's crowning as Miss Mzilikazi during the Rhodes Centenary Celebration, *Parade* (November 1953) wrote that "Miss Dorothy Masuka is better known for her lovely voice and music in which she has no equal in all Central Africa. Miss Masuka is such a polished singer that many find it hard to believe that she has not had overseas training. Her crooning has the American touch and she has always created terrific sensations wherever she has appeared on stage." Joni and "overseas" were imagined abodes of higher performative standards to which Africans elsewhere should aspire. Much of the music that Africans performed in early twentieth-century Zimbabwe revolved around this rich repertoire of imaginations of "overseas." These pervasive imaginations of "overseas" were as crucial a cultural portal for Black Atlantic identity self-fashioning among Southern African artists as the African homeland and inspiration were to diaspora artists like Louis Armstrong. Travel consummated such linkages in ways that complemented, rather than displacing, the significance of location (Tomlinson 1992, 28).

The Travel Motif: Arrivals, of Sorts

Performance tours helped artists and their compatriots to think about themselves in a global context. Having lived his life on the road, Mattaka claimed that he was one of the most traveled people in the country. His itineraries took him to Zambia, Botswana, the Congo, and his country of birth, Malawi, with his band, his family, and larger entourages that included teachers and their students. Transterritorial travel in Southern Africa required no passports, but only clearance from the district administrator's office, which Mattaka and the parents of his acolytes always found supportive. They were also received well by their hosts. He told me that in the Congo in the 1950s he had enjoyed "the best reception that we got from anywhere in the region. They invited people and hosted a big dinner for us after our performance. Huge crowds came."

It is symbolic of the significance of travel to his work and to African self-crafting that Mattaka composed two travel songs, which his group performed to announce their impending departure for a tour and then their return home when they toured abroad. Bidding farewell to their home fans, the band sang,

Sarai isu toenda	Good-bye, we are going
Toenda toenda	We are going, we are going
Toenda mhiri kwenyanza	We are going overseas.

And, concluding their foreign tours and preparing to return, they sang,

Tichafara tasvika	We will rejoice when we arrive
Tichafara tasvika muHarare	We will rejoice when we arrive in Harare
Harare iguta rakanaka.	Harare is a beautiful city.

For the singers, these songs constructed special moments to imagine both their foreign destinations and their own countries, as captured in the rejoicing they anticipated on their arrival back home. Geographical travel temporarily detached them from a place they may have taken for granted, and enabled them to conceptualize and identify their belonging to a "beautiful" home—Harare, the place that supported them and bade them farewell when they left. Like the special reception they received as visitors in far-away places, returning to this place they called home and the rejoicing that such a return entailed confirmed not only their belonging, but also a process of identity coconstruction as a relational process between "home" and an "elsewhere." Everybody rejoiced upon their return, as anticipated in "Tichafara Tasvika."

But why did Mattaka's band describe their destination in the farewell song as "overseas" when they never traveled beyond the continent? Perhaps this was their conceptualization of the indeterminate distance their music could take them: "because we were going to far-away places like the Congo," Mattaka explained. In everyday usage, "overseas" denotes far-off places, travel to which usually elicited much ceremony, anxiety, and good wishes, marking that important event and also imagining the great expectations that it evoked. As the ultimate form of travel, overseas travel symbolizes not only the conquest of great distances and cultural differences, but also a creative transfiguration of "roots in routes" in the production of new cultural meanings. As Stokes observes (1994, 4), music performs knowledge of other places that is borne out by subsequent experience. Masuku's tour of Europe and the United States represented this ultimate achievement in culturally significant ways. Her popular acclaim, for example in London's *Daily News,* fulfilled *Parade's* earlier hopes (January 1961), demonstrating that, indeed, "she could withstand the strain of the London stage," where she was expected, as a matter of course, "to be our ambassador." Because she was an ambassador, wrote *Parade,* "everyone is hoping she won't return without laurels to show she's what the old-timers like to call 'THE REAL THING.'" She was expected to demonstrate her *locus standi* by conquering the culture shock of and demystifying the imperial metropolis.

Mattaka's departure song captured this multidimensional conquest, which Masuku actualized. On another level, Mattaka's song represented his group's own widening travel horizons, as they must have seen themselves one day getting to the real "overseas." And considering the mesmerizing tap-dancing that accompanied the song, it may also have represented not only mental journeys, extending beyond what the singers could physically reach at the time, but, equally significantly, a "cultural arrival." Mattaka and his colleagues had appropriated and mediated "overseas" song for decades; they traveled outside of their own territories performing those songs for other people, who received the performers as accomplished modern musicians. Their performances in places like the Congo gave them the same accolades Zimbabweans anticipated upon Masuku's return from the UK and North America, thus certifying their status as having "reached," if only culturally by the aspired-to standards of the Congo's *évolues* or Southern Rhodesia's middle classes.

7 The Many Moods of "Skokiaan"

Criminalized Leisure, Underclass Defiance, and Self-Narration

Wherever colonization is a fact, the indigenous culture begins to rot and among the ruins something begins to be born which is condemned to exist on the margin allowed it by the European culture.

—Steve Biko, *I Write What I Like*

Hey! Black man,
You like dancing sideways . . .

—Nicolas Guillen, Algiers '69 *News Bulletin*

In the 1940s, Zimbabwean musician August Machona Musarurwa composed and subsequently recorded a saxophone instrumental, "Skokiaan," which quickly became an anthem in the country's teeming "native locations," *marukesheni*. Over the next two decades, dozens of western and regional musicians performed and created their own versions of the song. This appropriation of "Skokiaan" was part of a broader creative reading and misreading that helped to romanticize the song as a vernacular affirmation of the exoticized images of Africa prevalent in the western world. The romanticization was made possible by a decontextualization of the song which, in its original context of production and performance, can be read as a metaphor for African responses to, struggles, and creative engagement with harsh colonial Southern African urbanity.

"Skokiaan" was an underclass counterdiscourse that contested the colonial state's criminalization of an emergent urban African cultural economy that revolved around music, dance, and the independent brewing and consumption of alcohol. Africans responded to the criminalization of their beer by concocting a rapidly brewed drink, *chikokiyana*, or *skokiaan* in ghetto parlance, which they fortified with all manner of intoxicants. Musarurwa's song "Skokiaan" was therefore a metaphor not only for the tenuous existence and quick wit that African urban life demanded, but also for the popular African cultural contestation of discordant colonial modernity's attempts to reproduce and control racialized underclass African being both physically and ideologically. This contestation gave the brew its many coded monikers, not just *chikokiyana* and *chihwani* ("one-day"), but also the boldly declarative *chandada,* "I do whatever I like!" Its names indicate how the song indexed the African underclass's ability to celebrate defiance in self-fashioning registers that transcended colonial negation and alienation.

Yet "Skokiaan," the song, fascinated so many ears that it quickly became a song of many moods. It became subject to a multiplicity of readings and misreadings as it was refracted through various class and cultural lenses. I explore these readings and misreadings, arguing that the song is a crucial transcript of underclass African urbanity, which can greatly enrich our understanding of colonial power relations and racialized identity construction and contestation in mid-twentieth-century Zimbabwe and Southern Africa. If Biko is correct that colonialism decomposed African cultures, "Skokiaan" represented the fertilizing power of such rot. The song illustrates the creative potency of the underclass cultures that produced it, and of those that it inspired. Within the register of global cultural exchange, "Skokiaan" became a vehicle that brought the African American jazz legend Louis "Satchmo" Armstrong to Zimbabwe in 1960. I read the song from outside coming in—from its western (and diasporic) imagination back to the *rukesheni,* the Rhodesian African ghetto.

Cross-Cultural (Mis)readings

The performance of "Skokiaan" outside of its context of composition, particularly by North American and European musicians and audiences, provides a lens for examining the power of song in creating impressions of a people and their ways of life. "Skokiaan" was issued as sheet music in dozens of countries; an incomplete listing on Wikipedia (http://en.wikipedia.org/wiki/Skokiaan) counts close to a hundred cover versions. Musicians and groups who recorded their own versions include Louis "Satchmo" Armstrong, Roberto Delgado, Hugh Masekela and Herb Alpert, Nteni Piliso, Nico Carsten, Sam Klair, Ralph Marterie, Bill Haley, Joe Carr, the Mbira Marimba Ensemble, James Last, Spokes Mashiyane, Paul Lunga, Hans Carlings, Brave Combo, Perez Pedro, Hot Butter, Kermit Ruffians, the Four Lads, and the Soweto String Quartet. Several versions charted on the American Hit Parade. Wikipedia suggests that American artist Tom Glazer added English lyrics to the song for the Four Lads, a Canadian group, in 1954, who recorded it as "Skokiaan: South African Song." Armstrong recorded the song with the same lyrics the same year. Among the various versions of the song, it is Armstrong's rendition that most Zimbabweans are familiar with, even though it remains unclear whether that familiarity preceded or followed the artist's trip to the country during his 1960 African tour. Armstrong symbolized the African diasporic bond in the Black Atlantic musical world, hence my choice to foreground his reading and inscription of meaning into the song.

The transactions and translations of "Skokiaan" reinforced some of the messages implicit in Musarurwa's composition, but they also inscribed new meanings and images into it in ways that helped enrich conversations about and conceptions of Africa, particularly in the United States. And, while Meg Samuelson (2007, 31) rightly proposes that "Skokiaan" be read as an instantiation of African influence on African American modernity (rather than vice versa), I am interested in the manner of these transactions, particularly how they tended to reproduce western modernity's "othering" of Africa through appropriated and redeployed African idioms like "Skokiaan." The fact that Musarurwa's recorded version was an instrumental rendered the song open to (re)imagination and (mis)representation. The Glazer/Armstrong rendition, for instance, has not just lyrics, but English lyrics that are supposed to represent the meaning of the original song.

The primary effect of the musical representation of "Skokiaan," particularly the insertion and popularization of the English lyrics, was the distortion of the song's urban African social context, foregrounding instead the idea of carefree Africans celebrating life in "the jungle," merrymaking and partaking of "pineapple beer," as Brave Combo mistranslated *chikokiyana*.[1] An analysis of some of the versions of "Skokiaan" shows that while they did not entirely divorce the song from its original subcultural context, those versions were firmly anchored in an imperial romanticization of Africa. The Glazer/Armstrong version entreated listeners to take a ship to a far-away happy jungle called Africa to enjoy some carefree carousing to the beat of "hot drums," "hot strings," and "warm lips . . . kissful of *skokiaan*." There, the song enthused, anybody can "live along like a king," right in the jungle bungalow.[2]

Thomas Turino (2000, 41–42) observes that the reworking fitted the song into the "romantic, exotic imagery found in many popular songs drawn from the margins into the cosmopolitan circles," with imagery influenced by the "savannas, forests, high plateaus, mountains and deserts [that] characterize southern African topography." Significantly, it can be argued, with Veit Erlmann (1999, 60), that this "cosmopolitan" romanticization was a power play, part of a "massive project of global re-semanticizing that sought to inscribe . . . difference into the very syntax . . . of metropolitan discourse" in the age of knowledge imperialism. As a western lens for deciphering the human experience, cosmopolitanism tends to signify the coloniality of western-centered knowledge production, centering and reproducing the metropolitan self in and by decentering the nonwestern others, consigning their knowledges and lived experiences to inferiorized, racialized margins. Such inferiorization authorizes the imperial episteme by silencing questions of power and cultural alienation and by celebrating the transitional other as a success of the "civilizing mission." Ramón Grosfoguel (2008) explains that "the construction of 'pathological' regions in the periphery as opposed to the so-called 'normal' development patterns of the 'West' justified an even more intense political and economic intervention from imperial powers. By treating the 'Other' as 'underdeveloped' and 'backward,' metropolitan exploitation and domination were justified in the name of the 'civilizing mission.'" Thus inferiorized, as Frantz Fanon (1967a, 36) wrote, "The Negro is appraised in terms of the extent of his assimilation." The cosmopolitan incorporation and resemanticization of "Skokiaan" displaced African self-knowledge and valorized the gaze of the outsider and the object of his mystification.

To be self-sustaining, knowledge imperialism depends not so much on a total "obliterat[ion of] local forms of practice and knowledge [and their replacement] with supposedly universal forms" (Erlmann 1999, 60) as on debasement, appropriation, and caricaturing. That is how cosmopolitanism, as a liberal western canon for reading cultural difference through resemblance (the self), not just co-opts, but actually creates, the so-called margins. The Glazer/Armstrong rendition of "Skokiaan" poetically overplays, decontextualizes, and distorts the meaning of the local, vernacularized idioms in the song, such as the "hot drums," hot strings," and "warm, blissful lips . . . kissful of *skokiaan*," which can be imagined in the original song's artistic devices and context, as we shall see. Such (mis) reading and caricaturing can work as crucial instruments of knowledge imperialism, and they certainly were effective acts of creation, as can be witnessed in the fertile imagination that invented "Africa" in Florida in 1953. Implicit in the reworked "Skokiaan" is the (re)construction of Africa for Western ears (and eyes) as a not only geographically remote, but also nostalgically exotic, happy place inhabited by merry and overindulgent noble savages—a distant echo of an unspoiled western self that might yet be recovered through such appropriation. The representation of life in Africa as an unending kingly bliss, lived in inviting bush bungalows, resonated with both the Euro-American collective consciousness (conditioned by the imperial invention of Africa as an idyllic jungle) and the yearning of diasporic Africans for an unspoiled homeland.

The Invention of Africa in Florida: Africa U.S.A.

In a rather bizarre stretch of this imagination, these powerful imperial tropes inspired an American couple to create "Africa" in Florida in 1953. After listening to the reworked "Skokiaan," Jack and Lillian Pedersen decided to bring to life their thoughts about "what Africa might look like" on a piece of Boca Raton scrubland. The result was Africa U.S.A., a unique "zoo with no cages where visitors could safely interact with animals." Through it, the Pedersens transformed the "deadest town" they had ever seen into a novel tourist magnet (Africa-USA.com). The Pedersens imported not only a range of wild and domestic animals (zebras, kudus, wildebeest, lions, giraffes, leopards, donkeys, etc.), but also "natives," including "Machakas, a Masai [*sic*] warrior" from East Africa, who would exist as part and parcel of the fauna in the park. They opened the park in March 1953 to appreciative visitors who listened to Armstrong's "Skokiaan" pumped from the safari train, acoustically reinforcing the exhibition's thematic visuality, as they made rounds on the 350-acre veld of "Florida at its best."

This impression of Africa, like other "Africa-inspired" zoos and exhibitions in the western world, sprang from, and buttressed, the idea of Africa as knowable and appropriable exotica where humans existed not just in, but as, nature, interacting "face to face" with agreeable predators, drinking moonshine to pulsing music. Hot Butter's otherwise instrumental rendition ("Skokian," 1973) powerfully brought the jungle alive by adding the sounds of chattering primates, chuckling leopards, and other noises of the wilderness in the song's background, bolstering the double appropriation of both the intellectual property and the wild- and not so wild life. Yet the construction of Africa here was achieved by keeping intact key tropes of Musarurwa's song (made accessible through the "world music" portal) while freely reimagining them for "cultural" meaning. This is evident in the even wider representation of the song in films and concerts, ranging from Hans Carlings's "wild" choreographies to Eric Rasmussen's erotic short musical "Scrabble Rousers."

This analysis is conceptually significant. The discourses that songs like "Skokiaan" and South African Solomon Linda's "Mbube" generated illustrate not only the reciprocity but also the complexity of global cultural transactions. They require us to move beyond the notion of unidirectional transmission that, for instance, underlines Carol Muller's (2006) formulation of American musical "diasporas" in Africa. African musicians did not simply mediate products from America; they also created musical commodities that powerfully impacted the imaginations of American audiences, allowing them to adapt the songs and represent them in crucial ways that provide insight into not only the power of the mediated songs in America but also the workings of a deterritorialized, consummated, but often quite discordant virtual acoustic world. Thus, it was not only musicians from the supposed "margins of modernity" who yearned to travel to America to meet in person the makers of the songs that greatly influenced their early twentieth-century repertoires. As I explore in the final section, American musicians similarly desired to trace songs like "Skokiaan" back to their composers in Africa, in quest of what Penny M. Von Eschen (2000, 170) called "international sensibilities." Such songs functioned as optics for western musicians and audiences to visualize and create their own imaginations of Africa. Equally important, the power of "Skokiaan" also infused imaginations and contestations of African identities in Africa itself, revolving particularly around adoptive conceptions of class.

"Skokiaan" Straddling Cross-Class Fault Lines

I opened my first interview with "Professor" Kenneth Mattaka in 2006 by playing him "Skokiaan." My intent was not only to draw his mind back in time to the

1940s, but also to momentarily decenter his own works and frame the conversation within the larger context of Zimbabwean township music. While the song did frame our conversation as I expected, my tactic set us off on a discordant note. To him, "Skokiaan" conjured the blight of colonial African urbanity, which he was not too happy to be associated with back then or to remember in the present. Unexpectedly, I had managed to provoke some of the contentious cultural sensibilities of the time, revolving particularly around conceptions of class. I excerpt our conversation here to illustrate these contentions:

MC: Do you know this song?

KM: That's Musarurwa's "Skokiaan," of course. But I did not meet Musarurwa myself, because I didn't interact with many of those guys. I just knew them as people who played their own saxophones.

MC: Does that imply you played a different kind of music?

KM: Yes, mine was quite different.

MC: Did you ever perform a version of "Skokiaan," as many other musicians did, or did you listen to it in your own house?

KM: No, it did not augur too well with me; it was played at tea parties (also called tea meetings), an imitation of the parties that whites held, come-togethers. They were tea parties where tea was not drunk. Instead, they brewed beer, and that was done in the bush. So those songs weren't played in the halls.

MC: Why in the bush?

KM: They were saxophone players who entertained people in compounds. Here in Bulawayo, bands like the Black and White Band [led by prominent brothers Richard and Patrick Chipunza Makoni] were the ones that played in the halls. They played jazz music for ballroom dancers, tango, foxtrot, etc.—such dances. On the other hand, people who dwelt in the compounds invited Musarurwa and his colleagues to play there. And at the end, he had a contract with the Cold Storage Commission, so that he entertained people in the industries. He was famous for that. Personally, I didn't interact with him.

MC: You mentioned the bush . . .

KM: That was for the tea parties in the outskirts of town; these could not be held in the halls. The halls were for modern bands, you see? In most cases, only one banjo player played at tea parties, a small banjo and a small drum.

MC: And the music had a following?

KM: Yes, for those who enjoyed it. For one thing, there is no music that you can say is not entertaining. It is the audiences that differ. People loved some songs that you'd see as unenjoyable. People then loved things that would be difficult for modern people to appreciate, you see. We had grades of music: music that we were taught in school, then these saxophones and banjos. I don't know these days . . . because these things vary with age, but in our day we would have adults and church-going people coming to see our performances as families. They would come in and sit down to watch, clap their hands and call for encores, quietly sitting there. Nobody would get in drunk or holding a bottle (of beer). Not in the hall. And you see that nowadays everybody stands up dancing; we sang for seated audiences. You could hear a pin drop when we got onto the stage; everyone listened respectfully. There was no dancing.

MC: Why didn't the audiences dance?

KM: We the musicians danced, doing all the action, making gestures to express the meanings of the words. Nobody stood up. Church pastors and Christians were there. Respectable people would all come with their in-laws and we sang to them, *zvitsvene* [very smart], *zvisina tsvina* [no dirt], you see!

MC: What was dirt?

KM: That's Shona to refer to those grades that I was talking about; there were things that a respectable adult could not do. Can I stand up and jive here in the presence of my mother and father? Can I?

MC: What would it matter if you did?

KM: No, that can't do. I can't jive in the presence of my father, mother, or sister. That's not possible. That was in line with Christianity and education. That went hand in hand.

Tsaba tsaba dancing, which Mattaka considered a part of bush culture, upset the conventions of aspirant middle-class respectability. Mattaka frowned upon this urban subculture that mimicked white "tea parties" as a disguise for *chikokiyana* drinking, often in unruly places. However, this strident, urbane perspective elides the popularity of "Skokiaan," a syncretic tune that belied its underclass origins and context of composition. Implicit in Mattaka's statement is an assertion that "real tea parties" were those hosted by mission-educated "high society" elites who drank only nonalcoholic beverages, a particularly theoretical, protestant, orthodox "dryness." "High society" was a preserve of only "those people whose monthly or weekly incomes were above the African average salary," explained the modernist magazine *Parade* (November 1953). "Clean" classical music, church hymns, and foxtrots, tangos, and ballroom dances were the central tenets of the tea party culture; *tsaba tsaba* was disorder, immorality, and unrespectability. It was *tsvina,* (moral) dirt.

Musically, the modernist cultural tradition thus not only imagined itself as superior to indigenous musical cultures; it also despised syncretic underclass forms like *tsaba tsaba* and *kwela,* which Musarurwa's "Skokiaan" exemplified. In keeping with the broader European cultural ethos this tradition had adopted, "high society" tea parties were considered the heart of clean, "civilized" leisure, elevating the very act of drinking tea and "minerals" to an art form that excluded the *lumpenproletariat.* But this is essentially an alienated (and alienating) reading of "Skokiaan," a classical example of a dominant culture constructing a "low" of underclass self-articulations. So beyond the consigned, externalized readings, what did this culture mean on its own terms, to its own producers and the publics who were its primary audience?

"Skokiaan" in Context: *Mahobho* Carnivalesque as Underclass Self-Fashioning

The underclasses did much more than simply envy the "high society" cultures; they were ingenious cultural agents themselves who created and enjoyed their own ideas of leisure, inspired by both imported and indigenous registers. They borrowed and subverted the concept of the tea party to camouflage the brewing, selling, and consumption of beer in the *shebeens* (speakeasies) and out in the open veld, in the ruts of Mbare's Brickfields and the cactus scrublands of Mbombera in Makokoba. As N. Mtisi told Nathaniel Chimhete (2004, 56), "At a tea party everything was expected except tea." A perfect ruse, the teapot was appropriated to serve beer, not tea. In the locations, *chikokiyana* brewers sometimes gathered under the guise of birthday parties hosted by householders in turn, selling food and drinks to selected guests alerted through invitation cards to screen out potential *vatengesi,* police informers. Music blasted on the gramophone and patrons cast bets challenging each other to the dance floor. Together with illicitly sourced "European" beer (mostly obtained with the help of Coloreds), *chikokiyana* drove these gatherings. In an urban environment that pathologized and economically excluded African women and criminalized traditional beer cultures at the behest of municipal monopolies, women used the underclass tea parties to make quick money; Julia Moyo told me, "That is why *chikokiyana* was brewed now and consumed now," as *chihwani,* one-day brew. With the money earned, the women supplemented meager family incomes, bought property, and educated their children.

Subversively complicit, the underclasses appropriated and significantly decentered the tea party, unmaking its colonial significations and redeploying it to their own purposes. Middle-class condemnation thus reflected the intensification of struggle over a culture that, "for the poor majority . . . became one of the many institutions through which urban Africans tried to shape their own sociability and determine how they spent their leisure time against the backdrop of the aspirant middle class use of the tea party as a stamp to gain acceptance into settler society (Chimhete 2004, 56). Thus informed by this delegated gatekeeping and jostling to create and maintain cultural distance, the middle-class condemnation gave additional ammunition to the municipalities, which frowned upon the erosion of their claims to a monopoly on the brewing business by these criminalized African cultures. The language of respectability, order, sanitation, and health was a ready arsenal for municipal propaganda campaigns that justified violent punitive raids. Waging psychological warfare, the municipal brewers ran a series of illustrated articles in *Parade* in the 1950s, hailing "working men in Umtali [who] . . . successfully fitted themselves into the Western way of life earning themselves decency and respectability . . . drinking good, clean, healthy beer made by experts" in council beer halls, and contrasting them with the "sad men of Salisbury" who "brewed their own concoctions . . . usually that harmful liquid—SKOKIAAN—for a quick kick" (May 1954).

These "sad men" included the predominantly male domestic servants and shop attendants who lived in makeshift shacks close to their workplaces in white suburbs, and the brick-makers who inhabited the kilns and open pits of Brickfields (between Mbare and Arcadia). The Federal censor estimated that there were forty-five thousand of these men, who inhabited "unauthorized, crowded and unsanitary compounds [lacking] schools, hospitals, or . . . entertainment" (*Parade,* March 1961). For them, *chikokiyana* was business, entertainment, and socialization. It freed them from the expensive, watered-down "kaffir beer" and the captive beer hall. The underclasses made their own spaces: backyards and open velds where they created and defended their own freedom. Their liminal socialization, creative imagination, and visceral, arrogant boldness antinomically cast such spaces into margins of power dangerous to both themselves and the policing state. Tim Burke (2008, 365) criticized historians whose obsession with refuting colonial ideology led them to overlook the degree to which "some women adopted wickedness with considerable enthusiasm." Transgressive cultural dispositions—"wickedness"—served well not just women, but also the men who regrouped in the dunghills of modernity's exclosures. Recalling similar crowds in Joburg, Masekela observed that drinking helped the men forget not only the train that brought them to the mines, but also their parents, children, friends, wives, lands, and herds, all of which they would not see for months, if ever again (Masekela and Cheers 2004, 6–7). *Chikokiyana* carnivalized their irreverent, marginalized urban self-fashioning.

While the Native Affairs Department reassured itself that it had managed to suppress the specter of the "night dance" in 1930, the rowdy outdoor carnival dubbed the *mahobho* party needed no spokesperson. By the 1950s, the underclass tea party had actually morphed into a much more defiant and transgressive entertainment form. Often swelling to as many as two thousand, crowds drank and danced away weekends and the early days of the week (Gargett 1971, 48). Seeing like the colonial state—to quote James Scott (1998) out of context—many aspirant middle-class Africans felt scandalized by this boisterous subculture. A keen observer of African urbanity, journalist Lawrence Vambe (1976, 171–72) witnessed hardened *chikokiyana* queens turning Brickfields into "the heartland" of *chikokiyana* enterprise and a zone of chaos when they joined hands with their male patrons to defend their turf against police raids:

> These [raids] occurred . . . particularly at sunset when, often, nearly three-quarters of the compulsive drinkers from Harare congregated there; at that time of day, the official beer halls would be closed. Then all hell would be let loose; scores of policemen and patrons fought, fell and scattered in all directions, some injuring themselves in the holes or on the piles of bricks. . . . I did not have to mingle with these crowds, it being quite enough to stand on the Harare side of the Mukuvisi River to see men, women, the police, and their Land-Rovers, hats and batons flying all over the place in what amounted to small but intense battle engagements.

Patrons with a twisted sense of humor dubbed both the area and the brew "Poland," in light of the destruction wreaked on that eastern European nation during the Second World War.

Bulawayo, the industrial capital, was not spared the evils of "Poland" either. According to Hugh Ashton, the Director of African Housing in the 1940s,

> One of the social problems of the time was illicit drinking. There were shebeens all over the place on the Western Commonage. It was so bad that in an effort to try and control it the police used to have an aeroplane patrolling Bulawayo, to see where things were happening and then direct the [anti–illicit alcohol] squad. Because brewing and distilling had to be done quickly you got skokiaan—kill me quick, etc. Some of them were lethal.[3]

To paraphrase Cornel West's commentary (2005) on the pre–Hurricane Katrina New Orleans ghetto culture that blessed the world with Louis Armstrong, life in *elokishini,* being so close to death, had to be lived intensely, physically, sexually, and gastronomically. Thus, where Ashton elided coercive state agency by seeing people killing themselves with *skokiaan,* this was an extirpative struggle for the right to be. The crowd stood up to defend the subversive fringe cultures created at the point of collision between the criminalizing colonial political economy and African innovation, both driven by and producing this "art of not being governed" (Scott 2009).

For the underclasses, as Lawrence Vambe understood, there was no option but to craft lives on the margins, driven by the "recurring desire to flout the system that bore down so heavily on [them]." To Vambe, these *chikokiyana* battles were symbolic of the "bigger struggle between the ruling minority, whose will was paramount, and the majority, who wanted to break their chains" (1976, 172). For the colonized, the line between legality and illegality often meant injustice, hence their determined defiance. Ashton, Bulawayo's Administrative Chief for Africans and the enforcer of the alcohol bans, was quite aware that one solution could have been to allow people ordinary pubs. "But my job was not concerned with should have hads. That wasn't the way the government worked."[4] The stakes were quite high, since the government had passed the Harmful Liquids Act in 1949. The following year, the Salisbury Municipality's Native Administration Department reported "no less than fifty-seven convictions" under the law. Yet the municipality was already devising new deterrents. It reported, "The restraining of the brewing of skokiaan can only be managed by the expulsion of offenders from the location." Even this, the white administrators quickly conceded, was "not a long-term solution as it merely transferred the problem elsewhere."[5] Expelled *chikokiyana* queens occupied urban fringes to found whole new economies they stood up to defend. This *skokiaan* backlash qualifies Ashton's boast that "we were able to have our cake and eat it through the beer gardens."[6]

The queens of *chikokiyana* were often retired prostitutes. The potent mix of alcohol and song predictably fomented licentiousness. Thus, Sithole (interview) recalled how *mahobho* party organizers often "invited *omasiganda* musicians like John White to play for patrons, who loved to dance those kinds of dances, reminiscent of sexual courtship." *Parade* (May 1954) vividly depicted the typical scene as consisting of "hot rock 'n rolling to the music of the radiogram or gramophone, and there is a lot of Kwela jive to the music of the pennywhistle. . . . Pairs jive and rock 'n roll until dust almost completely envelops them." Of course, as Mattaka noted, nobody danced like that in the sanitized municipal halls, the domain of the municipality's "healthful, dignified, and respectable" recreation.

But despite the official promotion of the latter and criminalization of the former, *mahobho* won the battle for underclass hearts and minds, in the words of Ngugi (1997, 20), by redefining its own space in terms of both location and language. *Mahobho* was a rejection of permanent dislocation and sanitized silencing, as the Salisbury municipality tactfully conceded in 1958:

> With the exception of the last three months of the municipal year, concert parties remained very popular and well attended, the United African Melodians being by far the most popular, followed by the City Quads, the Safe Brothers, the Milton Brothers and the City Comedy Crooners. The Black Evening Follies remained almost dormant throughout the year.[7]

The city was more forthright in explaining the flagging attendance: "Five or six concerts were held each month, but takings began to drop sharply towards Christmas with the increasing grip of 'mahobo' parties on the townships population." The problem became so acute that "concert parties reduced their admission charges from 2/6d to 1/6d in an attempt to attract audiences, but to no avail. Only three concerts were held in each of the months April, May and June, 1958." Thus, by the late 1950s, underclass leisure had not only managed to transgress the colonial geographies of power by mapping its own spaces and entertainment register, it had also effectively broken down the colonial architectures of confinement and discipline. Through performativity, Africans disarmed proscriptive state power by inverting their marginalized urbanity, that is, both spaces and cultures, into sites of plebian power. "Tragedy," Achebe (1978, 5) wrote, "begins when things leave their accustomed place." Artistic escape from confinement crossed the *cordons sanitaires* and headed for the feared open velds.

In the 1950s, Faith Dauti composed a streetwise ditty, "Nzve," to a tune adapted from a South American song. Dauti's song articulated not only Africans' contestation of colonial usage of space, but also their generation and inflection of meanings from and into the voids of the urban built environment. The *nyaudzosingwi* (ideophone) *nzve* described their quick darting and ducking around street corners to avoid being seen and to see in an antinomic and spectacularly transitory usage of criminalizing space. Labeled "loiterers," "vagrants," "loafers," and "spivs" under the pass laws, African underclasses ventured into the city center and reappropriated the corner to subvert and contest their criminalization in ways that animated a rich poetics of embodied streetwise discourse. Barred—together with dogs—from certain streets, pavements, public parks, hotels, restaurants, shopping malls, and other spaces of urban leisure, they seized street corners, empty common spaces, and shopping arenas like the legendary Amato Shops on Kingsway Avenue (now Julius Nyerere) in Salisbury city center. They selectively occupied symbolic urban spaces and subverted them, turning them into transient rendezvous for shining, dating, shoplifting, soliciting, clandestine commerce, and political mobilization, transforming the cityscape into a site of intense cultural and political dissidence. This way, the margins persistently encroached onto the protected but porous center as Africans rehumanized colonial urban space.

Chikokiyana was a Black man's art of living sideways, but it was one star in a whole galaxy of symbols of transgressive innovativeness. The corner thus became both an unlikely physical meeting space and a metaphor for Africans' constricted and subversive lifestyles; Africans had to "cut corners" to make a living. They met at the street corner, turning it into an optic for a whole *tsvete* (illicit) cultural economy built around the conveyancing, repackaging, rebranding, and disposal of contraband, making a living beyond the line. Their innovativeness enabled them not only to survive, but also to thrive, despite the "wonderful poverty" (Shamuyarira 1965, 99) of colonial urbanity. Shops and factories formed sites for rich pickings to feed this political economy of subversion as each individual, like a goat, grazed where they were tethered. Shamuyarira (1965, 99–100) describes how this economy functioned:

> A man who works in a bakery brings a loaf of bread to his room in the evening, to exchange it for bicycle parts which someone who works in a bicycle shop brings along. Other workers come bearing spanners, pumps, shoes, shirts, groceries, meat straight from the butcheries. . . . A young man who works in a sweet factory will borrow from a friend oversize boots in order to stock his socks and boots of 2 lbs or more sweets. One man carries several sheathes of bacon under his vest. Another throws away half a dozen tins of condensed milk in the dustbin, covering them with rubbish from the floor. A fourth sticks an expensive fountain pen into a parcel of sugar he is taking

home. A fifth removes spanners in the boot of a car just come in for servicing. A sixth gives lifts to pedestrians.

To survive their sub-economic insertion into the colonial economy, Africans had to create a parallel, third space governed by barter, compassion, and mirth at beating the system. In these ways, the "loafers" and "spivs" of the colonial administrative counterinsurgency discourse were the heroes of *marukesheni*. They stole into the city, as Hugh Masekela (2015) put it, to "liberate" and courier goods from the shops, subverting the surveillance and policing functions of the street corner. Dauti's song was therefore symptomatic of, and a metaphor for, this creativity in the art of living and dancing sideways:

Ukati nzve, pachikona ndakuona	You dart around the corner, I see you!
Ukati nzve, paAmato ndakuona	When you dart by, at Amato, I do see you!

This is an exultant poetics of streetwise, subterranean disarmament of weaponized and statutory control of space, production, consumption, and leisure. The contestation is clearly boisterous, fleeting, self-conscious yet productive, enabled and disguised by disingenuous conformity. As it receded from the city center and elaborated itself into the fringes of *elokishini*, the self-fashioning became even more gastronomic, audacious, and exuberant.

On the urban fringe, the word *mahobho* denoted more than just the unruly crowd; it also meant "heaps," in a sexually suggestive sense. Lawrence Vambe observed that the name stuck after someone composed a hit called "Aya Mahobho Andakakuchengetera" (Here are the anatomical heaps and curves that I've been keeping for you), which leaves very little to the imagination:

Aya, Aya, mahobho	Here, here they are, big breasts and buttocks
Andakakuchengetera	That await you
Kushure mahobho	On my behind are big buttocks
Kumberi gaba rehuchi	On my front is a tin full of honey.[8]

The wicked tune stirred the sensual imagination of the disproportionately male *lumpenproletariat* and triggered moral panics among the respectable middle classes by its transgressive *funyungu*, cheerful vulgarity. The novelist Dambudzo Marechera adapted the song as "Shure Kwehure Kunotambatamba" (The buttocks of a whore shake) in his novella "The House of Hunger," and as Maurice Vambe (2007, 364) explains, the song was a powerful index of the depraved conditions of African life in the locations. As some NCs had charged a decade earlier, organizers of these "night dances" often featured hired girls as erotic dancers and sex workers who, as songs like "Aya Mahobho Andakakuchengetera" suggest, flaunted their anatomies in song and deed. Through these corporeal transgressions, African underclass women boldly defied middle-class, conservative African sensibilities and official criminalization of the sexual carnivalization and racialized eroticization of the female body to reinscribe a potent gender dynamic onto the very public realm of colonial urbanity. These were gendered modes of being that thrived by defying containment in the spaces of the displaced, where those disarmed through dispossession and scattering could be confined in *elokishini* and its kraals of re-creation.

Musarurwa and his Bulawayo Sweet Rhythms Band colleagues (who included the Mutyambizi brothers, Mutizwa and Muchemwa) saw themselves as the "kings of the tea parties" in the 1940s–50s. Ivy Mupungu, Musarurwa's daughter, could not remember her father ever spending a weekend at home, as he was always "playing at the tea parties, weddings, and other social functions in Bulawayo and its outlying rural precincts" (interview). These were the social circuits that produced "Skokiaan." As Muchemwa Mutyambizi told me (Mutyambizi family, interview), "We used to go out into the villages such as Mbembesi to drink *chikokiyana*. . . . We saw that our love for *chikokiyana* was so great, and we composed that song. Patrons loved the song very much. We all shared this *chikokiyana* mentality."

I have argued that "Skokiaan" should be read as a declaratively defiant *chandada* culture—an antinomic celebration of a repressed, criminalized leisure culture. It is common knowledge that Musarurwa's song is an instrumental. It is fascinating, then, that some claim to know the song's meaning in spite of its lack of lyrics. Bill Saidi (pers. comm.) claimed that he understood the song's meaning from its mood, its affect: "There is a part where Musarurwa's saxophone almost cries out for rescue from the devil drink." The intellectuals of the Organization of African Unity (OAU) gathered at the Pan-African Cultural Festival in Algiers in July 1969 commented of the "Black force" in African American jazz—Milford Graves's counterchant to Amiri Baraka's poem "Black Dada Nihilissimus" and his flogging of the cymbals: "This is violence, the violence of the slums" (OAU 1969, 26). One can similarly read the violence of "Skokiaan," an intoxicant that elicited "cries of pain and joy mingled in a strange orchestration," as the poet and revolutionary Agostinho Neto (1974, 43) described the underclass Saturday night in the Angolan *musseques* (slums). "Skokiaan" is a story of the defiant, tragic African struggle with the dehumanizing ghetto of colonial settler Africa.

In some ways, "Skokiaan" was therefore a symbolic manifestation of the internalized violation of colonized being, which Africans reinforced in a (self-) destructive struggle against external domination. In that sense, Musarurwa's wailing saxophone becomes a metaphor for the underclass's search for self-liberation and its bid to reject ultimate domination, the drowning of the colonized voice in its own misery. *Chikokiyana* was a sign of violence, or indeed a "violent sign," as Valentine Mudimbe (1988, 82) designated it. To colonial anthropologists like Malinowski (1959, xxi), *chikokiyana* was a trope for an aberrant mixture of the Same and the Other, a mixture "symptomatic and symbolic of culture change. . . . Anything which quickly increased the alcoholic content was added; calcium carbide, methylated spirits, tobacco, molasses and sugar." Mudimbe asks how anyone, "even an African, could survive after drinking such a poison?" Well, more than a violent sign, then, "Skokiaan" was also a text of violent culture change, a palimpsest of forced African unmaking and remaking, the very essence of dominated but stubborn African being. "Skokiaan" the silent text is more than a straightforward text of African survival. It is a subtext of disingenuous, complicit silence.

In Bulawayo, Sithole took me to the home of Kembo Ncube, a former comedian and pennywhistler who occasionally sessioned with the Bulawayo Sweet Rhythms Band. Ncube used to perform a version of "Skokiaan" with what are believed to be the original, unrecorded lyrics. Ncube serenaded me with a welcoming note right from the gate, playing the unmistakable "Skokiaan" on his pennywhistle, minus the lyrics! When he paused, I asked, "But I was told you did the song with lyrics?" He half-jokingly chided me, saying, "The words are in there; I was blowing them in there!" Saidi was right! I was intrigued. Happily, Ncube then obligingly crooned the words for me:

Baba naamai	Dear father and mother
Musambonwe chikokiyana	Don't ever drink *chikokiyana*
Chinokupedzai mapapu	It destroys your lungs
Musambonwe chikoki	Never drink *chikoki*
Nechikoki	Because of *chikoki*
Nechikokiyana	Because of *chikokiyana*
Nechikoki	Because of *chikoki*
Kupera kuti fu!	All of them, gone!

Ncube told me in 2012 that after listening to Musarurwa's song, he "saw that *paita chingwa chakapusa pano apa*!" (there is foolish bread right here!) He thus crafted his way into the Bulawayo Sweet Rhythms Band as a session vocalist. Six years later, I met Daramu Karanga, the founder of Hallelujah Chicken Run, who recruited Thomas Mapfumo and others into the Mhangura Mine band in the 1960s. Karanga grew up at Morris Police Depot in Salisbury, where he admired Musarurwa and the Police Band performing before the former left policing. Karanga closely followed Musarurwa's exploits on wind instruments. In July 2012, Karanga performed for me his own version of "Skokiaan," complete with lyrics that are strikingly similar to Ncube's:

Sekuru nambuya	Grandfather and grandmother
Ndakambokuyambirai	I once warned you
Musanwe chikokiyana	Do not drink *chikokiyana*
Mazuva ose	Each day
Munomukira chikokiyana.	You wake up to *chikokiyana.*

These two sets of lyrics similarly counsel against partaking of *chikokiyana.* If these are the original "Skokiaan" lyrics, composed by Musarurwa, why did he choose not to record them? Musarurwa composed a number of other works as instrumental pieces. But all my informants told me that "Skokiaan" was composed with lyrics. The puzzle, then, is to explain the exclusion of the lyrics from the studio. Was it a simple artistic decision, or did he perhaps dislike the lyrics, or their dissonance and apparent complicity with the system? Perhaps the lyrics were indeed Ncube's belated innovative contribution to Musarurwa's instrumental composition. But what did the former policeman really think about *chikokiyana,* the devil brew?

Musarurwa's daughter, Ivy, told me that her father "never touched *chikokiyana,*" preferring "European" beer in defiance of the racial laws that debarred Africans from consuming it. "He drove around with it in his car even at the pain of fines until the police eventually left him alone." However, Musarurwa's colleagues the Mutyambizi brothers laughed off the suggestion that Musarurwa did not touch *chikokiyana,* describing to me how they "all drank . . . so much that [Musarurwa] couldn't even direct his sax to his mouth! But once he did, ah, he was a gun, a bomb!" Whatever the origins of the lyrics, the antinomy of a "Skokiaan" that campaigned against *chikokiyana* in unrecorded lyrics and apparently celebrated it in a camouflaged studio version remains intriguing.

What complicates the "Skokiaan" narrative is the paradox of the underground popularity of a brew notorious for eating away the hands of its brewers and the lips and "lungs" of its consumers. Masekela's grandmother brewed *skokiaan,* which, he writes, made the faces of those who drank it to quench their thirst or to anesthetize themselves against the suffocating woes of their world distorted, and their legs, lips, cheeks, hands, feet, eyes, and livers swollen (Masekela and Cheers 2014, 10). The key might be located in the criminalization of both the deep traditions of African brewing and "native" consumption of "European" beer. Rejecting the stolen, diluted "kaffir beer" that the municipalities brewed for them, many urban Africans brewed and consumed the low-cost monstrosity in backyard hideouts and the comfort of their homes. As Lawrence Vambe (1976, 171) noted, "Having your beer freely, at any time and with whomsoever you liked was an essential part of that individual freedom that anyone looked for." If the loss of that freedom was symbolic of Africans' disenfranchisement, this *chandada* was a particularly (self-)destructive way to hit back. This is how, to borrow Tsitsi Dangarembga's (2004, 4) beautiful explanation, "Skokiaan" pointed unsystematic fingers at the conditions of the times, as popular music will.

The brew made drinkers *kenge* (high) at minimal financial cost. The Bulawayo Sweet Rhythms Band, the "kings of tea parties," imbibed it before their shows. Muchemwa Mutyambizi attested,

> *Chikokiyana* made one sharp so that when you start playing, you became cleverer because of the extra energy coming from it. That is why they called me Hellfire or Brimstone. I really caught fire with that stuff, and I would crack the sax! Before our shows at Stanley Hall we moved around the location rehearsing. You would see women abandoning their pots on the open fires outside their houses, joining the crowds that followed our vehicle as we blasted "Skokiaan." That song was a magnet.

A self-expressive organic ghetto register, the *skokiaan symbolique* furnished the dislocated and marginalized African underclasses with a common grammar by which they could fashion a sense of community, common belonging, social intercourse, survival strategies, and self-crafted identities in the otherwise alienating environment. Yvonne Vera (2000, 6) wrote that music enabled urban Africans to "create cracks within which to live." Perhaps one could go further to say that song itself was one such crack. Thus, the women of the locations could forget their worries about having no kitchens and cooking on open braziers to rally to a familiar language—"Skokiaan"—and in the process help thread registers of reciprocity and solidarity with both the musicians and the composite crowds that song mobilized. The power of the crowd, writes Vicente L. Rafael (2003, 415), is its capacity to disrupt the routinization of public space and send infrastructure into new alignments. Energized by intoxicating song, this "mob" brought alive the underclass power to remap *rukesheni* from an architecture of colonial dislocation and confinement into an open, creative workshop for self-reassemblage. The women's outdoor hearths served as both a physical and psychological optic through which to superimpose their own version of the city onto colonial designs, making it a collectively self-made, performatively mobile, and defiantly jovial acoustic space. As Mattaka observed, *tsaba tsaba*, the 1940s underclass musical convention that "Skokiaan" epitomized, had its followers, and these were fanatical crowds who talked to the music and took pleasure in the music's talking to them.

To commerce—ever lurking in the shadows of these creative subaltern commons—the same crowds that chased after the rehearsal trucks were a fertile market, already nurtured and ripe to generate profits for international capital. The ubiquitous gramophone was the universal canon. This was the medium that brought "Skokiaan" to Masekela long before he recorded his own version, growing up in Witbank's cacophonous stereosonic *elokishini* environment where householders who possessed the gramophone "blasted their music at full volume . . . leav[ing] their doors wide open so that the music would waft out over their yards and into the streets" (Masekela and Cheers 2004, 9; Masekela, interview). Walter M. B. Nhlope, a South African music journalist and talent scout for Gallo Records, was speaking the language of commerce when he decried the "abuse" of *tsaba tsaba*, a creation of the street and the township, urging that this music be promoted in place of the long-running American imitations:

> Everybody spoke of Tsaba Tsaba. . . . There were no radios to broadcast it all over; but everybody sang it. It had the spirit of Africa in it. . . . Regardless of torrents of scathing abuse, it swept the country. . . . In bioscopes we've seen Harlem dance the Big Apple, the Shag, and Africa's creation, La Conga . . . and these dances have not been recipients of abuse as Tsaba-Tsaba. . . . Europeans measure our development and progress not by our imitative powers but by originality. (Coplan 1985, 154)

David Coplan concurs with Nhlope that the composition of "Skokiaan" was a realization of the fledgling African creative confidence, a happy development for capital.

If commerce sought to capture this creative ghetto for financial profit, so also does Eurocentric epistemology seek to capture it for intellectual self-validation. In its selective approbation of this success, it realienates and depersonalizes certain of the icons of these marginalized cultures. For instance, the theory secretes Musarurwa away from the colonial ghetto and repositions him within the middle class because of his colonial education and training. He becomes a cosmopolitan, a theoretical paradigm that performs at least three related functions in this reading: it simultaneously sanitizes and perpetuates the alienation of the colonial ghetto—to buttress Zeleza (1997, 103)—by turning certain classes into caricatures of the European self, then it overcelebrates this western ratio, and, lastly, through inverse action, it overshadows, devalues, and inferiorizes those elements of African cultures that "global" culture cannot read, authorize, or appropriate into its own "margins." Acculturation, a crucial survival tactic for victims of violent colonization, is authorized and celebrated over the object of its violence. The countercultural ghetto sensibility was integral to, rather than apart from, Musarurwa's success even as, materially, his family became (according to his daughter) the "envy of the neighborhood."

Such was the intensity of this *skokiaan* subculture that it can be argued that Musarurwa was fortunate to escape the fate of his fellow musician, the legendary George Sibanda, who drowned himself in popularity-induced alcoholism. Like Sibanda, Musarurwa's everyday life and social consciousness escaped the trap of the adoptive notions of class. He rode to his beloved *chikokiyana* parties in his automobile, the quintessential symbol of the bourgeoisie, and, in spite of some puritanical vilification, his music appealed very much across class lines. "Skokiaan" was so popular, recalled Muchemwa Mutyambizi, that "everyone who had a gramophone had that record. You would hear it played at this house and the next and the next; people loved the song." Those with no gramophones benefited from the gregarious communal *madandaro* (platforms of entertainment) the song helped mobilize. For decades—indeed, until her passing in 2008—Miriam Mlambo (interview) used the song as the signature tune for her children's radio programs, even as she remained dubious about its message, which she would not explain to her young audiences, only emphasizing the artistic beauty of the song. The song's reception demonstrates that, while maintaining the context of its creation, it appealed to a broad spectrum of listeners by syncretically jumbling the fragile categories of class and culture that defined African consciousness in midcentury colonial Zimbabwe. "Skokiaan" was also a text of pent-up African political commentary.

"Skokiaan" issued from, and its context of performance invested it with, deep ideological significance. The song narrativized underclass creation of independent spaces on the unruly margins beyond the officially sanctioned and confining *madandaro*—the platforms of the entertainment hall, the beer hall, and the polite middle-class tea party. The song also mediated complex dialogues within the ghetto and the peri-urban communities that produced it. I have insisted on reading the song as antinomic because it can certainly be romanticized. Imbibers of the monstrosity knew that *chandada* was at best unhealthy and at worst toxic. Because of this, given a choice, Ncube would prefer "Seven Days," the traditional grain brew fermented naturally over seven days, or even the municipality's stolen version, "Kaffir beer," albeit begrudgingly because, he pointed out, "I personally didn't like the idea of buying that [Kaffir] beer and have my money used to build houses for which I again paid rent! But what could we do? We were a Y-E-S people, powerless . . ." (interview). Ncube resented this cannibal development, the colonial urbanization on the cheap that depended on and deepened African poverty. "Kaffir beer" was a hated, doubly articulated symbol of that underdevelopment.

This resentment foreshadowed activist attacks on these physical architectures of oppression and exploitation in the 1950s. Many Africans were conscious that they were perpetuating their own subjugation and disenfranchisement by patronizing the beer halls. They understood that the state's objection to their own independent brewing and drinking cultures was primarily economic. African autonomous beer cultures undermined the state's alcohol monopoly, the source of the only funds the settler state was willing to spend on African housing and amenities, including sports and other recreational facilities. Africans had limited means to resist the colonial state's illegitimate, institutionalized authority. They therefore resorted to their powerful a/moral discourses, alternative institutions, and transgressive performances and lifestyles. In that context, then, songs like "Skokiaan" were political, "talking about how Africans suffered to the extent of drinking *chikokiyana* and living on their feet, always pursued by police on horseback" (Sithole, interview). And the power of subversion was produced right there, at the point of criminalization. Criminalization helped to generate and enrich discursive texts of underclass subversion. Rich underclass discourses, such as "Skokiaan," articulated themselves through the register of the pleasurable margins—the open spaces, the street corner, and *musika*, the public market. How did

Louis Armstrong connect with this register when he visited colonial Zimbabwe in 1960? Did that visit reshape his musical consciousness?

The Turning Tide: Louis Comes Home

In October 1960, Armstrong crossed the Atlantic on a multicountry tour of Africa cosponsored by Pepsi and the U.S. State Department, which positioned him as one of Cold War America's "Jazz Goodwill Ambassadors" (Von Eschen 2000, 170). Armstrong presented the Southern Rhodesia leg of his journey as a trip "to see the famous composer of 'Skokiaan'" in a way that suggested the contestability of his assigned role in American diplomacy. But he was only one among many artists who had made the pilgrimage to pay homage to Musarurwa. South Africa's Spokes Mashiyane, the doyen of the pennywhistle, had come earlier to take a peek at the magical ways in which the virtuoso manipulated his sax (Mupungu, interview). Nonetheless, in many ways, Armstrong's visit was the most significant and symbolic. On a general level, it personified—in the powerful figure of Satchmo—the African American homage to the motherland, and on a more personal level it was the legend's "return to the source" to authenticate the song that had so inspired him and his American colleagues.

Images of the first glimpses of Armstrong have persisted. Musarurwa's daughter described to me how, right on the plane's staircase, "Armstrong performed the song, then asked Musarurwa to 'play it yourself,' after which he shook his head, dumb-struck by the man's dexterity on the horn. Then they shook hands." Thus satisfied, Armstrong handed Musarurwa a black-striped cream jacket that proclaimed on the back, "August Musarurwa: the famous composer of Skokiaan." Africans had greatly anticipated Armstrong's trip, with *Parade* running "Welcome home BROTHER" banners for several months. Beginning right at the airport, gifts changed hands and cameras captured the moments for posterity. De Black Evening Follies received him with the gift of a *ngomarungundu* (a gigantic drum), while the canvas artist Sambo had imagined the musician's departure for Africa in a huge painting of the man towering up from the horizons of an American cityscape, "blowing his huge horn across the Atlantic" (*Parade,* November 1960, January 1961). Crowds thronged Salisbury Airport, with *Parade* tying the cultural strings that connected the African American and African Black Atlantic in such famous images as the photograph of the "three greats": Musarurwa, Peter Rezant (the leader of South Africa's Merry Black Birds), and Armstrong.

Armstrong and Musarurwa went on to share the stage in both Salisbury and Bulawayo, thrilling crowds with their combined repertoire. Armstrong was already a legend in the country, and Africans attached much cultural and political significance to his visit. *Parade* marketed the tour by highlighting its potential implications for African struggles for racial equality. African Americans gave

Africans a model of self-redemption through race pride, self-help, and education, resignifying the African American iconicity beyond the U.S. government's diplomatic designs. Thus, harnessed by the voices of African progress that spoke through *Parade,* the Armstrong tour presented itself as an opportunity to further the cause of pan-African solidarity and development. In its November 1960 issue, the magazine exhorted readers to support the shows: "Half the proceeds of his shows will be given to the furtherance of our educational facilities. . . . With this in mind, PARADE feels everyone will make an effort to attend at least one of the shows." Armstrong's identification with Musarurwa also helped to bridge the seemingly intractable fissures of class and race (the latter enforced by law) in Rhodesian geographies of leisure. Middle-class Africans, the poor, and whites all traveled long distances both within Southern Rhodesia and from neighboring countries to watch Armstrong share the stage with Musarurwa.

Yet belying all this excitement was a palpable official anxiety about the huge experiment. To both white settler Rhodesia and Satchmo's American handlers, the tour was a challenge to the ingrained racial norms and practices that marked Rhodesia as "one of the most racially segregated places on earth" (Lewis 1996). Mark Lewis was the Director of the United States Information Service (USIS) for the Federation of Rhodesia and Nyasaland in Salisbury, and he claimed that the tour put him in a dilemma: "One morning I received an unexpected message marked 'urgent' from the State Department's Cultural Exchange Program in Washington: 'Louis Armstrong and All Stars in West Africa. Advise soonest if you wish performances.'" To Lewis and his USIS colleagues, the question was whether Armstrong was going to perform before segregated audiences, in accordance with Rhodesian custom, which would guarantee both white attendance and security, or would skip the country entirely. Apartheid South Africa did not even entertain the idea because, remembered Masekela, it was "not in the country's best interest" (Masekela and Cheers 2004, 82). Predictably, this stance infuriated Masekela, whose career had blossomed in part not only on Armstrong's songs but also, fortuitously for him, on the legend's used saxophone, which the latter had mailed him as a gift from the U.S. Similarly, the Rhodesians knew that, as Lewis said, "both blacks and whites . . . listened to his jazz on the Voice of America," and yet bringing the artist would test "the Rhodesian way of life," with uncertain political consequences.

They finally decided that a "visit by Armstrong would be an opportunity to dramatically demonstrate where America stood on racial discrimination. . . . Our goal has got to be non-segregated concerts if Armstrong is going to perform." An America cracking under the push by African Americans for civil rights seized on a famous African American as an envoy to an Africa increasingly swayed toward eastern ideologies, taking his visit as an opportunity to "give the United States greater credibility with the black majority" in Rhodesia, even if whites were to stay away. They were therefore pleasantly surprised that the Rhodesian government granted them permission for unsegregated concerts within a week, with Lewis reasoning that it had chosen to "keep the matter at a low level . . . to convey the impression that its decision was not a serious political problem . . . and that it was decided very quickly." But "insiders told us later that there was sharp debate within the highest levels of the government."

Armstrong performed on two consecutive nights; first in the Salisbury Showground (Glamis Stadium), which seated twenty-five thousand, then in the Queen's Cricket Ground in Bulawayo. An anonymous former Rhodesian reports a "fairly modest" crowd at Salisbury, perhaps as few as three hundred (versus the two or three thousand attendees in places like Kenya and Nigeria), and almost exclusively Black.[9] Miriam Mlambo attended the show with her husband, and she told me she saw "no whites, only blacks." On the other hand, the American diplomat—his memory admittedly refracted through this "brush with history"—recalled an overflowing crowd that shattered the color bar, and thus a big victory for U.S. Cold War jazz diplomacy:

> The standard ropes separating blacks and whites were gone; blacks were everywhere, not just at the far ends of the stadium . . . For the first time ever at an event of this magnitude in Southern Rhodesia, whites and blacks were sitting side by side completely filling the stadium: white government officials and business executives, black clerks, white farmers and black laborers who had come in trucks and buses from nearby rural areas, white and black students, white and black church leaders, white parliamentarians and black policemen, white army officers and black troops—all of them cheek by jowl in the stands. When Armstrong appeared, everyone rose and cheered together.

Lewis writes that Armstrong, apparently conscious of the epochal significance of the moment, captured the mood and sealed the new racial imagination in six words: "It's sure nice to see this." According to the anonymous memoirist, "some reports of the day suggest that there had been racial incidents or tension in the grounds, however, it is not known what the extent of this was."

Friday Mbirimi was a member of the Capital City Dixies, a boy band that welcomed Armstrong in "blackface" paint and costumes, proudly showing off the "American styles taught to us by our white manager, Eric Williamson" (Mbirimi, interview). They would learn only much later that Armstrong "was very disappointed to see Africans imitating American racist stereotypes, painting their faces like that!" Mbirimi remembered that "white people came, filling the stadium, and he performed and cried while doing so." He learned the reason for Armstrong's tears later: "He thought to himself, 'Here I am in Africa, performing to a stadium full of whites—with blacks sitting out there on the fringes.'" Was he crying, or only wiping profuse sweat from the early evening Salisbury heat, as the anonymous Rhodesian describes him doing? Whatever perception is correct, the

Armstrong shows painted a microcosmic picture of the Rhodesian way of life for Mbirimi: "You couldn't mix with whites; the seating there in large part reflected how people lived in this country."

Daramu Karanga also vividly remembered the Salisbury show. He did not recall any standard color-bar ropes, but he remembered well the "banana and orange peels that whites rained on us from their wooden stages as we sat on the ground opposite" (interview). These familiar little racial missiles might not have meant much to perpetrators accustomed to behaving worse, but they can be significant to their victims and to visitors. Thus, asked by a journalist what he thought of Rhodesia, Armstrong shot back "without missing a beat: 'Y'all sure know how to keep little black children in bare feet!'" (Lewis 1996). Armstrong's "desegregated" shows certainly opened gates for a tour of Rhodesia's racial terrain. And it does seem that national politics arrived on stage that Salisbury night, considering that Bob Gilmore and his Bobcats were one of Armstrong's supporting acts. Gilmore was a member of the National Unifying Force, a white liberal party that supported black majority rule in Rhodesia.

Lewis claimed more victories for American jazz diplomacy. He credited the Armstrong concerts with "spark[ing] new impetus toward desegregation." He correctly noted, "One of the first barriers to fall in Southern Rhodesia was segregated seating in entertainment, including movie houses. Next came the lifting of color bars in athletic teams, sports competitions, and in spectator seating at sporting events." The antisegregation movement had started a few years earlier under the banner of the Citizens Against the Colour Bar Association, or Freedom Sitters, co-led by Lovemore Chimonyo and Terence Ranger. Following the strategies of antisegregationists in the U.S. South, this group invaded public parks, cafes, hotels, restaurants, bars, public buildings, swimming pools, barbershops, churches, beauty contests, and other functions and spaces reserved for whites.[10] The first hotel to admit Africans was Salisbury's Federal, declared multiracial in 1965, soon to be followed by Jameson and Queens two years after the High Court and the Court of Appeals struck down segregation as *ultra-vires* municipal law.[11] Considering the decades-long history of desegregation activism, it is unlikely that Armstrong's tour carried the sort of political weight that Lewis attributed to it, and the fact that the Freedom Sitters won their court judgment just a year after Armstrong's tour was most likely coincidental. Yet its symbolic significance, particularly to Africans and American diplomacy, cannot be ignored.

However one may apportion credit for the victories, these forms of Black political action were deeply connected with the global Black struggles in which Armstrong—otherwise widely disparaged in American Black circles as an Uncle Tom—had just been controversially implicated, particularly after his scathing critique of the U.S. government over the shooting and molestation of Black kids in segregated Arkansas schools—the so-called Little Rock Crisis. Cultural politics is a terrain of symbolism. And it is testimony to the power of symbolism that, when Satchmo stepped off the boat on the Congo River, his African hosts serenaded him as Okuka Lokole, the "jungle wizard who charms wild beasts with his music" (Jones and Chilton 1971, 210). It was that magical symbolism that briefly stopped the war in Katanga; the foes reportedly declared a daylong truce, and fighters from both sides gave Armstrong armed escort and went on to enjoy his performance together. Musarurwa's reciprocating trip to the United States the following year might have further enhanced the transatlantic Black consciousness that took "Skokiaan" to America and brought Satchmo to Rhodesia. Unfortunately, the untimely death of his wife put paid to his plans (Mupungu, interview).

Nowhere in the accounts of Armstrong's eventful forty-five-concert tour of Africa is there any suggestion that he experienced Africa as a happy jungle of his and his western colleagues' imagination. Years later, Masekela asked Armstrong about the presumptuousness of the "happy happy Africa" lyrics, and Armstrong cryptically told him that he "just thought that was a jolly happy song, man!" (Masekela, interview). A son of the ill-fated Black townships in apartheid South Africa, Masekela told me that he would reflect on the ironies of the song before recording his own version with Herb Alpert in 1978, with scant lyrics that celebrate the ubiquitous Southern African *shebeen* culture. The power of "Skokiaan" is its capacity to capture the imagination, and it is precisely the gap between fantasy and reality that is the province of artistic creativity and symbolism.

August Machona Musarurwa, the composer of "Skokiaan." Courtesy of the Zimbabwe College of Music. Photographer, date, and place unknown.

Armstrong, who was with group — Trummy Young trombone), Danny Barcelona trumpet), Barney Leon Bigard clarinet), Mort Herbert (bass), Billy Kyle (piano) and Velma Middleton (vocalist) — stopped in Accra, then Lagos; then came to Kenya's Nairobi; Blantyre was next, then Salisbury, Bulawayo, Lusaka and Gwe. He then went on to trouble-torn former Belgian Congo where he met Katanga President Moise Tshombe. By

ght: three "greats" the music world ve a hearty laugh they pose together r this memorable hotograph. On the ft is Peter Rezant, ader of the eminent usicians, the Merry lack Birds of Johan-esburg; in the cen-e, the "Old Man" imself and on the ght the creator of at sensation hit-ne "SKOKIAAN", uite a trio, isn't it.

SATCH 'THE GREAT' MEETS OUR' GREATS'

The "Three Greats": Louis Armstrong (center) meets August Machona Musarurwa (right) and Peter Rezant (left). Courtesy of *Parade Magazine*.

Armstrong's palpable influence: Daramu Karanga with his grandson Louis, the son of Satchmo Karanga. Harare, 2012. Courtesy of the author.

"Skokiaan" is a significant piece of symbolic art that should be read as a text of historical experiences in its context of production but enriched and counter-poised by offshore imaginations. Carnivalized public drinking, dancing, sex, and raucous socializing constituted the bane of colonial "native administration." For many underclass Africans, engaging in transgressive "disorder" was a way to defy the expensive, politically constrictive municipal superintendence and to generate life and thrill. They sidestepped such strictures to remap their own terrains of leisure. *Chikokiyana,* which official discourse considered a bastard "bush" brew and the ultimate *elokishini* evil, antinomically reads as a metaphor for this African resistance against the colonial architectures of control, as subaltern transgression of white geographies of nervous power, as self-anesthetizing re-creation, and as a quest for sociopolitical autonomy. As such, "Skokiaan," the song that lyricized these processes, is a crucial transcript of not only underclass politics, but also the everyday, transgressive, and regenerative social counterhegemonic repertoires of the street corner, the ungovernable city margin that encroached onto the center, and the irreverent *musika.* And indeed, as Jack Wheaton (1994, 146) wrote in *All That Jazz,* great music transcends time and space.

8 Usable Pasts

Crafting Madzimbabwe through Memory, Tradition, Song

Yesterday I was a born again Christian. I lost my original name from Chandapiwa to Epiphania. . . . In the battle field I changed my name again. I became Afrikan. I remember the lions doing reconnaisance.

—Freedom Nyamubaya, "A Haunted Place"

[The] second phase of the struggle was inspired by the first and the image of Nehanda. One grew up with that image in songs.

—Yvonne Vera, interview with Eva Hunter

Decentering Gun-centric Historiographies of Chimurenga, Recentering the Self

In the book that earned him acclaim as a theorist of revolutionary self-liberation, Frantz Fanon (1967b, 45) visualized the "native" at the outbreak of the armed struggle against colonialism:

> At long last the native, gun in hand, stands face to face with . . . the forces of colonialism. And the youth of a colonized country, growing up in an atmosphere of shot and fire, may well make a mock of, and does not hesitate to pour scorn upon the zombies of his ancestors, the horses with two heads, the dead who rise again, and the djinns who rush into your body while you yawn. The native discovers reality and transforms it into the pattern of his customs, into the practice of violence and into his plan for freedom.

The history of the Second Chimurenga, the liberation struggle that lasted from the 1960s to 1980, makes clear that Zimbabwean ancestors were neither zombies nor the other fairy-tale figures that Fanon ridiculed, and that, in fact, they were the spiritual guides for the war. It is a story of how the ancestors and their progeny, the departed and the living, the past and the present, cooperated in a concerted self-liberation struggle (Lan 1985; Gumbo 1995).

Fanon's imagination of the African guerrilla as a hitherto "sleeping native" latterly roused from a deep slumber by "shot and fire" is both historically and intellectually misleading. Fanon fetishizes the gun and misunderstood the power and meaning of cultural armament in African philosophies and practices of self-liberation. He fails to make sense of the historical genealogies of resistance and of the liberation wars that Africans fought to stem European attempts at colonial occupation—which wars, if Fanon's argument is technological, employed the long-demystified gun and other (then) sophisticated weaponries of colonial and anticolonial warfare. Africans used guns in the First Chimurenga, which they were already manufacturing by the 1890s. The Second Chimurenga therefore symbolized cultural more than technological rearmament. Gun-centrism misrepresents the story of African self-liberation because guns were useful to the extent that the liberating self was culturally fully re/equipped. And it is that story of self-liberation beyond the gun that I focus on in this chapter. It locates the Zimbabwean liberation agenda in transgenerational self-knowledge and heritage, not the assimilation of colonial customs into African truths.

Claiming Usable Pasts, Forging Alternative Futures

Africans deployed their traditions and historical memories as usable pasts both to counter their construction as primitive "tribes" and to craft new national identities in a process that illustrates Edward Said's (1989, 219) conceptualization of anticolonial revolution as a "recla[mation of] traditions, histories and cultures from imperialism." In other words, Africans drew on their histories for cultural rearmament. While colonial ethnomusicology coopted "tribal dances" for ideological domination, nationalists antithetically deployed African traditions as an indigenous episteme to articulate different political ideologies and conceptions of selfhood.

The understanding of tradition here assumes the sense explicated by Dipesh Chakrabarty (2000, 15), that such cultures were "traditional only in so far as [their] roots could be traced back to the pre-colonial times, but [they were] by no means archaic in the sense of being outmoded." In other words, my conception of tradition refers to the "coexistence of past and present" (Shils 1981, 16). This versatility of African traditions—the reconstitution of the past into the present in the forging of viable futures—starkly contradicted the anthropological ossification of African being. I posit, therefore, that the popularity of Chimurenga music in the 1960s illustrated the emboldening of a preexisting, "unconquered site of on-going battles" (Chakrabarty 2000, 65) that had raged through various timbres in the preceding decades. Far from being a musical invention of the 1960s, Chimurenga was a historical sensibility and practice, a militant rearticulation and reaffirmation of a transgenerational awareness of national heritage and aspiration. It is this memory of the cultures that historically resisted imperialism that constituted a powerful usable past for the oppressed, a subaltern consciousness that has often eluded scholars intent on restoring African agency to histories of anticolonial struggles. Musical articulation of Madzimbabwe insurgency remains a fecund archive of African philosophies of self-crafting and power. It was precisely on the humus of these engaged cultures of resistance that political leaders fertilized cultural nationalism, the emotive consciousness that drove the liberation struggle in the second half of the twentieth century.

Jeffrey Olick (2002, 20) underlined the need to think about why pasts are usable at all. Pasts are archives of historical memory, which can constitute rallying points for struggles for self-restoration or for the crafting of different collective futures for subjugated peoples. African liberation struggles rallied popular support around collective memories of lost self-determination and brutalization by European colonizers. As Said (1989, 197) has observed, the legitimacy and cultural primacy of the nationalist parties that led the successful struggle against the Europeans depended on their asserting an unbroken continuity back to the first warriors who stood against the intrusive white man: "The Algerian National Liberation Front (FLN) which inaugurated its insurrection against France in 1954 traced its ancestry to the Emir Abdel Kader, who fought the French occupation during the 1830s and 1840s." Similarly, "in Guinea and Mali resistance against the French is traced back . . . generations to Samory and Hajji Omar."

On his 1962 continental tour to canvass support for armed struggle in South Africa, Rolihlahla Nelson Mandela (2013, 299) was struck by the spectacle of the FLN's intergenerational guerrilla apostolate on parade in Morocco. At the head of the march "sauntered proud, battle-hardened veterans in turbans, long tunics, and sandals, who had started the battle many years before. They carried the weapons they had used: sabers, old flintlock rifles, battle-axes, and assegais. They were followed in turn by younger soldiers, all carrying modern arms and equally proud." This spectacle of intergenerational resistance seemed to Mandela like a "walking history" of the FLN, with the past reinforcing the present. In Zimbabwe, guerrillas from ZANU (the Zimbabwe African National Union) and ZAPU (the Zimbabwe African People's Union) who took up arms against the colonial regime in the 1960s came in the name of—or, rather, came as—Murenga, Chaminuka, Mbuya Nehanda, Kaguvi, and other heroic ancestor figures from 1896–97 and even earlier. As the executioner's noose hung over her, Nehanda told the British colonists that her bones would rise again. Such a return represented self-reconstitution by a repressed transcendental African being.

The National Democratic Party (NDP) built its political program on this crucible of political and cultural renaissance, articulating a gallant past to authorize a sovereign future. Breaking the inherited reformist notions of colonial constitutionalism, the party urged Africans to abandon the mirage of misplaced hopes of inclusion in the exclusivist colonial system and instead to reconcile with their alienated pasts, seeing such reconciliation as one powerful means of freeing and recovering themselves as a people. The party rejected a flawed liberation agenda premised on the inevitability of subjection to colonialism and adoption of colonial customs, choosing instead one based on the wisdom and teachings of the ancestors (Alfred and Corntassel 2005, 612). Thus, the NDP discarded the evolutionary language of "civilization" and advocated the reclamation of the essence of despoiled African being: land, languages, names, dress, spirituality, food, music, and dance. Such self-reclamation involved renouncing the missionary miseducation that branded African cosmologies as heathenism and indigenous lifestyles as backwardness (Shamuyarira 1965, 62). It was the renaissance that saw Chandapiwa reborn as Freedom Nyamubaya, an Afrikan guerrilla whose assegai figuratively shredded the estranging *mushunje*—the burial shroud of epiphanic missionary witchcrafting.[1] Nyamubaya's rebirth was enabled only "by the radical and deep-seated refusal of that which others have made of us," in Sartre's reading (preface to Fanon 1968, 17) of Fanon's call to revolutionary violence.

Colonialism accentuated the power of dance as both a tool of alienation and a weapon of resistance and subversion. At the height of the *chimanjemanje* craze in the 1940s, wrote Nathan Shamuyarira (1965, 62), many "Africans had become ashamed of being seen performing [traditional] dancing, and preferred to learn ballroom steps." The story of Maurice Nyagumbo, told in chapter 4, is illustrative: he sought to climb the social ladder in Joni through ballroom dancing, his alibi against political activism. Similarly, Robert Mugabe recounted to Dali Tambo, on SABC's program *People of the South,* how he and his Fort Hare University colleagues—including Tambo's father, Oliver—would sneak into the neighboring Lovedale girls' school, pair themselves up with the female students, and imagine fashioning themselves into "African gentlemen" through quickstep and ballroom dancing.[2] Mandela—another close friend of Dali's father—acknowledged that in addition to physics, Fort Hare also taught him another precise physical science, ballroom dancing: "To a crackly old phonograph in the dining hall, we spent hours practicing fox-trots and waltzes, each of us taking turns leading and following. Our idol was Victor Sylvester, the world champion of ballroom dancing" (Mandela 2013, 47). Sponsored dancing and sporting had helped to undermine the Industrial and Commercial Workers Union's efforts to mobilize workers for political action in the 1930s (see chapter 4).

With the resurgence of radical cultural nationalism in the late 1950s, traditional dancing eclipsed the western dances as a tool for fashioning a self-liberating African personality. Nyagumbo, and later his fellow countrymen, "became patriotic" and returned home to form the Salisbury Youth League, a culturally conscious precursor to the NDP. They abandoned the European dances and deployed their own traditional dances to cultivate a feeling of pride in African indigenous identities. This cultural turn solidified in 1960 with Mugabe's installation as Publicity Secretary of the NDP upon his return from a sojourn in Ghana. Nkrumah had hosted him and a coterie of other pan-Africanist apprentices keen to understand the meaning of African independence. Mugabe came to better appreciate not only how imperialists manipulated class aspirations and ethnicity to partition the colonized into fictional and factional categories, but also, and more importantly, that culture could be harnessed to cultivate African solidarity to bridge such fissures. Enos Nkala, a cofounder of ZANU, recalled that Mugabe's legendary eloquence and oratory skill made him the natural choice for the job (interview).

At his first rally, in Mbare, Mugabe received a standing ovation when he announced the NDP's plan to overcome class barriers and build a truly participatory movement by admitting even members without much education into the party's leadership (Smith and Simpson 1981, 37). This was a radical departure from the movement's historical tendency to reinforce the crippling fetish for education by going out of its way to court "educated Africans" for leadership positions. The lesson was equally homegrown, not mere imported magic. Mugabe recalled that Joshua Nkomo, a founding leader of ZAPU, had grappled with critics who held to the entrenched myth of education, berating them:

> You are ignorant; to be educated is not always to be knowledgeable. You are an ignorant people if you do not realize that these people you call uneducated, dirty, are above you in reasoning. They have established that this country is theirs. They have established that this country does not belong to the British. They have established that the Africans of this country must unite and fight. You may have a degree or degrees. What do they matter if you are going to be a coward? (*Herald,* December 22, 2013)

The only degreed leader in the party then, Nkomo acknowledged that common people had initiated a mass nationalist revolution from below, overcoming the "educated" non-party members "who must have said Nkomo is doing what [Kenneth] Kaunda across the Zambezi [in Zambia] is doing, but Kaunda did not go to any university; we went to university. . . . That's the language they were taught." "Nkomo led them, Nyandoro, Chikerema, Nyagumbo and the people followed," reminisced Mugabe. "I only came in 1960 from Ghana." Mugabe was inspired by Nkrumah's overcoming of similar taunts from Ghana's Oxford graduates, who dismissed him as an uneducated "verandah boy." The equivalent of the delinquent piccanins, loafers, and hooligans of Rhodesian anti-African discourse, the "verandah boys" were unemployed youths who hung around and slept on the verandahs of roadside shops, surviving on petty thievery and pimping (Rathbone 2000, 24). They were the Black insiders, the wretched invaders of the colonial city. Nkrumah courted this rabble as representative of disaffected African society and as agents of participatory, urban mass politics. This way, the street became the brave school of commonsensical insurgency politics, whereas, as Mandela learned belatedly, "At university, teachers . . . shied away from topics like racial oppression, lack of opportunities for Africans, and the nest of laws and regulations that subjugate the black man" (Mandela 2013, 89). The "hooligan" stood up as the plebian who critiqued and exposed the immorality of overvalued colonial education and the chimera of its promissory modernity.

A fellow traveler on the nationalist road, Shamuyarira described how Mugabe ritually attacked the symbols of middle-class cultural alienation by asking crowds at political rallies to remove their shoes, socks, jackets, and ties. He told them at one rally, "Today you have removed your shoes. Tomorrow you may be called upon to destroy them altogether, or to perform other acts of self-denial" (1965, 67). Moreover, the incorporation and deployment of symbols of *chivanhu*—indigenous being, spirituality, and everyday epistemes—generated mass enthusiasm, as did the political identification with the *lumpenproletariat*. The public rituals—the staging of a metaphorical shedding of an alienating colonial civilization and the purposive crafting of the nation on the basis of an indigenous, inclusive moral ethos—electrified crowds. Ngwabi Bhebe (1989, 101) wrote, "On a cultural level, on Robert Mugabe's initiative, the party tried to inspire the spirit of 'self sacrifice,' which was marked by a rejection of European luxuries and habits and by emphasis on African culture in attire, music, diet, drinks, and religion." The idea was to inspire pride in African cultures, to cultivate "a spirit of self-discipline and to reduce unnecessary dependence on the white man." Thus, concluded Bhebe, "the NDP can be credited with having started to build a liberation culture and language, which was to culminate in the famous songs of liberation." Later on, I will problematize this teleology of revolutionary song trailing politics.

Implementing these ideas naturally fell onto the shoulders of the militant youth cadre, not only "to light a fire under the leadership of the party"—in Mandela's language—but also to marshal the urban crowds into an organized, disciplined mass through song, dance, spirituality, and oratory. Explained Shamuyarira (1965, 67–68),

> From the position of publicity secretary, Mugabe proceeded to organize a semi-militant youth wing . . . [which] started influencing and controlling some party activities. Thudding drums, ululation by women dressed in national costumes, and ancestral prayers began to feature at meetings more prominently than before. A public meeting became a massive rally of residents of a given township. The Youth Wing, with a small executive taking charge of units of fifty houses in each township, knocked at every door on Saturday evening to remind residents about meetings. Next Sunday morning, thudding drums, and singing groups again reminded the residents, until the meeting started. . . . At the hall, Youth Leaguers ordered attendants to remove their shoes, ties and jackets, as one of the first signs in rejection of European civilization. Water served in traditional water-pots replaced Coca-Cola kiosks. By the time the first speaker, a European in bare feet, took the platform, the whole square was a sea of some 15 000 to 20 000 cheering and cheerful black faces. The emotion-

> al impact of such gatherings went far beyond claiming to rule the country—it was an ordinary man's participation in creating something new, a new nation.

The colonial state conceded defeat to this new moral politics of the crowd that set the townships ablaze through a performative resocialization of power. The Salisbury Municipality "sadly admitted" in 1961,

> There has been an upsurge in politics on an unprecedented scale. Methods have been practiced on a mass basis where the image of the ruling African Nationalist party and its political beliefs and dogmas has been insinuated into almost every facet of township administration, and has been such that it has permeated into the lives of the whole community. Advisory boards, sport and recreation, youth club organizations, education, were all affected.[3]

By setting up parallel structures of anticolonial governmentality, Africans practiced self-rule and delegitimized colonial institutions.

The combative youth cadre was instrumental in fostering the cross-class alliances that this experimentation in majoritarian self-governance required. Nelson Chikutu, a former member of the Manyene Brothers Choir and a youth leaguer, told me that before the NDP was formed, the "idea of youth wasn't there. The youth wasn't very organized." They looked across the Zambezi to Zambia's United National Independence Party (UNIP) and its militant Youth League, led by Kaunda. A youth cadre crafted an image of the nationalist as a culturally confident, engaged, self-liberating being who consciously and proudly bore the generational mandate. Chikutu and other youths made forays into outlying white farms where they recruited adherents and sabotaged crops and livestock, and they brought back the pelts of wild game—of *majachacha, nzunza, tswetswe.* With these, they designed *madhukwa*—skin hats, aprons, and karosses—that party members and troupes of traditional dancers adorned as insignia of the nationalist movement and as cultural texts connecting them to both their history and their land.

Rebel missionary Ralph Dodge (1960, 44) observed Africans making this "definite turning to the past—a searching in the ashes for elements which have been resistant enough to survive the fires of westernization," and salvaging usable pasts that *madhukwa* symbolized:

> As one walks or drives along the streets of Salisbury . . . he may well see Africans wearing hats made of skins of various animals. These hats were associated with the now-banned Zimbabwe African People's Union and have become the badge of sympathy with the movement for African political independence. The African wearing the hat may have on a very up-to-date western suit; but the hat is a defiant assertion that he is no longer willing to abandon the age-old ways of his own people. The hat is the symbol of an emerging consciousness of values of the indigenous African culture; it implies a growing suspicion that

> no longer is everything western to be embraced and everything authentically African to be deprecated.

The power of this symbolism elicited Africans' emotion, excited their defiance, and threatened settlers, leading to the banning of the items. Chikutu recalled, "I wore that skin hat myself, before whites forbade them. Then you could be sent to jail for wearing them." Together with *midonzvo* (walking canes), *makano* (ritual battle axes), *fuko* (ritual cloths), *bute* (tobacco snuff), and *mbira* and *ngoma*, these ritual accoutrements came directly from the soil. They constituted an ecologically powerful umbilical cord and a deep connection to the land and its natural resources that colonialism alienated.

As well as an appropriation of the equally useful internationalist socialist rhetoric, this was a grassroots fashioning of ideologies of insurgent indigeneity to which all Africans, *vana vevhu* (children of the soil), could relate through lived experience. The cultural signification highlighted the problem of *vana vevhu vasina ivhu*—children of the soil who have no soil—a contradiction of terms that connected the cultural with the material, and that spoke to African disenfranchisement in a register that cried for revolution. The leaders of Chindunduma had similarly rallied their people across the country to resist colonial occupation on the basis of threats to their collective security in the 1890s. This argument has a bearing on the location of mass nationalism, both temporally and epistemologically.

If one is persuaded by Desai's (2008, 405) argument that Mugabe and his colleagues were "cosmopolitan leaders stooping to vernacular languages and idioms" to be understood by the masses, the significant point is that the strategy bore results by resonating with preexisting collective archives of African resistance or, one might even say, historical mass nationalism. Yet one must also ask: how is it "stooping" to commune with one's ancestors, with family, in a language enriched by one's own people's cultural symbolism? One symptom of African(ist) intellectual entrapment by western discourse is the tendency to unquestioningly define "educated" or "cosmopolitan" African identities by the western ratio, that is, according to the degree to which they have adopted western attitudes. The premise is that Africans' colonized bodies must be easily partitioned and categorized by the imperial authority. It is the same canon that alienated and surreptitiously immobilized the colonized who converted into *vatendi* (the "Christian natives" of missionary labors) by hailing them as elite, seeking to separate them from their own people. Commoners called converts who interiorized such partitioning *bafu*—traitors, white men's pets (Gurira 2013).

This was an era of anticolonial revolution increasingly driven by grounded pan-African feeling, rather than by rootless, tutored admiration of an imperial Europe. Aspiring leaders were quite conscious of the implications of the politics of self-representation, which is why they invested energy in rituals of ceremonial shedding of the signs of assimilationist being. The most effective leaders were those who had lived in or experienced what Mbuya Nehanda Charwe's niece, Mai Musodzi, called "the three places" that shaped African cultural consciousness by midcentury: the reserve, the mission, and the urban location. Tsuneo Yoshikuni (2008, 8) posited that these cultural spaces were incongruent or even contradictory to each other. Understood differently, however, these spaces were neither contradictory nor incongruent; as kraals of colonial enclosure, they actually reinforced each other—as they were intended to—in undermining African cultural and socioeconomic sovereignty. It was a mark of the resultant battles of inner consciousness touched off by this subversion that by midcentury, as Yoshikuni writes, "we witness the emergence of people who were both ardent Christians as well as cultural Nationalists, seeking 'pure' African traditions." Political leadership inhered in the ability to break free from the penitentiaries of these colonial physical and psychological kraals to command the whole "ragged, divided cultural terrain" in pursuit of self-liberation.

The orthodox dating of "mass nationalism" to the 1960s intellectually represses the historical processes of African self-making, and confuses the contemporary public rituals with the deeper historical realities. Collective engagement with localized and "national" threats was not new to twentieth-century Madzimbabwe. In fact, the legacy of Chimurenga as self-liberation dates back centuries, to ancestors like Murenga Sororenzou, a legendary hunter, fighter, and nation-builder, and Changamire Dombo, the famed vanquisher of Maputukezi (Portuguese) would-be colonists in the late seventeenth century (Mudenge 1988). Thus, the resurgence of the same nationalist spirit in the 1960s was legitimated by shared recollections of past histories of heroism, resilient transgenerational Murenga identities, and age-old struggles for autonomy. Little is derivative or peculiar to the 1960s about this resonant, usable African history.

These usable pasts constituted texts for staging public acts of performative politics, such as the carnivalizing of the otherwise private *bira* communion with ancestors and clandestine missions to national shrines of Mwari, such as Mabweadziva, Mutiusinazita, and Chirorodziva. Mass political leadership consisted in bridging these realms, restaging the sacred to animate public states of possession. Nobody but the transgenerational self performed such tasks. Chikutu told me that he had deeply experienced this cultural renaissance, which was marked by the "reemergence of *mbira* from the underground refuge it had been driven [to] by missionaries. VanaRwizi played *mbira*, ah, many people. Simon Mashoko. And many people were beginning to sniff *bute*. It was as if *mudzimu* [the ancestral spirit] had possessed everyone." It was through this register of collective possession by *vadzimu*, a powerful past and family, and therefore by transcendental self, that Africans made sense of their political consciousness and historical mandate to relaunch the armed effort for self-liberation. The new temporal and spatial states of being that are possession—*kubudirwa*—unite generations by bridging time, transporting the living back into the time of the ancestors and summoning the ancestors into the present for collective *matare* (communion) to forge the future. The Rwizi and other mbira-playing families reemerged with force during this period, summoning the national ancestral spirits to the agenda of self-liberation.

This *bira* register transformed the public rally and allowed the living to visualize how their inherited servitude had originated in the arrival of *madhunamutuna,* the wandering apparitions of a cannibal Europe. Their ancestor Chaminuka—the seer of dreams and caller of clouds—had foretold this fate in the 1870s:

Pasi pamera madhunamutuna	The earth has birthed apparitions!
Yowerere mukono unobva mudziva	A bull that emerges from the pool
Yowerere hahohaho pasi pane mhanda	The earth has birthed specters
Vakomana muchirere!	Boys, you are sleeping still!
Pasi pamera mhanda.	The earth has birthed specters.
	(Chikutu, interview)

Chaminuka's children had since lived the pain of the great seer's fearsome prophecy; *madhunamutuna,* a tribe of otherworldly beings, had emerged from the distant seas and devoured the land. Now, back into the seas the ashen ghosts must be driven. The militant youths sang verses that referenced the prophecy Chaminuka had made in the 1870s as they heeded his exhortation to fight to the death for self-liberation:

Children, beware!
Strangers want this land
Soon they shall arrive
From the west across the ocean
And you will have to fight
Children, to survive
You must be brave
You must be strong
Chaminuka *ndimambo* [is king]
Shumba inogara yega musango
[The lone lion that commands the forest]. (Maraire 1999)

They summoned the ancestors to guide them in continuing the war that the ancestors had fought before them.

By harnessing the material symbols and constitutive power and idioms of that heroic age, the nationalist leadership bridged generational gaps and inspired collective action. Many in the rank and file of the latter-day nationalist movement were the progeny of leaders and survivors of the First Chimurenga. The most cited example is the firebrand George Bodzo Nyandoro, grandson of a leader of the First Chimurenga and nephew of Ishe Nyandoro, whom the colonial state deposed from his chieftainship for insubordination. Similarly, the much younger Comrade Chinx (Dickson Chingaira) sang Chimurenga songs when he headed the ZANLA choir in exile.[4] He attributed his consciousness to both his own experience and troubled family history. His great-grandfather, Ishe Chingaira Makoni, was beheaded, as were Ishe Muchecheterwa Chiwashira, Chinengundu Mashayamombe, Nehanda Charwe, Kaguvi Gumboreshumba, and others who resisted Rhodesian colonialism. The telling and retelling of the colonial brutality at *matare,* the homestead schools of oral history, elicited transgenerational revulsion and immortalized the ancestors' valor. Now, emboldened by the Communist world's AK-47, the militant leaders self-consciously appealed to this transgenerational consciousness to build emotional capital for another mass assault on the rapacious aliens. As Shamuyarira (1965, 68) noted, Nyandoro "appealed in his speeches to the memory of the great prophet Chaminuka round whom the Shona rallied in the nineteenth century."

In a ritualized performance of these connections between the first anticolonial resistance of the century and the emergent movement, and of the generational and interspatial (spiritual) transference of the duty to continue the struggle, Nkomo, returning from a trip abroad in 1962, was met at the airport by ninety-year-old Sekuru Nyamasoka Chinamhora, a veteran of the First Chimurenga and uncle of Ishe Chinamhora (one of the chiefs who fell in the latter war). In a move that emphasized a symbiotic relationship between a generally sullied institution of chieftainship and the urban-led mass movement, Chinamhora presented Nkomo and his colleagues with a *gano* (ritual axe), *bakatwa* (sword), and *tsvimbo* (scepter) as symbols of the intergenerational call of the struggle, commanding, "Take this sword and these other weapons of war, and with them fight the enemy to the bitter end. Let the time be the same as those days when we used to keep as many cattle as we wanted. Also let it be that we shall plough wherever we like and as we like" (*African Parade,* March 1962).

The scepter that Nkomo was handed belonged to the Rozvi royal family. Fearing that all her sons would be captured after their defeat at the Battle of Marirangwe in 1896, Mutinhima's wife and spirit medium, Chikare, gave it to her daughter-in-law Takai, Chinamhora's sister, who kept it after consulting Mwari's priests at Chirorodziva Shrine. In 1961, the Rozvi royal family decided at a *dare* to give not only the scepter, but also the name Chibwechitedza, "The rock that never shifts," to Nkomo, blessing his leadership of Chimurenga (Dewa, interview). The airport ceremony was therefore a very public performance of this transgenerational investment in the project of self-recovery. The ritual weapons symbolized spiritual rearmament to continue the struggle that Chaminuka had prophesied, and whose front lines Nehanda, Kaguvi, and others had sanctified in blood and bones that refused to die. The *tsvimbo* reinforced the mystique of Nkomo's leader-

Adorning *madhukwa:* Robert Mugabe, Joshua Nkomo, and other leaders accept transgenerational blessing from Sekuru Chinamhora at Salisbury Airport. Courtesy of the National Archives of Zimbabwe.

Nelson Chikutu collected skins for *madhukwa*. Courtesy of the author, Harare, 2011.

Political demonstrators buoyed by song. Bulawayo, 1976. Courtesy of the National Archives of Zimbabwe.

The ZAPU troupe at the 1969 First Pan-African Cultural Festival in Algiers. Courtesy of Zimbabwe News.

ZANU is recreating the cultural heritage of Zimbabwe.

Traditional dancing and singing groups and artistic activities are encouraged and being developed in the liberated areas. The creativity of some is becoming that of all, men and women, young and old, from the North to the South – the new revolutionary Zimbabwe culture is being born.

Cde. Mayor Urimbo, the National Political Commissar. Combatants took part in traditionally cultivated revolutionary dances with indefatigable physical and mental involvment.

ZANU-Day Play: "The People Are Invincible"

A revolutionary play written, acted and produced by ZANLA combatants which exposes to the marrow and unequivocally condemns the so-called "internal settlement".

ZANU's Political Commissar Mayor Urimbo during a *pungwe* (nighttime political rally). Courtesy of the *Zimbabwe Times*.

ship, allowing him to style himself the Rozvi Mambo. Whenever he "talked politics" to gathered crowds, he would brandish the scepter, hang his jacket in the air on no visible hook, and mysteriously appear and disappear. These magical antics convinced some of his followers that here was a man whom even bullets would not harm, an emissary ordained to take back the country (Wright 1972, 368; also see Mavhunga 2014, 179). In addition to the drama of magic and ritual, the historical symbolism invoked usable pasts to reinforce the spirit of Chimurenga.

As Said (1993, 198) eloquently put it, by remembering the Madzimbabwe uprisings of 1896–97, the twentieth-century leaders honored their nationalist predecessors whose failures would enable later successes. History was the foundation for author(iz)ing and engineering new futures. The war would be fought in the name of, and guided by, the ancestors as a matter of duty to future generations, and the battle songs were composed in memory of, and in conversation with, *varidzi vepasi. Varidzi vepasi* were the ancestral owners of the soil, which their progeny must reclaim to utilize *pamadiro,* as they like. Africans' total and sovereign access to, use of, and authority over their own resources was *madiro,* freedom—the antithesis of colonial claims, expropriation, and enclosure.

Invoking the spirit of Chindunduma reinforced and consecrated the liberation task as a transgenerational responsibility blessed and guided by the pioneer fighters against colonialism, the ancestors. The process worked through the backward migration of spirit possession. The power of spirit possession inheres in the simultaneous epiphanic transmutation of the living body and lived ancestral knowledges and aspirations. As Kizito Muchemwa (2005, 198) explains, spirit possession effects "a momentary transformation of personality, a return to the past, a resurrection of the dead, and a metaphoric death of the living. . . . These outcomes of spirit possession are metaphors of suppressed discourses. These discourses contain memory and history. To allow these discourses to be rehabilitated is to allow memory and history pushed to the periphery to be relocated to the centre." A spiritual return to the past—"a world that is older than colonialism"—posited the defeat of the cruel regime of plunder, oppression, and injustice and the imagination of an autonomous future of *madiro.* That is how spirit possession signified the "return of the repressed" (Olick 2002, 22).

Through songs like "Chaminuka" and "Mbuya Nehanda" (discussed below), Madzimbabwe consciously invoked spirit possession, summoned the ancestors from a living past, and sought to overcome the tyranny of time and to build transgenerational solidarity. Tafataona Mahoso (1997, 17) explained this dynamism of African being:

> Before colonialism Africans overcame the tyranny of time by using the body as a medium. The ancestors refused to be obsolete and irrelevant by entering the bodies of young people, especially young women, and speaking to the future, for the future. . . . The first Nehanda is said to have lived more than

> 2000 years ago. The Nehanda whom the British executed in the late 1890s was actually Charwe, a medium of Nehanda. In the 1970s the same Nehanda spirit returned to possess more women who rallied youths in hundreds of thousands to join the liberation war.

Nehanda's vow to return was therefore the command of an intimate transgenerational "bonding cell"—to use Mahoso's phrase—that the Nehanda spirit represents in Madzimbabwe cosmology. The state attempted to co-opt chiefs, spirit mediums, and other cultural leaders in unsuccessful endeavors to break this African collective refusal to succumb to the colonial death wish. Epistemologically, this narrative interrogates the location of agency in African history and demands the decolonization of entrapped historiographies of African nationalism.

Zimbabwe Day: Reinforcing African Temporal Markers and Self-Knowledge

Festivals of founding seek to (selectively) re/define and unite a community, commemorate legacies, and claim and legitimate presents as foundations for creating futures on the basis of cumulative archives of lived experience and self-knowledge. National identity is thus often a statement of opposition to outside forces; it forms through protest. Africans encapsulated their contestation of Rhodesia-the-white-man's-country in a self-crafted identity as Zimbabweans. In doing so, they identified with the land whose *hoko,* physical pegs, were the historic Madzimbabwe stone castles (Great Zimbabwe, Khami, Daramombe, Mapungubwe) that settlers sought to alienate as mysterious footprints of some wandering white tribe. Nationalists' defiant evocation of this heritage by re/naming their parties, their country, and their cultures symbolized their ritual reclamation of alienated selfhoods, a cultural effort to decolonize. Reasserting sovereignty through endogenous roots and cultural heritages against discourses of colonial scattering was a powerful way to re/unify and self-craft.

This was the essence of ZAPU's proclamation of March 17 as "Zimbabwe Day" at the Afro-Asian Peoples' Solidarity Organization conference in Tanzania in 1963. It was part of this crucial process of discursive re-creation of a Zimbabwean national identity in opposition to colonial destruction:

> Colonialist historians have frequently characterized the military measures taken by our ancestor rulers against settler intrusion as a rebellion of tribes scattered, unorganized and without common purpose. This lie is dealt [with] in a single stroke by the early morning attack on Fort Mhondoro on the 17th of March, 1896, by a single military force put together by the gallant fighters Mashayamombe and Mukwati Ncube. These two generals, one from the northern part of the country and the other from the southern part, demonstrate the single-purposeness of the entire people of Zimbabwe in opposing settler attempts to impose their rule. (*Zimbabwe Review,* 1969)

It was on this terrain of powerful, usable pasts that individual leaders jostled for legitimacy.

Terence Ranger (1977, 128), one of the first Africanist historians of the First Chimurenga, derided the deposed ZANU leader Ndabaningi Sithole for greeting his audiences in the names of the leaders of 1896–97: Nehanda, Mukwati, Mashayamombe, Chingaira Makoni, and others. Abel Muzorewa also allegedly regurgitated these names. Sithole and Muzorewa wrote their own history, which included collaboration with the colonial regime. But Ranger also suspected that the names were lifted from his book *Revolt in Southern Rhodesia* (Ndlovu-Gatsheni 2011, 62).

This point demands a historiographical engagement with Africanist scholarship's proprietary privilege over Africans' self-knowledge (Zeleza 1996, 293). Where and to whom do African ancestors belong? One wonders, with Mudimbe (1988, 14), at the apparent epistemological ethnocentrism, namely, "the belief that scientifically there is nothing to be learned from 'them' unless it is already 'ours' or comes from 'us.'" The "modern," repackaged, yet essentially Hegelian discourse of an Africa without history before the coming of white liberal scholarship dogs the politics of knowledge production, clouding the agency for historical change in African history and reducing African nationalism to a derivative of, or a lesson learned from, the benevolent white "self," whether foreign or colonist.

This certitude allowed Turino (2007) to venture that "the Shona" did not have the word "nation" in their language, because "this was a cosmopolitan concept," until, of course, the good missionaries and other foreign tutors brought it to them. In his own words: "Through European and North-American-based missionary education, [the black middle class] learned the principles of nationalism—that each social group should rule itself through its own government." This is how the "white man's burden" not only justified apartheid in Southern Africa, but also appropriated its antithesis, as a comment by Hendrik Verwoerd, Prime Minister of South Africa, illustrates (quoted in Strickland 2012): "We represent the white men of Africa . . . who brought civilization here[,] who made the present developments of Black Nationalism possible, by bringing them education, by showing them this way of life. By bringing in industry and development." Verwoerd neatly connects the well-known, colonized historiography of science and technology in Africa with its corollary, the colonial intellectual imagination of African nationalism. African nationalism thus becomes a colonial project, a derivative. J. D. Hargreaves (1988, 3) boldly declared that the "most effective critics of racial injustice were always Africans who drew from their reading of European history a Mazzinian faith in the capacity of the independent nation-state to promote material progress and cultural renewal; in the euphoric 1950s the political parties they founded seemed natural heirs to colonial authority."

If one agrees with this reduction of African nationalism to its (anti)colonial elements, then its limits as a liberatory project become very clear. But as Zeleza (1997, 22) has observed, at base, this revitalized imperialist historiography of a planned decolonization seeks to "disrobe nationalism of its glories." The historiography reduces the Nkomos, Mandelas, Nyandoros, Chikutus, and Chinamhoras to well-rehearsed students of a now curiously benevolent decolonizing Europe and its naturalized settler offspring. In a double move, it banishes African (self-liberating) agency and millennia of independence, statecrafting, and self-rule. Banning Eyre, interviewing Turino (2007), extended the logic to proclaim that Zimbabweans lack a strong sense of history, and that this was why they had "failed" to preserve their cultures against colonialism. Clearly, Eyre and his colleagues are not conversant with such Madzimbabwe philosophies as *nyika vanhu,* that a nation is people. This basic *chivanhu* concept sums up the object of the First Chimurenga: the restoration of independence and self-rule, *kuzvitonga.* Needless to say, the Eurocentric thesis also elides the central role that missionaries—the implied agents of decolonization—played in founding and sustaining the colonial project.

This theory of donated nationalism also explains African middle classes' interest in their own people's music. It was also the gift of the white man, explained Turino (2007):

> During the late 1950s, the first attention on the part of the black middle class to indigenous musical practices does not come from the nationalists. But in fact, it comes from a group of white liberals, and white foreigners, who in the post–World War II era had become interested in indigenous African music. All of a sudden, the writers in African Parade started taking an interest in African music. . . . When a Zimbabwean group goes to London and performs indigenous music, that's what the Londoners are interested in. And so the idea takes root in Zimbabwe. Among the urban, middle class, all of a sudden, indigenous music starts to become chic.

Repetition and self-referencing canonized this idea into fact among Euro-American enthusiasts of Zimbabwean music. For example, one John O'Brien explained the revival of marimba music in Zimbabwe as if paraphrasing Turino:

> When the first American-based marimba band toured in Zimbabwe, many young people paid attention to Shona music for the first time in their lives, i.e., "America is cool, so if Americans think this music is cool, it must be." More than one musician at Zimfest credited this "re-importation" of the music back into Zimbabwe as reviving a dying tradition.[5]

Colonial ethnomusicologists rode the preservationist discourse to the "Dark Continent" to "save the primitive music of the savage tribes"; now they faithfully ride the same music to reteach and validate it to the still forgetful descendants of ancient Africans. Ethnotheory continues to credit the white self with teaching Africans to like their own music and averting an imminent "mbirapocalypse" or "marimbapocalyse" (Mark 2013). It replicates a deeply problematic epistemological exteriorism that encrusts histories of Africa, be it on nationalism, music, or science and technology.

In 1987, Ranger received "three Makoni dignitaries," who descended on London searching for the head of their ancestor Ishe Chingaira Makoni, who was murdered by the British during the First Chimurenga. They believed that his head, like those of many others similarly murdered, was brought to Britain as a gift for the crown. They turned to Ranger for help because, they reportedly told him, "Chingaira's beheading 'is written in your book.'" One imagines that the psychosocially orphaned children of Makoni would have greatly appreciated Ranger's assistance, seeing it as a matter of ethical responsibility to his subject of study. But Ranger was now fascinated by the stories of the African subaltern he had focused on in his recent book *Peasant Consciousness* (1985) rather than the hero-chiefs of his 1967 *Revolt in Southern Rhodesia,* and he scorned them, telling a western audience that *Revolt* had "mythic authority" to his visitors, despite the fact "that *Peasant Consciousness* is *about* Makoni and that there is no mention of a beheading in *Revolt.*" The doyen of British Africanist historiography also charged more recently that this "mythic authority" has helped ZANU-PF to "govern by [his?] historiography," exploiting the teleology of ancestrally ordained *zvimurenga*—the First Chimurenga of 1896–97 and the Second of the 1960s–70s, onto which ZANU-PF grafted the post-2000 Third Chimurenga of land repossession (Ranger 2004). His point is clear: African cultural nationalism is a donated sensibility.

With his efforts "to write a people's history, in which peasants rather than chiefs would be the protagonists, and in which change rather than tradition would be the theme," frustrated by the overwhelming presence (or rather absence) of Chingaira's head, Ranger confidently asserted that "Zimbabwe is not doomed to an exclusive diet of cultural nationalism" (1988). What his listeners do not learn about are the sources for the names and stories of the African ancestors that populate Ranger's book. Identifying these sources would not only move the historiography beyond the stubborn theme of cultural nationalism; it would also help decolonize Africanist research and resolve the apparent contradictions between chiefly and people's histories that colonialism exploited and exacerbated. By particularly referencing chieftainships that fell to colonial violence, Africans were seeking to reconstitute not mere traditions, but lost power, security, and self-determination; colonial change was not their project. And that history depended on African memory and family histories as archives and living knowledge, variously narrated at the household level, at the mass political rally, and in the mobilizing Chimurenga song. Rather than restoring them, Africanist scholarship still habitually distorts, displaces, ridicules, and colonizes African self-knowledge and agency.

Re/Placing African Self-Knowledge and Agency

The memory of the First Chimurenga and its heroes greatly inspired the Second: the memory of such battles as those fought at Fort Mhondoro, and that at Chigwagwagwa—the last battle that Kaguvi Gumboreshumba Kaodza fought against the colonial forces in Chivero. His grandson Gwenzi Gwanzura Gumboreshumba narrated in a documentary film recorded in 1975,

> Gumboreshumba, my father's father, was a very big medium, a [great] *svikiro*. . . . He was always hunted by white people, and as he was a medium, he would give warning to the families: "You must be careful; the *pfumo* (meaning the war) is coming!" He would forewarn the people during the wartime that we call Ndunduma; that "the white people are coming here tomorrow," and the white people would duly come tomorrow. . . . So the white people realized that it was he who was foiling their schemes. So they would say, "Surely, he is the lion's leg [*gumbo reshumba*]; he is very terrible." He fought them in the last war at Chigwagwagwa, where my home is today. (*Mbira Dza Vadzimu* 1978)

When he built himself a new home in the Chivero Reserve, Gwanzura brewed beer to consecrate it to Kaguvi Gumboreshumba and other ancestors, according to custom: "to let *vadzimu* know that I am here now." He summoned his grandfather Kaguvi and many other forebears through *mbira dzavadzimu*, the music of the ancestors, during the all-night *bira*. Kaguvi spoke through Gwanzura's sister (mbira player Stella Chiweshe's mother), and Gwanzura asked him and the other ancestors to look after their family in the new place and in the forests (of colonial hardship). The documentary brought out very clearly the African philosophy of being, which, as Basil Davidson (1977, 42) observed, is "founded in the relationship between living people and their ancestors who . . . guarded and guaranteed the life that any community could lead." Family matters are discussed, achievements consecrated, and knowledge transacted at the transcendental family *bira*.

Even at the family level, to which the documentary restricts its analysis, the *bira* cannot be dismissed as either "ancestor worship," as Eurocentric readings would have it, or, as Gwanzura reminded participants, as mere "entertainment." Rather, it is a transgenerational conversation and communion that is at the heart of the reproduction of self, and it is a living archive of that communion. The communion is familial, requiring the "return" home of the "departed," the ancestors. Basil Davidson (1977, 42) spoke eloquently to western reductionism when he argued that "what we reductively call religion . . . was for these communities the necessary regulator of all political and social action, just as it was unavoidably the mode in which every individual explained his world, and in which his culture acquired its meaning and its value." Because ancestors like Kaguvi Gumboreshumba worked to the benefit of more than one family, they were also *mhondoro*, national mediums of Mwari who guided larger endeavors, as Gwanzura implied in his careful choice of words in front of the American anthropologists' cameras that breached the privileged space of the sacred *bira*.

It is these realities of African being that cultural nationalists evoked in the 1950s and 1960s. Looked at through this cultural lens, the mass political mobilization required very little that was new except tackling the discourses of intimidation and estrangement that colonial epistemes fomented. To Nyandoro, Chinx, and Gwanzura, the personal was the national, and vice versa. Otherwise this popular nationalism not only survived colonial violence but was further stoked by it, as Basil Davidson observed:

> Through the 1930's and 1940's and later still, the masses continued with their efforts to use their own model as their means both of resistance to the cultural suffocation of the colonial enclosure and of reaching towards a regained freedom. The long ideological process of their movements of cultural resistance, whether inspired by purely indigenous beliefs, or by the assimilation of Christian beliefs . . . or by the imbrication of the one with the other in a host of messianic gestures and uprisings, throwing up new prophets, new doctrines, new songs, new dances, new modes of self-organization, holds a central place in the history of our century. And . . . there can be no sense in considering the phenomenon of nationalism as being somehow apart from the responses of indigenous culture. In so far as nationalism has acquired real substance, this is because the masses have breathed life into it. (1977, 44)

The nationalist leaders were children of the rural reserves, the bastions of cultural sovereignty that defied colonial violation. "When we went to the bush as guerrillas," wrote Herbert Ushewokunze (1984, 73), "we discovered that the . . . peasants still had their African culture in spite of the many years of cultural brutality perpetuated by the Rhodesian colonial state. We found that the spirit mediums of the 1890s had survived to the 1970s in defiance of the colonial orders to destroy." It was such enduring cultures of resistance that reequipped the fighters. Coming to terms with such archives of African self-understanding therefore means positing self-liberation as a broad-based continuum, a usable past, and an ideological corrective.

It is this sort of ideological synthesis that James Chikerema, the vice president of ZAPU, drew on in his 1974 Zimbabwe Day message, suggesting that the day transcended a theoretical challenge to colonial historiography by having a practical function:

> On this day, we reaffirm our dedication and determination and firmness to continue the fight against the white settler minority regime in Zimbabwe. On this day, we continue to admire our forefathers who started the confrontation with the white imperialists 79 years ago. . . . Our generation has picked up the

fight to free Zimbabwe from where it was left by our forefathers in 1897. (*Zimbabwe Review* 3, 1974)

This bristling confidence was surely boosted by the domesticated gun, which made all humans equal. But as a temporal marker, the idea of Zimbabwe Day also symbolized membership in and solidarity with the free, nonimperial world. More significantly, the ideologues conceptualized self-liberation as restoration of the "Zimbabwe culture—the entirety of the ways of life" of Madzimbabwe that colonialism had despoiled. The burden of the nationalist leader, in Fanon's (1967b, 214) words, was to undo colonialism's distortion, disfigurement, and destruction of the people's past. As Lazarus Mpofu of the ZAPU information department argued in a lengthy presentation to the Organization of African Unity (OAU)'s First Pan-African Cultural Festival, held in Algiers in 1969, "Zimbabwe culture" consisted of specific, purposeful indigenous spirituality and worldviews, marriage and family institutions, and the corresponding economic and political structures that underpinned these; it foregrounded self-reproduction.

These were attributes by which Madzimbabwe had defined themselves against foreign invaders since time immemorial. And that self-definition had to constantly take account of the changing horizons of the polities. At this particular moment, it implied resolving the violence of arbitrary colonial boundaries, both physical and mental. Africans' understandings of their being, self-perpetuation, and belonging were therefore historical processes of self-definition, that is, nationalism, not necessarily "modern" constructs, never mind the captured, unreformed post-colonial nation-state. And of course, historical depth does not mean stasis, because, as Mpofu wrote, every aspect of the culture was time-tested and evolving to serve the changing needs of the people (*Zimbabwe Review*, 1974). The regurgitated notion of mass nationalism does little more than simply denote the mobilization and carnivalization of these historically constitutive consciousnesses in the reverse engineering of the future at a specific historical time. Similarly, it makes little sense to map the whole history of African nationalism onto the templates of colonialism or European nationalism, displacing Africans' self-defined political communities and consciousness both before and beyond colonialism.

Ideologues had to reorient these philosophical truths of African being to contemporary tasks. Thus Mpofu asserted in the *Zimbabwe Review* (1974) that Zimbabwe culture was useful in the struggle: "Whether in curing the sick or in interceding for rain, or in festivities, Zimbabwe culture expresses itself ultimately in the form of song. Song is the colour of our culture. . . . The [essence] of Zimbabwe song and dance is that, whilst the melody might remain constant, wording is left to the song leader who, in the word construction, must issue a number of social correctives." African being under colonial rule consisted in constant striving to self-define and self-reproduce against colonial epistemes that sought to create a bewitched, ahistorical African subject. As Amadou-Mahtar M'Bow (2007, 102), a Senegalese scholar and a co-organizer of the 1969 symposium, argued recently, "It is culture, African culture, which has moulded our being, nourished our imagination and shaped our spirit and sensitivity . . . the basis of our innermost identity." "Its negation," he averred, "seemed to us a negation of our very being." Colonialism thrived on just such a negation.

African self-liberation called for the overthrow of these negations and the rearticulation of sovereign aspirations. The dynamism of African expressive culture lay in its ability to "become a way of expressing appreciation or rejection of a national event. In the circumstances of Zimbabwe," wrote Mpofu (*Zimbabwe Review*, July–August 1969), "our songs now contain abhorrence of oppression and a good many raise the spirit of war against the oppressors. When culture takes this form, it becomes the culture of resistance." One of the first tasks of the culture of resistance is to "reclaim, rename, and re-inhabit the land." This philosophy defined African self-liberation as a transnational agenda, as Nkrumah proclaimed in his midnight speech to the crowds that welcomed Ghana's independence at Accra's Polo Grounds and as Mugabe, his apprentice, reemphasized to crowds that represented an emerging post-colonial Zimbabwean nation in Mbare and Highfield. For Africans still battling recalcitrant settlerism, the transcendental spatial continuum that was Africa therefore constituted not so much an exile or a spiritual desert (as the colonial state wished it to, for African "demagogues") but a mobile *dare,* a space to plot and reengineer the post-colonial nation-state as a relational African entity beyond colonial taxonomies. This was the motive for the OAU's convening of the 1969 First Pan-African Cultural Festival in Algiers, animating African self-liberatory mobilities and solidarities beyond colonial interdiction.

Algiers '69: Staging Pan-African Mobilities and Solidarities

Presenting themselves in the national mode as the Zimbabwe delegation, the ZAPU delegates to Algiers included an appropriately costumed traditional dance troupe, which the Front de Libération Nationale (FLN)—the host country's liberation organization and now ruling party—hailed as "an emissary of the oppressed but fighting people of Zimbabwe" (*Zimbabwe Review,* July–August 1969). At the end of the proceedings, the FLN presented the troupe with a "cup of popularity," reinforcing pan-African revolutionary solidarity. ZAPU cast its cultural performativity as progressive, apparently critiquing the way that Rhodesia caricatured African being through the primitivizing "tribal dances." Thus, in a language contrapuntal to both the format of the festival and Rhodesia's "tribal dances," ZAPU wrote, "Our troupe did not go to Algiers to compete [because] it is difficult to make of a culture an object for competition. Culture is not like Olympic games where one can determine those who run faster or jump higher than others." Liberation performativity had little scope for staging cultural production merely for aesthetic competition. *Yainge isiri nyaya yekutamba*—revolutionary dance was no dancing matter!

The FLN seemed to share this philosophy, judging by its explanation for giving ZAPU the award: "This trophy to the ZAPU troupe has not so much been determined by the artistic performance of ZIMBABWE, rather it has been determined by the . . . Algerian [people's recognition] of the fact that ZAPU, faced with a ferocious enemy, has not surrendered" (*Zimbabwe Review*, July–August 1969). ZAPU reported that the troupe's performances moved women to tears. One can postulate that this was not the mystifying Negritudinal weeping of Africans' supposed emotionality and unreason, but rather the emotional product of self-sacrificial, combatant engagement (Lindfors 1970, 5; Shepherd 1969, 2). The dancing body generated intra- but also cross-cultural dialogue. Its simulation and anticipation of reality made it both a text and a weapon for desired change. The e/motive engagement was not only physical, but also mental and moral. The mental and physical creativity of revolutionary dance re/produced a miscellany of war dancing styles from around Madzimbabwe, all underpinned by the beat of "talking drums [which] represented a call to our people to continue the armed struggle" (*Zimbabwe Review*, July–August 1969).

ZAPU's Zimbabwe troupe, like the cultural troupes of its counterparts—the ANC, SWAPO, PAIGC, FRELIMO, and MPLA, as well as those of the newly independent African nations—deliberately shattered tribalizing ethnomusicological essentialisms by performing the diverse Madzimbabwe styles in ways that fostered unity through embodied communal memory and practice. Thus, at both the national and the global pan-African scale, the nationalist movements made conscious efforts to stage "ethnicity" as a positive resource rather than a springboard for retrogressive consciousness. This was a positive imagination of diversity whereby "ethnicity provided precolonial heroes for nationalists, platforms for political mobilization, and monuments that nationalists were able to turn into national symbols" (Msindo 2007, 269). Such performances of nationalism indicated an awareness of, and a self-critical endeavor to transcend, internecine frictions that bedeviled the delicate process of building a nation out of the rubble of precolonial divisions and colonial scattering and fragmentation. The same consciousness informed ZANU's popular and important mobilization strategy of singing and dancing at *mapungwe* (nighttime political vigils), with its fighters sharing the *dariro* with villagers. The fighters brought such dances as the *toyi-toyi*, a military dance-drill, and the energetic *kongonya*, combining them with preexisting *ngondo* (war) songs and dances in "liberated zones."

Itself both a technology of communication and a literary *dariro*, the *Zimbabwe Times* captured the combative dance *dariro* in a 1973 issue, depicting "ZANU . . . recreating the cultural heritage of Zimbabwe." Mayor Urimbo, the party's

National Political Commissar, was pictured thrusting himself into the sky, arms flying and feet commanding space in a spirited dance buoyed by a circle of singing and clapping coparticipants. This was a self-conscious, "indefatigable" physical and mental staging of embodied mass self-liberation. The *Times* explained, "Traditional dancing and singing and artistic activities are encouraged and [are] being developed in the liberated areas. The creativity of some is becoming that of all, from the North to the South—the new revolutionary Zimbabwe culture is being born."

The virile guerrilla song and *kongonya* dance fired rural morale and fertilized popular cultures of self-liberation, as Jonathan Murandu, who was a rural boy in the 1970s, reminisced:

> I first heard these songs being played by the comrades during mapungwe. They had brought them from Tanzania. They were very popular for raising morale. We learned how to dance to those songs during that time. . . . The comrades danced kongonya while holding their guns. . . . We then ended up mimicking them, carving our own wooden toy guns, which we also wielded under our arms as we danced. We had also given ourselves such [guerrilla] names as Mabhunu Muchadura, Mikonde Mina, Mudzimu Ndiringe.[6]

Vibrant social media have replicated the traditional *dare* today, allowing people who were but youngsters in the 1960s–70s to recount and share their memories and subsidiary contributions to Chimurenga as *jakwara,* participatory work.

The *jakwara* of self-liberation was a spectacle decidedly different from the "tribal gyrations" of colonial ethnomusicology that underpinned apartheid Bantustan philosophy. The effort to forge cultural unity and solidarity deconstructed the settler *herrenvolk* philosophy that posited African being in terms of distinct "tribes" and races, differently civilized and therefore warranting different treatment under state policy (*Zimbabwe Review,* July–August 1969). The nationalists' use of tradition was therefore revolutionary, retraditionalizing African culture for collective self-liberation. Such progressive revaluation of disparaged African selfhood constituted a minimal condition for throwing off colonial domination. Ali Mazrui and Michael Tidy (1984, 283) write that retraditionalization "does not mean returning Africa to what it was before the Europeans came . . . but a move towards renewed respect for indigenous ways and the conquest of cultural self-contempt."

This is why, at Algiers, the ZAPU troupe superimposed a new message on traditional tunes and dances to call into being new realities: "Even while all the songs and dances that the Zimbabwe troupe performed in Algiers had a traditional touch, the present war situation demanded a response and found it in such songs as 'Soja raNkomo tuma runhare kana ndozofa sara utore nhaka,' which means 'Nkomo's soldier send a telegraph, that when I die take the heritage'" (*Zimbabwe Review,* July–August 1969). As Cabral (1970, 3) taught, the heritage—

land and cultural self-recovery—could only be taken through guerrilla warfare. Therefore, Africans had to embrace their constitutive, quintessential heritage by identifying in themselves the transcendental self that had been pronounced through Nehanda's medium in 1898. With the backing of *masvikiro,* mediums, "the risen bones of Nehanda" resumed the ancestral mandate to fight to free the land. The Rhodesians had murdered Nehanda's medium, Charwe, in a futile effort to kill the spirit of African resistance, but to Madzimbabwe, the act constituted an investment in the more determined African will for restitutive justice, *ngozi.* What does this mean in practice?

The Returning Transcendental Guerrillas

When Zimbabweans recrossed the borders as guerrillas, their return was both physical and spiritual, symbolizing a critical moment in transgenerational reconstitution. Theirs was a return of the repressed in possession mode. Guerrilla deployment was led, accompanied, and guided by the ancestors. When instructor Comrade Khumalo (Joel Muzhamba) and his colleagues tried to recruit in and deploy from Zambia in the early 1960s, they faced immense difficulties until they received the ancestors' blessings and guidance. He told Munyaradzi Huni (*Sunday Mail,* October 27, 2012),

> We could not deploy troops into the country before consulting the spirit mediums. . . . While we were in Mbeya in Tanzania, one Tanzanian got possessed by an ancestral spirit and told us that amongst us was someone who carried an important national ancestral spirit, who could lead us back to fight and get Zimbabwe back. But we had to brew beer before we re-entered the country.[7]

Cde Khumalo and his colleagues conducted the requisite *bira,* and the spirit, which was the spirit of Chaminuka, came out to lead the incursion:

> Chaminuka's spirit came out through one young man called Makahwa. Makahwa was instructed to lead this group of seven, but he was told that there would be a battle in Karoi and he would not survive that battle. Makahwa led the group in 1968 knowing fully that he wasn't going to survive. Chaminuka's spirit that had possessed him had made a sacrifice that if the war effort was to succeed, Chaminuka's blood had to spill through Makahwa.

In Madzimbabwe cosmologies, a possessed person who has accepted *mudzimu,* the ancestral spirit, becomes a willing *svikiro,* a medium and host through whose body *mudzimu* executes its will for the greater good. Makahwa fell in the Battle of Karoi, and his colleagues proceeded to consult Ishe Chiweshe, Dotito, and others. The chiefs led them in conducting further rituals before consulting Mbuya Nehanda's medium in Musengezi. These were the protocols of Chimurenga, as Cde Khumalo explained: "We conducted the rituals before Mbuya Nehanda granted us permission to start the war, but we agreed that we were supposed to take her to Zambia so that the Smith regime could not trouble her." Then many people started joining the struggle, directed by the same *masvikiro.* People constantly invoked Nehanda in speech, song, and prayer. This is how, as Vera (2000) pointed out, children grew up with the image of Nehanda. An analysis of the songs that Africans—adults and children—sang on various platforms further illustrates this popularly shared culture of resistance that predated and rekindled the drama of war.

This argument moves us beyond the gun-centric analysis of African liberation that grounds itself on both Fanon's influential thesis about the revolutionary violence of the colonized and Bhebe's image of the mass nationalist program giving birth to Chimurenga song. If war was the foundation for revolutionary consciousness, that war was not necessarily the liberation war at the end of the twentieth century, nor was Chimurenga music merely a corollary of it. The suppression of Chindunduma in 1897 did not kill Madzimbabwe spirit and desire for freedom. African resistance simply took other forms, particularly cultural forms, and these forms inspired people to take up weapons when the military option became feasible again. The resurgent military option depended to a great extent on the cumulative cultural consciousness and rearmament that this differently combatant struggle had helped build over the decades.

9 Cultures of Resistance

Genealogies of Chimurenga Song

> Today in the semi-liberated zones, the songs, dances and history of the Zimbabwe nation, along with the new culture emerging from the liberation struggle, are making the people strong.
>
> —ZANU Solidarity Committee–NY

Chimurenga in Context

Zimbabwe's Chimurenga music has drawn much scholarly attention, partly because of the genre's imbrication with the Second Chimurenga, the 1960s–70s liberation war that finally dislodged Rhodesian settler rule in 1980. In a book dedicated to this huge ouevre, A. J. C. Pongweni (1982) hailed Chimurenga as the "songs that won the liberation war." What is remarkable is that, in spite of the acknowledged long history of Zimbabwe's cultures of anticolonial resistance, analysis of Chimurenga music tends to limit its purview to the liberation war. This raises two problems. Firstly, the scholarship wittingly or unwittingly gives credence to a self-congratulatory, exclusivist, ultra-nationalist post-colonial historiography of superpatriots who liberated everyone, as if the liberation war were a private enterprise (Moses Chikowero 2011). Secondly, it reinforces the equally uncritical view that the pre-1960s were essentially an age of cultural imperialism during which Africans merely mimicked western musical cultures—a view that is blind both to militant musical practices and to the subversive infra-politics of underclass engagement with colonial power since occupation.

This chapter traces the genealogies of Chimurenga music as a shared, public political sensibility and practice, conceptually tying the pre-1960s age of supposed "native pacifism" with the later era of overt militancy. It contextualizes the radical Chimurenga songs of the 1960s–70s within the historical continuum of politically engaged musical practices through which Africans had challenged their subordination to colonialism since occupation. Politically, Madzimbabwe understand Chimurenga as the collective, violent wars against European colonizers, particularly the 1896–97 antioccupation uprising and the 1960s–70s war that finally dislodged the recalcitrant colonial state. These wars form one continuing struggle for self-liberation. Thus, when the rumble of Chindunduma guns fell virtually silent in 1897, the people rearmed themselves culturally and spiritually for a future in which they would be able to resume the struggle on more solid ground. The songs that they sang constitute an archive of these continuing cultures of resistance, which inspired the second uprising.

"Ngombe Dzedu Dzatorwa": Texts of Violence and Memory

ZAPU invoked the power of transgenerational memory when it reminded its followers in 1974, "Old people may remember how three decades ago Zimbabweans used to sing a song called 'Ngombe Dzedu Dzatorwa'" (Our cattle have been seized):

Kwakatange chibharo	It started with forced labor
Kukauya mambure	Then came the nets
Kukauya nemigwagwa	And then the roads
Ngombe dzedu dzatorwa.	Now our cattle have been seized.

(*Zimbabwe Review*, February 23, 1974)

When I asked older Zimbabweans what historical events had shaped their political consciousness in the early twentieth century, most mentioned the land seizures and *nhimuramuswe,* cattle seizures (literally "tail-cutting"), mandated by racial land and ecological legislation. Cattle constituted a principal form of wealth for Africans. The seizures thus incited much anger and anguished protest, with songs like "Ngombe Dzedu Dzatorwa" becoming banks of transgenerational memory of the violence.

The nationalist parties mobilized recruitment by deploying and restaging such texts of popular memory. ZAPU recalled that villagers sang "Ngombe Dzedu Dzatorwa" in tears as colonial officials compelled them into *chibharo,* forced-labor gangs, while cherry-picking their herds at dip tanks in the seizure campaigns, which originated after the sacking of the Ndebele Kingdom in 1893. The Loot Committee of the British South Africa Company plundered more than 80 percent of Africans' cattle, on the assumption that its owners were Ndebele, and this seizure formed the basis of Rhodesia's beef industry (Banana 1989, 3). The BSAC's Land Commission of 1894 initiated land grabs by settlers, displacing Africans into crowded wastelands designated "native reserves," *maruzevha.* The Land Apportionment Act (1930), the Land Husbandry Act (1941), and related land and ecological laws would further this accumulation of property in settler hands and limit Africans to owning only a couple of beasts and a few acres of land, in the name of curbing environmental degradation and promoting "scientific agriculture" on the marginal "reserves."

Nhimuramuswe was tantamount to murder. In his autobiography, Chivanda Kennedy Manyika (writing as Kennedy Grant Dick Manyika; n.d., 66) remembered how elders, including his father, moaned as they wondered how they were going to feed their families when their herds were looted: "Amai vangu Shava, inga ndabaiwa pamwoyo. Jamburuti yaenda. Baba vangu Shumba, mhuri ndogoirera nei?" (Oh, my dear mother Shava, I have been stabbed at the heart. Jamburuti is gone. Tell me, dear father Shumba, how am I going to feed the children?) "Shava" and "Shumba" designate clan names and composite bloodlines (*madzinza*) that go to the roots of African personhood in Madzimbabwe cultures. Such personhood is deeply rooted in founding ancestries, and it is the material heritage of these transgenerational ancestries—*nhaka*—that colonists pillaged. Colonialism therefore violated not just the life of the individual, but also the reproduction of the transgenerational bloodlines of Madzimbabwe. For these reasons, Chivanda's father not only called on his own father, Manyika, to bear witness, but also ritually summoned the whole *dzinza* of the Shava people, which, through intricate networks of kinship and marriage, helps to form the nation. These are the culturally specific registers of African being and indigenous nationalism that missionary epistemicide sought to destroy.

Another Shava family, that of Ishe Chiwashira in central Zimbabwe, were rendered landless and cattleless by Nora Lee, the daughter of the British Prime Minister, Baron Atkin, when she alienated their entire homeland and turned it into Nora Lee Estates (Nhororiya) (Chikowero family, interview). This colonial plunder and enclosure laid solid foundations for a white capitalist economy and, in the process, as Hofisi Chikowero put it, "takasara tisisiri vanhu" (we ceased to be human). They became "livestock which went with the estate" (Luthuli 1962, 88) or scattered into newly carved "native reserves" like Mhondoro with only their dogs, there to lead new lives of hunting, gathering, and squatting. Cde Dambudzo (Chivandire), another great-grandson of Chiwashira and a fighter in the war for independence, remembered in an interview how his family moved to Njanja singing bitterly, "Mombe dzedu dzatorwa nemabhunu" (Our cattle have been seized by the Boers). Manyika's son, James, heard a variant of the song from one of his father's brothers, Shadreck:

Kwakatanga chibaro	First was forced labour
Kukawuya maraini	Then huts in lines
Kukawuya makomboni	Then compounds
Mombe dzedu dzapera.	Now our cattle are gone.
(J. Manyika 2001, 276)	

Pushed into the reserves, Africans were required to build houses in *maraini*, straight lines, for "native" administrative purposes.

Simon Muzenda experienced *nhimura* when Chivi was declared "overstocked" in 1938, with a white man they called Matigimu wreaking havoc:

> He would move around with white paint . . . and every beast he touched with his white paint he regarded as de-stocked. He did that for a long time and those cattle that had been de-stocked would be sold (to white farmers) for a song, for one pound, two pounds. . . . All those cattle that had been de-stocked found their way to those [settlers] who had opened butcheries. (Bhebe 2004, 33)

It is this history that recruited Chivanda Manyika and his brother Robson, Lungile Ngwenya, Josiah Tongogara, and Muzenda into political activism. Together with other Africans bearing similar wounds of settler primitive accumulation, they formed the National Democratic Party (NDP) as they inherited the leadership mandate from the generation of Benjamin Burombo, Masotsha Ndlovu, and others.

In western Zimbabwe, young Tshinga Dube (interview) listened as angry villagers, laboring in *chibharo* gangs, scolded the settlers in song: "Uyinj' uHulumende, uyinja, uyinj' uHulumende, Uyinja. Sithelela izinja, sitheleli nkomo, sithelela amadibha, sahlupheka!" (The government was such a bastard for taxing dogs, cattle, and dip tanks and making people suffer!) And young men summoned the energy to dig trenches and carry rails by heaping insults on the Boers: "Amakhiwa ngo dhemeti, amakhiwa ngo dhemeti!" (The whites are damned, the whites are damned!) Colonial injustice composed the text of African collective memories, grievances, and anger, and the mass nationalist parties tapped into these experiences through popular songs.

By the 1930s–40s, increasingly large numbers of African men were leaving the impoverished reserves for survival wages on white farms and in mines, urban industries, and settler homes. This urban drift was not the result of a natural attraction to a superior capitalist economy; it was a logical outcome of the combined effects of state-engineered rural poverty (Arrighi 1973). The state destroyed Africans' rural economies, thereby sowing the seeds of Chimurenga in the cities. The colonial scattering and shared grievances meant that the songs spread through every reserve, town, and mission school.

"Our Children Mourn": Village and Mission Guerrillas

Kwaramba (1997, 2) decried the replacement of the traditional role of music by the missionary school. Missionary designs to supplant African musical cultures with a grafted Christian hymnal hegemon did not always produce the desired results, as the students and teachers often repurposed and redeployed hymns to their own ends. They also composed counterhegemonic songs or brought them to the missions.

Lina Mattaka (Kenneth and Lina Mattaka, interview) sang in the Nyamandlovu School choir in the early 1930s. The wide repertoire she and her classmates sang included a hymn that grieved Africa's "death." The students chorused "Africa" to their teacher's funerary lamentation:

Lead:	*Vana vedu vanochema*	Our children mourn
Chorus:	*Africa*	Africa
	Vanochema nyika ye Africa	They mourn their country, Africa
	Vanochemera nyika yeAfrica	They mourn for Africa
	Isu tose tinochema	We all mourn
	Tinochema nyika yeAfrica	We mourn Africa, our country.
	Africa	Africa.

The sickness called colonialism brought death to Africans' socioeconomic and political sovereingty, throwing the people into grief. Their ancestors had been humiliated and their heritages wrested away. Yet missionaries' designs to enlist the disinherited children as deacons and have them assist in further self-destruction did not always succeed, since teachers and students sometimes sang—right under the noses of the missionaries—that the "civilizing mission" was death.

Miriam Mlambo recalled singing and marching during early morning physical education sessions conducted by her African teacher at Nyadiri Mission during the same period. One of her class's favorite tunes was "Urombo Hwemadzibaba," which they sang to the applause of the missionary overseers captivated by their "intelligent" singing and marching. The missionaries could not comprehend the message, sung in Shona:

Urombo hwemadzibaba	The poverty of our fathers,
Urombo hwemadzibaba	The poverty of our fathers,
Kutorerwa nyika nevasina mabvi	To be deprived of their country by the people without knees,
Urombo hwemadzibaba.	The poverty of our fathers.

These African literati stubbornly decried the colonial roots and transgenerational meaning of their condition—*urombo* (poverty)—political unfreedom and its concomitant material lacks. African poverty was not an aboriginal condition, but the heritage of colonialism, *nhaka yeurombo,* for the ill-fated African child. They named colonialism as the originary sin and thus similarly contested the notion that a charitable European civilizing mission could justify alien rule. The singers' culturally privileged figures of speech and metaphors coded their musical statements beyond the command of the "people without knees," the cultural outsiders and foreign usurpers of their heritage. Europeans were called "the people without knees" because they wore long trousers. But more significantly, they were a lazy and callous tribe that forced other people to do their chores, as if they had no knees and could not bend to work themselves. Through this linguistic armory, the students subverted colonial fetters on free speech, earning the approbation of the very targets of their critique, who were preoccupied with mere parading and chorusing and saw such displays as indicating "civilizing" order and discipline.

James Theodore Bent, the amateur archaeologist-spy whom Rhodes sent to excavate and "prove" the white origins of the ruined city of Great Zimbabwe, was struck by similar performances in 1891. He witnessed the women of one village "enjoying themselves round the drum, dancing a sort of war dance of their own." To him, "it was a queer sight to see these women . . . rushing to and fro, stooping, kneeling, shouting, brandishing battle axes and assegais, and going through all the pantomime of war, until at last one of these Amazons fell into hysterics" and the dance was over (Bent 1893, 75). The African men Bent and his invasive excavators employed as diggers also unnerved them with similar choreographies of "potential rebellion" (Apter 2002, 575). Bent recorded that "frequently on cold evenings our men would dance round the camp fire; always the same *indomba,* or war dance; round and round they went, shouting, capering, gesticulating. Now and again scouts would be sent out to reconnoiter, and would engage in fight against an imaginary foe, and return victorious to the circle." He and his colleagues reassured themselves by recalling the colonial myth that these "Mashona" were a "pusilanimous" people: "If one had not had personal experience of their cowardice, one might almost have been alarmed at their hostile attitudes" (Bent 1893, 75).

Another colonial spy, Frederick Selous (1896, xiii), was struck by similar theatrics of African resistance at the outbreak of the First Chimurenga six years later, but similarly reassured himself that they were only a manifestation of the perplexing "kaffir" mind: "If anyone had heard the natives . . . singing and dancing as they were wont to do on every moonlight night, he could not have maintained that they appeared to be weighed down by a sense of injustice and oppression, or, in fact, that they were anything but joyous and happy. It is very difficult to understand the workings of a Kafir's mind."

Uncomprehending and conceited, the settlers and missionaries variously dismissed, sought to suppress, or applauded the vitality of "kaffir" dances. African students did not leave their songs behind in the villages when they went to the missions, so that not even the mission school could prevent the transmission of these subversive transcripts. Many of the belittled "mission boys" were therefore guerrillas within the mission gates.

These mission guerrillas devised strategies to combat missionaries who could understand their languages. My fathers Tsuro, Musvutu, and Hofisi Chikowero remembered how, when they were students at Kwenda Mission in the 1950s, their teacher, Daniel Manyika—another of Chivanda Manyika's brothers—had to strategically post one or two sentries to make sure the missionary schoolmaster, a Mr. Heath, did not sneak up on them while they sang their "mischief." One of the songs they sang away from the missionary gaze was an emotive memorial to European and Arab enslavement. Tsuro broke down when they sang the song for me in 2012:

Makarekare
Madzitateguru edu akatambudzwa kwazvo
NemaArabhu naivo vachena
Vakatorwa vakatengeswa kunge huku nemombe
Vakatsaurwa vakaendeswa
Uko kure kure kwazvo kuAmerica
Vaisaziva kuti tiri vanhuwo saivo.

A long time ago
Our ancestors were violated immensely
They were enslaved
By the Arabs and the whites
They were alienated and taken away
To the faraway land, America
There to be sold like chicken and cattle
They did not think we too were people like themselves.

As Jane Lungile Ngwenya explained (2012 interview), these songs are very different from the "Negro spirituals" that missionaries foisted on them, presenting them as expressions of enslaved Africans' gratitude for their redemption through the gifts of Christianity and "civilization"—thanks to the slave trade. These songs represent continental African memory of that historical violation. She and her schoolmates sang them in deep sorrow and anger, remembering their alienated ancestors. The Chikowero brothers and other great-grandchildren of Chiwashira sang many similar songs as the Chiwashira Brothers Choir. After beheading Ishe Muchecheterwa Chiwashira in the 1890s, the colonial state disbanded his chieftainship and banned his name, together with those of Kaguvi Gumboreshumba and others, in a bid to kill the memory of the African hero-martyrs of the anticolonial resistance. It was thus daring for Chiwashira's progeny to call themselves by it (as Muchineripi Chiwashira discovered when he was sent to Whawha Prison for doing so in the 1960s). Quite clearly, then, Madzimbabwe did not perceive their colonization as a civilizing mission or as a *Pax Britannica* imposed to stem an "African" slave trade.

Mlambo encountered youths staging *jenaguru* festivities on her nursing tours in Rusape. Their songs were neither merely joyful nor bewildered. She recalled one that asked,

Tinofarirepi?	Where do we find happiness?
Nyika yedu yarasika	Our country is lost
Tinofarirepi munyika yedu?	Where can we be happy in our country?
Kuti zvibharo,	With the rampant forced labor,
Zvimadhibhi nepapa,	Damned dips here,
Uku zvimapurazeni!	Wretched prazos [farms] there!

Together with a broad regime of extirpative taxes and levies extracted through both judicial and extrajudicial force, *chibharo* underpinned the political economy of colonialism, and African families were compelled to work as labor tenants for colonial farmers like Nhororiya. They were forced to build roads, railways, dip tanks, dams, drainage works, and contour ridges without payment and using their own equipment, as the "irregular" missionary Arthur Cripps recorded (1936, 35–36). They decried the rapine in songs like "Nhamo Yemakandiwa" (The travails of contour ridges), singing to lighten the punitive tasks.[1] Mines, factories, and missions all requisitioned *chibharo,* and demands for it mounted as white immigrants and white war veterans came in droves in the post-WWII "settlement schemes." Meanwhile, Native Commissioners and dip tank supervisors exploited the mandatory dipping law to perpetrate *nhimura.* Because of that, Africans swept *zvimadhibhi,* dip tanks, in the sabotage campaigns that heralded the guerrilla war in the 1950s; as the songs warned, dip tanks were a hated symbol of legislated theft.

With colonial plunder continuing, many songs went beyond vain pleas for humane treatment to advocate war. Mlambo also heard the children of Rusape sing *ngondo* (war) songs:

Tinorwa	We fight
Tinorwira nyika yakatorwa nemabhunu	We fight for the country taken by the Boers
Tinorwira nyika yedu	We fight for our country
Yakatorwa nemakiwa	Which was taken by the whites.

This song might have been a new composition or part of the First Chimurenga heritage. In any case, the African voices clearly conceptualized their independence, loss of which they never conceded to the settlers. In the 1970s, villagers in Chivero sang a traditional Korekore ditty, "MaTonga Munogarovirimira Vamwe/Tondobayana" (Tongas, you habitually molest others), which took on a new salience; moving on from its precolonial reference to the pesky Tongas, it now spoke to a new menace, the blood-sucking "Vana VaPfumojena" (white settlers) who ate by the gun, surviving by plundering. According to Kaguvi Gumboreshumba's grandson Gwenzi, who performed the song with his wife, his nieces Stella and Francesca Chiweshe, and his brother Fanuel Chitinhe for the 1978 documentary film *Mbira Dza Vadzimu,* the song "warned an abuser who always molested us that 'today we are ready; we have got a plan to fight you.'" Gwenzi danced spiritedly to the song as if covertly propagating *marehwarehwa ehondo,* the rumors of war that had reached the depths of Chivero—the backyard of the colonial capital, Salisbury—by the 1970s. These Chimurenga songs reinforce the argument that the foundational militancy of Chimurenga music cannot be located in the 1960s; it predated the "drama of war" by decades. Some of the songs constituted a continuing (First) Chimurenga, and some derived from even earlier repertoires. Mlambo cogently summarized the argument: "[Protest songs] started many years before the Second Chimurenga. That is because people always knew that they were oppressed, right from the beginning."

Chimurenga in the Ghetto

Many urban musicians emerged as professionals in the "location" recreation halls, where they congregated on weekends to "expend their excess energies" and relieve the strains of the urban labor regimen. These were the people who experienced colonialism most intimately, because they worked for, and interacted daily with, the white settlers. Their lifestyles and cultural sensibilities were most deeply introjected with the cultures and behaviors of the colonists; because of this, it was their performances that the colonists found most unnerving and hence considered to require the closest "welfarist" oversight. Their performances had the greatest potential to dramatize colonial interactions and to subvert settler hegemony.

One of the most popular early political compositions to incite a mood of mass defiance in the locations was "Lizofika Nini Ilanga?" (When will the day come?), a protest tune by the City Quads, led by Sam Matambo. Its message was direct and unambiguous (Jenje-Makwenda 2004, 22):

Lizofika nini ilanga lenkululeko?	When will the day of freedom come?
Lizofika nini ilanga lenjabulo?	When will the day of happiness come?
Abantu abansundu bayahlupheka	Black people are suffering
Kudhala, kudhala, kudhala	It's been too long, it's been too long, it's been long.

Matambo worked for the African Service of the Federal Broadcasting Corporation (FBC) in Salisbury. He failed to satisfy his white supervisor when queried about his lyrics, and had to sanitize the song into a generalized appeal to God to help the suffering *abantu abansundu,* Black people, before he could play the song on the radio ([Saidi] 2007). The sanitization subverted the song, which now implied that "blackness" was the problem that naturally explained Africans' suffering, and that only God could ameliorate it, through the sympathetic agency of whites, thus reinforcing the doctrinaire civilizing mission. That is how radio, as a tool of empire, sought to kill independent African voices.

However, the song was not that easy to suppress or appropriate. Andreya Masiye (1977, 24) remembered that a Zambian group translated the song into Nyanja as "Lidzafika Liti Dzuwa Lopulumuka?" Masiye was also an FBC announcer, based in Lusaka, where his colleagues and he employed music to propagate the nationalist sentiment in the whole region, subverting colonial radio's imperial agenda: "Listeners in Nyasaland and Southern Rhodesia joined others in Northern Rhodesia to request the song. . . . Programme announcers joined in singing over the recorded version, they intoned and stressed, or stretched, what they considered to be the right message." African employees of colonial radio utilized their linguistic armory to disarm imperial radio, repurposing it into a technology of self-liberation.

Bill Saidi and his Milton Brothers, Andrew Chakanyuka, and others faced the same predicament when they decried the Federation:

Honai rudzi rwevatema runongochema	Witness how Africans continue to cry
Nokuti takagara nevachena	Because of whites' presence here
Honai vatema vanongotambudzika	See how Africans continue to suffer
Ngatichemeyi kunababa wedu-wo!	Let us all cry to our father!

The FBC producer at Mbare, Dominic Mandizha, who was also a regular sessionist with the Milton Brothers, demanded they change the lyrics, which they did under protest. The song ended up celebrating the Federation as a beneficial racial partnership in accord with state rhetoric (Saidi, pers. comm.). Radio was the chief instrument for promoting the Federation to Africans (Mhoze Chikowero 2014).

A huge nightmare in the colonial state's welfarist urban entertainment project was that Africans appropriated—and even renamed—the recreational halls and turned them into rendezvous for political struggle. In Bulawayo, they renamed Stanley Square Lumumba Square (Nehwati 1970, 251). They congregated there and set off singing and marching on the city in labor and political demonstrations. Maurice Nyagumbo nostalgically recalled how in the 1950s ANC youths sang and danced all night at Joshua Nkomo's Mpopoma house—the "State House"—then proceeded onto Lumumba Square the next morning. In Salisbury, processions were launched from Mai Musodzi or Highfield's Cyril Jennings Hall to the city center. Demonstrators brandished sticks (as weapons with which they reinforced their occupation of public space, but also as "passports" that organizers demanded to see, in the place of the colonial pass, before someone could proceed) as they repetitively sang and danced in call-and-response patterns, lionizing their leaders and denouncing the government. "Mukono Unobaya Dzose" (The champion fighter bull), an adaptation of a rural herding song, was a favorite of Maurice Nyagumbo (1982, 105). It excited crowds and fired up leaders like Leopold Takawira, "the Bull of Chirumhanzu":

Tewera mukono unobaya dzose	Follow the sharp-horned bull
Tewera, baya wabaya.	That gores any hapless challenger.

Presenting the party leaders as champion bulls in this rural register generated a subversive counternarrative that performatively dislocated the center of power and reinforced African claims to self-rule.

Displaced by a deep-rooted African register of self-reclamation, the colonizing, "civilizational" discourse was no longer the reference, even to Nyagumbo, a former ballroom dance champion. Unlike the *chimanjemanje* tradition, which tended to vaunt the foreign European as the modern, this cultural nationalist tradition fed on pan-African, transnational self-valuation and solidarity articulated through song. Thus, the political songs by South African composer Herbert Caluza were translated and sung at mission schools and location halls. Caluza's "Silusapho lwase Africa" (We are the children of Africa) had been adopted as a political anthem by the South African Native National Congress, and it traveled to Rhodesia with mine laborers, hotel workers, teachers, students, and political organizers. Similarly, schoolteacher Enoch Sontonga's deceptively pacific "Nkosi Sikelel' iAfrica" ("Ishe Komborera Africa," God bless Africa) grew beyond its South African origins to become the "African national anthem," reinforcing the commonality of African identities and destinies crafted on the front line of struggles against oppression. Thus, African teachers and students, and children in colonial Zimbabwe, composed their songs as part of this broader, transterritorial, pan-African conversation about the African quest for self-liberation. The sense of collective loss and the call to restore plundered heritages challenged the "children of Africa" to stop pleading and to stand up and take their freedom. With the increasing radicalization of the nationalist movement from the late 1950s, "Ishe Komborera Africa" captivated crowds and disturbed settlers' self-deluding notion that "all what the natives really have is rhythm" (Pongweni 1997, 70). Nyagumbo was also fond of "Ishe Komborera Africa," which he rendered thus:

Mwari komborera Africa	God bless Africa
Ngaitunhidzwe zita rayo	Hallowed be her name
Inzwai munamato wedu,	Hear our prayer,
Mwari komborera	God bless us,
Isu mhuri yayo,	Its family
Hu-uya mwiya	Come down, Holy Spirit
Huya mwiya	Come down, Holy Spirit. (Nyagumbo 1982, 162)

Africans sang vast repertoires of such songs on the march, at rallies, and during meetings in the location halls and villages.

The power of song unnerved the colonial state, forcing it to acknowledge (to itself) African politics for the first time in 1958. The Native Affairs Department confessed, "It has always been the policy of the department when preparing its annual reports to avoid, as far as possible, any observation on the current political situation." But censoring reportage had not stemmed the escalation of the insurgency, obliging the department to change course: "However, if a true picture of the life and activities of the African section of the city's community is to be presented, the course previously followed must be departed from." African politics had reached "almost fever pitch throughout and Africans participated to an unprecedented degree as one crisis followed another." The Southern Rhodesia African National Congress and trade unions were the culprits, using song to "experiment with mob psychology" and disturbing public order, the state explained. State officials had lauded the beautiful singing of "Ishe Komborera Africa" as a sign of "native progress" at concerts and welfare events they superintended within the confines of the halls. Now unleashed by raucous crowds on the march, the song touched off settler panic with its communicative power, eliciting condemnation as disorder:

> An interesting characteristic of these processions has been the universal adoption of the hymn "Mwari Komborera Africa"—"God Bless Africa"—which many Africans like to postulate as their National Anthem—which demonstrators now persistently chant as they go. Sophisticated Africans who like this piece of music are already becoming embarassed at the manner in which it is thus being prostituted, however, and deprecate its use as a mob madrigal.[2]

On July 19, 1960, the state arrested NDP leaders Michael Mawema, Sketchley Samkange, Leopold Takawira, Jane Lungile Ngwenya, and others, alleged fomentors of the endemic disorder, and "exiled" them to Gonakudzingwa Restriction Camp, deep in the wilds of Gonarezhou Game Reserve, bordering Mozambique. In response, seven thousand Africans marched from Highfield into Salisbury, but the Whitehead government violently repulsed them. Similarly, very early on July 24 a crowd gathered at Lumumba Square in Bulawayo. It swelled to about five thousand as it snaked through Makokoba, heading for the city a mile away. Again the protestors were scattered by police batons, gun butts, dogs, and tear gas, touching off a rampage of violence as Africans targeted government property and that of alleged quislings. For three days, they looted, crushed, and burned things to the chant of "Zhii!" an onomatopoeic call to destroy utterly (Nehwati 1970, 250). State agents killed more than a dozen and jailed hundreds. The crowds seemed possessed by the spirits of the First Chimurenga of sixty-three years earlier.

The war cry "Zhii" had unnerved settler forces during the First Chimurenga, as Frederick Selous (1896, 161), a colonial soldier, recorded: "The Kafirs . . . commenced to shout out encouragingly to one another and also to make a kind of hissing noise, like the word 'jee' long drawn out." "Zhii" never left the African anticolonial repertoire, becoming a popular ZAPU slogan that captivated the imaginations of both urban and rural crowds. According to Francis Nehwati and other foot soldiers, the so-called Zhii riots were an act of spontaneous popular heroism and a call for all-out war against dogged settlerism, while in settler imagination they confirmed the colonial myths of "native savagery" (Frederikse 1982, 38). Allan Wright (1972, 373), who was then *mudzviti* for Nuanetsi, was alarmed to hear the slogan echoing around Gonarezhou, clandestinely propagated by the same wily nationalists the state had condemned to live with wild animals at Gonakudzingwa.

Abel Sithole and his Cool Four made sure Zhii was destined to live forever in African memory. They reconstituted the chant into a song feting Africans' show of valor, setting it to the tune of Faith Dauti's "Nzve," which celebrated the more mundane African defiance of urban criminalization in the earlier decades. In "Zhii," the Cool Four chronicled the brutality and Africans' bravery in confronting the colonial state, "all for the sake of Africa":

> Zhii!!!
> *Madod' akithi alizaz' inkathazo*
> *Ezavela kithi la e Africa*
> *Kwadibana, 'bamnyama nabamhlophe*
> *Bebanga i nkululek' e Africa*
> *Ingane za zifihliw' emakhaya*
> *Omama be lila izinyembezi*
> *Babehamba bebaleka bevik' inhlamvu*
> *Abanengi babehamba bethwel' induku*
> Kwalwiwa, kwafiwa ngal' amalanga
> *Baphela abantu, babotshw' abantu.*
>
> Zhii!!!
> Our fellow men, you don't know the tribulations
> That emerged among us here in Africa
> Blacks and whites confronted each other
> Quarreling over African freedom
> Children were hidden in homes
> Mothers were wailing, in tears
> They were going, running away, dodging bullets
> Many prowled around with knobkerries
> There was fighting, there was death those days
> People were finished, people were arrested.[3]

To Sithole (interview), "Zhii" signified an emboldening spirit of popular Chimurenga: "We were saying how hard we fought, throwing rocks and things at the whites. The song eventually led to our exiling." He and his group were sent not to Gonakudzingwa, but out of the country altogether.

The exiling of Sithole and his colleagues heralded an increasingly drastic state response to urban insurgency. The government enacted the Law and Order (Maintenance) Act (1960), the mother of colonial counterinsurgency laws, which reinforced a slew of other "terrorism" laws. These laws, the Native Affairs Department crowed, constituted an additional tool to "deal with hooligans, spivs and loafers." The state could now impose immobilizing curfews, ban African political parties one after another, outlaw public meetings, and arrest, restrict, or detain people without trial. The state had seen its greatest fear come true: Africans had transformed the locations from concentrations of domesticated labor into battlefields within the gates. It had to fight, occasionally "arranging for the entry of troops into the townships *on peaceful missions*."[4] Over the first four decades of colonial rule, "native administration" had largely been a matter of social control—the preemptive management of African anger through confinement in recreation halls, the promotion of diversionary "native" entertainment programs, and the deployment of police and army bands to charm residents. By the late 1950s, Africans had seized these architectures of soft domination and surveillance and turned them into spaces and instruments of resistance, prompting a drastic statutory shift from soft domination to overt repression, from guitars to guns. Even the Censorship and Entertainment Control Act (1967) operated on the premise that art was seditious, authorizing the Censorship Board to blank out newspaper columns and ban books, magazines, and records, and empowering the police to break up musical shows and to whip and detain musicians.

These preexistent cultures of resistance fertilized "mass nationalism" in the decisive stages of the liberation struggle. Protest song transformed mission schools into hotbeds of student activism and guerrilla recruitment. Max Mapfumo, who became a singer and a fighter for liberation, was certainly politicized by his Black teachers, but the white missionaries at Silveira Mission in Bikita also had a perhaps unexpected effect on him. He recalled some of them scolding him and his schoolmates: "'You are stupid! That is why you are ruled by 2 percent while you are 98 percent.'" This forced him to think, "'If I am not stupid, how come I am ruled by 2 percent of the population?' Many students then left for the war" (interview). As Max Mapfumo and other youngsters crossed the borders to become guerrillas, they carried with them the deep traditions of militant song, which they deployed to communicate the message of guerrilla struggle, to recruit, to spread counterpropaganda, to boost morale, and to articulate their collective self-assertion. The trajectory of Cde Chinx (Dickson Chingaira) illustrates this engineering of Chimurenga from exile through both gun and song.

Guerrilla Artists at the Front Line: Cde Chinx

Explaining his decision to cross into newly independent Mozambique to become a guerrilla in 1977, Cde Mabhunu Muchapera (interview) credited, *inter alia,* the freedom songs he listened to on the Voice of Zimbabwe's "Chimurenga Requests" program. He remembered the songs sung by youths like himself: "Kune Nzira Dzemasoja" (Soldiers' code of conduct), "Muka, Muka!" (Wake up, wake up!), and a tune punctuated by a rattling AK-47, "Ndiro Gidi" (It is the gun). Composed by a young female guerrilla, Cde Muchazotida, "Ndiro Gidi" hailed the equalizing power of the gun, a tool that, like the radio, the colonizers brought to subjugate Africans but which the latter domesticated into a technology of self-liberation. Each time young Mabhunu Muchapera listened to the militant songs, speeches, didactic dramas, and news updates the program broadcast, he was overcome with desire to join the action; "Mabhunu Muchapera" is a *nom de guerre* meaning "Boers, you will be wiped out." The powerful voices that drew Muchapera and thousands of other youths across the borders also belonged to Cdes Chinx, Murehwa, Sando Muponda, Jack, Mhereyarira MuZimbabwe, Mupasu, George Rutanhire, Max "Esteri" Mapfumo (a former student at Silveira Mission), Vhuu, Serima, and Juliet Xaba, and groups like ZIPRA's Light Machine Gun (LMG) and ZANLA's Takawira Choir. Many youths convinced themselves of the rightness of the cause, crossed into Zambia and Mozambique, and, through song, inspired multitudes to follow suit. African freedom was now a matter of life or death, the youths sang in such songs as "Somlandela, Somlandela uNkomo, Somlandela Yonke Indawo" (We will follow Nkomo, everywhere he goes) and "Vakomana Vehondo Tinofira Pamwe Chete" (We will die together as guerrillas) (Dube, interview).

Cde Chinx, who was a great-grandson of a First Chimurenga martyr, Ishe Chingaira Makoni, developed a keen interest in his own troubled history from an early age (interview). Like other African youngsters, he got the education that mattered from the village *dare,* the professorial structure that withstood the destructive missionary project, providing a complete reinterpretation of the colonial Rhodesian school accounts that disparaged his ancestor, Chingaira, Nehanda Nyakasikana, Kaguvi Gumboreshumba, Muchecheterwa Chiwashira, and others as "wicked rebels and murderers who were rightly punished for opposing civilization." His account of coming of age conveys the impression that Chinx was a bold young man who took himself very seriously. Working at a Salisbury engineering firm in the late 1960s, he frequently quarreled with his employer, one Nichodemus Jacobus Schumann, over the country's recent history. "I debated him a lot, standing my ground. . . . He would just call people 'You terrorist, you terrorist!'" Chinx would retort, "You are the terrorist; you came here and colonized us, killing our ancestors. This is our country." And Schumann would eventually taunt him into silence: "Go join your fellow terrorists in Mozambique, and come back to fight for your country if you think you can get it back!" In 1974, Chinx stepped up to the challenge, using a letter of leave that Schumann himself had issued him to go visit his parents in Rusape as his pass to join the guerrillas in the mountains of eastern Zimbabwe.

Writing on the self-legitimating Rhodesian historiography that defined colonial education, Anthony Chennels (2005, 131) observed that Rhodesian history was culled from travel journals like William Charles Baldwin's *African Hunting and Adventure from Natal to the Zambezi* (1868), Frederick Selous's *A Hunter's Wanderings in Africa* (1881) and *Travel and Adventure in South-East Africa* (1893), and subsequent romantic accounts of conquest. This founding Rhodesian corpus was codified in the journals of Robert Moffat and the Inyati Journals, the Oppenheimer Series, and the Rhodesiana Reprint Library after the Second World War, all these publications helping to constitute a discrete white Rhodesian national identity shaped by its own narratives of heroism and discovery. Further, as white supremacist notions stiffened in the 1960s–70s, noted Dan Wylie, for a white Rhodesian to "subscribe to [the Rhodesiana Reprint Library felt] like a mild act of patriotism. One could find [therein] unlimited justification for present attitudes" (quoted in Chennels 2005, 132). These patriotic histories of perceived white invincibility and racial arrogance drove the Rhodesians to take up arms to defend their colonial claim that Rhodesia was a "white man's country," thus dashing Africans' expectation of independence at what should have been the "moment of arrival" (Chatterjee 1986, 131). Like their Zambian and Malawian counterparts, Madzimbabwe had expected independence with the breakup of the Federation in 1963.

In story and song, Africans countered this Rhodesian colonizing discourse. And buoyed by the Communist world's AK-47, they stood up to challenge colonial certitudes with military force. Thus, the guerrillas went beyond simply countering the self-justifying imperial Rhodesian history to urge the destruction of the colonial project by armed force. They outranged the immobilizing strictures of the violent state by camping in the pan-African neighborhood of the independent African state. From there, they not only attacked, but they also boldly named, taunted, and insulted the enemy in their guerrilla radio broadcasts, songs, and newsletters, engineering a new post-colonial nation-state from exile.

One of Cde Chinx's first compositions was the blockbuster "Maruza Vapambepfumi" (You have lost the war now, plunderers), which, as he boasted to his mentor, Cde Mhere, he could sing "from Rusape to Harare without repeating a stanza!" It was simultaneously an elegy to colonialism and a new, ennobling narrative hailing the imminent era of self-determination. In a double move, the song narrates and celebrates the heroism of African resistance, and similarly narrates and immortalizes colonialism as an unforgettably shameful act of European barbarism. Barney and Mackinlay (2010, 9) note that a counterstory, or countersong, contains elements of repudiation, resistance, deconstruction, correction, and redefinition. In "Maruza Vapambepfumi," Chinx deconstructs the Rhodesian narrative of a founding white civilization, pointing out how the colonists, led by spies like Selous (who pretended to be a hunter), deserted their overpopulated and hunger-ravaged Europe and the neo-European slave empire of America to plunder Zimbabwe, the Africans' land of milk and honey:

Vakauya muZimbabwe	They came into Zimbabwe
Vachibva Bhiriteni	Coming from Britain,
Vachibva kuAmerica	Coming from America,
Vachibva kuFrance	Coming from France,
KuGermany kwavak atandaniswa nenzara	From Germany, chased by hunger
Vati nanga-nanga neZimbabwe	They made for Zimbabwe
Havazivi kuti inyika yavatema	But this country belongs to the Blacks

Izere uchi nemukaka	It's full of honey and milk
Ndezveduka isu vatema	But it's ours, us Blacks
Vakapinda muZimbabwe vaine gidi	They brought their guns to Zimbabwe
Kekutanga vachiti vanovhima	To hunt, they claimed,
Vodzokera, iko kuri kunyepa	Then go back, the liars!

Through intimidation and dubious treaties, the purported hunters twisted the arms of African leaders and claimed exclusive rights over African lands and minerals, trampling the rights of locals, taxing and enslaving them. They even spurned the offer of peaceful coexistence, "taxing humans, dogs, chickens, cattle, donkeys, and houses!" So now, through the armed counterviolence of African self-liberation, the colonists were learning their painful lesson. The comrades were going to hit them hard, driving them all the way back to Britain, sang Cde Chinx.

Chinx deployed the pedagogical tool of orality to "challenge the authority of the [colonizing] written word" (Muchemwa 2005, 198). Thanks to the guerrilla movement's emphasis on history in its intensive political programs, Chinx was able to reclaim and retell African history from an African perspective to an audience brought up on a starvation diet of white supremacy and fear. "Maruza Vapambepfumi" belongs to the huge Chimurenga oeuvre that boosted guerrilla recruitment, as Chinx nostalgically recalled: "I taught the choir the song during *mapungwe* [nighttime political meetings] and we kept polishing it, hitting it until people went crazy; we then sent it over to Maputo, where every one of my compositions was requested for recording and radio play. And man, what recruitment that song inspired!" Songs like "Maruza Vapambepfumi" and "Ndiro Gidi" resonated powerfully with Africans both at the war's front and listening to the guerrilla radio at home. They critiqued and put into historical perspective the African predicament as rooted in the originary sins of Rhodesia: the "plunder, greed and mendacity" of the settlers that Rhodesian history books extolled as courage, self-sacrifice, and patriotism (Pongweni 1997, 69).

African song traditions are inclusive and participatory. Any member of the musical community can participate in the familiar styles of call and response, the yodeling, *makwa* clapping, and dance refrains, thereby molding the song narrative in the performative *dariro*. Thus, Cde Mhere, who assembled the Takawira Choir with Chinx, added a short preface to the nine-minute song. He felt that the song's plot omitted a crucial aspect of the popular understanding of the advent of colonialism and African resistance—Chaminuka's prophecy. Chaminuka is believed to have thus prophesied the invasion of the land before he was captured and murdered by the Ndebele in the nineteenth century. So, Cde Chinx told me, Cde Mhere sang,

Paivapo nemumwe murume	There was once a man
Zita rake Chaminuka	His name Chaminuka
Waigara muChitungwiza	Who lived in Chitungwiza

Munyika yedu yeZimbabwe	In our country Zimbabwe
Wakataura achiti	He foretold that
Kuchauya vamwe vanhu	There shall come a people
Vachange vasina mabvi	with no knees
Munyika yedu yeZimbabwe.	Into our country Zimbabwe.

Chinx started singing Chimurenga songs as a local *mujibha,* a guerrilla helper, during *mapungwe* before crossing into Mozambique. He recalled, "I started as a *mujibha,* right in the mountains of eastern Zimbabwe. I was singing right there . . . when we went to open new bases, raising *morari* [morale]. Such songs as "Sendekera" [Keep pushing], I would sing them and keep on embellishing them with my own words, depicting what I would be seeing wherever I patrolled. People liked that so much."[5] In Mozambique, Chinx's fame solidified with "Rusununguko MuZimbabwe" (Freedom in Zimbabwe), a composition that used the tune of a Christian hymn, now repurposed to predict the coming not of Jesus but of African freedom, and sooner rather than later. "I was taking those gospel tunes which I used to sing in church with my mother, emptying them of all the words about [the Christian] God and filling them with Chimurenga words." In this way, the guerrillas domesticated and redeployed the pervasive and often insidious Christian hymn.

This process of domestication and redeployment was informed by Africans' revaluation of their own cultures. The Madzimbabwe high god Mwari and the martyr ancestors, both outraged by colonial slight, were substituted for Jesus and the Christian God, thanks partly to the intoxicating influence of the Marxist ideology in which the recruits were steeped during political lessons, and partly to the resurgence of African belief systems at the height of the war. ZANLA had *masvikiro,* including the medium of Nehanda, in the Dare ReChimurenga (War Council), who gave them *miko nemitemo* (regulations and taboos) and advice on major war decisions. Similarly, the guerrillas also worked with *masvikiro* on any new battle fronts. Cde Shungu reminisced, in conversation with Munyaradzi Huni,

> Before we fought any battles in any area, we would consult masvikiro in that area so that they could give us permission to fight in their area. We would tell them, "Our grandfathers, we have come. . . . And we may spill blood in your area." We would then place tobacco snuff into a *chiumbwa* [figurine] and supplicate to Mbuya Nehanda and other national spirit mediums, including the medium of the particular area. They would then tell us: "Our children, you may now go on and fight the war." They would tell us that this was an unfinished war that must be fought, started by Mbuya Nehanda and other ancestors. (*Sunday Mail,* August 25, 2012)

Thus, both the guerrillas and the ancestors fought the liberation war as the same unfinished Chindunduma. Before they left home, many fighters supplicated their ancestors, asking for guidance and protection. Cde Dambudzo described his departure for Mozambique in 1976 (interview): "I knelt down and prayed to my ancestors—our traditional prayer—telling them that 'I have decided to go to fight the war that you fought long back, the war of the ancestors that our forebears always told us about.'" Similarly, in the context of war, song, and particularly *mbira* music, summoned the guiding and protective hand of the ancestors. When Mabhunu Muchapera and his comrades decided to launch a daring attack on a Rhodesian military camp in Mt. Darwin in 1979, they first consulted *masvikiro,* who led the mission under the cover of the music of the ancestors, played by *magwenyambira* (mbira players). *Vadzimu* gave them spiritual camouflage to raid and annihilate the Rhodesian camp, which was absorbed in an afternoon parade; the comrades suffered not a single casualty (Muchapera, interview). Cde Mhere's *mbira* group often performed this role in Mozambique, helping to convene *matare* with *vadzimu* whenever necessary (Jeyacheya, interview).

ZANLA anthems like "Titarireyi" (Watch over us)—popularly known as "Mudzimu Woye"—and "Mbuya Nehanda" constituted transgenerational conversations between the ancestors and their progeny in the prosecution of the war. In "Mbuya Nehanda," Cde Muchazotida evoked the spirit of the heroine and matriarch of Madzimbabwe resistance through her own words, "My bones shall rise again":

Mbuya Nehanda kufa vachitaura shuwa	Mbuya Nehanda died telling us
Kuti ndonofire nyika	That I am dying for this country
Shoko guru ravakatiudza	The one important word she left us:
Tora gidi uzvitonge	Take the gun and rule yourself
Wawuya kuhondo here	Welcome to the war front
Vakamhanya-mhanya nemasango	They jogged through the bushes
Vakabata anti-air	Holding the anti-air [missiles]
Kuti ruzhinji ruzvitonge	So the masses could rule themselves.
(*ZANLA Chimurenga Songs,* 2011)	

Cde Muchazotida would fall in action in the Man-to-Man Battle of Monte Cassino in 1979, but not before downing a Rhodesian helicopter (one of the seven that ZANLA reportedly gunned down; *Sunday Mail,* October 27, 2012). The bones of Nehanda had risen and wielded the gun to demand self-determination. "Mbuya Nehanda" is therefore a memory song (T. Mahoso 1997, 17). Hers was not a forgetful progeny; it took heed of her living word, a transgenerational command whose time had come.

Cde Dambudzo explained that many of the songs they sang during the war, including "Mbavarira," came from the First Chimurenga: "Mbavarira inoda vane dare; ndiwe wakarova paMashayamombe" (The spirit of bravery demands unity; isn't it you who hit the Boers at the Battle of Mashayamombe). Cde Dambudzo had sung this song at home during *mapira,* celebrating Chiwashira and Chinengundu's joint assault on the settlers at the Battle of Mashayamombe during the First Chimurenga. In singing the same song in the heat of war seventy years later,

Cde Dambudzo enlisted the spirit of his ancestor, Chiwashira, to come and lead him along the old paths of anticolonial warfare. He also loved "Ridza Gidi Rako, Chaminuka," (Fire your gun, Chaminuka), which invoked the spirit of independent, precolonization African being and heroism that Chaminuka epitomized.

Most Africans who did not carry guns nonetheless fought in various capacities: feeding, sheltering, clothing, and camouflaging the guerrillas, and reconnoitering. A Hwedza woman, Lisa Teya, recalled getting caught up in a battle after she and fellow villagers had gone into the local hills to feed the guerrillas:

> Suddenly, we were surrounded by Dakotas. . . . There were helicopters and jets everywhere. . . . *Vakomana* [the boys] ran in all directions, dodging the planes and disappearing. They were like people possessed by their *vadzimu*. We, the onlookers, started singing traditional songs such as *Tatora Nyika Taramukai* [We have taken our country, so you better disperse!] and *Mikono Inorwa* [The fierce fighter bulls]. And so it was a battle of the fittest. There was heavy gunfire all around us. We sang the praises of our ancestors and urged them to give courage to our young fighters. So we sent our praises to *Mbuya* Nehanda and *Sekuru* Chaminuka and then went back home. (Staunton 1990, 99–100)

Teya teased out the depths of the culturally specific registers of African being that informed the liberation struggle. The "mothers of the revolution" dutifully wielded *migoti* and other cooking utensils to feed the children they sent to win back the country. The African family therefore played its role as a central institution of self-reproduction through liberation. Victories, escapes, and sacrifices owed much to this collective transgenerational effort. Thus, when they escaped the Hwedza Mountain battle, Teya and her companions thanked the ancestors in prayer and song, singing "Mudzimu Woye." The blood of the martyrs of the First Chimurenga nurtured both the spirit of resistance and an immortal collective memory that drove Chimurenga as a historical, transgenerational mission. This sense also suffused the songs that professional musicians—guerrilla artists at home—sang within the country.

Guerrilla Artists on the Home Front

True to the times, even the singers who became synonymous with Zimbabwe's Chimurenga song groomed themselves into professional recording artists by covering popular American songs, imitating Elvis Presley, Bruce Springsteen, and Jimi Hendrix. However, in music as in politics, the 1960s–70s gave birth to revolution. Thomas Mapfumo, Dorothy Masuku, and Zexie Manatsa emerged as some of the most significant singers to front the Zimbabwean popular musical revolution, discarding the foreign "copyrights" and reclaiming their African roots. They steeped themselves in indigenous musical forms, or selectively infused the local with elements of the foreign to create wholly new popular sounds, giving birth to some of Zimbabwe's unique commercial genres, like *sungura* and *jiti.* This cluster of guerrilla artists is interesting not only for their musical innovation, but even more for the cultural and political significance of their work. While they did not wield the gun like Cde Chinx, Cde Mhere, and Cde Max Mapfumo, they wielded the guitar, *mbira,* and *ngoma* to drive the revolution from inside the country. Using Thomas Mapfumo and Manatsa as my principal case studies, I analyze the work of these guerrilla artists and its significance to the liberation struggle.

Thomas Tafirenyika Mapfumo

Thomas Mapfumo was born in 1945 and raised by his mother's people, the Munhumumwe family in Marondera. His musical consciousness never strayed too far from the strong Zimbabwean song cultures, despite the pervasive American influences that he encountered when he returned to live with his parents in Salisbury (Mapfumo family, interview). Thus, it did not take too much imagination for him, his Sekuru Marshall Munhumumwe, Jonah Sithole, Joshua Hlomayi Dube, Daramu Karanga, Leonard "Picket" Chiyangwa, William Kashiri, Robert Nekati, and other friends in the Acid Band—and especially the Mhangura Mine group, Hallelujah Chicken Run, with which he performed—to make a professional switch to indigenous music by the 1960s. When Gallo's Chrispen Matema invited them to a music competition at Skyline Motel, they came out on top and drew the crowd's attention with their indigenous-language songs buoyed by heavy *ngoma* drumming and trumpeting, replicating the model of the West African Afro-rock group Osibisa, which was very popular then (Karanga, July 2012 interview).

Their decision to switch was part of a deliberate quest for self-discovery and relevance. Mapfumo asked himself, "'Where is our own music?' What I had been singing was not my culture. I then decided to do my own culture; to play my own people's music as Thomas Mapfumo; for I cannot be called Elvis Presley." Rediscovering his own identity and singing his own people's music meant communicating their aspirations in their own register: "I realized . . . that I must use my own African language to send a message to my own people." The innovative hands of Jonah Sithole and Leonard Chiyangwa coaxed the *mbira* sound out of the guitar at the start, inventing the Chimurenga or mbira-guitar, before boldly incorporating the *mbira* itself, giving them the confidence to discard the *chimanjemanje* tradition of foreign "copyrights." They reclaimed the rich languages they could skillfully use to "conceal what we were saying . . . but our people understood the language[s] that the whites didn't understand" (quoted in Frederikse 1982, 106). This was the quest for relevance for which one Emman Mhuru had called back in 1945 in a letter from Waddilove Institution (*Bantu Mirror,* September 22, 1945): "No foreign music can serve the purpose for which our own music can stand. I should like to advise my fellow Africans that we should not only be satisfied with the music of other races, which does not reproduce African life. We must try hard to improve our own music to express our own feelings." Mhuru argued that it was only African music that "binds the elements of our social origins," making it possible to reproduce African being. The wisdom belongs to the historical canons of African cultural nationalism, best represented by Edward Wilmot Blyden's 1887 charge to Africans to do "our own work and we shall be strong and worthy of respect," for to imitate others would only court weakness and contempt (Blyden 1967, 92). Africans had come to realize that no people ever liberated themselves using other people's cultures, particularly the same cultures that enslaved them. Cultivating Africans' pride through their own music was therefore a foundation for restoring and reasserting their maligned being. For Mapfumo, such reclamation was akin to answering the call of his own name, Mapfumo, "the spears" that must liberate his people.

Mapfumo proclaimed this self-rediscovery with a significant battle cry in 1974, "Murembo" (Trouble), which would be followed by a string of other similarly themed singles. For instance, "Chaminuka Mukuru" (Chaminuka is great), "Mudzimu Ndiringe" (Watch over me, ancestral guardian), and "Shumba Inobva Mugomo" (The mountain spirit lion) appealed to the ancestors to protect the nation in this great endeavor and entreated Africans to value their traditions as the only platform for self-liberation (Hallelujah Chicken Run Band, 1974). This was the African voice repudiating the limits of colonial assimilation. Mapfumo and his colleagues encoded this spirit of self-liberation in a new band name, Blackman Unlimited, later refined to Blacks Unlimited. *Ngoma, hosho, mabhosvo, mbira,* and especially Chimurenga or *mbira*-guitar rhythms began to define a uniquely Blacks Unlimited beat. African symbolism permeated the music and Mapfumo's stagecraft; he wore *fuko nengundu* (a spirit medium cloak and headdress), wielded *gano* (ritual axe) and scepter, and sported *mhotsi* (dreadlocks) and *ndarira* (copper armbands). In this way, as Webster Shamhu wrote in the *Radio Post* (January 1974), Mapfumo and his group personified the African cultural revolution sweeping the continent. Ghanaian Kwadwo Danso-Manu proudly declared from distant London (*Parade,* July 1959) that such cultural renaissance was testimony that "Black Africa too has got a cultural heritage to bequeath to the world treasury of cultures." More important to Madzimbabwe, this pan-African consciousness framed a purposeful cultural rededication to the imperative of the liberation war.

Mapfumo declared in "Murembo" that the time had come to take up "my weapons to prosecute the historic war that is upon us," in order to restore his people's dignity. While the people were wont to lose heart at the entrenched white settlerism, Mapfumo reassured them of the certainty of victory in "Musawore Moyo" (Don't lose heart), for the suffering and desperation of decades were surely coming to a close:

Musawore moyo musawore	Don't lose heart, never
Musawore moyo muchazofara	Don't lose heart, you shall surely rejoice
Musha ndewenyu musawore	The home [country] is yours, don't lose heart
Upfumi ndehwenyu musawore	The wealth is all yours, take heart
Musawore moyo muchazofara	Don't lose heart, you shall surely rejoice.

(Hallelujah Chicken Run Band, 1974)

The song implored Madzimbabwe not to lose heart, because they were surely going to "eat with liver!" Eating liver had become an unimaginable luxury to a people accustomed to "boy's meat"—entrails and other second-grade meats that whites fed to dogs—and the substitute "soya meat for Africans" the settler rebel regime invented for them when sanctions were imposed on it (*Zimbabwe Review*, November 2, 1974). Settler plunder devastated African wealth and food cultures, eroding the people's happiness. However, in the song, Mapfumo reclaimed the expropriated land, livestock, and home (the country). Africans were going to get them back so they could eat liver again—a powerful metaphor for a new life of *madiro*, an abundance Africans imagined would come with the overthrow of the colonial system. Meanwhile, that system removed them *en masse* into concentration camps to break the lines of guerrilla support.

Mapfumo reinforced the imagery of suffering in "Pfumvu Paruzevha" (Trouble in the reserve; Mapfumo 1999). By chronicling the evils of African underdevelopment through "reservation," Mapfumo called for armed assault on evildoers that he had no need to name, merely saying, "Father has seen trouble at home" and asking, "Did you hear that grandmother died?" "Did you hear that brother was taken?" "Did you hear that grandfather ran away?" "Did you hear that there is no more land?" "Did you hear that the cattle were taken?" "Did you hear the rains no longer fall?" Mapfumo utilized *bembera*, the Madzimbabwe tactic of undirected, nonconfrontational public shaming, to decry this litany of *pfumvu*, troubles, that made him a *rombe*, an outcast with neither family nor a heritage. The song required no elaboration to Africans who, since the 1890s, had been made *marombe* in great numbers through land and cattle seizures, taxation, and destruction of their homes in forced removals and punitive raids, and whose young men disappeared in the dead of night at the hands of colonial soldiers and police (the so-called Security Forces).

Thus made wretched by colonial savagery, African life became a diametrical contrast to that of the luxuriating "blessed Others" who, as he put it in "Pfumvu Paruzevha," lived in towns, traveled by car, had money in their pockets, enjoyed good health, had comfortable places to sleep, ate hot meals, and lived in electrified houses. As Kwaramba (1997, 42) observed, most of Mapfumo's wartime songs are overlexicalized with trouble, suffering, destitution, and death—a powerful indictment of the settlers and their system. As a communication technique, the rhetorical questions in "Pfumvu Paruzevha" were intended to jolt people to action, chiding them for folding their hands while the settlers threw sand into their eyes. Mapfumo's lamentation was no African self-pity, but a call to armed uprising.

Similarly, in "Kuyaura" (Suffering), Mapfumo articulated popular grievances—the arbitrary killings, the spiteful destruction of homes, and the resultant impoverishment—then made impassioned pleas for advice, wisdom, sacred weapons, and charms from the nation's grey heads, ancestors, martyred leaders of the revolution, the herbalists and medicine men and women, and even from local witches, who might perhaps redeem themselves by redeploying their witchcraft to honorable ends. This was an indication that, as Oliver "Tuku" Mtukudzi put it in "Ndiri Bofu" (I am blind), the country was trudging through desperate spiritual darkness that required divine intervention. While Tuku cloaked his plea for mobilization in a gospel ditty, apparently asking for personal redemption from the Christian God in the harsh environment bereft of free speech, Mapfumo tended to boldly declare African defiance and intentionality. Amidst all the lamentation born of extreme suffering, an unfaltering confidence and reassertion of the popular vision of victory ran through his songs.

The warning to the settler government was clear: "I have drawn out my sword and war axe," Mapfumo sang in "Hokoyo" (Watch out). He became even more daring as the war progressed, penning a string of songs like "Tumira Vana Kuhondo" (Send the children to the war) and "Pamuromo Chete" (Mere big mouthing), a response to the bravado of Rhodesian Prime Minister Ian Smith about crushing the terrorists and maintaining the white supremacist state "for a thousand years." "This song was sung directly," explained Mapfumo. "I was telling Smith that there are people in such trouble that all this talking was mere words—talk without substance. The people understood. They knew what I was talking about" (Frederikse 1982, 108). In addition to his own compositions, Mapfumo adapted some songs from their *chidzimba* (hunting), *ngondo* (war), and *mabasa* (work) contexts into recruitment calls for this greatest of tasks, frightening the regime and earning himself jail time.

So influential was Mapfumo's music that the state variously tried to disarm him through brutal suppression, appropriation, and subversion. As it had dealt with the City Quads and the Milton Brothers, so also it sought to deal with Mapfumo. Naturally, as W. Bender (1991, 158) wrote, "On suspicions of subversion, Shona songs that were . . . popular with the people and the guerillas were excluded from the [RBC's radio] system," but they were also banned from the formal market. Radio was a natural weapon, yet the censorship proved a double-edged weapon, fueling underground sales. The state tightened its grip on record companies, which in turn compelled musicians to tone down their rhetoric, as Tony Rivet of Teal Records pointed out:

> Thomas' music! Phew! If you only knew what the words were before—we'd to change some of the words . . . to a certain extent . . . so that the songs could be

> acceptable to the government. I remember they came along to me and said, "The terrs [terrorists] are getting all the tribes-people to sing gook songs." The one they really didn't like was Tumira Vana Kuhondo . . . I told them it was a bloody RAR [Rhodesia African Rifles] marching song, an old military marching song. (Frederikse 1982, 108)

The state's agents may have been fooled, leading Rhodesian soldiers to adopt the song for a bloody RAR marching song: "You see, the RF [Rhodesian Front] soldiers thought the song was meant to support them—that was the whole trick. They used to sing this very same number, only meaning it the other way round. We pulled their leg, at the same time encourag[ing] our people to fight." Or Mapfumo may have celebrated too soon, as the regime repeatedly arrested and detained him for aiding the "terrs" through his songs. But the charges never stuck, because his lyrics were sly and couched in innuendo. Mapfumo's songs helped send multitudes into the guerrilla camps. His shows at popular spots, like the Mushandirapamwe Hotel in the nationalist hub of Highfield and the peri-urban Skyline Motel, became sites of guerrilla recruitment: "People came to the shows, spent the whole night dancing to Chimurenga and towards dawn got into hired buses and set off straight for guerrilla training" (Mapfumo family, interview). Moreover, Mapfumo's interaction with the guerrillas was much more personal and intimate. He helped underground recruiters like Matema to raise funds. One night in the late 1970s, Matema came to collect him for a solidarity meeting with guerrillas camped in the Hwedza Mountains. Up in these *makwindingwi,* the guitar guerrilla was amused to meet one self-styled "Cde Jimi Hendrix," whose exploits with the AK-47 apparently mimicked the guitar poetics of the African American superstar! As guerrilla artists, Chimurenga artists operated at the front line of popular consciousness, helping to breach the zones of colonial criminalization of both the guerrillas and the communities that deployed and hosted them, and breaking the vice of state propaganda.

In 1979, the Zimbabwe-Rhodesia regime detained Mapfumo for three months without trial and then coerced him to perform for Bishop Abel Muzorewa, the Prime Minister of the discredited and short-lived "Internal Settlement" government. Two decades later, in the pages of *Parade* (January 2000), Mapfumo looked back:

> I was detained continuously on the pretext that I was working [with] and aiding "terrorists." They had detained me before but did not lay charges, and released me without any explanation. They again detained me in 1979 for about three months. . . . A condition for my release was that I should accompany Bishop Muzorewa for a rally in Bulawayo. I was told to support him to avoid harassment. I sang at his rally, and the next day I was splashed on the front page of *The Herald,* with Muzorewa.

Back in Harare, angry fans denounced Mapfumo as a sellout and boycotted his shows. Mapfumo was rightly worried, realizing that the regime was out to ensnare him and confuse the people who regarded him as a voice of the disenfranchised: "They managed to get even some in ZANU to denounce me, saying all sorts of unpleasant things; writing letters to newspapers." Mapfumo averred that he had to comply, "because they had guns and we didn't have guns." But the compliance was disingenuous:

> Those that came to that show can tell you that I never sold out, I was singing the same Chimurenga beat, the same critical lyrics and the same protest. . . . I continued producing heavy Chimurenga music and then people started asking themselves, if I had sold out, how come I was still playing the same revolutionary songs. It was one incident that disturbed me in those days but people soon found out that I was not a sellout.

Moreover, Muzorewa's United African National Congress (UANC) party hijacked Mapfumo's songs, blaring them from helicopters together with announcements that the singer had deserted ZANU and now backed Muzorewa.[6] Ben Musoni was the chief African propagandist for the Rhodesian and Zimbabwe-Rhodesia governments, and he recounted to me how they bombed villages and guerrilla camps to pulsating Mapfumo tunes. But Mapfumo overcame this soiling of his reputation, he told me, "because the people knew who the real liberators were; and, moreover, the music they were playing was actually criticizing them. It never said Muzorewa and Smith are good." Listeners who bought his music from underground sources or who listened to it on pirate guerrilla radio must have found this musical bombing confusing. Part of the government's strategy was to bolster its call for a ceasefire in 1978, but the only people who responded were Muzorewa's own Auxiliary Forces—Madzakutsaku, whom Mapfumo went on to mock in another song, "Bhutsu Mutandarika" (Oversize, disfigured boot), "because we did not want anything to do with that phony Internal Settlement thing." Chimurenga song pulsed with power and inflamed the battle for hearts and minds.

Zexie Manatsa

Like Mapfumo, Zexie Manatsa turned around his musical career when he abandoned American cover versions in the late 1960s, and his work also became deeply absorbed with the war (Manatsa and Manatsa, 2012 interview). Manatsa's musical history goes back to his birthplace, Mhangura, where he grew up building guitars out of oil tins before dropping out of primary school and heading to Bulawayo with some friends. After a stint playing for Jairos Jiri's charitable organization for the disabled, he formed the Green Arrows and soon left for Salisbury. For years, he camped at Borra Township (kwaBhora) outside the city, entertaining travelers on their way home to Murehwa, Mutoko, or Nyamapanda for the weekend. Many of those who heard him interrupted their trip, thanks to his bewitching music, which was driven by the heart-piercing lead guitar played by his younger brother, Stanley, and the bass guitar that he played himself.[7] The Green Arrows were only dislodged from the popular township by the war that encroached from that side of the country. They subsequently camped at the legendary Jamaica Inn on Mutare Road, among other places.

Like Mapfumo, Manatsa was deeply concerned with the war, and this got him into trouble—detentions, arrests, beatings, and assassination attempts. Trouble started for him with an arrest at the Jamaica Inn in 1975 after performing his song "Vakomana Vaye" (Those boys). The song hailed "the boys," who, he boldly declared, "are here!" The problem was not simply the suggestive lyrics, but specifically the action of Shamhu, a Rhodesia Broadcasting Corporation DJ, who skipped onto the stage, grabbed the microphone, and announced, "Yes, those boys are here! This is a band of the soil. It's a band for Zimbabwe!" He put the microphone down and left. Special Branch operatives promptly arrested Manatsa, who was only saved by an informer who was enamored with a band girl. Two weeks later, they heard that Shamhu had fled the country for the guerrilla camps in Zambia, inspiring another equally suggestive chart topper for Manatsa, "Waenda" (He is gone):

Waenda, ah	He is gone
Waenda chose	He is gone forever
Waenda mwana	The child is gone
Haachadzoki	He is not coming back.

Manatsa tried to disguise this "guerrilla odyssey" behind the mask of marriage, adding a stanza that said, "Baba vairamba kuti ndiroore kure" (Father refused me permission to marry far away). Exile had become the only space from which to engineer Zimbabwe, and many children left parents—supportive or not—in tears.

The threadbare poetic veil did not keep trouble away from the Green Arrows. Again, in 1978, they courted trouble by performing their song "Madzangaradzimu" (Apparitions) in Headlands. The song called the settlers apparitions who took away the people's happiness:

Chii chinenge madzangaradzimuwe?	What is that which looks like ghosts?
Chinenge Madhunamutuna,	Like apparitions
Chiiko Madhunamutunawe?	What, the ghosts?
Atishaisa mufaro	Which took away all our happiness.
Ndiwayo Madhunamutuna	It is indeed the apparitions
Ndiwayo madzangaradzimu!	The ghosts!

Overexcited roadies pointed fingers at colonial police and soldiers in the audience while chorusing, "Ndiwayo Madhunamutuna, ndiwayo madzangaradzimu!" The outraged *madhunamutuna* stormed the stage, whipped the musicians, and took away a few.

Two of Manatsa's most famous Chimurenga pieces are "Musango Mune Hangaiwa" (Guinea fowls in the forest) and "Nyoka Yendara" (The ominous snake), both composed in the mid-1970s. "Hangaiwa" hailed the guerrillas who swarmed the forests as ancestral guinea fowls. Nehanda had sent these sacred birds on a mission. If Manatsa could hide behind the innuendo in the song when he was asked, "Does Mbuya Nehanda have guinea fowls?" his actions onstage left very little to the imagination. Zexie and his wife Stella described their shows at Gwanzura Stadium, Highfield, to me:

> Sometimes we took Chipo, our daughter, to Gwanzura, clothed her in black cloths similar to those worn by *mhondoro* [spirit mediums], and sat her on the stage. We gave her nestling guinea fowls before playing "Hangaiwa." So when we sang the lines that said "Tangai mabvunza VaNehanda" (Consult Nehanda first), she would take the birds and release them into flight, enacting the song's message. That electrified the crowds and people cried, thinking about their relatives who had gone off to the war. Others, gripped by the emotive spirit, got possessed.

Chipo was Manatsa's niece and the subject of his first hit, "Chipo Chiroorwa" (Get married now, Chipo), which exhorted the girl to settle down since she had come of age, so that "our parents may eat cakes and celebrate." While this was a quite personal song, to many Zimbabweans Chipo was Zimbabwe, whose moment of triumph was due so that everyone might celebrate.

In "Nyoka Yendara," Manatsa defiantly reasserted Africans' conviction that they were going to beat the Rhodesian forces and crush Smith, the "ominous snake" that brought death on the people: "Vachairova musoro nyoka yendara. Baba muzimba iro. Tendai vakomana vanoridza hosho, baba muzimba ramambo" (They are going to crush its head, this ominous snake, dear father, in that big house. Thanks to the boys who shake the rattles, in the king's house). Smith was the *nyoka yendara* that had portended death in ancestral Madzimbabwe, the sacred house of stone. By the late 1970s, the comrades—the boys who rattled *hosho* (a musical euphemism for the gun)—were indeed crushing the colonial serpent's head. Manatsa could not say "Zimbabwe," so he chose the figurative *zimba*, an unnamed big house: "I could not say 'in Zimbabwe' explicitly! But our people knew. Even the settlers knew. They had their own people, including one white RBC guy who knew Shona. He would listen and ban these songs. Many of our songs were banned on radio."

The guerrillas had progressively penetrated the country, creating liberated zones, hence the sense of imminent victory. But this was also a time of much political intrigue and opportunism, with some emergent or failed leaders cutting deals with the Smith regime. Manatsa captured the resulting confusion in "Vaparidzi Vawanda" (The preachers have become too many). He recalled,

> When I performed "Vaparidzi Vawanda," I would sometimes hoist a bed onto the stage so as to enact the message of the song: "We no longer know who to follow; there are just too many preachers; father, tell us in our dreams," then I would go onto the bed and simulate sleep. Baba! That drove people crazy. And the songs enjoyed tremendous sales. Everybody who had a record player bought them; everybody was so taken over by this defiant political spirit—that "now we don't want anything to do with Rhodesia." Everyone!

Mapfumo and Manatsa were among the giants of 1970s Zimbabwean music, and they did not shy away from their people's burning concerns. Indeed, it is this engagement that made them stand out. Four decades later, one Jekanyika would comment on a YouTube posting of Manatsa's song, "Chipo Chiroorwa," saying, "his song musango munehangaiwa still holds the record of staying on top of the charts the longest in zimbabwe. he truly is a legend. he contributed a lot to the zimbabwean music as well as the liberation struggle. Another commentator, Chrispen Matsilele, agreed: "Chipo Chiroorwa reminds me of my early years . . . Christmas time when those who used to work in town will come back home to the village with gramophones and this is one of the songs that was constantly churned out" (Green Arrows 2010).

It was this popularity that Muzorewa, the "stooge" Prime Minister of the Internal Settlement government, blamed for "sabotaging" one of his Salisbury campaign rallies in 1979 when only a small crowd turned up. Zexie and Stella had staged their wedding reception in Rufaro Stadium the same day, attracting an astounding sixty thousand paying guests and earning themselves a princely $19,000. Thomas Mapfumo and Tineyi Chikupo played music during the wedding. The Manatsas' popularity and unequivocal support for the liberation war made them targets of more serious threats than the routine harassment and occasional arrests and beatings. For instance, at Mushandirapamwe Hotel in 1978, Zexie believed assassins were waiting in ambush near his car, and he had to escape through the back door and into a friend's car. Even more seriously, one night in Victoria Falls in 1979, he and Stella were stunned as they listened while soldiers sprayed bullets into a motel room they had just vacated: "We had booked a guest house, but the girls who worked there moved us out into another room which had a good bed. Then to our horror, we listened as soldiers fired bullets into the room that we had vacated earlier, shooting through the door, intending to kill us in there. We observed the numerous bullet holes on the door and the walls the next morning. We would certainly have died had we not been moved" (Manatsa and Manatsa, 2014 interview).

Song inspired Africans to boldness in the communal *jenaguru* and school *dariro,* in urban concerts, in street protests, at political rallies and *mapungwe,* on the guerrilla trail, in training camps, at the front lines, and in the settler jails. I end this chapter by exploring Chimurenga song in Rhodesia's gulag.

Reliving the Chiwashira Brothers Choir days. Left to right: Josh (the author's brother), Tsuro, Hofisi, and Musutu Chikowero. Mhondoro, 2012. All images in this chapter are courtesy of the author unless otherwise noted.

The *dare* professoriate: telling history at the Chikowero homestead. Mhondoro, 2012.

Cde Chinx at a rehearsal. Chitungwiza, 2012.

Chris Matema (center) and Zexie Manatsa (right), with Gallo Records's Mr. Rose, celebrating Gold Disk Awards for "Chipo Chiroorwa" and "Musango Mune Hangaiwa." Courtesy of the Manatsa family. Photographer unknown.

The wedding of Zexie and Stella Manatsa. Harare, 1979. Courtesy of the Manatsa family. Photographer: Jimmy Salani.

Thomas Mapfumo, spearheading the cultural revolution. Courtesy of Thomas Mapfumo, c. 1970s.

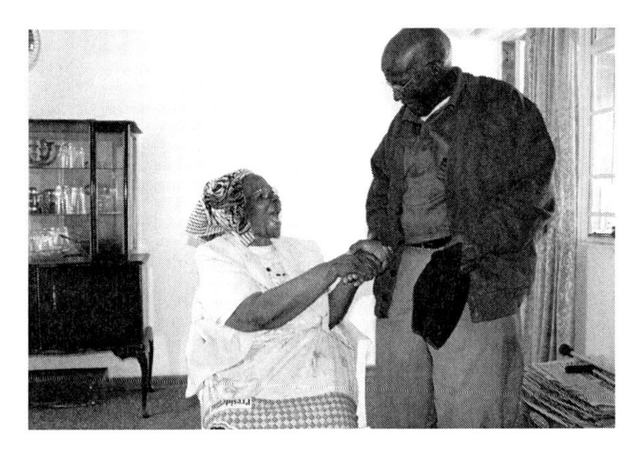

Old pals reunite: Jane Lungile Ngwenya and Abel Sinametsi Sithole. Bulawayo, 2012.

Chimurenga in the Stocks

During his fund-raising performances for ZAPU in exile in Zambia, Abel Sithole (interview) endured taunts from some of his uncharitable hosts, who told him, "Go back to your country and fight Smith." He eventually did. In 1969, after training for a year in Tanzania, Sithole was deployed as part of a ZIPRA reconnaissance and recruitment unit. He was captured in battle and sentenced to death under Rhodesia's terrorism laws, but his sentence was later commuted to life imprisonment and he was interned at Bulawayo's Khami Maximum Security Prison. Empire brought its jail to reinforce its authority and African subjugation.

To Sithole and his guerrilla compatriots, the pain of colonial jail was aporic, testing their resilience and convictions. Culturally, it proved a transcendental opportunity to deepen the imagination of the struggling, self-liberating African. Rather than depoliticizing African consciousness, imprisonment often achieved the opposite. Thus, when Mapfumo was detained for singing "terr" songs, he reportedly dared his jailers to kill him, for that would be easier than forcing him to stop "singing Chimurenga songs—our own African traditional music" (Frederikse 1982, 110). The Chimurenga sensibility was defiantly lodged in the African desire for freedom. The songs also provided a psychological antidote to the harsh treatment and uncertainty of jail.

Colonial imprisonment was particularly tough for political prisoners, who had to sleep on bare cement floors and undertake punitive make-work tasks like crushing rocks. Song remained one way to ease the psychological toll. Sithole and his colleagues thus formed prison bands:

> I formed a band called Down Beat, with K. Shumba and Zizi—the three of us. Another five colleagues formed a separate group, Merry Makers. So we took turns to entertain prisoners, encouraging them not to worry too much, because death hung over our heads and also because of the ill treatment. We grouped together as ZIPRA and ZANLA to sing Chimurenga songs until it was time to sleep. That helped the inmates not to lose their heads; though five or six did! (Interview)

Unlike prison writing, singing was a more communal mode of marking time and collectively contesting the mental paralysis that the authorities intended. The songs helped reinforce the inmates' political beliefs and cement their struggles and ideals. This defiant guerrilla agency disarmed the colonial jail and transformed it from a spiritual desert into a space from which to collectively (re)imagine the nation. It allowed Sithole to compose, learn, and share songs and experiences with fellow countrymen from different political parties and other parts of the country: "I composed some of the songs, and learned a lot from my fellow inmates like Mbengeranwa, who taught me *mbira* songs. . . . There was much scope to exchange these songs and also to share thoughts and experiences."

One of the songs that Mbengeranwa taught Sithole was "Tsenzi" (Honeybird), a deeply spiritual *mbira* piece:

Gogogoi tasvika isu nherera	We have arrived, we the orphans
Musango dema rinochema tsenzi	In the dark forest of the chirping honeybird
Mhondoro dzesango dzinozarura	The guardian spirits will open the way
Musango dema rinochema tsenzi	In the dark forest of the chirping honeybird
Vakadzi musarase dota mariri	Women, don't dispose of ash in it
Musango dema rinochema tsenzi.	The dark forest of the chirping honeybird.

Tsenzi is a chirping honeybird that escorts hunters to bee colonies so that it may also enjoy the spoils. Zimbabwe cultures revere this bird, as they do *mhondoro,* the spirit lion, and *chapungu* (pl. *zvapungu*), the bateleur eagle, often interpreting their sighting as epiphanic. During the war, *vadzimu* deployed these creatures as messengers and signs to guerrillas, as Cde Shungu explained (interview):

> To us, these were not ordinary birds. They were *zvitumwa* [messengers] of the ancestors. . . . When you see approaching bateleur eagles hitting each other, know that a battle is imminent and be on standby and alert. Sometimes *chapungu* would come shrieking and flying very close to the ground. That was a sure sign that the enemy is close and you should leave that place and follow in the direction of its flight; that was your safe route.

Harming these sacred creatures would desecrate the forests and upset the ancestors.

In "(Gwindingwi Rine) Shumba" (Gwindingwi Mountain has a predator lion), Mapfumo used the dark forest as a metaphor for the confusion and uncertainty that had struck the Africans. However, in "Tsenzi," the dark forest is also the holy abode of the ancestors, who maintain the balance of nature and manifest through symbols like *tsenzi, zvapungu,* and *mhondoro* to guide people through such confusion and uncertainty as long as they uphold ancestral precepts. People do not ordinarily venture into the dark forest save in a desperate search for refuge from a life-threatening invasion, for an organized hunt, or because they are lost. In all such circumstances, they would supplicate their ancestors for guidance and observe the precepts that govern the sacred forests as both a refuge and a resource, as the ancestors are the ultimate guardians of the land and African ecology. To Madzimbabwe, the independence war was a desperate bid to drive out obstinate invaders who imperiled their very existence, so they took both literal and psychological refuge in the dark forests, as Mbengeranwa sang.

The same meaning is shared by "Haisi Mhosva yaChinamano" (It's not Chinamano's fault), composed by Lot Nyathi, Dennis Dhlamini, and Ken Ndhlovu, ZIPRA captives also held at Khami:

> It is not the fault of Chinamano,
> It is not the fault of Musarurwa
> That the children of Zimbabwe must carry guns to fight in Zimbabwe

> Truly we have suffered;
> Our relatives are in the wire,
> Others are orphans,
> Their riches have vanished
> Let's fight in Zimbabwe,
> Let's be brave and fight the war of our ancestors,
> The war of Chindunduma;
> Let's be brave—we, the Africans—to finish the war of liberation in Zimbabwe.
> (Frederikse 1982, 110)[8]

Chimurenga song assuaged the pain of imprisonment and inspired even those thus shackled to fight on. Thus, as Nyathi and his colleagues told Julie Frederikse, "Those who were released earlier had to convey the message to the people outside. They had to sing those songs and let the people get to know them. We knew that they were going to be sung and that we, too, were going to sing them outside one day." Prison songs, therefore, perpetuated the spirit of the historical revolution which Nyathi and colleagues conceptualized as the war of the ancestors, *hondo yeChindunduma.*

Imprisonment could not kill this transgenerational spirit of Chindunduma. Nelson Chikutu (interview) was imprisoned briefly in Chikurubi in 1976 for public stoning and sabotage. He was amazed to find that inmates in the notorious prison were jovial, defiantly singing such songs as "Tinoda Nyika Yedu"—"Tinoda nyika yedu nehupfumi hwayo hwose; Zimbabwe; Nyika yedu yakatorwa nevauyi; Zuva rayo rasvika" (We demand our country—the whole of it together with all its wealth; Zimbabwe; Our country colonized by aliens; Its day has come). The experience was incisive to Chikutu: "When you are in jail and those sorts of songs are sung, you see that *jeri racho harina zvariri kushanda*" (the jail is serving no purpose). In other words, Chimurenga song disarmed the colonial jail and rendered it not only ineffectual but, nightmarishly for the colonial state, one of the many unlikely spaces from which guerrillas propagated the revolution and held the colonial state to account.

Throughout the near century of colonial overlordship, Africans wielded song to articulate their cultures, their overwhelming sense of loss and unhappiness, and their defiant celebration of life, hope, resistance, and self-liberation. Ngwenya summarized the power of song best when she noted to me in 2012, "Song made life easier. When you go to a *jakwara* or *nhimbe* [communal work party] the task does not go smoothly without song. All collective endeavors are driven by song." Chimurenga was a *jakwara* of self-liberation, mobilized only by a few, "as others still doubted its feasibility, doubting whether we were really going to beat *mabhunu.*" Yet the thrill of militant *jakwara* summoned and intoxicated participants, steeling them to confront their fear of the cannibalistic settler state. The genealogy of Chimurenga song draws from the depths of African historical independence, spanning the decades from the First Chimurenga (1896–97) through to the outbreak of the second in the 1960s, and it exists today as interwoven historical memory. Between the two wars, Africans largely expressed their opposition to colonialism nonviolently, with villagers, schoolteachers, and students as well as professional musicians weaving a rich repertoire of musical cultures of resistance that eventually inspired armed struggle. Leaders of the nationalist movement drew on this vault of defiant arts of self-liberation to marshal a discourse of mass cultural nationalism and to mobilize for the war that finally dismantled colonial rule. Song, then, constituted an indispensable arsenal in Africans' struggle for freedom.

10 Jane Lungile Ngwenya

A Transgenerational Conversation

Gogo (Grandmother) Jane Lungile Ngwenya's life story and sociopolitical striving inject a vivid personal perspective into the multivalent story of African being, song, and power in colonial Zimbabwe. Ngwenya was born at the crest of the Rhodesian settler system, when the impact of missionary education and colonial policies had drastically reshaped African life. The trajectory of her life, from young girl growing up in the "native reserve," to student, teacher, mother, politician, and, ultimately, a guerrilla who questioned and stood up to fight the colonial system, is instructive about the resilience of African consciousness under the assaults of colonial epistemes and the expression of that consciousness through traditions of song.

Like many other people discussed in these pages, Ngwenya is not a "professional musician," a category that derives from European culture. Like them, she sang and used song at home, in church, at school, and at political rallies. But more than most, she also sang and used song in detention, in jail, in the guerrilla training camps, and as a guerrilla broadcaster playing Chimurenga songs on pirate radio from exile in Zambia to mobilize support for the independence

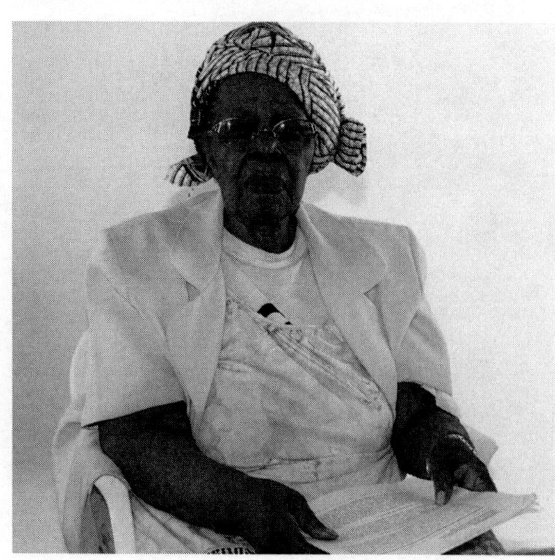

Guerrilla of many *doeks:* Gogo Jane Lungile Ngwenya. Bulawayo, 2012.

struggle. Ngwenya's rich life story is therefore tightly enmeshed in the African struggles that this book narrates through the lens of song. Because of this, she is too important to either skim over in a few pages or speak for. The transcription that follows combines two conversations I had with her, in July 2011 in Esigodini and in August 2012 in Bulawayo. The transcript takes the reader to the *dare*, the professorial African communal space where history—as knowledge and consciousness—is transacted communally across generations. It is a doubly authored, transgenerational dialogue that reframes the location of knowledge in the African collective experience and, in so doing, implicitly interrogates scholars' universally adopted and rather alienating "modernist" claims to single authorship by virtue of research and retransmission through print culture. Gogo Ngwenya coauthored this chapter, by which I mean more than that she was interviewed and shared her life experiences as merely an "interviewee" or an "informant," terms that are implicated both in Eurocentric research framings of "natives" and in the counterinsurgent strategies of colonial intelligence gathering. She cowrote this chapter, and edited and corrected it for errors of fact and inexactness of translation and transcription as a grandmother writing her own history. The desire that we merely gesture at here is to decolonize research by recentering African cooperative modes of self-authoring.

MC: Gogo, let us start by talking about your name, childhood, and schooling.

JLN: My name is Jane Lungile Ngwenya. My real name is Lungile, and my grandparents called me Rungire, because, as you know, in ChiKaranga they don't have an "L." I was born on June 15, 1935, in Buhera, Manicaland. I have only one sibling, a younger sister. My father came from down south, Lesotho. Unfortunately, he died when we were still young, so we don't know much about him. We grew up in Buhera under the care of our maternal grandfather. For schooling, I first went to Gwebu School for my Sub A, B, and Standard 1. And for Standard 2, I went to Madende School, there in Chief Gwebu's area. Chief Gwebu had come from Matabeleland with a group of his people after being displaced by land-grabbing white settlers, and he resettled in Manicaland. The chiefs of the latter area welcomed him.

MC: It was expected that children should go to school by the time you were born. Is that a correct characterization of affairs in those days?

JLN: Yes, but the schools were few, scattered, and very far apart. One area would have Standard 1, another up to Standard 2 only, and so, like other children, I would go from place to place, staying with either relatives or family friends in pursuit of education. But you know, we Africans showed so much love to each other. The fact that you could stay with total strangers as your parents greatly demonstrated our culture of love, unity, and oneness as Africans. This was done without any payment—any child was treated as the child of the family looking after it. Our family systems were broad-based—extended, as we have been taught to call them. But unfortunately, that is now almost extinct because of the influence of the incoming cultures, particularly the western. They taught us to hate each other, to refuse, to neglect, and to discriminate; and those evils were inculcated into us as virtues—"civilization." You can see the legacies of that in the languages that we have adopted—"half-brother," "cousin-sister," etc. In our cultures, a brother is a brother, a sister a sister. Our cultures became badly corroded.

MC: Clearly. Did you go beyond Standard 2 in your schooling?

JLN: Yes, and my schooling history is quite checkered. From Madende, I went to Kwekwe's Globe and Phoenix for Standard 3 and to Shurugwi for Standards 4–6. When I finished my Standard 6, I then taught for a while as an untrained teacher while I awaited training. I was still too young then, so I could not go to train straight away. And remember there were only two career options available to Africans—teaching and nursing. Almost every educated African was either a teacher or a nurse. No more.

But you know, I love being a Black Zimbabwean. We loved and respected each other. During those days of lack of educational facilities that I have mentioned, those with as little as Standard 1 or 2 would teach others how to read and write in those segregated schools and communities. You are blessed these days to be learning and teaching freely in schools with whites. We never rubbed shoulders with whites either as children or adults, save for those pastors who came to our schools on some select Sunday or Saturday to brainwash the Africans, whom they labeled pagans and heathens.

MC: Let's talk about those pastors later. But for now, tell me: did you eventually train as a teacher?

JLN: I did teacher training because I was too young to be a nurse, which displeased me. My mother wanted me to be a nurse, because it was the parents' decision what course you took; you know in our culture how much we listen to and obey our parents. But I didn't stay for long in teaching because—it seemed that I was an arrogant child, but I didn't want to do something that I didn't quite understand. I had this independent mind that questioned things. This is my approach to life. For instance, when a teacher was teaching I always insisted that he explain things to me in detail so that I do the right thing. But I discovered that teachers were some of the most brainwashed people in our society then. Their questioning of things was very limited, and they were being separated socially from their people.

MC: What do you mean? My impression is that teachers were idolized as models.

JLN: They were molded thus, but they were models of what? Most of them were slaves to their profession and the colonial system. They were made to believe that they were different from other Africans: the idea that a teacher should not be seen eating, or just opening his or her mouth unnecessarily, save the music teacher who conducted the tonic sol-fa. And even the latter sang in those stilted European pitches and when doing those Negro spirituals that drove all of us to tears.

MC: OK. Tell me more about the so-called Negro spirituals.

JLN: You know, we all cried singing the Negro spirituals, thinking about the slave trade. But our missionaries and teachers did not consider that the slave trade was evil; they mystified it. There was so much confusion with the Negro spirituals. They were presented to us as a sentiment of a grateful people who had now found light as a result of their enslavement, and expressing pity for us who had remained here in Africa, as if they were now better humans and nearer to God by virtue of their enslavement. So they were now singing songs praising God for redeeming them from heathenism in Africa. Yet here we sang songs pitying the slaves. So the missionaries' idea was that when we sang those songs, we should actually wish we were slaves too. The songs were twisted to imply that enslaved Africans found God across the ocean, when in fact they were being tormented and sold away from each other at slave markets and appealing to God for deliverance from the cruelties. But missionaries and many of our teachers used to perpetrate lies and brainwash people.

MC: I know many teachers also did *makonzati*. Can we learn anything about their political consciousness through the songs?

JLN: Yes, and their consciousness changed over time. God, perhaps having seen the oppression of the Black person, equipped him to articulate his thoughts through singing, because if you spoke your views, the colonists charged you for talking politics. So if you listen to the songs closely, you will see that many of them revolved around suffering. And even the songs that we ended up singing with the children in the guerrilla camps in exile evolved mostly from the hymns and *makwaya* songs. Such songs as "Nyika yedu yeZimbabwe ndomatakazvarirwa" [Zimbabwe our birthright] originated from church hymns, just with changed words. The transformation was quite natural.

MC: You talked about the displacement of people like Chief Gwebu. How did such policies affect African lives?

JLN: People lost their lands and herds, of course. But our own grandfather was very rich; he had a lot of livestock. So money was not a big problem as we grew up. They no longer had young children, so they looked after my younger sister and me. Our grandparents understood the need for education, which was rare at that time. My aunt had gone to Makumbe Mission, where she was among the first Africans to rub shoulders with the Donnas and Jethros of the white world. Ah, it was quite something! Going to a mission school, ah, and they sang too, those church hymns. The idea was that schooling should transform us into a new people. The design was to convert us, because the colonists said that to win an African over, you have to destroy his culture first, so that he or she can hate himself or herself. This became a serious problem among those who were given bursaries by missionaries. When they came back, many of them had been removed from their people—now seeing heathens in their elders, simply because they were uneducated. The system was like that, without pronouncing itself so.

MC: Do those ideas explain the changing of names by Africans? You told me Jane is not your real name. Why did people get renamed?

JLN: That was part of the process of changing Africans' identities, so that you really felt that, yes, you have been cleansed; you are now a new person, different from your old dirty self. That was the meaning of conversion. There came a time when that became a real disturbance in our country. At that time, when you didn't have an English name, not having been baptized, you were regarded as raw, uncivilized. When I think about it I can still feel the hand that slapped me on the cheek, here! I remember this one time when I took a message to this sister of ours, Sibongile, shouting out her name, and she hit me, telling me, "Don't you know that I have been baptized? I am no longer Sibongile. I am Elizabeth!" We had not witnessed her baptism. People thought they were being despised to be called by their African names. They had become Mildred, Mary, Eve . . . To be called Mazvidzeni, Makurirwei, Mudzingwa, ah! Nobody liked that anymore! So it became very difficult.

MC: Some of us—your grandchildren—were born in the last decades of the colonial era, and we still got "Christian" names. I remember my mother thumbing through the Bible a few days before my younger brothers started school, sounding out various names—"Cyprene? No, David?"—until she found the right-sounding name for school. Fortunately, none of us got renamed after any of the more notorious Bible villains; neither did we get burdened with the more outlandish of the Bible names, perhaps because my mother actually read her own Bible and knew the various stories associated with the characters. But why was all that necessary?

JLN: The Bible was the first book that Africans were taught, and for many households it became the only book they proudly owned. The people who were patted on the shoulder were the champions in the Bible. To be baptized meant to be reborn, so you had to be renamed. All that was necessary if you were to be accepted in school, or to get a birth certificate at the *mudzviti*'s office—which means to look for a job or to deal with any official at all in order to survive. You needed an English name. I remember my friends used to chide me for my name, Lungile, telling me that was an uncivilized name. The same thing with our languages: when I was in Shurugwi it became compulsory that you don't speak your "vernacular" in the schoolyard. You would be punished for it, spending the whole day out of class serving punishment for speaking Ndebele or ChiKaranga. We were too young and we didn't think too much about it but we would still feel it somehow, that we were being oppressed. Unfortunately, speaking English gave some of us an attitude, so that we started despising people back at home simply because we spoke English, wanting to speak English to parents. We were being transformed into rude children, cultural misfits. We had been obedient to our parents before we went to school. Yet the irony is that we were being taught to be obedient to the missionaries and teachers at these new schools, and to turn the other cheek if you are slapped; not to care about the litany of real injustices in this wicked world, because heaven is beautiful, with green grass and all. But I questioned some of those things, which almost got me expelled from school once.

MC: Tell me about it. What had happened?

JLN: Our school was nondenominational, so that many different priests would come to preach every Sunday. One Sunday VaMupanze of the Methodist Church came, together with John Trusdale, Reverends Thompson Samkange and Henry Kachidza, and some British colonial officials who were visiting in connection with their Federation [the Federation of the Two Rhodesias and Nyasaland]. VaMupanze started preaching, telling us about the green valleys, the golden gates, etc.: "Ah, heaven is beautiful!" He finished his sermon before time, and invited questions. I was one of the youngest pupils at the school, and I looked around to see if anyone was going to ask a question, but nobody raised their hand. So I raised mine and asked the reverend whether this heaven was meant for Black people only or for everybody. I didn't know that offended Mufundisi [the missionary]. He expressed his displeasure to my teachers, and they punished me. These were African teachers getting angry on behalf of the missionary. They said I had embarrassed *murungu* [a white person, pl. *varungu*], you see, because when a white person came you would see them worshipping him, and they had so much faith in the sermons and Bible that they saw themselves in those fantastic green valleys. So asking that sort of question was seen as disrespecting Mufundisi. The idea was to be told and keep quiet; but I wanted to know, after what I had seen over the few months at that school and in my young life. At the school we had worked very hard preparing for John Trusdale. We had planted green grass (as we called lawn), cleaned and scrubbed and made swings for his children. So I was wondering if these people who lived in these nice places that we made for them would again live in similarly nice places in heaven, or whether that new world would now be meant for us oppressed Black people. That offended Mufundisi and he expelled me from school. Luckily, I was reinstated after Reverends Samkange and Kachidza intervened and pleaded with the authorities that I was only a child genuinely seeking knowledge, and should be taught the right thing, rather than being expelled.

MC: So your teachers did not question what seemed like indoctrination to your young mind?

JLN: I was only curious, but it is very clear that the British really intended to blind us with their tailor-made education for servitude, which we were required to regurgitate without thinking. I remember as kids . . . we were quite naughty, you know. We used to take a chicken and fold its neck and bury its head under its wing, and we would lull it to sleep with song: "Chipudugwa, ramba wakadaro; chipudugwa, ramba wakadaro . . ." [*Chipudugwa,* stay like that; *chipudugwa,* stay like that . . .], clapping our hands. And the dumb chicken [*chipudugwa*] would stay like that virtually for the whole day, you know, never mind the hunger and all! Thinking back and reinterpreting that now, I can clearly see that Mwari had given us the parables, because you can make a person a fool and she or he would be proud of it. The colonial system sought to mold us into proud fools, particularly us the teachers. Teachers were the worst victims of colonial indoctrination. It was a very deliberate design to kill us.

MC: But what did your teachers charge you with, when you posed that naughty question?

JLN: There is this term that I only came to understand when I grew older; they were saying I was politically minded. I had no idea what that meant then; I was only an African child brought up in the village, but I was inquisitive. When things were done I always wanted to understand their logic.

MC: Well, I would probably have said the same; you were politically minded. But how did someone, particularly a child like you then, become "politically minded?"

JLN: My grandfather had many cattle, as I have said, but they were taken while we looked on, my grandchild. We looked on as the whites ferried the cattle into Bedford trucks, because we were told to pave way for *murungu* who must live in nice areas. Our herds were forcibly bought off at five bob [shillings], ten bob. And our grandparents were force-marched into those fierce trucks to be thrown away—*kunoraswa*—in some barren wastelands they designated "native reserves." So I would ask why they were treating our people with such cruelty and violence. The cattle were ours but they were just taken, and I would want to know why. So I kept asking those questions without ever getting a satisfactory answer. I would ask villagers who lost their cattle why they were taken and they would say, "Ah, they have been taken by the whites." "But are they yours?" "Yes, ah!" At the same time, young men your age were bound up and conscripted for *chibharo* [forced labor] while their parents were beaten up before them. And their goats and chickens were left wandering into the wild with nobody to look after them. Houses were burnt down and bulldozed. So those things really troubled me as I grew up; they really hurt our people.

MC: The cattle seizures. Was that *nhimuramuswe*—"*ngombe* counting," as the British called them in Kenya?

JLN: Yes. Forcible cattle seizures. Then when I had gotten married to my Catholic husband, one day I came across B. B. Burombo addressing a gathering of people, about twenty-five men. I was coming from church. I came over and sat down. I was the only woman there, carrying my little baby on my back, and these men were looking at me with quizzical eyes as if saying, "Where is this crazy woman coming from; is she OK?" BB did not stop addressing the meeting. When he talked about the seizures of our land, homes, and cattle, that really touched me. That was my first political rally, and it greatly stimulated me. One of my challenges had been that I would fail to find someone to discuss these sorts of issues with, as people were so frightened that they just looked on even when they saw a Black person being beaten up. Whites would randomly beat up people those days, you know.

MC: So we learned. But what about the church; did it help you to articulate these grievances or, as you implied, did you see it as a partner in the oppression of our people?

JLN: The church taught us to sing those self-denying hymns—"Negro spirituals" like "It Is Well with My Soul," "Swing Low," and the national anthem, "God Bless the Queen!" Nothing was well with our souls, or bodies. Fear was drilled into us. We sang those songs at schools standing still. You would not move even when a pesky fly bothered you. I don't despise the churches, but it was the church that was used to really destroy us. Those who were lucky to be chosen to go to far-away schools, some of them came back only to reject their parents. They came back to their parents' homes, to the homes they grew up in, and pitched up tents, stretcher-beds, and

Primus stoves where they cooked food only they ate. Right at their parents' homes! Some really educated people, including one who later became a vice chancellor of the University of Zimbabwe after independence. Many did that, including graduates and teachers from Fort Hare. [The only historically black university in South Africa, Fort Hare admitted students from around the continent.] Many of the teachers who taught us did not want their houses to be entered by people who came from homes where floors were smeared with cow dung. That was the sort of transformation that was being foisted on us. That was the meaning of "civilization"—to be "civilized" [meant] to be lost. Even the singing, you had to sing in those fake European accents and tones, not the freely expressive African singing voices, but to sing like "Missis" [the proverbial white woman]. That was the colonial school. Our mothers had been beaten up and cajoled to go to school, whenever missionaries found them herding cattle or doing other errands. Then they became the ones who persuaded us to go to school, because schooling was good.

Yet, on the other hand, while the church was transforming people in all these ways, there were other people who continued to sing their own traditional and drunken songs after beer drinks, etc., unaffected by the church. There was this one song sung by one villager which said,

What can I does for country for Rudhizha?
What can I does . . . ?

Other people sang it in Shona:

Ndoita sei nenyika yeRudhizha?	What can I do with the country, Rhodesia?
Ndoita sei nenyika yababa?	What can I do with the fatherland?

MC: How drunken was that song?

JLN: Not very drunken, if you really think about it! People were seeing all these problems and they didn't know what they could do, or how to say it out [loud], but that's how they spoke. They were told that the country is not theirs, and they had nowhere to go. Eventually the song was suppressed.

MC: Who suppressed the song?

JLN: Those who declared themselves the owners of the country. People were not told that you are singing a subversive, hateful song because the authorities did not want to drum into Africans' heads, even in a reverse sort of way, the idea that they were oppressing us. So they would just say, "Ah, what does that mean? It's a stupid song." They wanted to pretend that Africans were happy—Smith would infamously proclaim that "our natives are the happiest Africans on the continent!" But our situation was like that of an orphan. Nobody teaches an abused and neglected orphan to sing, "Dai ndiinamaiwo;

mai vangu vainditambira; dai ndiinamaiwo, nhasi uno vaindibereka" [If only I had a mother, she would surely accept me; If I had a mother, she would surely carry me on her back today]. Such songs just spring from the subconscious while the orphan does her chores, and whoever might be abusing her will begin to think she is making political statements, and may wish to suppress her voice: "Do you think I am the one who killed your mother, heh? What sort of thing are you singing?" A villain is always troubled by his guilty conscience—*kuvhunduka chati kwatara hunge uine katurikwa,* as we say. That is how context can shape a person's mind, and the Rhodesian system was founded on African dispossession, oppression, and denial—so they had a lot hanging, and so the sound of anything falling startled them. Those songs, we found them there, speaking to Africans' situation.

Unfortunately there are some alienating songs that our parents also sang and some of us continue singing even today in church, such as

Hatina musha panyika . . .

We do not have a home on this earth;
We yearn only for the home in heaven . . .

MC: Where did that song come from?

JLN: Such songs came with the hymnbooks. When we asked, we were told that each church—except the Roman Catholics, which had no hymnbooks—asked their African trainee pastors to compose those self-alienating songs. One thing that you will see when you look at the hymnbooks is that some of these songs you don't find in the original white missionaries' hymnbooks. For instance, the one that we have in our Methodist hymnbook:

Wauya wauya mucheki,
Vakaipa vachapiswa vakati maiwe . . .

Behold, the gory reaper has come,
The evil ones are going to be burned eternally until they cry, "Oh my dearest mother!"

MC: I know that one too, quite well; various churches sing it.

JLN: Such songs were weapons that were deployed to destroy African cultural self-confidence and self-worth through fear. When you are thus destroyed you devalue yourself and start to imagine that you should be someone else, because Africans were taught to discard their old selves and cultures that anchored their being and identified them transgenerationally with their ancestors and *madzinza* [bloodlines]. So by despising yourself, it means you are despising your mother and father for giving birth to a thing like you, and you are being estranged from yourself. Do you know what I mean?

MC: That is still quite evident even today. You said some people despised their parents when they came back from the missions, and the same attitudes have persisted to a good degree, so we can then say *chakabaya chikatyokera* [the bewitching colonial thorn became permanently lodged in our souls]. But I also get the sense that these mission students were applauded when they brought back all that cleverness, speaking like the white man. No?

JLN: They were, so that many were sending their children to learn, but others did not like it. Some of the ideas about education did our people no good. For example, you would see somebody looking up a tree speaking English to a dove, demonstrating their "education" in crazy ways. Even today that still happens. You hear youngsters asking each other which university they went to, and when somebody mentions Oxford, those who went to less important colleges back off. It took time for our people to use education to engage the evils of the system, such as asking why the *bhurakuwacha* ["black watchmen"—African policemen of the colonial state] were brutalizing our people, for example. I stood up to such injustice, but I didn't know that it was politics.

MC: So it seems you were an insurgent at a young age. But what else shaped your political consciousness?

JLN: The racial indignities of the colonial system were innumerable, and many people stood up to them. When I got married I left teaching and started doing dressmaking. I had learned dressmaking, and I once worked for Hardon and Sly, and a white woman whom I had actually taught to make even a hem was supervising me, just because her skin was white! Such things disturbed me to no end. And I remember one day I hit a white woman when I was pregnant.

MC: Nobody dared do that! Tell me more about it.

JLN: I was buying things for my baby and this shop attendant was preventing me from unwrapping the clothes so that I could inspect them properly. And she pushed me away. I put my wallet down and we started fighting. We were arrested and taken to the Charge Office, but I refused to climb into the back of the truck while she got inside the passenger cabin of the police jeep. We were both arrested for public fighting and I insisted that we be treated the same. We were taken for interrogation, and the officer asked if I had the money to buy the things that I said I wanted to buy, and I showed him. The other people there wished that I be punished for hitting a white person, because, as you suggested, you couldn't so much as touch a white person then, let alone beat them up. The officer was reasonable and cautioned the shop people that they'd just lost a genuine customer because of their bigotry, and I was set free.

MC: Were Africans allowed to enter the shops? Because I know that they could only buy from the back door or from a side hatch. Or was that during an earlier period?

JLN: That was after we had fought those rules, my child, in the late 1950s. After we had fought them, otherwise before then a Black person was only allowed up to Amato, on the fringe of Salisbury CBD [central business district], and in Bulawayo only up to the Indian shops meant for Africans on Lobengula Street. Otherwise we didn't shop where whites shopped. We then sorted that out during the time of the NDP [National Democratic Party]. We invaded the places in the Freedom Sitting movement. We would come into the shops, restaurants, hotels, and salons and sit down, all the while singing our freedom songs. The police would come and beat us up, using butts of guns and kicking us, but we refused to shift. (I still suffer now in old age from the injuries that I sustained from the savage beatings then and during my prison years.) By the late 1950s we were now able to get into the shops—OK, Meikles, etc. Those demonstrations started with people like Masotsha Ndlovu back in the 1920s, when they stubbornly walked on the sidewalks instead of sharing the roads with cars, and they were taken up by later generations and then by ourselves under the leadership of Lovemore Chimonyo and others. We won the war through being arrested, beaten up, and murdered. You don't even mention swimming pools—you want to do what, who? You? Ah! Only domestics who lived in their employers' backyards knew swimming pools. You could not even suckle your baby in the city, sullying the white people's air. The police would beat and arrest you; and now these are the same people who are telling us through the newspapers and their NGOs to breastfeed our children until they are two years old! That knowledge, which they were despising as primitive, is now theirs to teach us. What cheek!

MC: You spent some time in jail. Can you explain?

JLN: I was imprisoned for my hard-headedness, fighting the police, etc., and for being a leader in the NDP, the Njube branch of the party. I was arrested and served jail time for that. I did not join the party; the party found me here, already active. Before the NDP there had been the Southern Rhodesia African National Congress [SRANC], which had started in South Africa, spread to Northern Rhodesia and Nyasaland and then here. I would go to political meetings whenever I heard where they were taking place, listening to people like Burombo and others. We were banned as the ANC in February 1959, in the whole of Southern Africa (except South Africa).

MC: Is that when you were arrested?

JLN: Yes, I was arrested together with my infant child, and that destroyed my marriage because my husband put his foot down, declaring that his home was not going to be run by a woman. And the sort of wife who gets arrested and taken to prison while her husband remains at home with the children, eh! That's shameful! And he got support even from my relatives, who asked what kind of a wife would want to come to rule her husband's home. Things like that. But the way I was born, I said to myself, "Let this man divorce me for my love of Zimbabwe." So the day that the NDP was formed, on January 1, 1960, I was already a member. And I was elected at the National Congress the same day that we chose Nkomo, Mugabe, Sithole, and others to be leaders. Nkomo was outside the country, in Ghana, for a meeting, the All-African People's Conference. That is the year we were arrested together with the Malawian leaders, Kamuzu Banda and others, who were transferred from Malawi to be imprisoned here.

MC: OK, that was during the Federation. How easy was it for a woman to be elected into positions of leadership in the nationalist movement?

JLN: It was not easy, and I don't even know how my name made it to the top, but I suppose those who knew me had a full profile of how I was arrested, harassed, but remained resolute, so that they took me as one of the boys, fighting in the trenches. Yes, political activity was regarded as a male concern . . . but I refused the indoctrination that "you are a woman and so you can't touch this or can't do that."

MC: So it was difficult, but not impossible for women to assume leadership positions. What about their general involvement?

JLN: Women really supported the movement, but it was difficult for them to assume leadership roles. The truth must be told that it was difficult, looking at these things from a cultural perspective: what would happen to the children if both father and mother were arrested? And the wretched goats and cows? Women were the majority supporters, but these were some of the constraints. I think some of us got elected because we were found everywhere *takachanjamara kunge minzwa yegaka* [raising our spikes like the prickly cucumber]! Men preferred that they be arrested because the better orphan is the one who has a mother, but women were really avid supporters because even the property that the colonists were plundering was theirs. And when people like myself were elected into positions of leadership, we stood as national leaders but also representing women's presence in the hierarchy. I am very happy now that we have women in very high positions in the country and across Africa, and I am happy that we were able to overcome the little oppressions that were heaped on us by our men; now that's mostly gone. But the key thing is that it was then difficult to assume leadership positions, because once you were known as a leader you became a target of the Special Branch (the notorious colonial secret police). So, culturally, we value the protection of the children and the family. But that does not mean women could not be, or were not, in leadership positions.

MC: I want us to go back to song. What role did music play in political mobilization? You mentioned the rallies . . .

JLN: We sang songs celebrating our leaders and articulating our grievances—our land, our cattle, our country. I remember George Nyandoro's song that almost became the national anthem, which said, "It is a good, honorable thing to die for your country":

Zvakanaka kufira nyika yako
Zvakanaka kufira nyika yako
Zvakanaka, kufira nyika yako

After singing that song, you felt possessed by a spirit and you became bold, no longer mindful of whatever adversity you came up against. There was nothing that we did without song—just like our grandmothers when they ground, they would be singing songs denouncing their proverbial *mukadzin'ina* [the junior wife] or articulating something that bothered them. Morale. We always sang, and it happened naturally that the song would quickly have *vabvumiri nevatambi* [dancers and backup singers]. We sang many songs, the majority of which denounced the police, Smith, Welensky, Whitehead, etc., and songs about *ivhu redu* [our soil]:

Ivhu nderedu
Tipei nyika yedu

The soil is ours
Give us back our country

And we also sang another one that says, "Vanababa vedu vakatambura kutorerwa mombe dzavo" [Our fathers suffered when their cattle were seized].

MC: Protesting against the seizure of livestock?

JLN: Yes, and also one that said, "Tsuro tsuro iwe wapera; tsuro tsurowe naNkomo" [The cunning hare; you are now finished; Nkomo is going to get you]—utilizing the rich Madzimbabwe folktale register. We were telling the whites that you thought you monopolize knowledge, but we also know what you thought you only know. You are too clever for your own good; now we are on your tail like a hound!

MC: But did these people hear the songs? Or what was the idea?

JLN: They heard them because they ended up recording us secretly in order to prosecute us. That is how they gathered evidence against us, but we still contested their interpretations, arguing, "I don't know that the songs mean what you're making them to say in your translations."

MC: So your militancy could be gleaned from the songs. What about other cultural accoutrements, such as *tsvimbo* [walking sticks] and skin hats? I have seen photographs of people holding and wearing those at rallies.

JLN: Yes, men carried *tsvimbo* and we all wore hats made of skins of small animals. I wore one myself. The statement we were making was that every man carries *tsvimbo* as his weapon. That was the symbol of manhood, the African manhood that we were reclaiming from colonialism. Traditionally, we also used to wear *nhembe* [animal-skin aprons] and we utilized our animals not only for meat but also for clothing items, but now we couldn't make *nhembe* or utilize our livestock as we had done historically because our agropastoral economy had been plundered. Those things were symbols of our identity, connecting us directly to our ecologies and ancestors. That is why we wore the fur hats. We were saying we want our resources and wealth back. Nkomo was given several *tsvimbo nemakano* [scepters and ritual battle axes], especially when we met chiefs around the country. Culturally these things constitute regalia given to a chief. Most chiefs gave Nkomo such things, except a few, such as Chief Kaisa Ndiweni, who were overzealous colonial puppets.

MC: Where were you when the war started?

JLN: The war started while I was in Gonakudzingwa [a restriction camp] with most of the nationalist leaders. It was then that I decided that once I got out I wanted to be an ordinary supporter of the party, because my mother was getting old and needed someone to look after her. We were then moved to Whawha Prison. But we drove the struggle from inside. We had our informers within the system just like they had their own in our midst. We were politically very active in the detention centers and prisons. We would sing in those jails, sometimes employing the funeral guise, as if mourning someone, to camouflage our activities. And that ended up becoming like a tradition. Some of the things that you see in the townships today—such as the flying of the red cloth—we did that when we held meetings *kurasisa muvengi* [to throw off the enemy], dancing *shangara* and *mhande* dances. That is how we domesticated the colonial jail to make it serve our own purposes. I spent seven and half years in detention, but others spent more—eleven years, etc. I was first arrested in 1959, together with our Malawian counterparts and other locals, and then again in 1964 with many more of the leaders—Mugabe, Nkomo, Nyagumbo, etc. I was then released in 1970.

MC: The colonial jail was meant to break down the colonial insurgent, but it seems you remained quite active, continuing to wage Chimurenga in the stocks, so to speak. Can you describe to me how life was in detention or restriction more broadly?

JLN: Ian Smith, Dupont, and their friends were hiding behind semantics, labeling those prisons—Whawha, etc.—as restriction camps, as if we were only restricted. We had suffered restriction here at our own homes, and been proscribed from speaking to more than five people, even our own relatives. Then in places like Whawha we were detained and lived behind barbed security razor wire, guarded at a small gate. If you crossed that line you got arrested right there in detention and sent to prison under the Law and Order (Maintenance) Act (1957). Most women detainees and prisoners were arrested during those street demonstrations, during which they sang defiant songs after being set upon by dogs, and they would spend from five days up to a month before they were released. So female political prisoners rarely numbered beyond twenty at any one time.

MC: Can you describe to me the conditions in the detention centers?

JLN: We lived in tin shacks that were similar to railway workers' makeshift roadside shacks, within the security fences. These did not protect us from the elements. We usually shared, two to such a shack, at any one time, and they gave us lice-infested blankets—the dirt bred lice with very long tails! And they stank like hell! So we preferred the blankets that our relatives brought us from home. For food, we got *sadza* prepared from rotten mealie-meal. That we rarely ate. We cooked for ourselves instead of eating that dirt. Otherwise the officials gave us a bit of mealie-meal, *zvisauti* [some lousy salt], and beans and said, "Ponai kana muchipona" [Survive, if you will].

MC: I suppose the terrible conditions were an aspect of the punishment. So how did you keep your sanity?

JLN: We kept our *morari* [good spirits] because, for one thing, we never regretted that whatever we had done was wrong. We were actually proud of ourselves, addressing each other as *mwana wevhu* [child of the soil] to encourage each other and to propagate the spirit of resistance. We maintained a jovial mood and laughed amongst ourselves because we knew that we were already in detention. So we spoke very freely, telling ourselves that we are fighting this child of a donkey who came to steal our father's country. The policemen, those so-called *majoni,* could hear us, but what could they do? Nothing!

MC: You were quite arrogant prisoners, weren't you? Did you also sing in detention and the prisons?

JLN: Very much. We sang very much. Even when you were alone in prison, you would still sing. In Gweru there were no female political prisoners. It was only me, and *kungoti dinhu rwiyo jeri rose roimba kwoitwa zvisingaitwi* [once I started on a song, the whole prison would go up in flames, and we would do what could otherwise not be done]. Then the jail guards would threaten everyone, that they should not listen to this mad woman, but everyone would sing even more. We sang that even death we were prepared for and proud to face for our country.

MC: And then you were released after seven years.

JLN: Then I was released and returned home for a year, but because of the colonial laws the whole country was virtually an open prison, and so the danger did not abate for us. Many people were disappearing. Fortunately, we had fairly intricate intelligence and communication systems. We had people inside the colonial security apparatus, as I have said, and they passed information on to us through a system of codes. That saved many of us. We give due respect to those who were in the police force for giving us the information. They wore the uniform, yes, working for the enemy, yes, but most of them supported us. Most Africans supported each other and were behind what we were doing. This was because no one escaped the atrocities of the colonial system—those forced and violent removals, cattle expropriations, etc. Everybody suffered that fate and understood the meaning of the struggle. Of course there were others who had evil hearts and did not respect themselves; you could not do much about those. But there were policemen who helped, and we know them. We were not allowed newspapers, but these policemen smuggled radios for us so that we could hear the news.

MC: Which broadcasts did you listen to—the Rhodesia Broadcasting Corporation?

JLN: Sometimes the RBC, but mostly the BBC because that was the station that flattered *varungu*, broadcasting to the world that "the nationalists are in restriction camps" when in fact we were in detention camps. So the radios kept us well informed, and that confused the enemy agents planted amongst us, wondering at how much we knew but not knowing the source. We assigned one individual to go and listen to the radio and monitor what it said and then inform everybody, because we knew that we had infiltrators in our midst. Over time, however, we would flush these out, because we had people who were trained for those jobs. Some became converts to the cause by the time they were released, after having been arrested together with us as plants. Many of them would pretend to be nationalist zealots. Only one or two individuals listened to the wireless, to prevent these plants from getting to our sources of information. Then in the evening we sat outside within the fence singing and sharing the news. And no one would know how we got the information. We used the radio for news only, not for listening to music. We also passed messages on the slender toilet paper, while one pretended to go to the lavatory, or on our palms. We used all kinds of methods, codes and language, such as someone saying, "I am going home tomorrow; I don't know if I might pass through your grandmother's," and we would reply, "OK, that's fine, please pass our regards. Here is a letter for her." And the next day someone wakes up in Zambia while the security focused on searching cooked food that our relatives were bringing us.

MC: You were part of the ZAPU exile in Zambia. When did you leave?

JLN: That was after a year out of detention, when our boys discovered a long list of people to be disappeared, and my name topped it. There are many people who were disappeared and never found. The list was prepared within the security structures and one of our plants within the system saw it and copied it, then advised us to leave promptly. So I left the country on a Monday, then I heard that on the following Wednesday they had reached Buhera looking for me; and they also searched my sister's place here in Bulawayo. They wanted to get me by all means. They would come in the dead of the night and you are gone—never to be seen again—like Choga, Edison Sithole, and others. They knew the hotheads and spitfires, and they targeted them. Their information gatherers, whom we called *mbeu* [seeds], were quite astute, but we had also trained ourselves so much with the support of those countries that had also fought the colonists, such as Algeria, Cuba. We sent our fighters to friendly countries like Yugoslavia, Russia, China, and others for specialized training.

MC: How did you get out, because the Rhodesians claimed that they sealed the country's borders, and we know that they shot people on sight for breaking "curfews" in these "no-go" border areas?

JLN: I was told I must leave urgently, and I was assisted by people who were specialized in smuggling people out. I left by bus, through Botswana. I went through several relays, and we had representatives in Botswana who had been preinformed that someone was coming. Seretse Khama had given us camps in Dukwe, Selibe Pikwe and so on (as did the Zambians and later the Mozambicans). The Batswana police worked with our representatives to check all newcomers, to verify who was a genuine recruit and who was a traitor coming to wreak havoc on our people. But I had no problem because I was a known leader of the struggle. So I was taken to State House, where I waited for my ticket from Zambia, when the message was relayed that I was waiting. The Botswana government provided us with planes, as did the Zambian government. It was tougher for those who left on their own. The vetting process was strenuous on them, and they also risked being captured or shot on the way out.

MC: So now, in exile, what was your major role?

JLN: I was already a leader here at home, even before my detention. So in exile I simply joined my fellow leaders. But first I found a scholarship waiting for me to go to Canada to study law. But the party was in shambles after George Nyandoro, James Chikerema, and others had split to join FROLIZI and others had gone on to ZANU. Jason Moyo, George Silundika, Edward Ndlovu, and others had remained, and I joined them, forfeiting the scholarship because I decided that I was not fighting for myself, but for the country. The war had heated up, and there was a great need for broadcasting, so I went on radio to train broadcasters and also to call people from home to join the struggle, to say, "Look here, please come and take up your own gun and fight for our country. The country is waiting for you; the war will not be won without your input, but even if it is won by others while you just sit there, what are you going to say you did for the fatherland which was taken by the Boers [whites]?"

MC: So the radio was a key recruitment tool for the struggle?

JLN: It was key. And remember, you are telling this to someone who knows that their cattle were confiscated while they looked on helplessly, their homes destroyed and families broken up by colonial vice. You don't tell that person twice. I was not exactly a broadcaster, but I was in administration more broadly, performing various functions and going to radio only occasionally. But I also trained various people for the task, such as one girl called Ratidzo, who continued to use my name. She was later killed at Mkushi when the Muzorewa-Smith government bombed our camps. I was lucky, myself, to also survive the letter bomb that took Jason Moyo. This skin on my hands is not mine; it was grafted on after the injuries. Myself, Dumiso Dabengwa, John Nkomo, one man called Ngwenya, a young man called Dingane, Carlos Mangwana, and others, we were all injured in that letter bomb blast. But those are the vicissitudes of war, guerrilla warfare. You don't parade yourself that you are a soldier. War is ugly, but we had a country and lives to liberate.

Epilogue

Postcolonial Legacies: Song, Power, and Knowledge Production

In his preface to Fanon's influential *The Wretched of the Earth* (1968, 20), Jean-Paul Sartre aptly captured the psychological impact of colonialism when he wrote that the condition of the colonized is a nervous condition. Colonists sought to subjugate Africans both through their own European cultures and also through subverted African cultures, and Africans responded variously through assimilation, inculturation, accommodation, and resistance. All of these responses reinforced the cultural front as a creative site for a dialectical fashioning of the colonizing self, the colonized subject, and the self-liberating being. African engagement with colonial epistemicide was invariably aporic, producing new orders and spaces that equally subverted the colonial designs. As both weapon and byproduct of the cross-cultural encounters, African music bore the marks of this bruising struggle to script and to contest European hegemony. This epilogue reflects on some of the key legacies and implications of this history for contemporary African consciousness and knowledge production, gesturing toward new directions for further work.

Legacies of Colonialism and Its Cultures

While the tide of cultural nationalism and the liberation wars deeply shook some of the foundational certitudes of colonial evangelical Christianity, its legacy continued to dog African cultural consciousness in the new era of political independence. Writing about Zimbabwean music at independence in 1980, Paddy Scannell (2001, 13) pointed out that the new political dispensation authorized a new African musical identity recognizable as Zimbabwean. However, amidst the euphoric celebration of that political independence—appropriately buoyed by song and dance—artists soon expressed dissatisfaction with signs that the status quo would endure and there would be no revolutionary change in national cultural dispositions. Musicians, including the guitar guerrilla and veteran of Zimbabwean cultural nationalism Thomas Mapfumo, decried the continued dominance of foreign music over indigenous songs and musical consciousness, which persisted on the new nation's electronic media, from Rhodesia into Zimbabwe (Moses Chikowero 2008).

Similarly, in spite or because of its symbolic cultural significance (particularly exhibited during the liberation war), *mbira*, the quintessential Madzimbabwe instrument, was still treated as a throwback, a symbol of backwardness and "heathenism," by sections of a populace that largely remained under the sway of an entrenched Eurocentric cultural sensibility. The legacy of missionary violence remains deep-seated to this day, with Christian identities often defined in opposition to African cosmologies (Moses Chikowero 2007; Mano 2009). The internalized identities of shame, inferiority, and Euro-centered definitions of class exclusivism persisted, underpinning the paradox of the unreformed African postcolonial condition. State policy did little to alter these realities (Mhoze Chikowero 2007).[1]

Much of the historiography on missionary evangelization emphasizes both the mission's denominational heterogeneity and its doctrinal unity of purpose. Foundational mission stations like Lovedale represent that organizational unity in Southern Africa. My exploration of missionary policy benefited from a diverse archive generated by a cross-section of denominations and orders. In exploring it translocationally, I have implicitly tackled this critical question: what did denominational differences matter in terms of missionary attitudes toward African cultures? I have argued that the differences mostly amounted to divergent strategies contingent on Africans' responses, particularly their critique of missionary ethnocentrism and collusion with the colonial state. Otherwise, denomination, as Es'kia Mphahlele (1985, 179) wrote, made little difference to missionary domination from the African subject's end of the power equation. When the Catholic and other missions made small concessions to African cultures—such as incorporating aspects of African music into the church and occasionally turning a blind eye to certain allegedly repugnant customs—such concessions reflected African resistance and efforts to domesticate the church as much as they did the church's self-serving, selective appropriation and deployment of African cultures to lure converts and redeem an imperiled future. They did not reflect a Damascene respect for African cultural sovereignty. Because of this, the compromises hardly fundamentally altered the constitutive missionary orders of knowledge, faith, and objective.

In any case, a provincial, denominational approach to church histories provides crucial insight into the implications of missionary fracturing of African identities. Vying missionary sects produced both devout and nominal African Anglicans, Methodists, Catholics, Masavadha (Seventh-Day Adventists), Salvationists, Madhachi (Dutch Reformists), and so on in ways that paralleled ethnomusicologists' and the Native Affairs Department (NAD)'s capturing of African musical traditions to produce factional "tribes" out of the dancing African body. Thus, while the NAD marshaled the rival "tribes" that sang and danced in the marginal, dusty urban spaces to steer these "tribal dances" onto the captive, sanitized official platforms, the various mission churches similarly projected intra-African differences and enmities onto African communities through the distinctive, disciplining uniform and hymnbook. Overall, the alienating register of "heathens" and "animists" solidified and has retained its currency as a tool for approving and disapproving African identities, valuing and devaluing musics, and allocating and denying privileges. Thus, the discursive power of the "civilizing mission" in engineering new, conflicted African identities persisted even under the motive force of adoptive (and often reified) African agency. As early as the 1930s, some African mission converts had zealously received the externally imposed discourse and internally reinforced it by urging the colonial state to stamp out what they regarded as evil African musical cultures. At the same time, sly African converts appropriated Christian hymns and dances, repurposing them innovatively to enrich the Southern African musical repertoire with the *kwaya,* the *konzati,* and the subversive tea party.

Epistemicidal Aftertastes: The Politics of Knowledge Production

While African agency intervened in conflicting ways that reshaped the nature of colonialism, the colonial cultural nervousness proved as resilient as the physical structures of intensive resource extraction. Some of the alienating cultural attitudes that early generations strived to resist became progressively normalized as part of the larger western hegemonic order of the African everyday that would soon go unremarked, if it was visible at all. This unreformed social consciousness has become one of the treacherous pitfalls of African independence. Achille Mbembe (2002) made a similar point when he decried the post-colonial African subject's continued entrapment by the cultures and thought-systems of his or her colonial founding, thereby (and unsurprisingly) earning the admonition of African(ist) intellectuals (see, for instance, the essays collected in "African Modes of Self-Writing Revisited" in *Public Culture* 14 [3]). This is not to argue that the criticism was baseless; rather, it is to suggest that its sheer torrent signaled the pertinence of dialogue against the backdrop of the defensiveness of the postcolonial African dispositions. The Afro-pessimist retort frequently thrown at Mbembe suggests the indignation of a postcolonial African(ist) intellectual positionality that is still at some level too proximate to the foundations of its colonial creation to either critique itself or face squarely the implications of its epistemological discomfort.

I encountered a strong sense of this discomfort at my alma mater, the University of Zimbabwe, in July 2012, in responses to a working paper on the missionary factor. The paper elicited heated debate, which clearly signaled the need for even more robust research on the subject. One of the most thought-provoking critiques came from one of my former history professors in the form of a rather sarcastic, living irony that appropriately reduced matters to the personal. He chided, "You are here; with an Apple [computer] in front of you. . . . Now, how can you tell us that missionaries were bad?" How dare I question the benevolence of missionaries who "brought hospitals and treated some diseases that we could not treat," indeed, some diseases that might have laid my forebears (or me) low in infancy? Emerging scholarship on science and technology in Africa has begun to robustly interrogate the meaning of some of the technologies and knowledges that missionaries—as vested technologists and moralists—brought to (and gained and pirated from) Africa in the context of African indigenous knowledge systems. My paper sought to interrogate the epistemological implications of the missionaries' dialectical "civilizing mission" for African knowledge systems, cultures, and self-worth, as I have discussed in the first four chapters of this book. In other words, what were the rationales, mechanics, and impact of a "civilizing mission" that was an alibi for colonialism?

My analysis here is restricted to musical cultures, colonialism, and self-liberation, and the treatment will hopefully reorient debate on a subject that, despite the voluminous scholarship, is often treated as a *fait accompli,* reducing its African subjects to appreciating its blessings while decrying but willingly forgiving the collateral infractions committed in quest of a supposed ultimate good. By training my focus on the so-called civilizing mission's epistemicidal quest to disarm the African subject, I have advanced the argument that the men and women of God who allegedly sacrificed their own lives to bring "light" through the church, the school, the hospital, and the plough were not simply apolitical beings intent on redeeming some benighted "heathens" from their alleged deficiencies in technology, religion, and history. They were also, very significantly, confessing colonial crusaders who wrought much destruction in an effort to re-create a new African being in their service, and almost in their image.

With the aid of historical hindsight, we can see that the cultural crusades that generations of Africans struggled for centuries to resist or domesticate now seem to be tacitly approved of, or at least their outcome is accepted with resignation. Indeed, the apparent effectiveness of the colonial educational scheme in fashioning a new, grateful, and testifying African subject is uncritically marveled at. Writing as an African—the dehumanized subject—it is germane to interrogate what seems like acquiescence to all those designs of colonial scheming. Or what feels like a fulfillment of the *Kaffir Express*'s prophecy in July 1871: that after the missionary has kindly and gradually won "the Kaffir" over "from barbarism and heathenism to civilization and Christianity," then "the Kaffir himself will only too gladly and willingly seek to be subject to the same laws and regulations which govern a civilized community." The colonial design and process of witchcrafting African subjecthood constituted creative violence that, as the Comaroffs (1991, 18) have observed, not only reified cultural orders, but also gave rise to a new hegemony amidst (and despite) cultural contestation. For Africans, it remains a matter of self-knowledge to engage this hegemony, this uncomfortable fact that, to a significant degree, we remain stepchildren—even if reluctant stepchildren—of the missionaries, both culturally and intellectually. The question then is: how do we know and deal with this stepparentage? *Toramba tichidya uroyi nekunyara here*—did the epistemic witchcraft succeed to the degree that Africans became both too proximate and too implicated to name the witchcraft of their "stepparents?"

How does this witchcraft affect African historical consciousness and knowledge production today? The power of this colonial witchcrafting can be located at the intersection of cognitive and expressive culture, historical memory, and, indeed, knowledge production. When this book had neared completion, I asked one Zimbabwean publishing house if it might be interested in copublishing it, to help its distribution in the region. The publishers asked for the table of contents. Assuming that no publisher would seriously consider granting a book contract merely on the basis of a table of contents, I sent it together with a proposal outlining the book's argument. The editor promptly wrote back, informing me that, "judging by the table of contents" (although the same sentence admitted that "perhaps one should not!"), the press had decided not to take the manuscript. While I was none too impressed by the quick verdict on the unseen manuscript on the basis of its table of contents, I was struck by the publishers' suggestion that rather than focus on colonial Zimbabwe, I should write instead about what has happened since independence, "which is very interesting, not least the way in which traditional dance is used and performed as part of the nationalist rhetoric of patriotic history." Here was the common demand—often unvoiced—to "explain Mugabe." The gospel of modernization expects the African scholar-deacon to fight the zombies of post-colonial "savagedom," a combat often manifesting in something called Afro-pessimism.

Since 2000, the ZANU-PF government has sponsored national musical galas, inviting popular musicians to perform before large audiences during nights of unfettered revelry (Muchemwa 2010). The government utilizes this platform, together with the state-controlled broadcast media, to reinforce its hold on power and to drum up support for the contested land redistribution program, which transferred vast swaths of the country's prime farmland from a few thousand white former Rhodesian settlers to hundreds of thousands of dispossessed African families. Chimurenga memory suffused the songs that reiterated the revolutionary significance of the massive land transfer, dubbed the Third Chimurenga (Mhoze Chikowero 2011). The editor's implication was that I might get published more easily if, instead of writing about Rhodesia's harnessing of song and dance to construct colonial hegemony, I advanced the fashionable "(anti-)patriotic" historiographical bandwagon that ridiculed the post-colonial state's latter-day use of the same cultural tools in the service of contested post-colonial statecrafting.

This advice was instructive, raising important questions about contending historical memories, the working of authorized historiographies, power, and knowledge production in post-colonial Zimbabwe's ailing publishing industry. In the post-2000 historiographical battles for Zimbabwe, both the state and massive oppositional forces (including vested publishing capital) commissioned musical works, documentary films, and books to advance competing ideological stances.

A key feature of these battles is that Robert Mugabe's name became a guarantee of sales. The deluge was set off by Terence Ranger's (2004) belated, valedictory indictment of his erstwhile Zimbabwean nationalist comrades at the onset of the so-called Zimbabwe crisis at the turn of the millennium. With the condemnation of Mugabe, academics and artists who had proudly sung his name during and shortly after the liberation war now rushed to disassociate themselves from him and disavow their former praise. The monstrification of Mugabe found ready sponsorship particularly in a global north now spinning a newfound discourse of the supremacy of human rights and the right of (white) private property in the global south. Needless to say, there is no shortage of writing on contemporary Zimbabwean politics and culture. Yet, as Blessing-Miles Tendi (2010) has pointed out, a good proportion of the post-2000 writing is caught up in the narrow dialectical matrix of "patriotic" historiography (focusing on ZANU-PF) versus "oppositional" historiography, which often lacks historically grounded analyses of power and its structural and cultural materialities.

This book has hopefully helped locate this contested present historically beyond the reductive seduction of the presentist, post-2000 Mugabe discourse. One of the book's key lessons is that very little of what has happened in cultural politics since independence in 1980 is novel. The more contemporary transfigurations of the politics of music and power have clear historical antecedents and genealogies that can be analyzed most fruitfully through the *longue dureé* of colonial cultural politics and African self-crafting. Yet I do not seek to foreclose the argument here. I thus want to end the book by destabilizing the orthodox colonial national framing of song and power in scholarship by underlining African self-fashioning through mobility and the imagination of African identities that outranged colonial taxonomies of a colonized, contained African object and subject being—a salient theme in the book.

Registers of African Self-Crafting through Mobility

The stories that I have told in these pages feature and revolve around a wide range of African musicians, singers, songs, and users of song, whose essence transcends the geographies of colonial (and post-colonial) national sovereignties. "Colonial Zimbabwe," the book's locational designation, suggests an antinomic, territorial boundedness even as the personal histories of many of the musicians, songs, and transmissional networks indicate that translocation, mobility, and interconnectivity are key threads in African self-fashioning. Thus, I wish to stress that the African subject of this book is a creative, and at the least pan-African, being. Dorothy Masuku related to me the story of a young Zambian Lozi chef who catered to white passengers on the trains that tore Southern Africa in the 1920s–30s. On one trip, the young man met a beautiful Zulu nanny tending the children of her white South African employers. He later followed her to South Africa, where they married. The Lozi man's life on the railway tracks took them to colonial Zimbabwe, where they made a home and raised a family. Thus was born Dorothy in 1935, the girl who grew up singing in the languages of, and in the recreation halls of, Southern Africa's locations. Dorothy's own odyssey to Joni in her late teens heralded a peripatetic life in which she transcended the colonial lines as an entertainer and guerrilla vocalist, hounded by the Southern African settler regimes.

Madzimbabwe say *kukava datya huriyambutsa,* kicking a frog helps it across otherwise difficult hurdles. Similarly, rather than deflating her, state persecution buoyed Masuku's revolutionary voice beyond the command and containment of the settler state as she traveled with the region's nationalist leaders around the continent, performing on such platforms as the Organization of African Unity's Pan-African Cultural Festival in Algiers in 1969. In an interview with Wonder Guchu in 2005 (*Herald,* November 12), Masuku recalled, "I never held a gun but my voice was as powerful as a gun. It took me a few moments to send my revolutionary messages home to millions of people. When I sang 'Tinogara Musango' [We live in the bush] and 'Dr. Malan,' it was like being with the people." She embraced her Zambian ancestral roots, utilizing them as a guerrilla platform to fight the settler regimes in South Africa and Rhodesia, and she triumphantly reclaimed all of these homes with the fall of the regimes. Her story is both personal and metonymic. It tells a tale of one woman's complex identity and aspirations, a tale of a woman who rehumanized herself and helped craft collective futures through mobility and political engagement with colonialism across its arbitrary borders, the chief immobilizing instrument of its illegitimate sovereignty. For these significations, Masuku's story is also the story of Abel Sinametsi Sithole, Jane Lungile Ngwenya, Kembo Ncube, Hugh Masekela, and other singers whose names are also a multidimensional metaphor of Africans' troubled self-making.

These are identities that no provincialized notion of Zimbabwean, South African, Malawian, or Zambian history could do justice to. They constituted ways of being that were self-crafted on an awareness of an Africa and a world that both transcended and weaponized colonial notions of sovereign space and nation in quest of individual and collective African freedom. They are sovereign identities constituted through mobilities and affinities that follow the spatial and temporal itineraries of African history in ways that interrogated the colonial hegemonic transfiguration and consignment of Africans into alienated "natives" and doubly alienated "alien natives" through the violence of arbitrary geographical and cultural borders. Masekela (2015) spoke to this reality when he told me how, "in Africa, we live inside so many walls that were made not by us, but in Berlin." And a large part of our recent histories of making life, singing, and traveling have been, to borrow Ayi Kwei Armah's (2010) conceptualization, rearticulations of our dismembered societies, livelihoods, knowledges, and cultures despite Berlin's walls. Maurice Vambe (2008) rightly noted how songs like "Aphiri Anabwera," by the Zambian singer Nashil Pitchen Kazembe, can help us map African musical diasporas into a broader Southern African imaginary. Many African musical styles, such as Zimbabwean *sungura,* Congolese rhumba, and Kenyan *benga,* emerged out of shared pan-African sensibilities and solidarities with wider continental and extracontinental musical innovations. Musical interactions elaborated African agency beyond the colonial cages of "tribes" and arbitrary settler borders. Methodologically, then, mobility elaborates the production of cross-cultural African wholeness.

Lupenga Mphande (2001, 210) posed the challenge in a review of Turino's *Nationalists, Cosmopolitans, and Popular Music in Zimbabwe,* criticizing it for having a "narrow restriction in scope and interpretation of Zimbabwean musicians." Mphande pointed at Masuku and the Zambian Alick Nkhata as some of the musicians who "used to perform during political rallies addressed by luminaries such as Hastings Kamuzu Banda, Kenneth Kaunda, and Joshua Nkomo," and he was surprised that Turino dismissed such musicians either as non-Zimbabweans or as having resided only briefly in Zimbabwe. As Mphande observed, while Masuku was hounded back and forth across the settler borders, Nkhata was pursued and assassinated in Lusaka by the Rhodesian Air Force, a tragic acknowledgment of his regional cultural and political influence. African (musical and political) guerrilla mobilities challenged colonial legitimacy in ways that can only be understood through methodologies that transcend orthodox epistemic structures of valuation and inquiry.

For this reason, predominantly colonial "nationalist" and western "cosmopolitan" canons often exclude, rather than illuminate, these mobile guerrilla insurgencies and processes of self-making and self-rehumanizing. Some of the guerrilla artists of the Zimbabwean independence struggle, such as Thomas Mapfumo, have recently become domiciled in distant exiles, thanks to the inherited, unreformed post-colonial state that is still obsessed with disciplining citizens' dissident thoughts and voices. This is a story for another day, yet the connections must be located in the recalcitrant legacies of state victimization and strategies of resistant struggle. More importantly, the mobility optic should help account for such exiles beyond just geospatial presences and absences. The breaching of space—through body, voice, and mediative technologies—belongs to the deep histories of resistance and self-making this book has only engaged in part.

Some of the pains and pleasures of Southern Africans' histories of creative resistance and a(nta)gonistic dances with power are captured in the locomotive sensibility of songs like "Stimela," which tells of the Joburg train that Zimbabwean young men sang about and mimicked in Chibububu dances in the 1930s, the train in which Masuku's parents found love on the move in the 1920s, the train that took Masekela's Karanga father from Zimbabwe to Joni, the train that Masekela saw disgorging African men from the mines to quench their thirsts in the locations every Sunday (Masekela and Cheers 2004), and indeed the train that Masekela cussed in that haunting song of distress for stealing African men from their families for the vampire Witwatersrand Native Labour Association. The African identities of pain, pleasure, and adventure are narrativized in the various agonized and melancholic repertoires of labor migrancy, *nthandizi,* that Malawians composed en route and as they labored in the settler farms and mines in Southern Rhodesia and South Africa (Lwanda 2008). African identities were historically crafted on the move, again symbolically encoded in the multiple "ethnicities" that constitute Masuku's composite individual identity: to Zambians, Masuku is a Lozi; to South Africans, she is Zulu; and in Lesotho and Zimbabwe, she can answer to both Sotho and Ndebele, and compose Shona songs. Historically, nothing is false or intrinsically ethnic about any of these versatile, fluid identities. Masuku captured this significant historical consciousness and her own consciousness of history by self-identifying as "a citizen of Southern Africa" and by spending her time at home in Joburg, exploring her ambitions for farming in Zambia, and constantly trekking to and from Zimbabwe, whence both her *rukuvhute*—umbilical cord—and her mother's bones call her (interview). Her multilingual repertoire, transterritorial belonging, lived experiences, and standing as a heroine of regional liberation all underscore the need to rewrite the stories of African self-making and cultural consciousness beyond the alienating colonial boundaries, taxonomies of "tribes," bounded nation-states, and codified official languages. The itineraries of the African traveling body and knowledge register transcend these taxonomies.

Historically, these mobilities were often a matter of necessity. Africans culled a living—*kushava*—"on the loose foot," *rutsoka.* Their more recent itineraries gave Southern Africa such migrancy folk songs as "Stimela," "Aphiri Anabwera," and "Shosholoza." In the same ways that the migrant labor routes fed guerrilla recruitment, these songs could be transformed into liberation anthems. Thus, struggling against the apartheid state, South Africans now sang "Stimela" and "Shosholoza" to reimagine and celebrate the repurposed train, now bringing back trained guerrillas disguised as cheap mine laborers. To the call and response of these reimagined tunes, Mandela and his fellow inmates dug quarry and crushed rocks at the "university of revolution," Robben Island jail:

> We were singing the song "Stimela," a rousing anthem about a train making its way down from Southern Rhodesia. "Stimela" is not a political song . . . but it became one, for the implication was that the train contained guerillas coming down to fight the South African army. . . . [We also sang] "Tshotsholoza," a song that compares the struggle to the motion of an oncoming train. (If you say the title over and over, it mimics the sound of the train.) (Mandela 2013, 407–408)

These guerrilla repertoires followed the same migratory networks and rearticulations of regional cultures that produced and transmitted the defiant *shebeen* cultures that Zimbabwean August Machona Musarurwa captured and shared with the world in "Skokiaan," and the early pan-African strivings for freedom that South Africa's Enoch Sontonga gave the continent in "Nkosi Sikelel' iAfrika." To read these circuits of song, cultural consciousnesses, and mobilities, one must follow the cyclical trails as far as the Congo. Here, beginning in the 1950s, the Zimbabwean saxophonist Isaac Musekiwa buoyed Congolese rhumba as a member of the T.P.O.K. Jazz, playing with such legends as Franco Luambo Makiadi, Madilu System (Jean de Dieu Makiese), and the great Sam Mangwana, who identified himself as a Central African. In reverse flows, many Congolese musicians and groups moved from country to country, with their Lingala-driven musical registers cross-fertilizing with other African styles in ways that influenced such genres as Zimbabwean *sungura* and Kenyan *benga* (Perman 2012). These realities trouble provincializing notions that, for instance, seek to portray Congolese rhumba as unique to the Congo on the African continent (White 2008).

It was on the same fecund *rutsoka* and to the pulsating beat of the Congolese and East African rhumbas that Zimbabwean guerrillas invented the *kongonya* and *toyi-toyi* dances in their training camps in Tanzania, Zambia, and Mozambique. Imported to Joni by the defiant street guerrillas, the *toyi-toyi* gave a new edge to the freedom song that helped to paralyze the apartheid state in the 1980s. Moreover, returnee war veteran–musicians Simon "Chopper" Chimbetu, Marko Sibanda, Ketai Muchawaya, and other members of the Kasongo Band fused the east African beat and the Swahili linguistic touch into their music, enriching the Zimbabwean township creativity since the 1980s. In these multiple ways, the guerrilla trail extended and fed into the regional itineraries of colonial labor extraction. It was the migrant labor trails that brought Kenneth Mattaka to Zimbabwe in the early twentieth century, never to go back, as powerfully evoked in Kazembe's *kanindo* song "Aphiri Anabwera." Thus, foot and song mapped these transterritorial imaginations. In Zimbabwe, the migrant workers constituted the songscapes around the farm and mine compounds. Jonathan Murandu, who was a rural boy in the 1970s, recalled the force of these migrants' musical cultures:

> Growing up, my rural area was surrounded by commercial farms such that some of my schoolmates and classmates were children of the farm laborers.

> These schoolmates sang some of these songs. Even some of the rural people used to go to the farms during harvest time to work as cotton pickers. It was during these sojourns that they brought back home songs by Malawian and Zambian singers. "Aphiri Anabwera" was one of the popular songs to diffuse into rural Zimbabwe this way. It was even played *pamasitoro* [at rural stores]. We would spend a number of weeks singing these songs in the hills and vleis as we herded cattle and tapped *hurimbo* latex [natural rubber for trapping birds].[2]

More of these songs were also imported by the guerrillas and diffused amongst rural and urban populations through *mapungwe,* whose repertoires the young would-be guerrillas like Murandu also imitated.

In all these ways, Southern Africans interwove composite songscapes that today constitute rich texts of history, pan-African solidarities, and transterritorial identities. Formed by processes of state formation over millennia, memories of capitalist European and Arab enslavement and colonialism, the missionary enterprise, and the transterritorial liberation movement, these cultural itineraries mapped Southern Africa into an important cultural matrix. These are templates that transgressed the colonial remapping of space and the assignment of subservient identities, and they can therefore most fruitfully be accounted for through theorization of knowledge that equally bravely transcends the postcolonial anxiety about inherited physical and mental borders. This is an enterprise that demands the decolonization of research methodologies beyond the cages of obstinate colonial frameworks. In that regard, I hope this book has contributed one drumbeat to a song that already has complex rhythms.

Notes

Introduction

1. *Zino irema* means "the tooth is a fool"—because, Madzimbabwe say, "it unwittingly smiles even on him whom it does not like." I use "Madzimbabwe" in this book to refer not only to the geospatial Zimbabwe plateau but also to the collective African linguistic and cultural groups that inhabited the territory. It is interchangeable with the Anglicized "Zimbabweans." I use the problematic, anachronistic, colonial "ethnic" ascribed identities such as "Shona" only sparingly.

1. Missionary Witchcrafting African Being

1. An example is *Hymns Ancient and Modern Revised* (Norfolk: Canterbury Press, 1875), published in translation as *Ndhuyo Dzokudira* (Mt. Selinda: Mission Press, 1907) by the Rhodesian branch of the American Board Mission in South Africa.

2. There have been vociferous pressures to disinter Rhodes's remains since independence. In February 2013, veterans of the war for liberation descended on Malindadzimu, intending to remove them for "causing drought in the region." In a Voice of America broadcast debate in which I participated, however, a local chief and a rival group of veterans intriguingly argued that Rhodes was their ancestor and also attracted tourists, and must therefore be left alone (Nyaira 2012). The tombstone was subsequently desecrated in 2014 in an apparent failed attempt to remove the remains.

3. National Archives of Zimbabwe (hereafter cited as NAZ) Oral History Collection, Mushure, 1981.

4. See, for instance, *Rugwaro Rwe Citanhatu* (Chishawasha: Mission Press, 1953), one of the Chishawasha Readers series published by the Jesuits.

5. Father Biehler himself was posthumously identified as the author of the *ZMR* article. Indeed, missionaries planted most of the reportage on the band.

6. NAZ Oral History Collection, Mushure, 1981.

7. NAZ N3/32/1/1, NC Rusape to CNC, September 12, 1916.

8. NAZ N 3/33/3, Sup. Natives to CNC, April 24, 1915.

2. Purging the "Heathen" Song

1. As well as Dodge, John White and, to an even greater degree, Arthur Shearly Cripps stood out among the white missionaries, critiquing colonial injustice and adopting elements of African cultures for liturgical purposes very early in the century. Cripps venerated the Madzimbabwe prophet Chaminuka, encouraged the sacred spiritual playing of *mbira*, adopted the Great Zimbabwe and roundavel architectural styles for his stone churches, and rejected government subsidies for his African schools (Steere 1973). For their unusually open-minded

stances, these handful of white missionaries were indeed “irregular” and unpopular among their peers.

2. This problem has persisted. Musodza (2008, 333–34) recommended that “the Diocese of Harare adop[t] a vigorous program of grouping all the gifted musicians, provide them with further training in the need to conceptualize God in African perspectives using African . . . thought patterns and come up with music that encapsulates such conceptions,” using African instruments, dance forms, and liturgical gestures.

3. “Too Many Don’ts”

1. NAZ S4150N/MISS, H. M. G. Jackson, August 29, 1930.

2. Howard Moffat was a grandson of John Moffat of the London Missionary Society and a son of Robert Moffat, the missionary who helped squeeze the Rudd Concession for the British South Africa Company from Lobengula, the Ndebele King, in the late 1880s, allowing for the settler occupation of the country in 1890. The Moffats thus personify the confluence of church and colonial state in Southern Rhodesia.

3. NAZ S12/364/30, NC Gutu to Sup. Natives, Victoria, September 22, 1930.

4. NAZ S98/30/C, NC Mzingwane to Sup. Natives, Bulawayo, October 1, 1930.

5. NAZ S12/364/30, NC Gutu to Sup. Natives, Victoria, September 22, 1930.

6. NAZ S215/30, NC Gokwe to Sup. Natives, Matabeleland, September 27, 1930.

7. NAZ S215/30, NC Gokwe to Sup. Natives, Matabeleland, September 27, 1930.

8. NAZ S683/30, Assistant NC Bindura to NC Amandas, September 20, 1930.

9. NAZ S683/30, Assistant NC Bindura to NC Amandas, September 20, 1930.

10. NAZ C58, NC Sinoia to CNC, September 8, 1930.

11. NAZ S683/30, Assistant NC Bindura to CNC, September 20, 1930.

12. NAZ S132/708/49/30, NC Gwanda to Sup. Natives, Bulawayo, November 5, 1930.

13. NAZ S132/4442, NC Marandellas to CNC, September 22, 1930.

14. NAZ S4442, NC Inyati to Sup. Natives, Bulawayo, September 18, 1930; NAZ S151/56, Sup. Natives, Matabeleland, to CNC, September 18, 1930.

15. NAZ S885/30/C, NC Hartley to CNC, September 12, 1930.

16. NAZ S235/393, NC Plumtree to CNC, September 11, 1930.

17. NAZ S408/63/30, NC Mtoko to CNC, September 10, 1930.

18. NAZ S408/63/30, NC Mtoko to CNC, September 10, 1930.

19. NAZ S110/434/30, NC Range/Enkeldoorn to CNC, November 21, 1930.

20. NAZ S235/393, NC Mrewa to CNC, September 8, 1930.

21. NAZ S132/4442, NC Marandellas to CNC, September 22, 1930.

22. NAZ S98/30/C, NC Mzingwane to CNC, October 1, 1930.

23. NAZ S98/30/C, NC Mzingwane to CNC, October 1, 1930.

24. The law reduced African chiefs and headmen into “constables” of the NC.

25. NAZ U5115/4150/N/M, CNC to Sec. Premier (Native Affairs), December 6, 1930.

26. NAZ C/58, NC Sinoia to CNC, September 8, 1930.

27. NAZ C58, NC Sinoia to CNC, September 8, 1930.

28. NAZ S110/434/30, NC Range/Enkeldoorn to CNC, November 21, 1930.

29. NAZ S12/364/30, NC Gutu to CNC, September 22, 1930.

30. NAZ S98/30/C, NC Mzingwane to CNC, October 1, 1930.

31. NAZ S235/393, NC Nyamandlovu to CNC, September 13, 1930.

32. NAZ S110/434/30, NC Range/Enkeldoorn to CNC, November 21, 1930.

33. NAZ S110/434/30, NC Range/Enkeldoorn to CNC, November 21, 1930.

34. NAZ S235/393, NC Shabani to CNC, September 13, 1930.
35. NAZ S235/393, NC Mrewa to CNC, September 8, 1930.
36. NAZ S1/993/30, NC Chipinga to CNC, December 11, 1930.
37. NAZ S127/30, Assistant NC Melsetter to NC Chipinga, December 4, 1930.
38. NAZ S1/993/30, NC Chipinga to CNC, December 11, 1930.
39. NAZ U5115/4150/N/M, CNC to Sec. Premier (Native Affairs), December 6, 1930.
40. NAZ S5740/164/30, F.M.C.S., Private Secretary, to Secretary, Southern Rhodesia Missionary Conference, December 24, 1930.
41. His friend Esau Nemapare eventually broke away to form his own rebel diocese.

4. Architectures of Control

1. Southern Rhodesia, *Debates of the Legislative Assembly,* 1944, vol. 24, col. 2501.
2. NAZ S246/782, Bulawayo Native Society, Application for Assistance towards Recreation Hall for Natives in Bulawayo Location, Bulawayo Town Clerk to the Secretary, Department of Internal Affairs, May 25, 1935.
3. NAZ S246/782, CNC, Salisbury, to the Native Welfare Society of Matabeleland, May 2, 1935, Recreation Hall.
4. Southern Rhodesia, *Debates of the Legislative Assembly,* 1934, col. 533.
5. Hugh Ashton, interview by Mark Ncube, June 1, 1994, Bulawayo Oral Interviews, part of the (Bulawayo) Oral History Project of the National Archives of Zimbabwe. Thanks to Ennie Chipembere for sharing the transcripts with me.
6. NAZ S/FE 21, Federation of African Welfare Societies of Southern Rhodesia, December 11, 1943, 11.
7. Hugh Ashton, interview by Mark Ncube, June 1, 1994, Bulawayo Oral Interviews.
8. Masotsha Ndlovu, interview by Mark Ncube, October 8, 1981, Bulawayo Oral Interviews.
9. Masotsha Ndlovu, interview by Mark Ncube, October 8, 1981, Bulawayo Oral Interviews.
10. Hugh Ashton, interview by Mark Ncube, June 1, 1994, Bulawayo Oral Interviews.
11. NAZ LG 191/12/7/6, Superintendent, Stodart, to M. O. H., Band Performance by BSAP Police Band, March 10, 1941.
12. NAZ S/SA 6175, Salisbury, Annual Report of the Director of Native Administration, July 1, 1960–June 30, 1961, 13.
13. NAZ S/SA 6175, Salisbury, Annual Report of the Director of Native Administration, July 1, 1950–June 30, 1951, 16.
14. NAZ S/SA 6175, Salisbury, Native Administration Annual Report, July 1, 1948–June 30, 1949, 6.
15. NAZ S/SA 6175, Salisbury, Native Administration Annual Report, July 1, 1948–June 30, 1949, 6.
16. Hugh Ashton, interview by Mark Ncube, June 1, 1994, Bulawayo Oral Interviews.
17. NAZ ZAN 1/1/1, Thornton, Evidence to the Jackson Commission, January 1930.
18. Dan Skipworth-Michell, contribution to a Facebook group discussion, Rhodesians Worldwide, July 20, 2013.
19. NAZ F148/AGF/72/1, Federal Attorney General Robinson to Secretary for Law, May 13, 1958. I am grateful to Allison Shutt for sharing this reference and case summary.
20. NAZ LG 191/10/633, Director of Native Administration to B. J. Neale (Town Clerk), Multi-racial Clubs & Hotels, Aug 28, 1958.

21. See also NAZ LG 191/11/788, Federal Hotel to Provide Accommodation for Africans, undated.

5. The "Tribal Dance" as a Colonial Alibi

1. NAZ S/SA 6175, Salisbury, Native Administration Annual Report, July 1, 1948–June 30, 1949, 6.
2. NAZ S/SA 6175, Salisbury, Native Administration Annual Report, July 1, 1953–June 30, 1954, 22.
3. NAZ S/SA 6175, Salisbury, Native Administration Annual Report, July 1, 1953–June 30, 1954, 22.
4. ILAM website, http://ilam.ru.ac.za.
5. NAZ S1003, Indaba at Government House: Visit of his Royal Highness the Prince of Wales, circular from the Superintendent of Natives to all stations in Matabeleland, January 22, 1934.
6. I am grateful to Allison Shutt for identifying Savanhu as the anonymous journalist. Savanhu subsequently became one of the few Africans elected to the colonial Federal Parliament.
7. NAZ S/SA 6175, Salisbury, Native Administration Annual Report for July 1, 1952–June 30, 1953, 32.
8. Masuku's name is sometimes misspelled "Masuka" in the press, but as she has indicated, this is incorrect (*Rhodesia Herald,* November 19, 2007).
9. NAZ F121/H3/52, Songs about Federation, 1960–61. Thanks to Allison Shutt for generously drawing my attention to this archive.
10. City of Harare Department of Housing and Community Services (DHCS), Ha/ri/1, P. Kriel, Community Services Officer, to Deputy Director, November 5, 1974.
11. DHCS, Ha/ri/1, Report of Rufaro Stadium, November 30, 1974.
12. DHCS, C/26/6/5, Director of African Administration, F. P. F. Sutcliffe, to General Manager, Liquor Undertaking Department; DHCS, C/26/6, Salisbury Traditional African Association, Rufaro Tribal Dancing Festival, undated.
13. DHCS C/26/6/5/30, J. P. Courtney, Sup., City of Salisbury, Harari, to Director of African Administration, Nyau Dancing, Harari Township, October 26, 1972, emphasis mine.
14. DHCS, C/26/5/13, Memo from Manager (Rhodesia), WENELA, Salisbury, to Director of African Administration, October 8, 1975.
15. Such "exchange" was escalating at this time, as Zambian and Malawian labor migrants returned to their newly independent countries after the collapse of the ill-fated Federation in 1963.
16. Salisbury Municipality, DHCS, File 11, Basil Chidyamatamba (for African Choral Society) to Director of African Administration, October 1968.
17. DHCS, File 11A, Townships Officer (Martin), to Director of African Administration October 17, 1968.
18. DHCS, C36, Harare Arts Council, Report on First Cultural Leadership Course Held at Ranche House College, April 7, 1984.
19. NAZ S/SA 6175, Salisbury, Native Administration Annual Report, July 1, 1948–June 30, 1949, 6.
20. DHCS, 1 HA/RI/1, Letter from Mrs. Jean Crooks, Advertising Promos, to Mr. P. Kriel, November 1974; Report of Rufaro Stadium, November 30, 1974; Shaya interview.

6. *Chimanjemanje*

1. Colonial etiquette required that Africans remove their hats and step out of the way when they met white people, and address them as "Nkosi."

2. Mattaka and Mattaka, interview. The year is that of the colonial occupation of Zimbabwe. Throughout the following discussion, quotations are taken from my interviews with the Mattakas unless otherwise indicated.

3. NAZ S/SA 6175, Salisbury, Annual Report of the Director of Native Administration for the Mayoral Year July 1, 1951 to June 30, 1952, 6.

4. NAZ LG 191/11/414, Ministry of Internal Affairs, The development of Music in the Rhodesians, its significance as a social and national attribute: a plea for collaboration and cooperative action, and proposals to that end, 1955.

5. This is one of the many songs that, in his comedic jargon, he said were in "top gear," i.e., his head. He signed away too many to Gallo for nothing during his time in Joburg.

7. The Many Moods of "Skokiaan"

1. *The Machine's Pump* 8 (8), newsletter of Brave Combo, http://brave.com/bo/volume-8-8-august-2005/.

2. The English lyrics that Armstrong sang can be found on Lyricszoo.com and other websites.

3. Hugh Ashton, interviewed by Mark Ncube, June 1, 1994, Bulawayo Oral Interviews.

4. Hugh Ashton, interviewed by Mark Ncube, June 1, 1994, Bulawayo Oral Interviews.

5. NAZ S/SA 6175, Salisbury Native Administration Annual Report, July 1, 1949–June 30, 1950.

6. Hugh Ashton, interviewed by Mark Ncube, June 1, 1994, Bulawayo Oral Interviews.

7. NAZ S/SA 6175, Salisbury Native Administration Annual Report, July 1, 1957–June 30, 1958.

8. The translation is by Maurice Vambe (2007, 364).

9. "Satchmo's Visit to Rhodesia 1960," an anonymous contribution to Rhodie Music, a website commemorating (white) Rhodesian popular music ("Recollections & Memories," Rhodie Music, June 19, 2005, http://www.rhodiemusic.com/memories.htm).

10. NAZ S/SA 6175, Salisbury, Native Administration Annual Report, July 1, 1961–June 30, 1962.

11. NAZ LG191/11/647, Jameson Hotel: Multi-Racial Hotel; LG 191/11/788, Federal Hotel to Provide Accommodation for Africans, undated.

8. Usable Pasts

1. A guerrilla *nom de guerre,* Nyamubaya means "the one who stabs." The revolutionary anger is aptly captured in the then fashionable Afrocentric spelling "Afrikan," a sign of the times.

2. Robert Mugabe, interview by Dali Tambo, *People of the South,* SABC 3, June 2, 2013.

3. NAZ S/SA 6175, Salisbury, Native Administration Annual Reports, July 1, 1961–June 30, 1962.

4. ZANLA, the Zimbabwe African National Liberation Army, was ZANU's army. ZANU was formed in 1963 by a faction of nationalist leaders who had left ZAPU. ZAPU's own army was called ZIPRA, the Zimbabwe People's Revolutionary Army.

5. John O'Brien, "Trap Drums," message posted to the Dandemutande mailing list, March 3, 2014.

6. Facebook comment, March 24, 2014.

7. Cde Khumalo weaved together English and ChiKaranga as he spoke; I have translated the ChiKaranga here.

9. Cultures of Resistance

1. Thomas Mapfumo (1992) recorded a version of this song in the 1970s.

2. NAZ S/SA 6175, Salisbury, Native Administration Annual Report, July 1, 1957–June 30, 1958.

3. Transcription by Glen Ncube.

4. NAZ S/SA 6175, Salisbury, Native Administration Annual Report, July 1, 1961–June 30, 1962, emphasis mine.

5. "Sendekera" was composed by Cdes Murehwa and Sando Muponda, if Stalin Mau Mau (interview), a former Voice of Zimbabwe presenter, remembered correctly.

6. This tactic is reminiscent of the regime's intimidatory practices of "raining pamphlets" and "flying corpses," in which it dropped propaganda leaflets on villages and dangled dead "terrorists" from helicopters or dragged them behind army trucks.

7. Zexie and Stella Manatsa confessed to disrupting many a home through their music, because some men gave up their plans to go home for the weekend and instead camped with prostitutes in the areas around the township, enjoying the music from Friday evening to Sunday morning and then begging bus fare from Zexie himself to go back to work.

8. Josiah Chinamano and Willie Musarurwa were prominent ZAPU leaders. "Wire" refers to the concentration camps into which the state kraaled villagers to deprive the guerrillas of support.

Epilogue

1. I use the non-hyphenated form "post-colonial" to refer to the epistemological condition since colonial occupation, and the form "postcolonial" to refer to the time after the supposed end of colonial occupation. Thus, the postcolonial state is also the colonial state—Rhodesia—while the post-colonial state is Zimbabwe. This distinction reflects my critique of the concept of "postcolonialism."

2. Comment in a Facebook discussion, March 24, 2014.

Selected Bibliography and Discography

Interviews

Interviews were conducted, and translated when necessary, by the author except where indicated.

Banda, Pauline. Bulawayo, July 2012.

Chikowero family. Interviewees were the brothers Tsuro Chikowero, Musutu Chikowero, and Hofisi Chikowero. Mhondoro, July 2012.

Chikutu, Nelson. Harare, July 2011.

Chinx (Dickson Chingaira). Chitungwiza, December 12, 2006.

Chiweshe, Stella Rambisai. Email communication, November 12, 2009.

Dambudzo. Interviewed by Mugove Chikowero. Chikomba, August 2012.

Dewa, Tendai Terrance Mutyambizi. Facebook conversation, March 30, 2014.

Dube, Tshinga. Harare, July 2011.

Jeyacheya, Farai. Skype interview, September 2013.

Karanga, Daramu. Harare, July 2012, August 2012.

Mafika, Nyamasvisva Tichaona. Harare, July 2012.

Manatsa, Zexie, and Stella Manatsa. Harare, July 2012, November 2014.

Mandishona, Gibson. Harare, November 2014.

Manyika, Chivanda Kennedy. Gweru, July 2012.

Manyika, Chivanda Kennedy, and Rahab Manyika. Gweru, July 2012.

Mapfumo, Max. Harare, July 2012.

Mapfumo family. Interviewees were the brothers Thomas Mapfumo (main respondent), William Mapfumo, and Lancelot Mapfumo. Eugene, Oregon, November 25, 2011.

Masekela, Hugh. Santa Barbara, March 2015.

Masuku, Dorothy. Johannesburg, August 2012.

Mattaka, Kenneth. Bulawayo, November 19, 2006.

Mattaka, Kenneth, and Lina Mattaka. Bulawayo, January 7, 2007.

Mau Mau, Stalin. Harare, July 2012.

Mbirimi, Friday. Harare, November 10, 2006.

Mlambo, Miriam. December 3, 2006.

Moyo, Mavis. Harare, July 2012.

Muchapera, Mabhunu. Interviewed by Mugove Chikowero. Chikomba, July 2012.

Mupungu, Ivy. Norton, November 2006.

Musarurwa, Peter. Harare, December 2007.

Mushawatu, Neddington. Facebook conversation, January 27, 2015.

Musoni, Ben. Harare, June 2011.

Mutyambizi family. Interviewees were the siblings Muchemwa Mutyambizi, Mutizwa Mutyambizi, and Julia Mutyambizi Moyo. Bulawayo, January 4, 2007.

Ncube, Kembo. Bulawayo, January 3, 2007, July 2012.

Ngwenya, Jane Lungile. Esigodini, July 18, 2011; Bulawayo, August 2012.

Nkala, Enos. Bulawayo, July 2011.
Shamuyarira, Nathan. Harare, July 2011, July 2012.
Shaya, George. Harare, July 2011.
Shungu. Interviewed by Munyaradzi Huni.
Simemeza, Herbert. Harare, July 2011.
Sithole, Abel Sinametsi. Bulawayo, January 3, 2007.
Zikhali, Norman. Domboshava, July 2011.

Newsletters and Newspapers

These periodicals are cited in the text.

African Daily News
African Parade
African Weekly
Bantu Mirror
Christian Express (continues the *Kaffir Express* from January 1876)
Evangelical Visitor
Herald
Kaffir Express
Mashonaland Quarterly
Native Mirror
Newsletter of the African Music Society
Parade (continues the *African Parade*)
Port Elizabeth Herald
Radio Post
Rhodesia Herald
Rhodesia Herald Weekly Edition
South African Outlook (continues the *Christian Express* from January 1922)
Star
Sunday Mail
Zambesi Mission Record
Zimbabwe Review
Zimbabwe Times

Books, Journal Articles, and Audiovisual Materials

Achebe, Chinua. 1978. "An Image of Africa." *Research in African Literatures* 9 (1): 1–15.
"African Modes of Self-Writing Revisited." 2002. Special section of *Public Culture* 14 (3).
Agawu, Kofi. 2003. *Representing African Music: Postcolonial Notes, Queries, Positions.* London: Routledge.
Ajayi, J. F. Ade. 1965. *Christian Missions in Nigeria, 1841–1891: The Making of a New Elite.* London: Longmans.
Alfred, Taiaiake, and Jeff Corntassel. 2005. "Being Indigenous: Resurgences against Contemporary Colonialism." *Government and Opposition* 40 (4): 597–614.
Allen, Lara. 2001. Review of *Nationalists, Cosmopolitans, and Popular Music in Zimbabwe,* by Thomas Turino. *Notes* 58 (2): 378–79.
Andrew, Father. 1933. *My Year in Rhodesia.* Westminster: The Society for the Propagation of the Gospel in Foreign Parts.

Apter, Andrew. 1999. "Africa, Empire, and Anthropology: A Philological Exploration of Anthropology's Heart of Darkness." *Annual Review of Anthropology* 28: 577–98.

———. 2002. "On Imperial Spectacle: The Dialectics of Seeing in Colonial Nigeria." *Comparative Studies in Society and History* 44 (3): 564–96.

Armah, Ayi Kwei. 2010. "Remembering the Dismembered Continent." *New African Magazine* 493, February.

Armstrong, Louis. 1994. *Louis Armstrong's All-Time Greatest Hits.* Sound recording, MCA.

Arrighi, Giovanni. 1973. "Labour Supplies in Historical Perspective: A Study of the Proletarianization of the African Peasantry in Rhodesia." In *Essays on the Political Economy of Africa,* edited by Giovanni Arrighi and John Saul, 180–234. New York: Monthly Review Press.

Askew, Kelly. 2002. *Performing the Nation: Swahili Music and Cultural Politics in Tanzania.* Chicago: University of Chicago Press.

Badenhorst, C. M., and C. Mather. 1997. "Tribal Recreation and Recreating Tribalism: Culture, Leisure and Social Control on South Africa's Gold Mines, 1940–1950." *Journal of Southern African Studies* 23 (3): 473–89.

Badenhorst, C. M., and C. M. Rogerson. 1986. "'Teach the Native to Play': Social Control and Organized Black Sport on the Witwatersrand, 1920–1939." *GeoJournal* 12 (2): 197–202.

Baden-Powell, R. S. S. 1970 [1897]. *The Matabele Campaign, 1896, Being a Narrative of the Campaign in Suppressing the Native Rising in Matabeleland and Mashonaland.* Westport: Negro Universities Press.

Ballantine, Christopher. 1991. "Music and Emancipation: The Social Role of Black Jazz and Vaudeville in South Africa between the 1920s and the Early 1940s." *Journal of Southern African Studies* 17 (1): 129–52.

Banana, Canaan S. 1989. Introduction to *Turmoil and Tenacity: Zimbabwe, 1890–1990,* edited by C. S. Banana. Harare: College Press.

Barney, Katelyn, and Elizabeth Mackinlay. 2010. "'Singing Trauma Trails': Songs of the Stolen Generations in Indigenous Australia." *Music and Politics* 4 (2): 1–25.

Beach, David N. 1973. "The Initial Impact of Christianity on the Shona: The Protestants and the Southern Shona." In *Christianity South of the Zambezi,* edited by J. A. Dachs, 25–40. Gweru: Mambo Press.

Bekkum, W. v. 1957. "The Missionary Potential of the Liturgy." *Worldmission* 8 (1): 83–96.

Bender, W. 1991. *Sweet Mother: Modern African Music.* Chicago: University of Chicago Press.

Bent, J. Theodore. 1893. *The Ruined Cities of Mashonaland: Being a Record of Excavation in 1891.* London: Longmans, Green.

Berman, E. H. 1975. "Christian Missions in Africa." In *African Reactions to Missionary Education,* 1–53. New York: Teachers College Press.

Bhabha, H. 2001. "Of Mimicry and Man: The Ambivalence of Colonial Discourse." In *Race Critical Theories: Text and Context,* edited by Philomena Essed and David Theo Goldberg, 113–22. Malden, MA: Wiley-Blackwell.

Bhebe, Ngwabi. 1980. "Christianity and Traditional Religion in Western Zimbabwe, 1859–1923." *African Affairs* 79 (316): 441–43.

———. 1989. "The Nationalist Struggle, 1957–1962." In *Turmoil and Tenacity: Zimbabwe, 1890–1980,* edited by C. S. Banana, 50–116. Harare: College Press.

———. 2004. *Simon Vengesai Muzenda and the Struggle for and Liberation of Zimbabwe.* Gweru: Mambo Press.

Biko, Steve. 2002. *I Write What I Like: Selected Writings.* Chicago: University of Chicago Press.

Blyden, Edward Wilmot. 1967. *Christianity, Islam and the Negro Race.* Edinburgh: Edinburgh University Press.

Bucher, Hubert. 1980. *Spirits and Power: An Analysis of Shona Cosmology.* Cape Town: Oxford University Press.

Bulawayo Municipality. 2000. *Siye Pambili.* January.

Bullen, Josephine. 2008. *Empandeni Interlude, 1899–1903: Journal of a Woman Missionary, Josephine Bullen, SND de Namur, at the Turn of the Century in Rhodesia.* Transcribed and edited by Brigid Rose Tiernan, SND de Namur. Pietermaritzburg: Cluster Publications.

Burke, Timothy. 1996. *Lifebuoy Men, Lux Women: Commodification, Consumption and Cleanliness in Modern Zimbabwe.* Durham, NC: Duke University Press.

———. 2008. "The Modern Girl and Commodity Culture." In *The Modern Girl around the World: Consumption, Modernity, and Globalization,* edited by Alys Eve Weinbaum, Lynn M. Thomas, et al. (The Modern Girl around the World Research Group), 362–70. Durham, NC: Duke University Press.

Burns, James M. 2002. *Flickering Shadows: Cinema and Identity in Colonial Zimbabwe.* Athens: Ohio University Press.

Cabral, Amilcah. 1970. "National Liberation and Culture." Eduardo Mondlane Memorial Lecture, delivered at Syracuse University for the Program of Eastern African Studies of the Maxwell School of Citizenship and Public Affairs, February 2.

Carrol, K. 1956. "Yoruba Religious Music." *African Music* 1 (3): 45–47.

Césaire, Aimé. 1972. *Discourse on Colonialism.* Translated by Joan Pinkham. New York: Monthly Review Press.

Chadya, Joyce M. 1997. "Missionary Land Ownership: The Case of the Roman Catholics at Chishawasha." MA thesis, University of Zimbabwe.

Chakrabarty, Dipesh. 2000. *Provincializing Europe: Postcolonial Thought and Historical Difference.* Princeton, NJ: Princeton University Press.

Chatterjee, Partha. 1986. *Nationalist Thought and the Colonial World: A Derivative Discourse.* Tokyo: United Nations University.

Chennels, Anthony. 2005. "Self-Representation and National Memory: White Autobiographies in Zimbabwe." In *Versions of Zimbabwe: New Approaches to Literature and Culture,* edited by R. Muponde and R. Primorac, 131–46. Harare: Weaver Press.

Chikowero, Mhoze. 2010. "A Historian's Take on Thomas Mapfumo and Robert Mugabe." Interview by Banning Eyre. Part of the Hip Deep program "Thomas Mapfumo 2: The Mugabe Years." Afropop Worldwide. http://www.afropop.org/wp/7041/thomas-mapfumo-2-the-mugabe-years/.

———. 2011. "Thompson Samkange: An Early Zimbabwean Nationalist." In *Dictionary of African Biography,* edited by Emmanuel Akyeampong and Henry Louis Gates, Jr. New York: Oxford University Press.

———. 2014. "Is Propaganda Modernity? Press and Radio for 'Africans' in Zambia, Zimbabwe, and Malawi during World War II and Its Aftermath." In *Modernization as Spectacle in Africa,* edited by Peter J. Bloom, Stephan Miescher, and Takyiwaa Manuh, 112–34. Bloomington: Indiana University Press.

———. See also Chikowero, Moses.

Chikowero, Moses. 2007. "The State and Music Policy in Post-colonial Zimbabwe, 1980–2000." *Muziki: Journal of Music Research in Africa* 4 (1): 111–28.

———. 2008. "'Our People Father, They Haven't Learned Yet': Music and Postcolonial Identities in Zimbabwe, 1980–2000." *Journal of Southern African Studies* 34 (1): 145–60.

———. 2010. Review of *Rumba Rules: The Politics of Dance Music in Mobutu's Zaire,* by Bob White. *Canadian Journal of African Studies* 44 (2): 431–35.

———. 2011. "The Third *Chimurenga:* Land and Song in Zimbabwe's Ultra-nationalist State Ideology, 2000–2007." In *Redemptive or Grotesque Nationalism? Rethinking Contemporary Politics in Zimbabwe,* edited by Sabelo J. Ndlovu-Gatsheni and James Muzondidya, 291–313. New York: Peter Lang.

———. See also Chikowero, Mhoze.

Chimhete, Nathaniel. 2004. "The African Alcohol Industry in Salisbury, Southern Rhodesia, 1945–1980." MA thesis, University of Zimbabwe.

Chitando, Ezra. 2001. "Music in Zimbabwe." Review of *Nationalists, Cosmopolitans and Popular Music in Zimbabwe,* by Thomas Turino. *Zambezia: The Journal of Humanities of the University of Zimbabwe* 29 (1): 82–91.

———. 2002. *Singing Culture: A Study of Gospel Music in Zimbabwe.* Research report no. 121. Uppsala: Nordiska Afrikainstitutet.

Chitauro, M., C. Dube, and L. Gunner. 1994. "Song, Story and Nation: Women as Singers and Actresses in Zimbabwe." In *Politics and Performance: Theatre, Poetry and Song in Southern Africa,* edited by Liz Gunner, 111–38. Johannesburg: Witwatersrand University Press.

Churchill, Ward. 2004. *Kill the Indian, Save the Man: The Genocidal Impact of American Indian Residential Schools.* San Francisco: City Lights.

Cohn, Bernard. 1987. "The Command of Language and the Language of Command." In *Subaltern Studies IV,* edited by R. Guha, 45–88. Delhi: Oxford University Press.

———. 1996. *Colonialism and Its Forms of Knowledge: The British in India.* Oxford: Oxford University Press.

Cole, Catherine M. 2001. *Ghana's Concert Party Theatre.* Bloomington: Indiana University Press.

Comaroff, Jean, and John Comaroff. 1991. *Christianity, Colonialism and Consciousness in South Africa.* Vol. 1 of *Of Revelation and Revolution.* Chicago: University of Chicago Press.

———. 1997. *The Dialectics of Modernity on a South African Frontier.* Vol. 2 of *Of Revelation and Revolution.* Chicago: Chicago University Press.

Comaroff, John, and Jean Comaroff. 1992. *Ethnography and the Historical Imagination.* Boulder, CO: Westview Press.

Conrad, Joseph. 1950. *"Heart of Darkness" and "The Secret Sharer."* New York: New American Library.

Cool Crooners. 2006. "Zhii." *Blue Sky.* Sound recording.

Coplan, D. B. 1985. *In Township Tonight! South Africa's Black City Music and Theatre.* London and New York: Longman.

Cripps, Arthur Shearly. 1936. *How Roads Were Made in the Native Reserves of Charter District of Mashonaland, Southern Rhodesia, 1934–35.* London: N.p.

Daneel, M. L. 1970. *The God of the Matopo Hills: An Essay on the Mwari Cult in Rhodesia.* Leiden: Afrika-Studiecentrum.

Dangarembga, Tsitsi. 2004. *Nervous Conditions.* New York: Seal Press.

Daniélou, Alain. 1969. "Cultural Genocide." *African Music* 4 (3): 19–21.

Davidson, Basil. 1977. "Questions on Nationalism." *African Affairs* 76 (302): 39–46.

Davidson, Frances. 1915. *South and South Central Africa: A Record of Fifteen Years' Missionary Labors among Primitive Peoples.* Elgin, IL: Brethren Publishing House.

Desai, R. 2008. "Introduction: Nationalisms and Their Understandings in Historical Perspective." *Third World Quarterly* 29 (3): 397–428.

Devittie, Thomas D. 1976. "The Underdevelopment of Social Welfare Services for Urban Africans in Rhodesia, 1929–1953, with Special Reference to Social Security." Henderson seminar paper, no. 32. Department of History, University of Rhodesia.

Diawara, Manthia. 1990. "Reading Africa through Foucault: V. Y. Mudimbe's Reaffirmation of the Subject." *October* 55: 79–92.

Documents on the Portuguese in Mozambique and Central Africa, 1497–1840. Harare: National Archives of Zimbabwe.

Dodge, Ralph E. 1960. *The Unpopular Missionary.* Westwood, NJ: Fleming H. Revell Company.

Duncan, Graham. 2006. "Winning Hearts and Minds: Character Formation in Mission Education with Special Reference to Lovedale Missionary Institution." *Studia Historiae Ecclesiasticae* 32 (1): 1–47.

Dutiro, Chartwell. 2007. "Chosen by the Ancestors: Chartwell Dutiro." Interview by Keith Howard. In *Zimbabwean Mbira Music on an International Stage: Chartwell Dutiro's Life in Music,* edited by Chartwell Dutiro and Keith Howard, 1–7. Burlington, VT: Ashgate.

Erlmann, V. 1994. "'Africa Civilized, Africa Uncivilized': Local Culture, World System and South African Music." *Journal of Southern African Studies* 20 (2): 165–79.

———. 1999. *Music, Modernity and Global Imagination: South Africa and the West.* Oxford: Oxford University Press.

Fabian, J. 1990. "Presence and Representation: The Other and Anthropological Writing." *Critical Inquiry* 16 (4): 753–72.

Fanon, Frantz. 1967a. *Black Skin, White Masks.* New York: Grove Press.

———. 1967b. *The Wretched of the Earth.* Harmondsworth: Penguin.

———. 1968. *The Wretched of the Earth.* New York: Grove Press.

Finkle, H. C. 1962. "History of Education in Southern Rhodesia." Survey Report on Adult Literacy and Christian Literature in Southern Rhodesia. Southern Rhodesia Christian Conference.

Fleming, Tyler, and Toyin Falola. 2011. Introduction to *Music, Performance and African Identities,* edited by Tyler Fleming and Toyin Falola, 1–34. New York: Routledge University Press.

Foucault, Michel. 1979. *Discipline and Punish.* New York: Viking.

———. 2007. *The Politics of Truth.* Los Angeles: Semiotext(e).

Frederikse, Julie. 1982. *None but Ourselves: Masses vs. Media in the Making of Zimbabwe.* Harare: Oral Traditions Association of Zimbabwe in association with Anvil Press.

Freire, Paulo. 1970. *Cultural Action for Freedom.* Cambridge, MA: Harvard Educational Review.

Gargett, E. S. 1971. "Welfare Services in an African Urban Area, Bulawayo." PhD diss., University of London.

———. 1973. "The Changing Pattern of Urban African Welfare Services." Paper presented to the Rhodesian Provincial Division of I.A.N.A., April 26.

———. 1977. *The Administration of Transition: African Urban Settlement in Rhodesia.* Mambo Press: Gwelo.

Gbeho, Philip. 1954. Letter to the editor. *African Music Journal* 1 (1): 82.

Gorer, Geoffrey. 1935. *Africa Dances: A Book about West African Negroes.* New York: Alfred A. Kopf.

Granger, Todd. 2012. "Bernard Mizeki, Catechist and Martyr in Mashonaland, 1896." *For All the Saints,* blog, June 12. https://forallsaints.wordpress.com/2012/06/18/bernard-mizeki-catechist-and-martyr-in-mashonaland-1896-2/.

Gray, R. 1960. *The Two Nations: Aspects of the Development of Race Relations in the Rhodesias and Nyasaland.* London: Oxford University Press.

Gray, S. Douglas. 1923. *Frontiers of the Kingdom: The Story of Methodist Missions in Rhodesia.* London: Cargate Press.

Green Arrows. 2010. "Zexie Manatsa—Chipo Chiroorwa." Song, uploaded by YouTube user lavender on August 2. https://www.youtube.com/watch?v=G70vnzGtZX0&feature=related.

Grier, Beverly. 1994. "Invisible Hands: The Political Economy of Child Labour in Colonial Zimbabwe, 1890–1930." *Journal of Southern African Studies* 20 (1): 27–52.

Grosfoguel, Ramón. 2008. "Transmodernity, Border Thinking, and Global Coloniality." *Humandee: Human Management and Development.* http://www.humandee.org/spip.php?article111.

———. 2013. "The Structure of Knowledge in Westernized Universities: Epistemic Racism/Sexism and the Four Genocides/Epistemicides of the Long 16th Century." *Human Architecture: Journal of the Sociology of Self-Knowledge* 11 (1): 73–90.

Gumbo, Mafuranhunzi. 1995. *Guerilla Snuff.* Harare: Baobab Books.

Gurira, Danai. 2013. *The Convert.* Washington, DC: Woolly Mammoth Theatre Company.

Gwekwerere, Gadziro. 2010. *A Study of Zimbabwean Gospel Music, 1980–2007: The Development and Evolution of Zimbabwean Gospel Music as Shaped by the Political and Socio-economic Climate.* Saarbrücken: VDM Verlag Dr. Müller.

Hallelujah Chicken Run Band. 1974. *Murembo.* Sound recording, Teal Records. Reissued as *Take One* (Gramma Records, 2006).

Hamm, Charles. 1995. *Putting Popular Music in Its Place.* Cambridge: Cambridge University Press.

Hargreaves, J. D. 1988. *Decolonization in Africa.* New York: Longman.

Heise, D. R. 1967. "Prefatory Findings in the Sociology of Missions." *Journal for the Scientific Study of Religions* 6 (1): 49–58.

Hernández-Avila, Inés. 2003. "The Power of Native Languages and the Performance of Indigenous Autonomy: The Case of Mexico." In *Native Voices: American Indian Identity and Resistance,* edited by Richard A. Grounds, George E. Tinker, and David E. Wilkins, 35–77. Lawrence: University of Kansas Press.

Hodgson, Dorothy L., and Sheryl A. McCurdy, eds. 2001. *"Wicked" Women and the Reconfiguration of Gender in Africa.* Portsmouth, NH: Heinemann.

Hostetter, John Norman. 1967. "Mission Education in a Changing Society: Brethren in Christ in Southern Rhodesia, Africa, 1899–1959." PhD diss., State University of New York at Buffalo.

Houser, Tillman. 2007. *Let Me Tell You: A Memoir.* Charleston, SC: Booksurge.

How the British Stole Zimbabwe. 1984. Documentary video, uploaded by YouTube user rasorder, December 6, 2008. http://www.youtube.com/watch?v=1HIoZoaMjoM.

Hunter, Eva. 1998. "Shaping the Truth of the Struggle." Interview by Yvonne Vera. *Current Writing* 10 (1): 75–86.

Ibbotson, P. 1942. "Native Welfare Societies in Southern Rhodesia." *Race Relations* 9 (2).

Jaji, Tsitsi Ella. 2014. *Africa in Stereo: Modernism, Music and Pan-African Solidarity.* Oxford: Oxford University Press.

JanMohamed, Abdul R. 1985. "The Economy of Manichean Allegory: The Function of Racial Difference in Colonialist Literature." *Critical Inquiry* 12 (1): 59–87.

Jenje-Makwenda, Joyce. 2004. *Zimbabwe's Township Music.* Harare: Self-published.

Jones, Max, and John Chilton. 1971. *Louis: The Louis Armstrong Story, 1900–1971.* Boston: Little, Brown and Company.

Kadalie, Clements. 1970. *My Life and the ICU: The Autobiography of a Black Trade Unionist in South Africa.* London: Cass.

Kahari, George K. 1981. "The History of the Shona Protest Song: A Preliminary Study." *Zambezia: The Journal of Humanities of the University of Zimbabwe* 9 (2): 79–101.

Kapenzi, Geoffrey. 1979. *The Clash of Cultures: Christian Missionaries and the Shona of Rhodesia.* Washington, DC: University Press of America.

Kauffman, Robert. 1960. "Hymns of the Wabvuwi." *African Music* 2 (3): 31–35.

Khan, Katy. 2008. "South-South Cultural Cooperation: Transnational Identities in the Music of Dorothy Masuka and Miriam Makeba." *Muziki: Journal of Music Research in Africa* (5) 1: 145–51.

Kirby, Percival. 1959. "The Use of European Musical Techniques by the Non-European Peoples of Southern Africa." *Journal of the International Folk Music Council* 11: 37–40.

Kisiang'ani, Edward Namisiko Waswa. 2002. "Decolonizing Gender Studies in Africa." Paper presented at African Gender in the New Millennium, a conference of the Council for the Development of Social Science Research in Africa (CODESRIA), April 7–10, Cairo. http://www.codesria.org/spip.php?article579.

Klein, Naomi. 2007. *Shock Therapy: The Rise of Disaster Capitalism.* New York: Picador.

Kruger, L. 1994. "Placing 'New Africans' in the 'Old' South Africa: Drama, Modernity and Racial Identities in Johannesburg, c. 1935." *Modernity/Modernism* 1 (2): 113–31.

Kunonga, Nolbert. 1996. "Roots of the Zimbabwe Revolution: A Biographical Study of the Reverend Ndabaningi Sithole." PhD diss., Northwestern University.

Kwaramba, A. D. 1997. *Popular Music and Society: The Language of Protest in Chimurenga Music; The Case of Thomas Mapfumo in Zimbabwe.* Oslo: University of Oslo.

Lan, David. 1985. *Guns and Rain: Guerrillas and Spirit Mediums in Zimbabwe.* Berkeley: University of California Press.

Larkin, Brian. 2008. *Signal and Noise: Media, Infrastructure and Urban Culture in Nigeria.* Durham, NC: Duke University Press.

Lenherr, J. 1967. Review of *Ndwiyo Dzechechi Dzevu (Hymns of the Soil),* by John Kaemmer. *African Music* 4 (1): 75.

Lewis, Mark B. 1996. "My Brush with History." *American Heritage Magazine* 47 (3).

Lezra, Esther. 2014. *The Colonial Art of Demonizing Others: A Global Perspective.* New York: Routledge.
Lindfors, Bernth. 1970. "Anti-Negritude in Algiers." *Africa Today* 17 (1): 5–7.
Livingstone, David. 1857. *Missionary Travels and Researches in South Africa.* London: John Murray.
Lobley, Noel. 2010. "The Social Biography of Ethnomusicological Field Recordings: Eliciting Responses to Hugh Tracey's 'The Sound of Africa' Series." PhD diss., Oxford University.
Louw, Johan K. 1956. "The Use of African Music in the Church." *African Music* 1 (3): 43–44.
———. 1958. "African Music in Christian Worship." *African Music* 2 (1): 51–53.
Louw, Johan L., and Johan K. Louw. 1956. "Notes and News." *African Music* (1) 3: 75.
Lury, E. E. 1956. "Music in African Churches." *African Music* 1 (3): 34–36.
Luthuli, Albert. 1962. *Let My People Go.* New York: McGraw-Hill.
Lwanda, John. 2008. "The History of Popular Music in Malawi, 1891 to 2007: A Preliminary Communication." *Society of Malawi Journal* 61 (1): 26–40.
MacAloon, John J. 1984. "Olympic Games and the Theory of Spectacle in Modern Societies." In *Rite, Drama, Festival, Spectacle: Rehearsals toward a Theory of Cultural Performance,* edited by John MacAloon, 241–80. Philadelphia: Institute for the Study of Human Issues.
Mafeje, Archie. 1991. *The Theory and Ethnography of African Social Formations: The Case of the Interlacustrine Kingdoms.* London: Codesria.
Mahoso, Langson Takawira. 1979. "The Social Impact of Christian Missions in Zimbabwe, 1900–1930: A Case Study of American Board Mission, Brethren in Christ Mission and the Seventh Day Adventist Mission." MA thesis, Temple University.
Mahoso, Tafataona. 1997. "Visualizing African Memory: The Future of Zimbabwean Sculpture." *Journal of Social Change and Development* 42–43 (August).
Makeba, Miriam. 2004. *Makeba: The Miriam Makeba Story.* In conversation with Nomsa Mwamuka. Johannesburg: STE Publishers.
Malinowski, Branislow. 1959. "Introductory Essay on the Anthropology of Changing African Cultures." In *Methods of Study of Culture Contact in Africa.* London: Oxford University Press.
Mamdani, Mahmood. 2012. *Define and Rule: Native as Political Identity.* Cambridge, MA: Harvard University Press.
Mandela, Nelson. 2013. *Long Walk to Freedom: The Autobiography of Nelson Mandela.* New York: Little, Brown and Company.
Mannan, Hamza. 2014. "Liberty through the Lens of Music." Paper written for the Re/Membering Mandela Pro-seminar on Colonial and Post-colonial Southern Africa, Department of History, University of California, Santa Barbara, winter.
Mano, W. 2009. "'Thank God It Is Friday': Responses to Music Scheduling on Radio Zimbabwe." *Muziki: Journal of Music Research in Africa* 6 (2): 192–220.
Manyika, James. 2001. "Re-encounters: Rhodes, Rhodesia and Scholarships." In "Discipline and the Other Body," special issue of *Interventions: International Journal of Postcolonial Studies* 3 (2): 266–95.
Manyika, Kennedy G. D. n.d. *Beyond My Dreams: An Autobiography.* Gweru: Destiny Focus Publications.

Mapfumo, Thomas. 1992. "Nhamo Yemakandiwa." Reissued as "Makandiwa," on *Spirits to Bite Our Ears: Singles Collection, 1976–1986*. Sound recording, Gramma Records.

———. 1999. "Pfumvu Paruzevha." *Live at El Rey*. Sound recording, Anonymous Records.

Maraire, Chiwoniso. 1999. "Pasipamire." *Ancient Voices*. Sound recording, Grammar Records.

Maraire, Dumisani, and Ephat Mujuru. 2003. "Chemutengure." *Tales of the Mbira*. Sound recording, Sheer Sound.

Mark, Andrew. 2013. "Mbirapocalyse: A Reappraisal." In "Papers Collected in Commemoration of Mbira Month," an unpublished collection edited by Mhoze Chikowero.

Masekela, Hugh, and D. Michael Cheers. 2004. *Still Grazing: The Musical Journey of Hugh Masekela*. New York: Crown Publishers.

Masiye, Andreya S. 1977. *Singing for Freedom: Zambia's Struggle for African Government*. Lusaka: Oxford University Press.

Mathabane, Mark. 1986. *Kaffir Boy: An Autobiography*. New York: Simon and Schuster.

Mavhunga, Clapperton Chakanetsa. 2014. *Transient Workspaces: Technologies of Everyday Innovation in Zimbabwe*. Cambridge, MA: MIT Press.

Mazrui, Ali A., and Michael Tidy. 1984. *Nationalism and New States in Africa*. Seattle: University of Washington Press.

Mbembe, Achille. 2002. "African Modes of Self-Writing." *Public Culture* 14 (1): 239–73.

Mbira Dza Vadzimu: Religion at the Family Level with Gwanzura Gwenzi. 1978. Video, dir. Andrew Tracy. University Park, PA: Pennsylvania State University.

M'Bow, Amadou-Mahtar. 2007. "Culture, Integration and African Renaissance." A translated and edited version of an address to the First Pan-African Cultural Congress organized by the African Union, Addis Ababa, November 13, 2006. *International Journal of African Renaissance Studies—Multi-, Inter- and Transdisciplinary* 2 (1): 101–106.

McHarg, James. 1958. "African Music in Rhodesian Native Education." *African Music* 2 (1): 46–50.

Methodist Episcopal Church. 1917. *Minutes of the Second and Third Sessions of the Rhodesia Mission Conference of the Methodist Episcopal Church, Held in Old Umtali, Rhodesia, South Africa*. Methodist Episcopal Church.

Mitchell, Timothy. 1988. *Colonising Egypt*. New York: Cambridge University Press.

Mokoena, Hlonipha. 2009. "An Assembly of Readers: Magema Fuze and his Ilanga lase Natal Readers." *Journal of Southern African Studies* 35 (3): 595–607.

Moorman, Marissa. 2008. *Intonations: A Social History of Music and Nation in Luanda, Angola, from 1945 to Recent Times*. Athens: Ohio University Press.

Morrison, J. H. 1969. *Streams in the Desert: A Picture of Life in Livingstonia*. New York: Negro Universities Press.

Mphahlele, Es'kia. 1985. *Down Second Avenue*. London: Faber and Faber.

Mphande, Lupenga. 2001. Review of *Nationalists, Cosmopolitans, and Popular Music in Zimbabwe*, by Thomas Turino. *Research in African Literatures* 32 (2): 209–11.

Msindo, Enocent. 2007. "Ethnicity and Nationalism in Urban Colonial Zimbabwe: Bulawayo, 1950 to 1963." *Journal of African History* 48 (2): 267–90.

Muchemwa, Kizito. 2005. "Some Thoughts on History, Memory and Writing in Zimbabwe." In *Versions of Zimbabwe: New Approaches to Literature and Culture,* edited by R. Muponde and R. Primorac, 195–202. Harare: Weaver Press.

———. 2010. "Galas, Biras, State Funerals and the Necropolitan Imagination in Reconstructions of the Zimbabwean Nation, 1980–2008." *Social Dynamics: Journal of African Studies* 36 (3): 504–14.

Mudenge, S. I. G. 1988. *A Political History of the Munhumutapa State, c. 1400–1902.* Harare: Zimbabwe Publishing House.

Mudimbe, V. Y. 1988. *The Invention of Africa: Gnosis, Philosophy and the Order of Knowledge.* Bloomington: Indiana University Press.

Mugo, Micere. 1992. Introduction to *Songs from the Temple,* by Emmanuel Ngara. Gweru: Mambo Press.

Muller, C. B. 2006. "American Musical Surrogacy: A View from Post–World War II South Africa." *Safundi* 7 (3): 1–18.

Mungazi, Dickson, A. 1983. *To Honor the Sacred Trust of Civilization: History, Politics, and Education in Southern Africa.* Cambridge, MA: Schenkman.

Musodza, Archford. 2008. "An Investigation of the Process of Indigenisation in the Anglican Diocese of Mashonaland (1891–1981), with Special Emphasis on the Ministry of Indigenous Christians." DTheol diss., University of South Africa.

Musururgwa [i.e., Musarurwa], August. [1940s?]. "Skokiaan." Sound recording, Gallo.

Ndlovu-Gatsheni, Sabelo J. 2011. "Introduction: Redemptive or Grotesque Nationalism in the Postcolony?" In *Redemptive or Grotesque Nationalism? Rethinking Contemporary Politics in Zimbabwe,* edited by Sabelo J. Ndlovu-Gatsheni and James Muzondidya, 1–32. New York: Peter Laing.

Nehwati, Francis. 1970. "The Social and Communal Background to 'Zhii': The African Riots in Bulawayo, Southern Rhodesia in 1960." *African Affairs* 69 (276): 250–66.

Neto, Agostinho. 1974. "Saturday in the Musseques." In *Sacred Hope,* translated by Marga Holness. Dar es Salaam: Tanzania Publishing House.

Ngara, Constantine. 2007. "African Ways of Knowing and Pedagogy Revisited." *Journal of Contemporary Issues in Education* 2 (2): 7–20.

Ngugi wa Thiong'o. 1997. "Enactments of Power: The Politics of Performance Space." *Drama Review* 41 (3): 11–30.

Nkomo, J. 1984. *The Story of My Life.* London: Methuen.

Nkrumah, Kwame. 1998. *Africa Must Unite.* London: Panaf.

Nyagumbo, Maurice. 1982. *With the People: An Autobiography from the Zimbabwean Struggle.* London: Allison and Busby.

Nyaira, Sandra. 2012. "Zimbabwe Monuments Officials Block Removal of Cecil Rhodes Gravesite." Voice of America–Zimbabwe, February 22. http://www.voazimbabwe.com/content/zimbabwe-monuments-officials-block-call-for-removal-of-rhodes-gravesite-139997423/1468169.html.

Nyamubaya, Freedom. n.d. "A Haunted Place." In *Ndangariro,* edited by Freedom Nyamubaya and Irene Mahamba, 77–78. Harare: Zimbabwe Foundation for Education with Production.

Nzenza, Sekai. 1988. *Zimbabwean Woman: My Own Story.* London: Karia Press.

OAU [Organization of African Unity]. 1969. "New Music and the Paths of Revolt." Algiers: First Pan-African Cultural Festival, May 1.

O'Callaghan, Marion. 1977. *Southern Rhodesia: The Effects of a Conquest Society on Education, Culture and Information.* Dorset: UNESCO.

O'Farrell, Josephine. [1930?]. *Dedication of a Christian Home in Rhodesia.* New York: Agricultural Missions Foundation.

Olick, Jeffrey K. 2002. "From Usable Pasts to the Return of the Repressed." *Hedgehog Review,* summer, 19–31.

Ortner, Sherry B. 1995. "Resistance and the Problem of Ethnographic Refusal." *Comparative Studies in Society and History* 37 (1): 173–93.

Ouden, Amy E. 2007. "Locating the Cannibals: Conquest, North American Ethnohistory, and the Threat of Objectivity." *History and Anthropology* 18 (2): 101–33.

Palley, C. 1970. "Law and the Unequal Society: Discriminatory Legislation in Rhodesia under the Rhodesian Front from 1963 to 1969, part 1." *Race and Class* 12 (1): 15–47.

Parrinder, E. G. 1956. "Music in West African Churches." *African Music* 1 (3): 37–38.

Parry, Richard. 1999. "Culture, Organisation and Class: The African Experience in Salisbury, 1892–1935." In *Sites of Struggle: Essays in Zimbabwe's Urban History,* edited by Brian Raftopoulos and Tsuneo Yoshikuni, 53–94. Harare: Weaver Press.

Peaden, W. R. 1970. *Missionary Attitudes to Shona Culture, 1890–1923.* Local series pamphlet 27. Salisbury, Rhodesia: Central Africa Historical Association.

Perman, Tony. 2012. "Sungura in Zimbabwe and the Limits of Cosmopolitanism." *Ethnomusicology Forum* 21 (3): 374–401.

Peterson, Bhekizizwe. 2000. *Monarchs, Missionaries and African Intellectuals: African Theatre and the Unmaking of Colonial Marginality.* Asmara: Africa World Press.

Phillips, Ray E. 1937. *The Bantu in the City: A Study of Cultural Adjustment on the Witwatersrand.* Alice, South Africa: Lovedale Press.

Phimister, I. 1994. *Wangi Kolia: Coal, Capital and Labour in Colonial Zimbabwe, 1894–1954.* Johannesburg: Witwatersrand University Press.

Pongweni, A. J. C. 1982. *Songs That Won the Liberation War.* Gweru: Mambo Press.

———. 1997. "The Chimurenga Songs of the Zimbabwean War of Liberation." In *Readings in African Popular Culture,* edited by Karin Barber, 63–72. Bloomington: African International Institute in Association with Indiana University Press.

Radasi, John. 1966. *The Life and Labours of a Native African Missionary.* Gisborne, New Zealand: Gisborne Herald.

Rafael, Vicente L. 2003. "The Cellphone and the Crowd: Messianic Politics in Contemporary Philippines." *Public Culture* 15 (3): 399–425.

Ranger, Terence. 1967. *Revolt in Southern Rhodesia.* Evanston, IL: Northwestern University Press.

———. 1970. *The African Voice in Southern Rhodesia, 1898–1930.* Evanston, IL: Northwestern University Press.

———. 1977. "The People in African Resistance: A Review." In "Protest and Resistance," special issue of *Journal of Southern African Studies* 4 (1): 125–46.

———. 1985. *Peasant Consciousness and Guerrilla War in Zimbabwe: A Comparative Study.* London: James Currey.

———. 1987. "Taking Hold of the Land: Holy Places and Pilgrimages in Twentieth-Century Zimbabwe." *Past and Present,* no. 117: 158–94.

———. 1988. "Chingaira Makoni's Head: Myth, History and the Colonial Experience." Eighteenth annual Hans Wolff Memorial Lecture, March. African Studies Program, Indiana University, Bloomington.

———. 1993. "Thompson Samkange: Tambaram and Beyond." *Journal of Religion in Africa* 23 (4): 318–46.
———. 1999. *Voices from the Rocks: Nature, Culture and History in the Matopos Hills of Zimbabwe*. Bloomington: Indiana University Press.
———. 2004. "Nationalist Historiography, Patriotic History and the History of the Nation: The Struggle over the Past in Zimbabwe." *Journal of Southern African Studies* 30 (2): 215–34.
———. 2010. *Bulawayo Burning: The Social History of a Southern African City, 1893–1960*. London: James Currey.
Rathbone, Richard. 2000. *Nkrumah and the Chiefs: The Politics of Chieftaincy in Ghana, 1951–60*. Athens: Ohio University Press.
Rea, W. F. 1961. "The Missionary Factor in Southern Rhodesia." Paper delivered at the Second Conference on the Study and Teaching of History, University College of Rhodesia and Nyasaland, August–September.
Report of the Commission Appointed to Enquire into the Matter of Native Education in All Its Bearings in the Colony of Southern Rhodesia. 1925. Salisbury, Rhodesia: Government Printer.
Rex, John. 1974. "The Compound, the Reserve and the Urban Location: The Essential Institutions of South African Labour Exploitation." *South African Labour Bulletin* 1 (4): 4–17.
Root, Deborah. 1996. *Cannibal Culture: Art, Appropriation, and the Commodification of Difference*. Boulder, CO: Westview Press.
Ruzivo, Munetsi. 2005. "Elizabeth Musodzi: The Catholic Woman Agent of the Gospel." http://hdl.handle.net/10646/348 (preprint of article appearing in *Studia Historiae Ecclesiasticae* 31 [2]: 63–75).
Said, Edward. 1989. "Representing the Colonized: Anthropology's Interlocutors." *Critical Inquiry* 15 (2): 205–25.
———. 1993. *Culture and Imperialism*. New York: Knopf.
[Saidi, Bill.] 2007. "Africans Still Singing to Be Freed from Persecution." Sowetan Live, November 23. http://www.sowetan.co.za.
Samkange, Stanlake. 1975. *The Mourned One*. Nairobi: Heinemann.
Samuelson, Meg. 2007. "Yvonne Vera's Bulawayo: Modernity, (Im)mobility, Music, and Memory." *Research in African Literatures* 38 (2): 22–35.
Sartre, Jean-Paul. 1967. Preface to *The Wretched of the Earth*, by Frantz Fanon. Harmondsworth: Penguin.
Scannell, Paddy. 2001. "Music, Radio and the Record Business in Zimbabwe Today." *Popular Music* 20 (1): 13–27.
Scott, James. 1990. *Domination and the Arts of Resistance: Hidden Transcripts*. New Haven, CT: Yale University Press.
———. 1998. *Seeing Like a State: How Certain Schemes to Improve the Human Condition Have Failed*. New Haven, CT: Yale University Press.
———. 2009. *The Art of Not Being Governed: An Anarchist History of Upland Southeast Asia*. New Haven, CT: Yale University Press.
Selous, Frederick C. 1896. *Sunshine and Storm in Rhodesia: Being a Narrative of Events in Matabeleland both before and during the Recent Insurrection up to the Date of the Disbandment of the Bulawayo Field Force*. London: Rowland Ward and Co.
Shamuyarira, Nathan. 1965. *Crisis in Zimbabwe*. London: Andre Deutsch.

Shepherd, George W. 1969. "Reflections on the Pan-African Cultural Conference in Algiers." *Africa Today* 16 (4): 1–3.
Shils, Edward. 1981. *Tradition.* London: Faber and Faber.
Shopo, T. D. 1977. "Social Welfare or Social Control?" *Zambezia: The Journal of Humanities of the University of Zimbabwe* 5 (2): 203–12.
Shutt, Allison. Forthcoming. *Manners Make a Nation: Racial Etiquette in Southern Rhodesia, 1910–1963.* Rochester, NY: University of Rochester Press.
Shutt, Allison K., and Tony King, 2005. "Imperial Rhodesians: The 1953 Rhodes Centenary Exhibition in Southern Rhodesia." *Journal of Southern African Studies* 31 (2): 357–79.
Smith, D., and C. Simpson. 1981. *Mugabe.* London: Sphere Books.
Smith, Linda Tuhiwai. 1999. *Decolonizing Methodologies: Research and Indigenous Peoples.* London: Zed Books.
Smith, Reginald. 1950. *Sketches from Penhalonga.* London: S.P.G.
Somé, Malidoma. 1994. *Of Water and the Spirit: Ritual, Magic and Initiation in the Life of an African Shaman.* New York: G. P. Putnam's Sons.
Souvenir of the Centenary of Loyola Mission Chishawasha. 1990. Gweru: Mambo Press.
Stanlake, J. W. 1903. "Missionary Meetings in Matabeleland." *Work and Workers in the Mission Field* 12.
Staunton, Irene, ed. 1990. *Mothers of the Revolution: The War Experiences of Thirty Zimbabwean Women.* Harare: Baobab Books.
Steere, Douglas V. 1973. *God's Irregular: Arthur Shearly Cripps; A Rhodesian Epic.* London: S.P.C.K.
Steinberg, Stephen. 2007. *Race Relations: A Critique.* Stanford, CA: Stanford University Press.
Steyn, Melissa E. 2001. *"Whiteness Just Isn't What It Used to Be": White Identity in a Changing South Africa.* New York: State University of New York Press.
Stokes, M. 1994. "Introduction: Ethnicity, Identity and Music." In *Ethnicity, Identity and Music: The Musical Construction of Place,* edited by Martin Stokes, 1–28. Oxford: Berg.
Strickland, Nathanael. 2012. "Hendrik Verwoerd on Separate Development." Faith and Heritage: Occidental Christianity for Preserving Western Culture and Heritage. http://faithandheritage.com/2012/08/hendrik-verwoerd-on-separate-development/. Accessed March 23, 2014.
Summers, Carol. 1997. "Demanding Schools: The Umchingwe Project and African Men's Struggles for Education in Southern Rhodesia, 1928–1934." *African Studies Review* 40 (2): 117–39.
———. 2002. *Colonial Lessons: Africans' Education in Southern Rhodesia, 1918–1940.* Portsmouth, NH: Heinemann.
Swartz, J. F. A. 1956. "A Hobbyist Looks at Zulu and Xhosa Songs." *African Music* 1 (3): 29–33.
Taylor, C. T. C. 1968. *The History of Rhodesian Entertainment, 1890–1930.* Salisbury: Collins.
Tendi, Blessing-Miles. 2010. *Making History in Mugabe's Zimbabwe: Politics, Intellectuals and the Media.* Bern: Peter Lang.
Thomas, N. 1994. *Colonialism's Culture: Anthropology, Travel, and Government.* Princeton, NJ: Princeton University Press.

Tlou, Josiah S. 1975. "Rhodesia, Religion and Racism: Christianity's Dilemma in Southern Africa." In *African Reactions to Missionary Education,* edited by Edward H. Berman, 182–205. New York: Teachers College Press.
Tomlinson, J. 1992. *Globalization and Culture.* Cambridge: Polity Press.
Tracey, Hugh. 1929. "Some Observations on Native Music in Southern Rhodesia." *NADA: The Southern Rhodesia Native Affairs Department Annual,* 96–103.
———. 1933. "Songs from the Kraals of Southern Rhodesia." Unpublished paper deposited at the National Archives of Zimbabwe.
———. 1961. "The Importance of African Music in the Present Day." *African Affairs* 60 (239): 155–62.
———. 1966–67. "Musical Appreciation in Central and Southern Africa." *African Music* 4 (1): 47–55.
———. 1970. *Chopi Musicians: Their Music, Poetry, and Instruments.* London: Oxford University Press.
———. 1973. "Catalogue: The Sound of Africa Series; 210 Long Playing Records of Music and Songs from Central, Eastern and Southern Africa." Transvaal: International Library of African Music.
Turino, Thomas. 2000. *Nationalists, Cosmopolitans and Popular Music in Zimbabwe.* Chicago: Chicago University Press.
———. 2007. Interview by Banning Eyre. Part of the Hip Deep program "Thomas Mapfumo 1: The War Years." Afropop Worldwide. http://www.afropop.org/wp/6408/thomas-mapfumo-the-war-years/. Accessed October 2, 2013.
Urban-Mead, Wendy. 2008. "Negotiating Plainness and Gender in the Creation of an African Rural Elite: Christian Weddings in Matabeleland, 1913–1944." *Journal of Religion in Africa* 38 (2): 209–46.
———. 2010. "Negotiating 'Plainness' and Gender: Dancing and Apparel at Christian Weddings in Matabeleland, Zimbabwe, 1913–1944." Paper presented at the Northeast Workshop on Southern Africa (NEWSA) Conference in Burlington, VT, October.
Ushewokunze, Herbert S. M. 1984. *An Agenda for Zimbabwe.* Harare: College Press.
Vambe, Lawrence. 1972. *An Ill-Fated People: Zimbabwe before and after Rhodes.* London: Heinemann.
———. 1976. *From Rhodesia to Zimbabwe.* London: Heinemann.
Vambe, Maurice. 2007. "'Aya Mahobo': Migrant Labour and the Cultural Semiotics of Harare (Mbare) African Township, 1930–1970." *African Identities* 5 (3): 355–69.
———. 2008. "Diaspora, Music, Identity and Desti/Nations in Southern Africa." *Muziki: Journal of Music Research in Africa* 5 (2): 284–97.
Van Onselen, Charles. 1976. *Chibaro: African Mine Labour in Southern Rhodesia, 1900–1933.* London: Pluto Press.
Vera, Yvonne. 2000. *Butterfly Burning.* New York: Farrar, Straus and Giroux.
Von Eschen, P. M. 2000. "Satchmo Blows Up the World: Jazz, Race and Empire during the Cold War." In *Here, There and Everywhere: The Foreign Politics of American Popular Culture,* edited by R. Wagnleitner and E. Tyler, 163–78. Hanover, NH: University Press of New England.
Waterman, Christopher. 1991. "The Uneven Development of Africanist Ethnomusicology: Three Issues and a Critique." In *Comparative Musicology and Anthropology of Music: Essays on the History of Ethnomusicology,* edited by Bruno Nettl and Philip V. Bohlman, 169–86. Chicago: University of Chicago Press.

Weinbaum, Alys Eve, Lynn M. Thomas, et al., eds. 2008. *The Modern Girl around the World: Consumption, Modernity, and Globalization.* The Modern Girl around the World Research Group. Durham, NC: Duke University Press.

Weman, Henry. 1960. *African Music and the Church in Africa.* Uppsala: Universitets Arsskrift.

West, Cornel. 2005. "Exiles from a City and a Nation." Interview by Joanna Walters. *Guardian,* September 11. http://www.theguardian.com/world/2005/sep/11/hurricanekatrina.comment.

Wheaton, Jack. 1994. *All That Jazz.* New York: Ardsley House.

White, Bob. 2008. *Rumba Rules: The Politics of Dance Music in Mobutu's Zaire.* Durham, NC: Duke University Press.

Wilde, Guillermo. 2007. "Toward a Political Anthropology of Mission Sound: Paraguay in the 17th and 18th Centuries." *Music and Politics* 1 (2): 1–29.

Wilson, David. 1935. "Dr. Boyd on the Native Problem." *South African Review,* February 1.

Witz, L. 2003. *Apartheid's Festival: Contesting South Africa's National Pasts.* Bloomington: Indiana University Press, 2003.

Wright, Allan. 1972. *Valley of the Ironwoods: A Personal Record of Ten Years Served as District Commissioner in Rhodesia's Largest Administrative Area, Nuanetsi, in the South-East Lowveld.* Cape Town: Cape and Transvaal Printers, Ltd.

Yoshikuni, Tsuneo. 2008. *Elizabeth Musodzi and the Birth of African Feminism in Early Colonial Zimbabwe.* Harare: Weaver Press.

ZANLA Chimurenga Songs. 2011. Harare: Gramma Records.

Zantzinger, Gei. 1999. *Mbira: Njari, Karanga Songs in Christian Ceremonies with Simon Mashoko.* Video recording, Constant Spring Productions.

Zeleza, P. T. 1996. "Manufacturing and Consuming Knowledge: African Libraries and Publishing." *Development in Practice* 6 (4): 293–303.

———. 1997. *Manufacturing African Studies and Crises.* Dakar: Codesria.

———. 2009. "African Studies and Universities since Independence." *Transition,* no. 101: 110–35.

Zindi, Fred. 1985. *Roots Rocking in Zimbabwe.* Gweru: Mambo Press.

Index

Note: Page numbers in *italics* refer to illustrations.